THE IRVING BERLIN COLLECTION

ISBN 0-7935-0440-6

C O N T

E N T S

Alexander's Ragtime Band

Registration 5
Rhythm: Fox Trot or Swing

Words and Music by
Irving Berlin

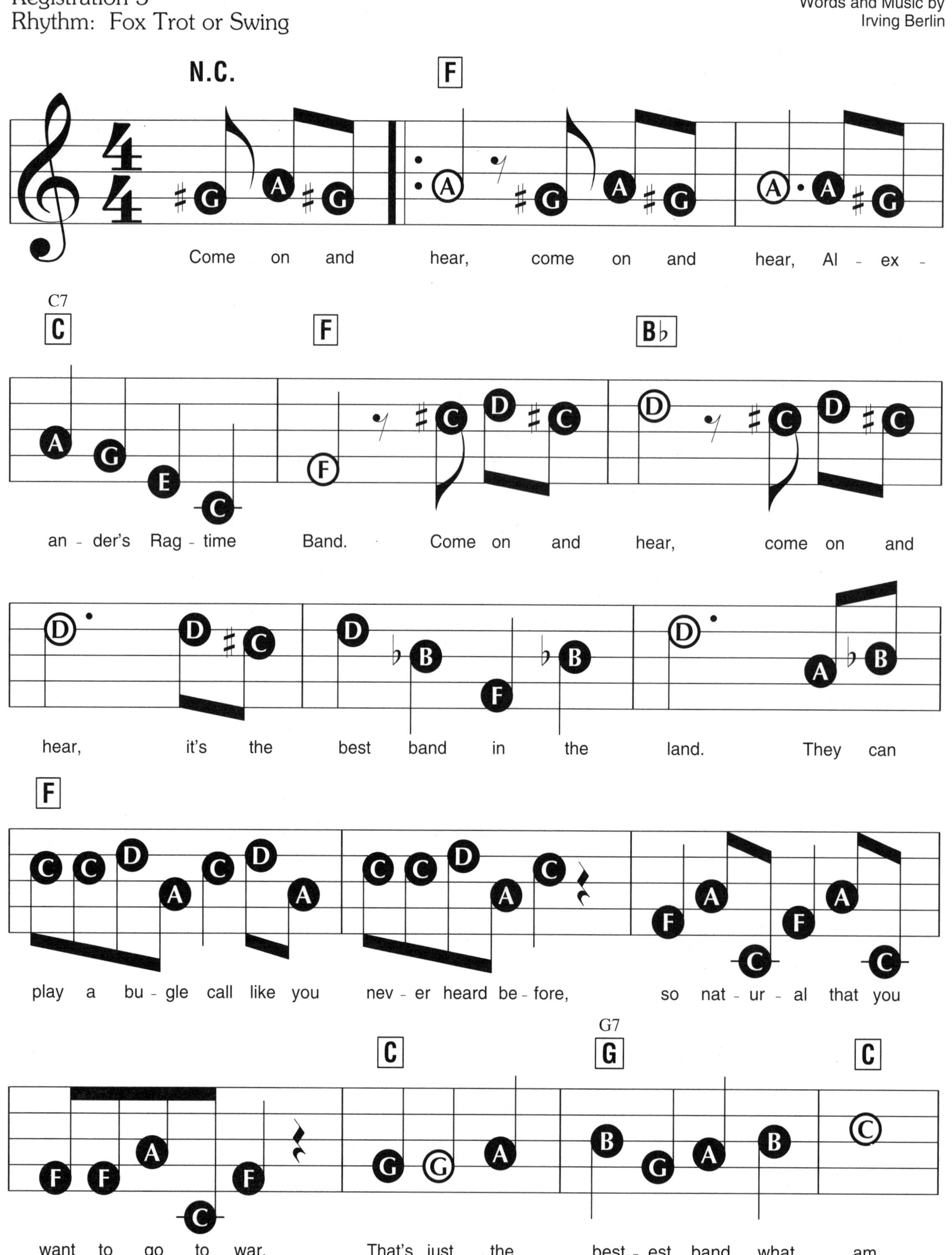

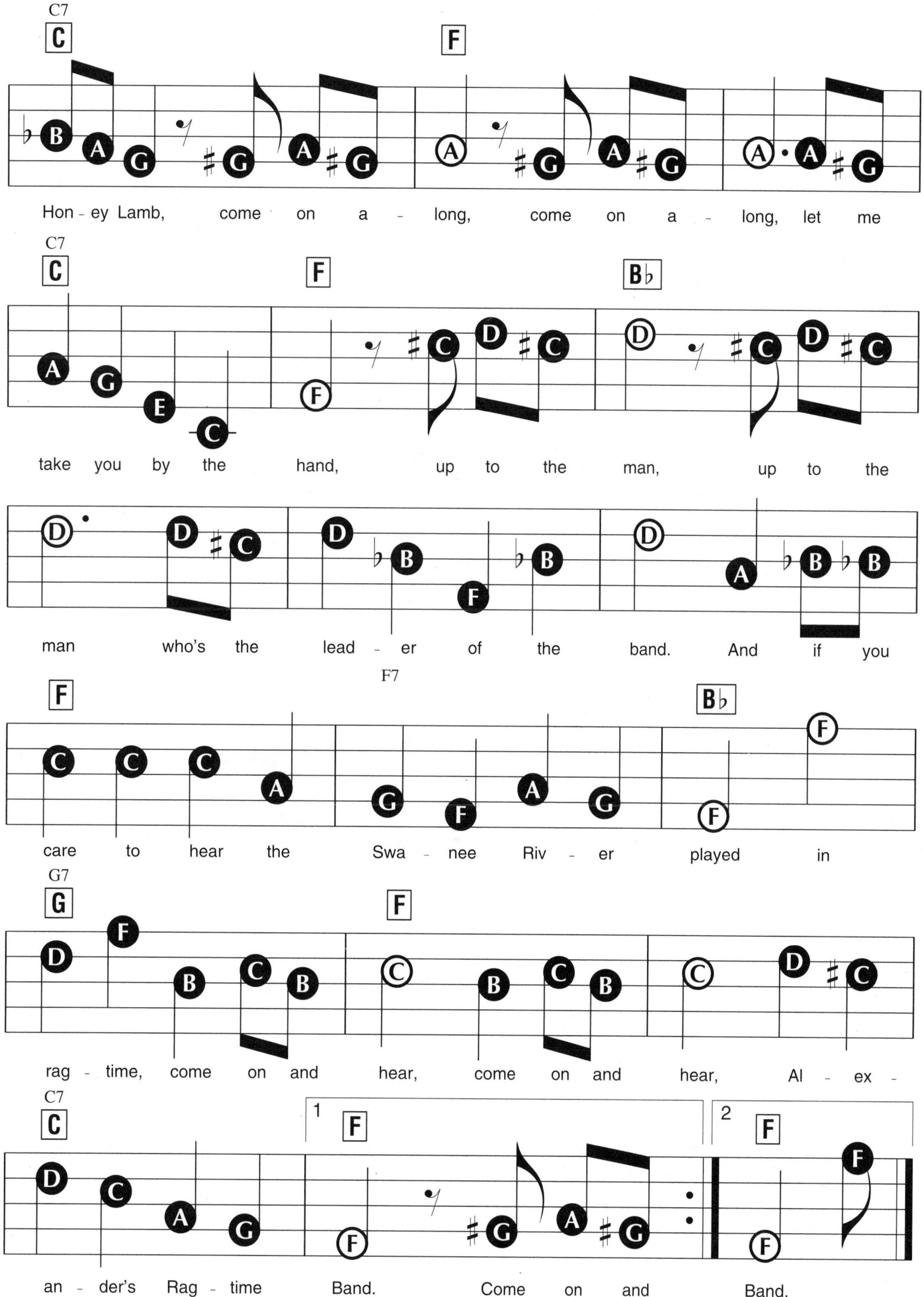
C7
C
F
Hon - ey Lamb, come on a - long, come on a - long, let me
C7
C
F
B♭
take you by the hand, up to the man, up to the
man who's the lead - er of the band. And if you
F
F7
B♭
care to hear the Swa - nee Riv - er played in
G7
G
F
rag - time, come on and hear, come on and hear, Al - ex -
C7
C
1
F
2
F
an - der's Rag - time Band. Come on and Band.

All Alone

Registration 5
Rhythm: Waltz

Words and Music by
Irving Berlin

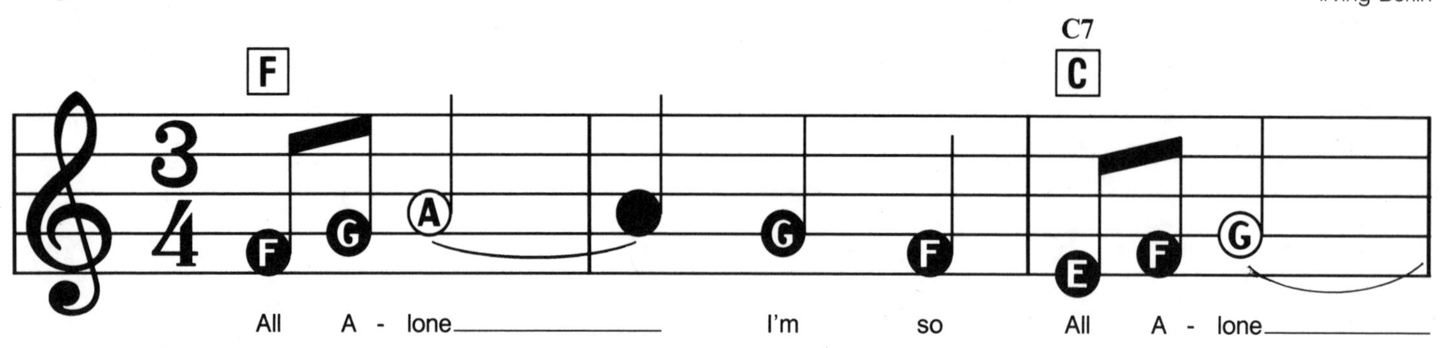

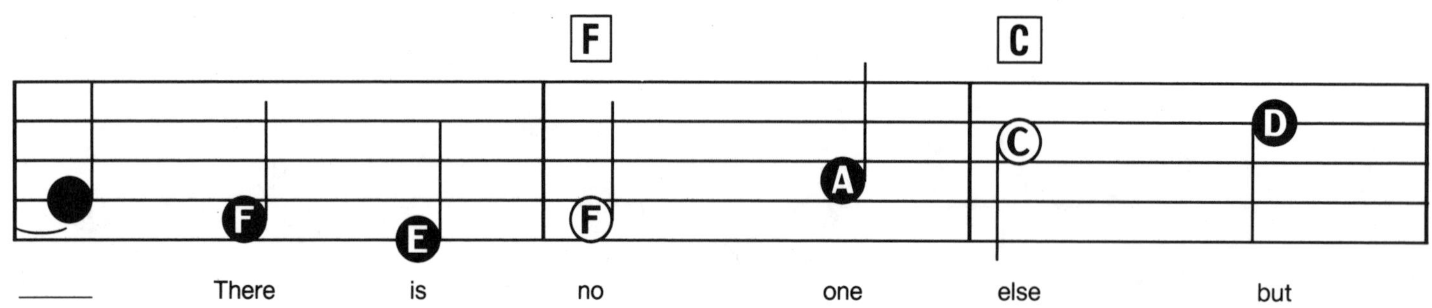

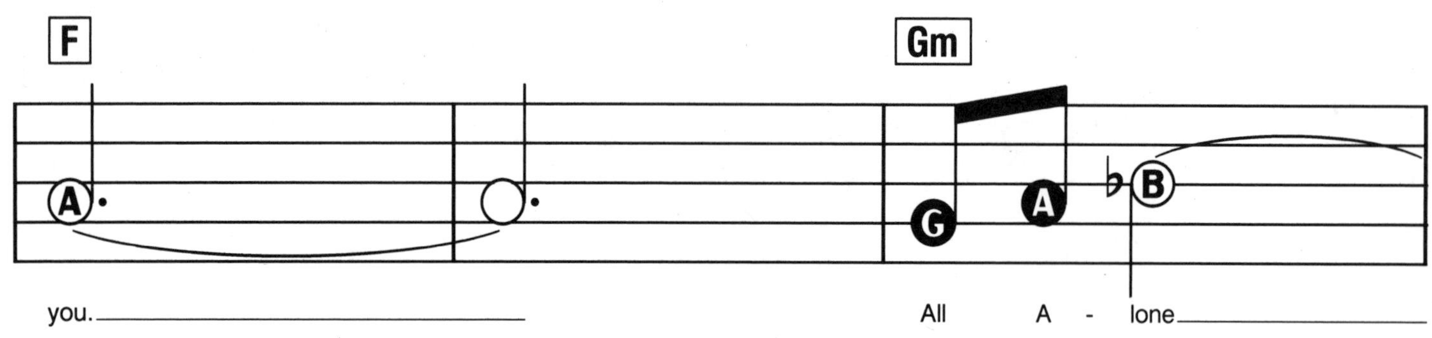

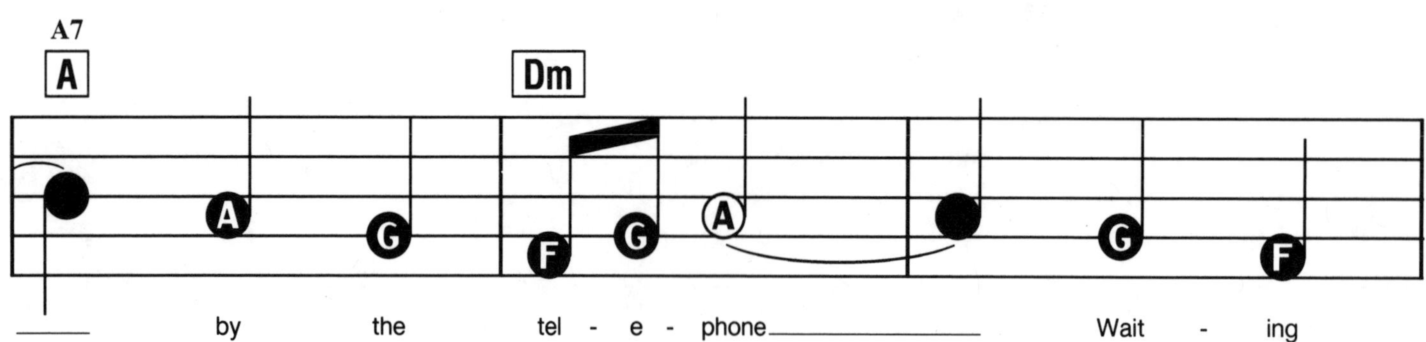

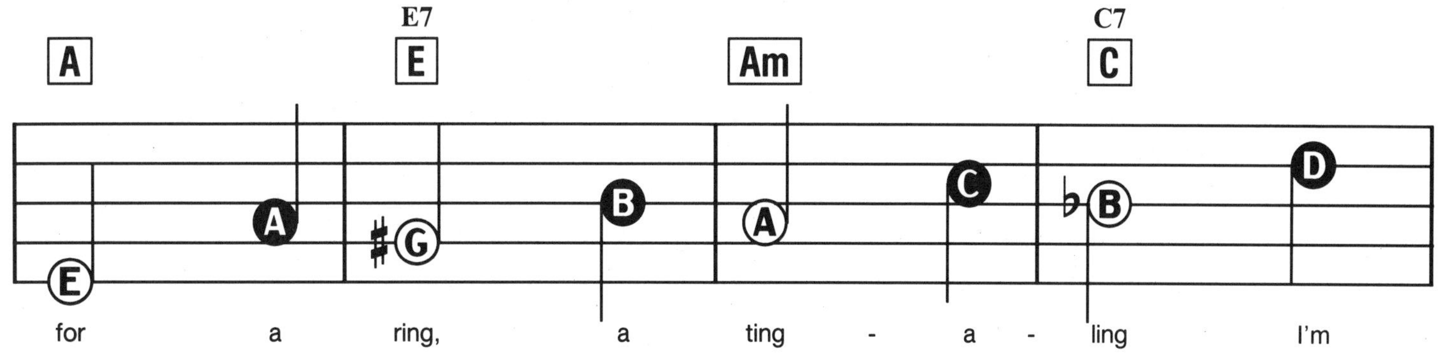
E7
C7
A
E
Am
C
E
A
G
B
A
C
B
D
for a ring, a ting - a - ling I'm

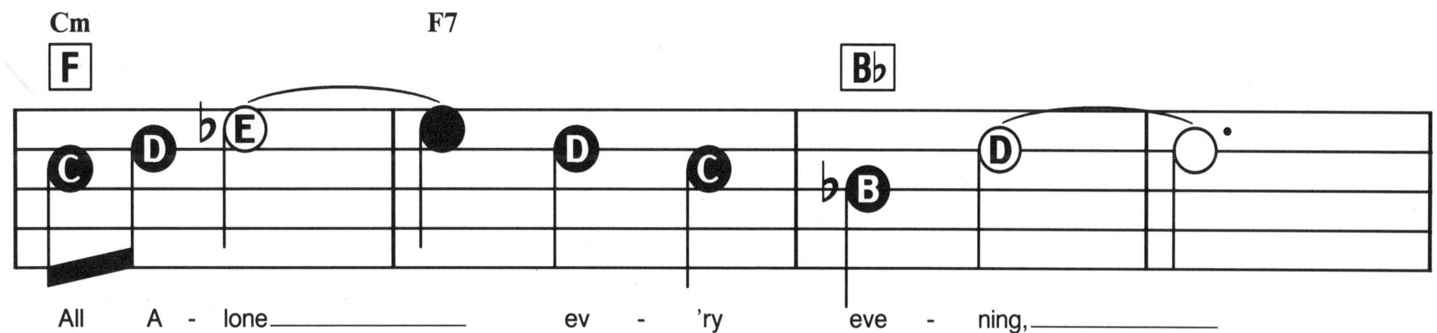
Cm
F7
F
B♭
C
D
E
D
C
B
D
All A - lone ev - 'ry eve - ning,

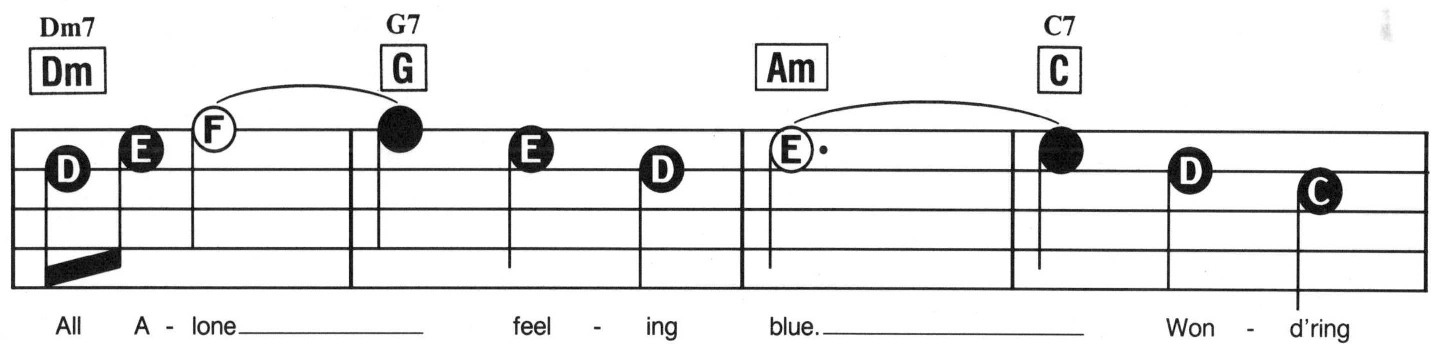
Dm7
G7
C7
Dm
G
Am
C
D
E
F
E
D
E
D
C
All A - lone feel - ing blue. Won - d'ring

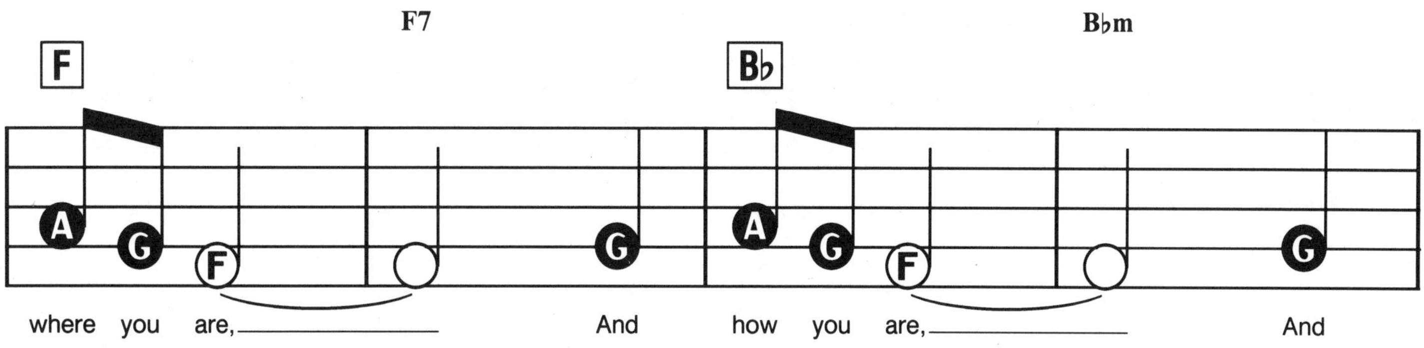
F7
B♭m
F
B♭
A
G
F
G
A
G
F
G
where you are, And how you are, And

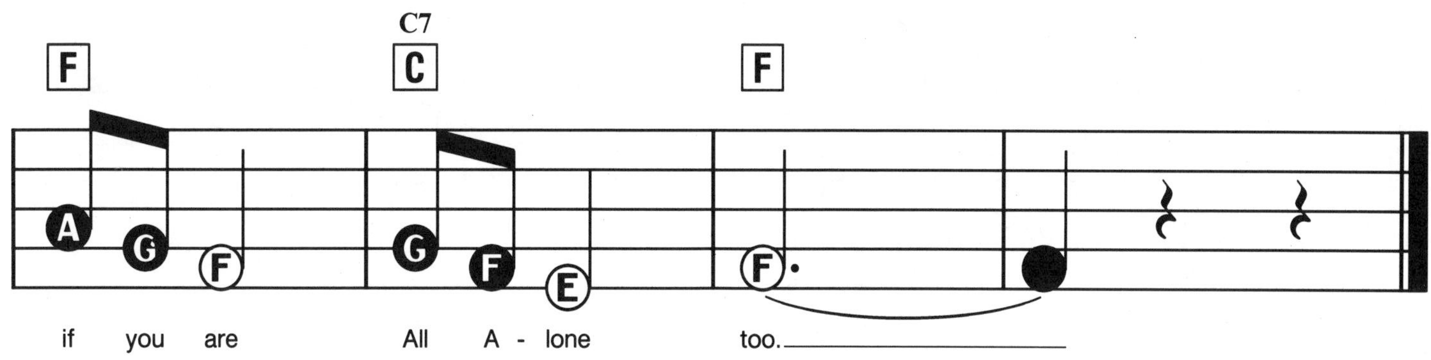
C7
F
C
F
A
G
F
G
F
E
F
if you are All A - lone too.

All By Myself

Registration 4
Rhythm: Swing

Words and Music by
Irving Berlin

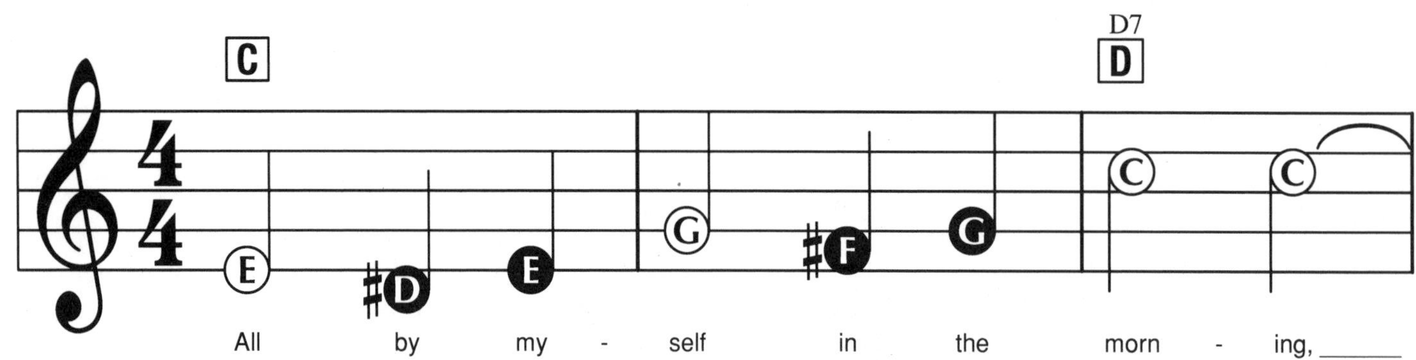

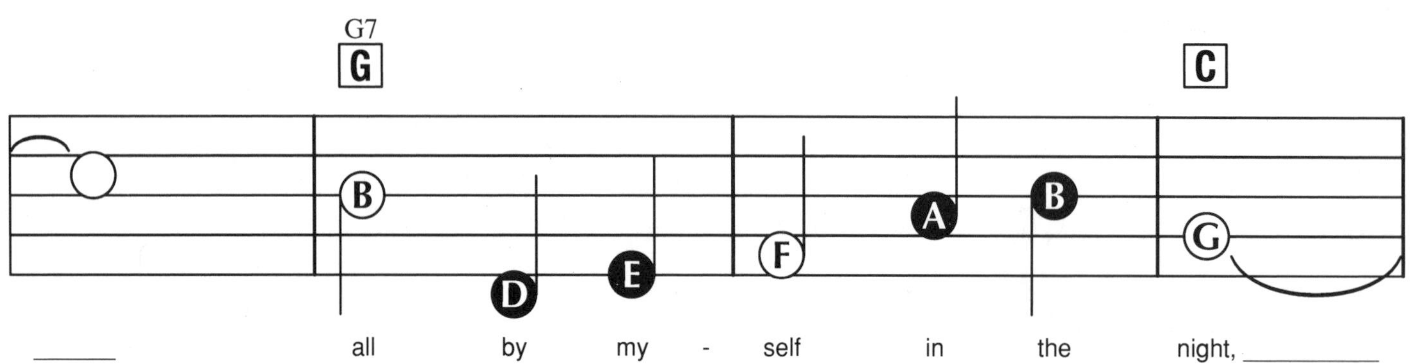

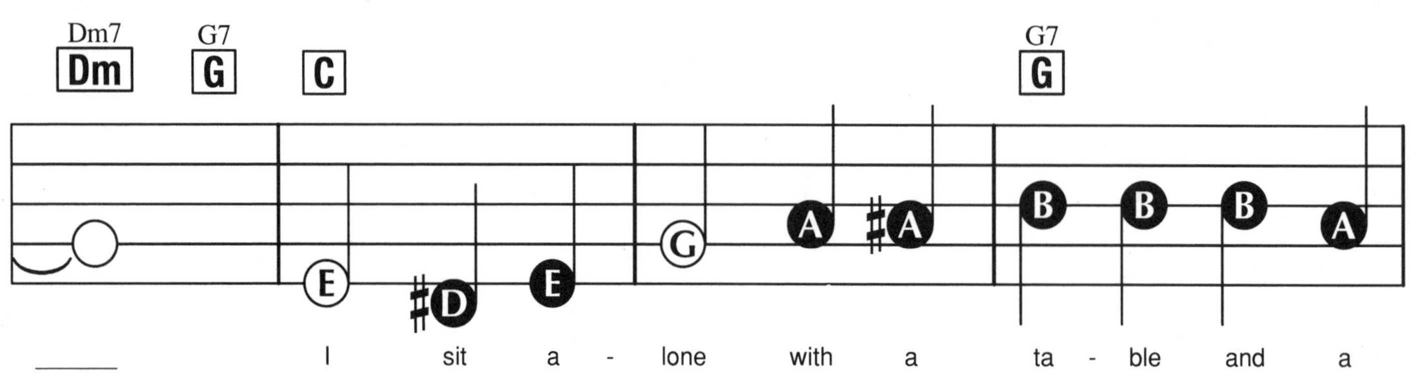

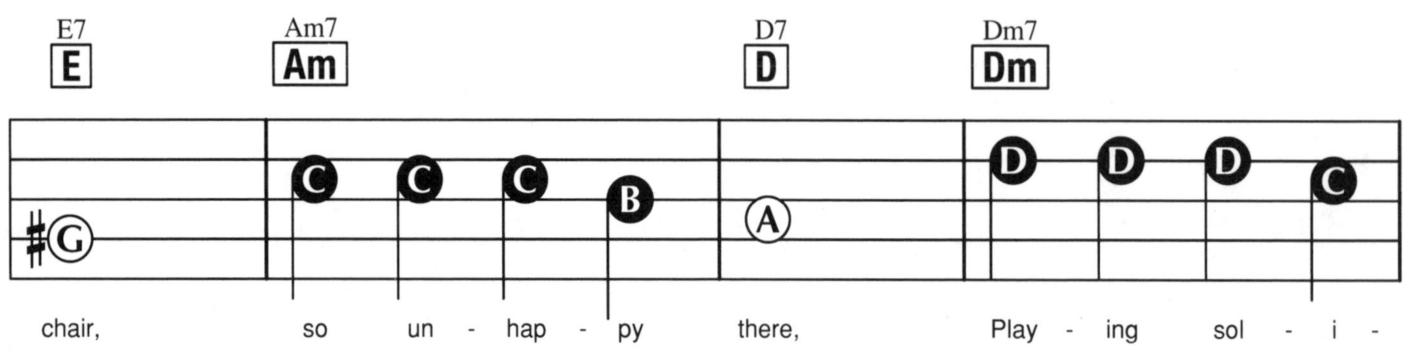

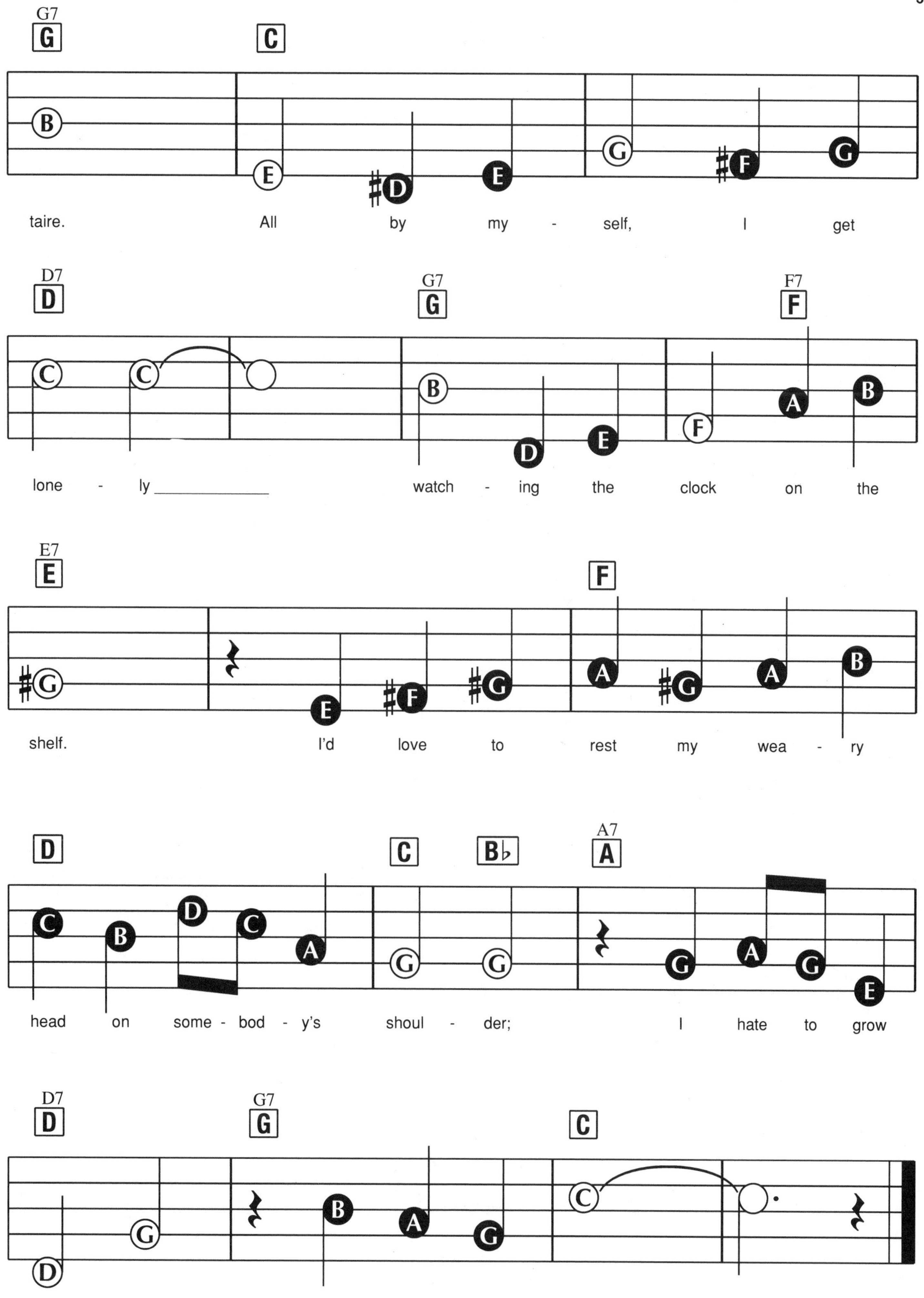
G7 G
C
taire. All by my - self, I get
D7 D
G7 G
F7 F
lone - ly watch - ing the clock on the
E7 E
F
shelf. I'd love to rest my wea - ry
D
C
B♭
A7 A
head on some - bod - y's shoul - der; I hate to grow
D7 D
G7 G
C
old - er all by my - self.

Always

Registration 2
Rhythm: Waltz

Words and Music by Irving Berlin

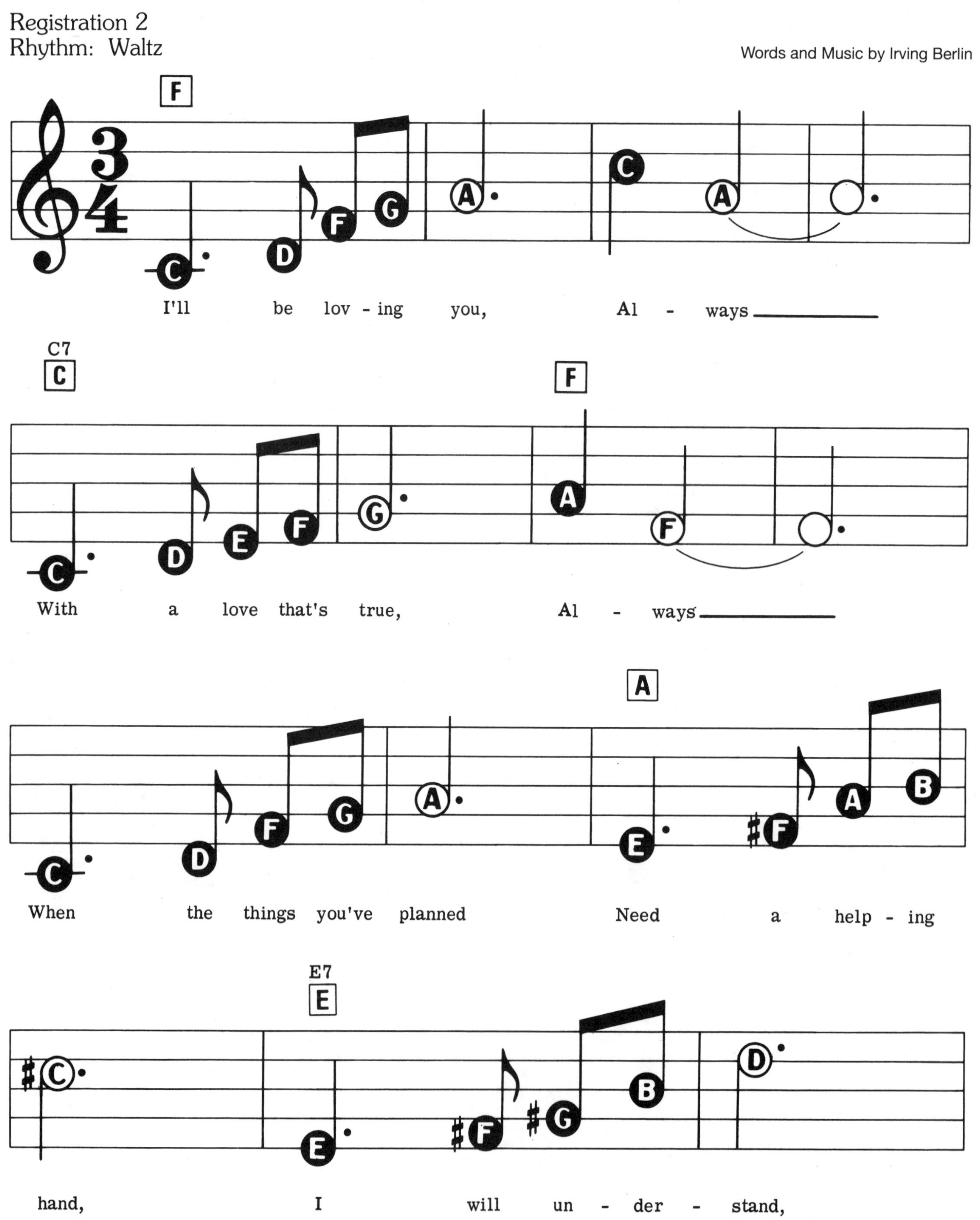

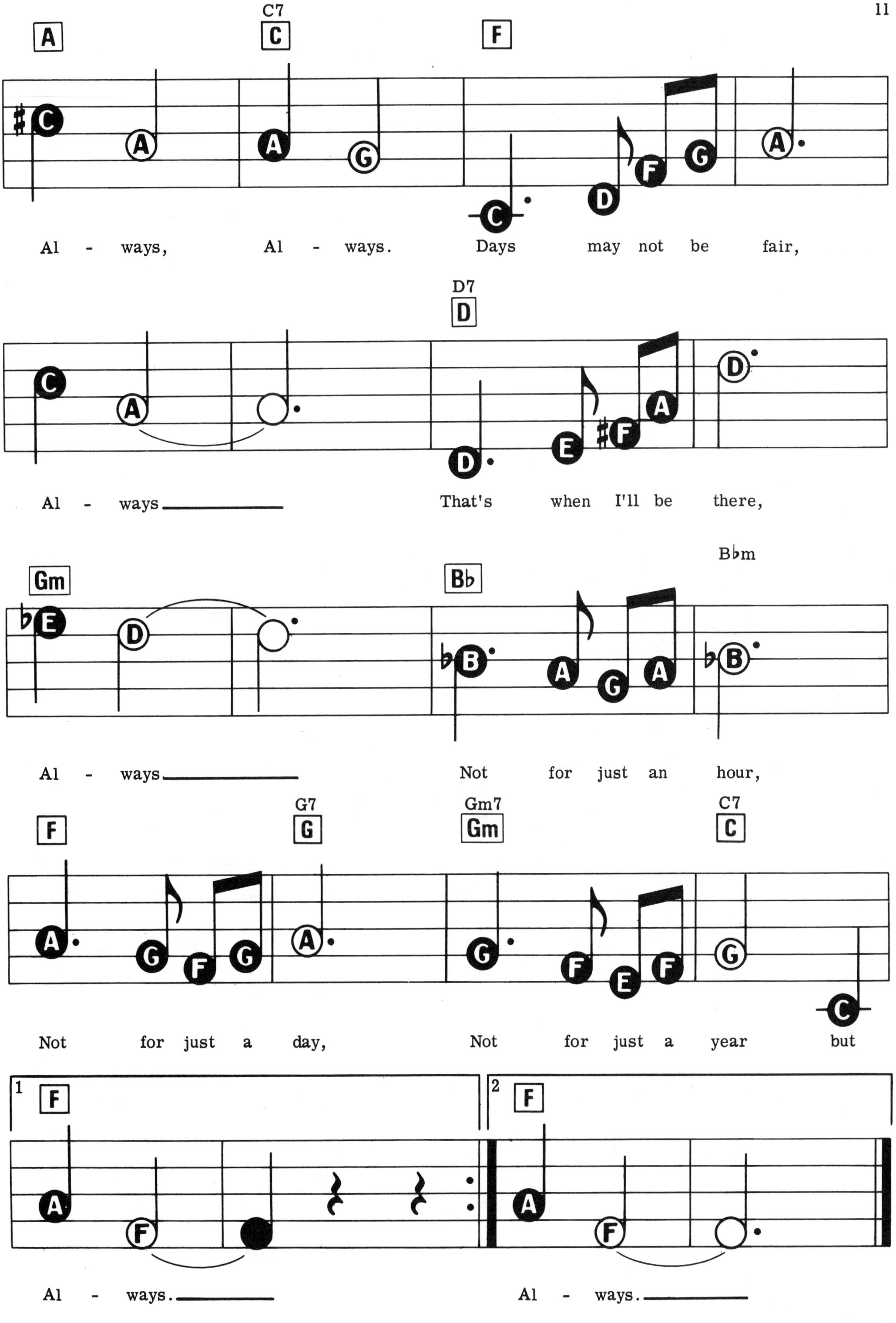

A C7 C F

Al - ways, Al - ways. Days may not be fair,

D7 D

Al - ways ________ That's when I'll be there,

Gm Bb Bbm

Al - ways ________ Not for just an hour,

F G7 G Gm7 Gm C7 C

Not for just a day, Not for just a year but

1 F 2 F

Al - ways. ________ Al - ways. ________

Be Careful, It's My Heart

Registration 1
Rhythm: Swing

Words and Music by
Irving Berlin

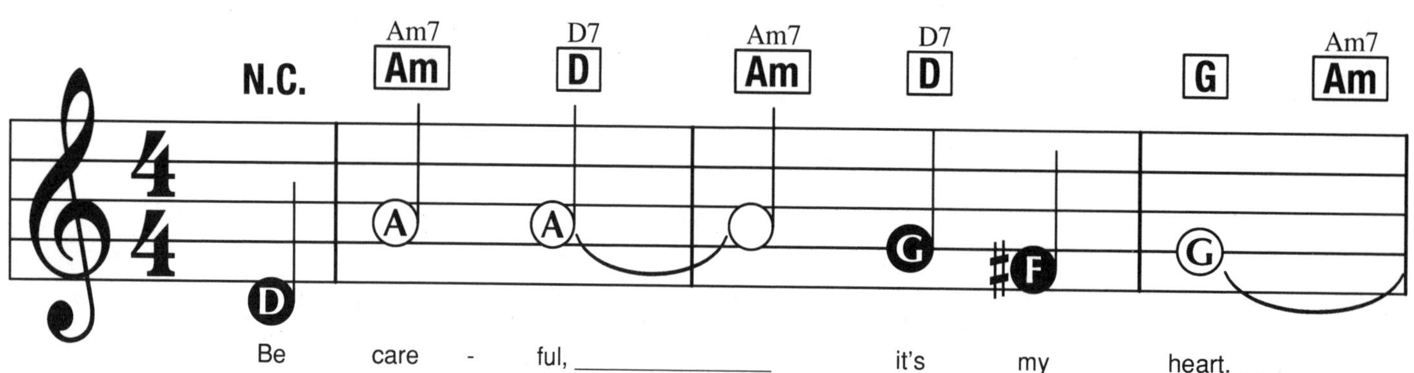

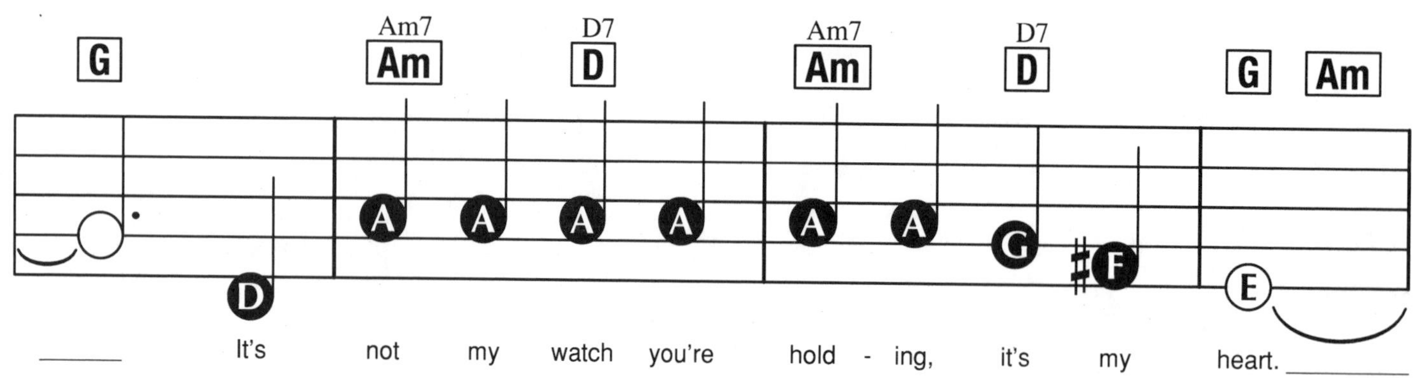

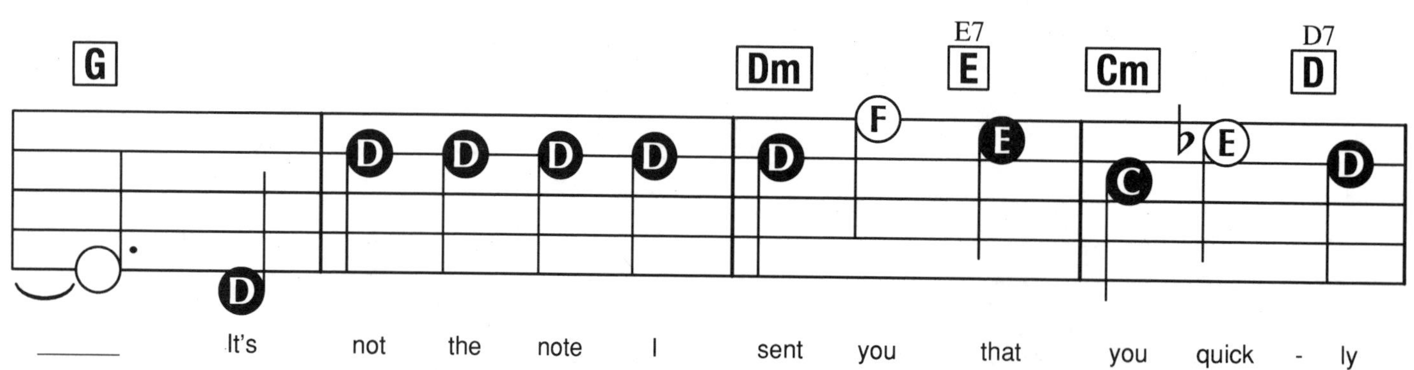

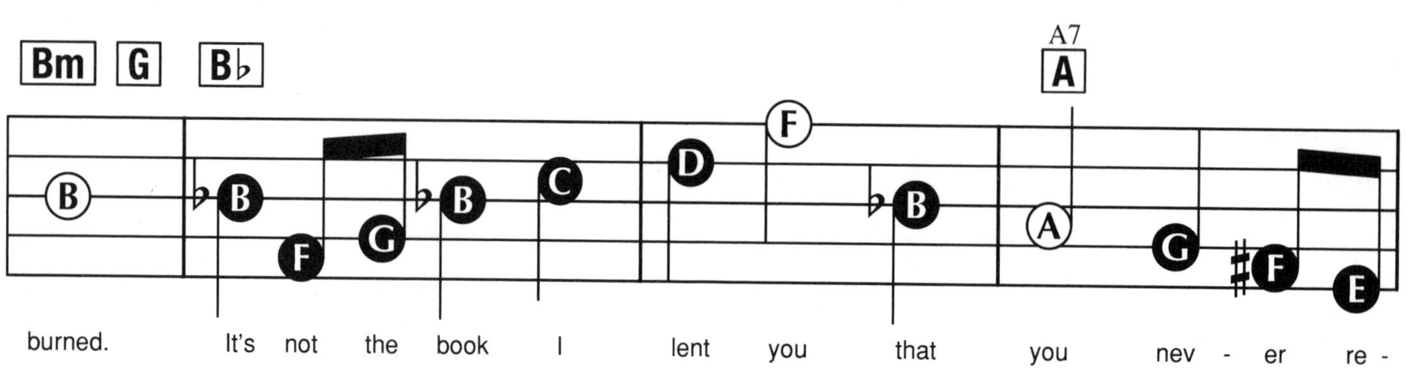

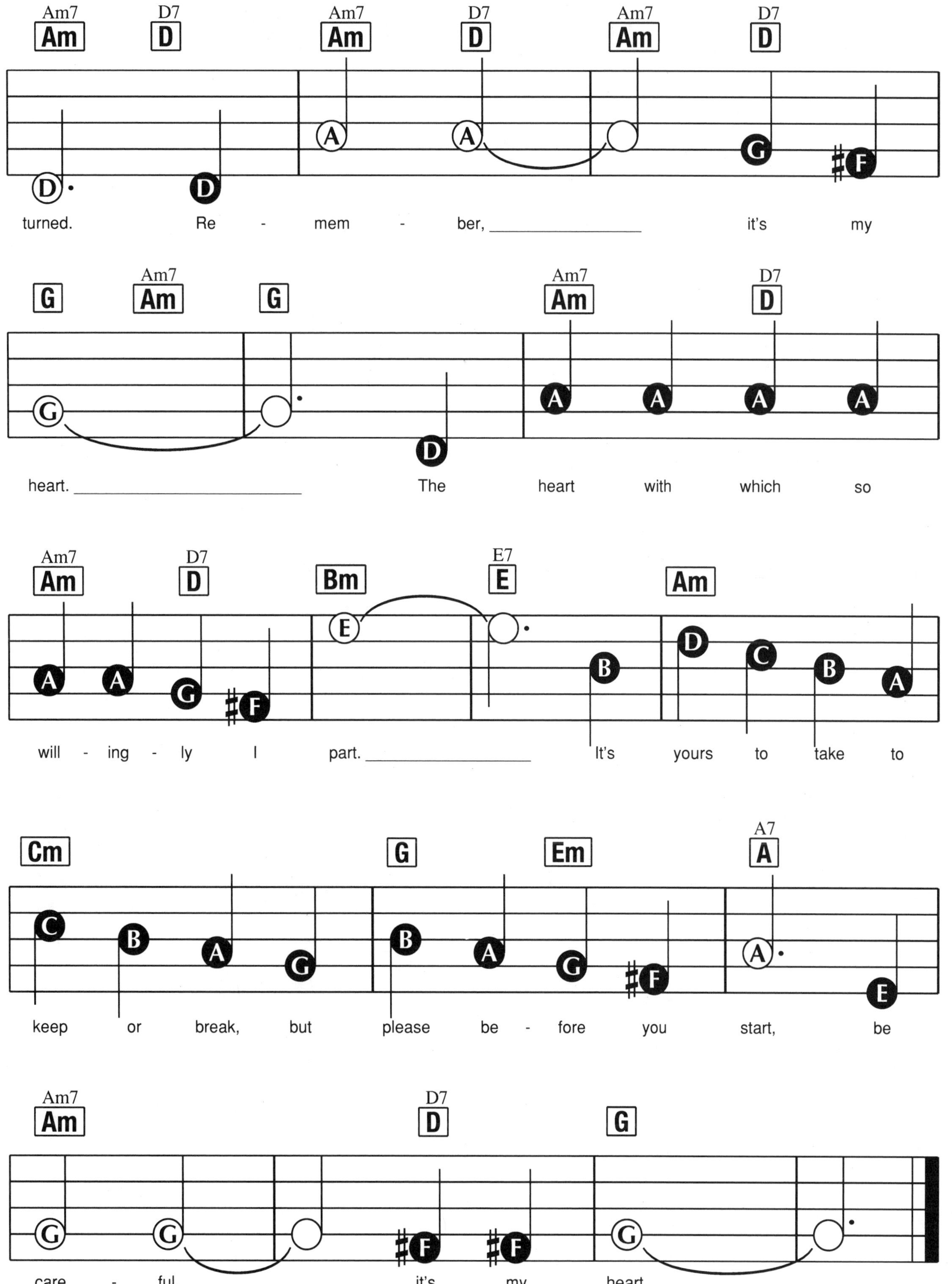
Am7 D7 Am7 D7 Am7 D7
turned. Re - mem - ber, it's my
G Am7 G Am7 D7
heart. The heart with which so
Am7 D7 Bm E7 Am
will - ing - ly I part. It's yours to take to
Cm G Em A7
keep or break, but please be - fore you start, be
Am7 D7 G
care - ful, it's my heart.

Because I Love You

Registration 2
Rhythm: Waltz

Words and Music by
Irving Berlin

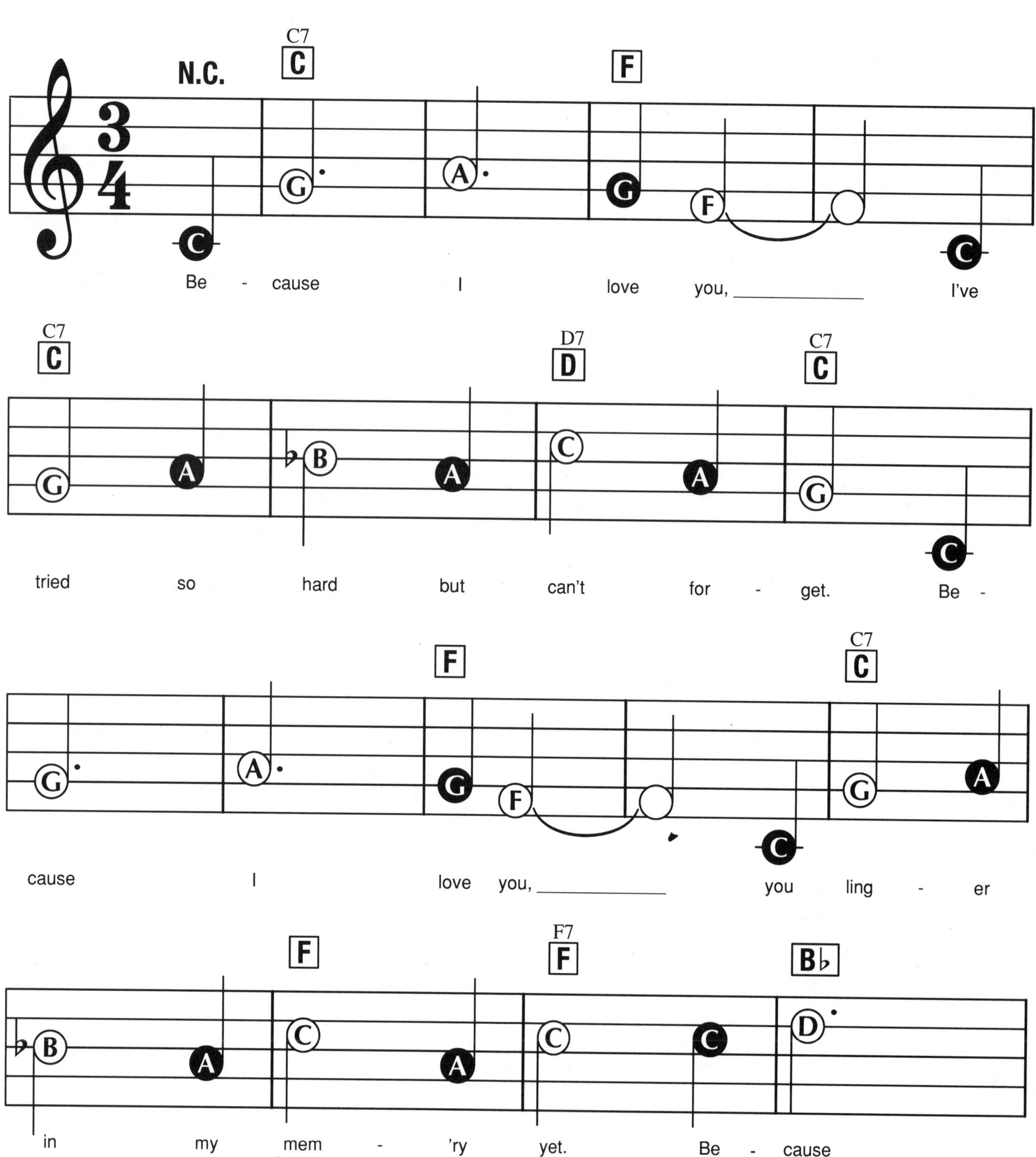

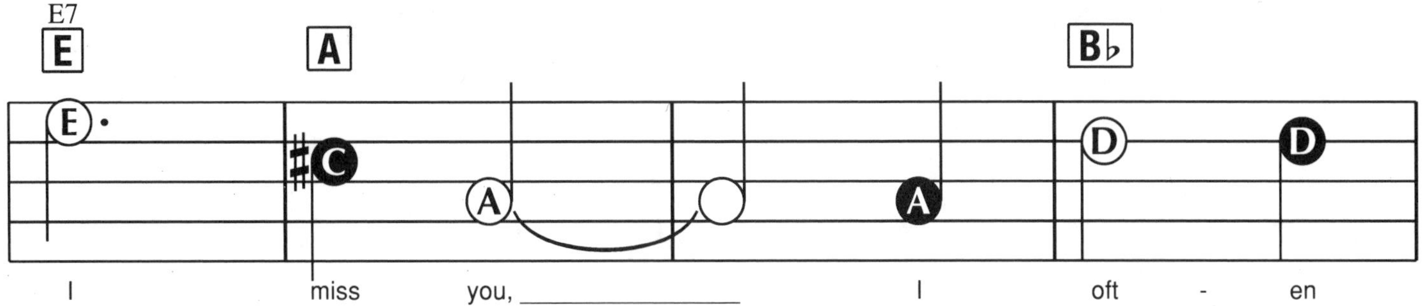
E7
E
A
B♭
E
C
A
A
D
D
I miss you, I oft - en

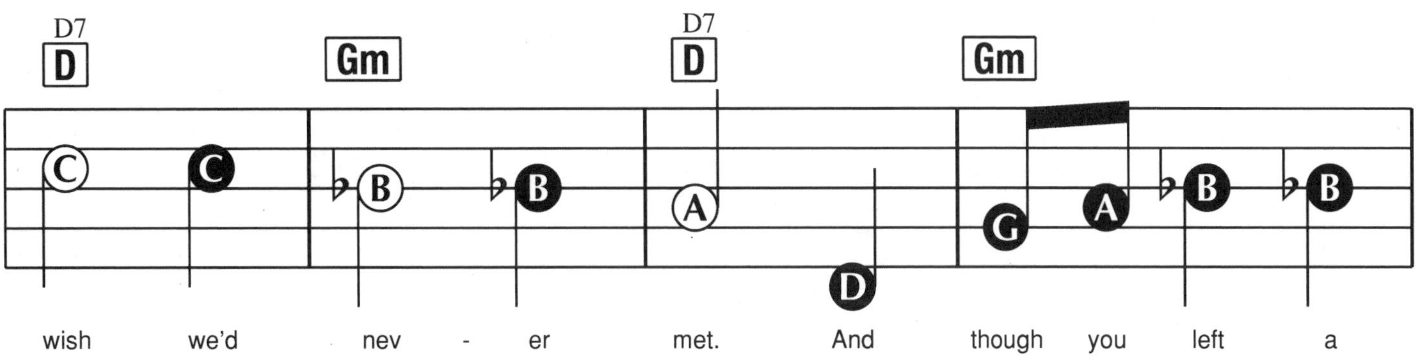
D7
D
Gm
D7
D
Gm
C
C
B
B
A
D
G
A
B
B
wish we'd nev - er met. And though you left a

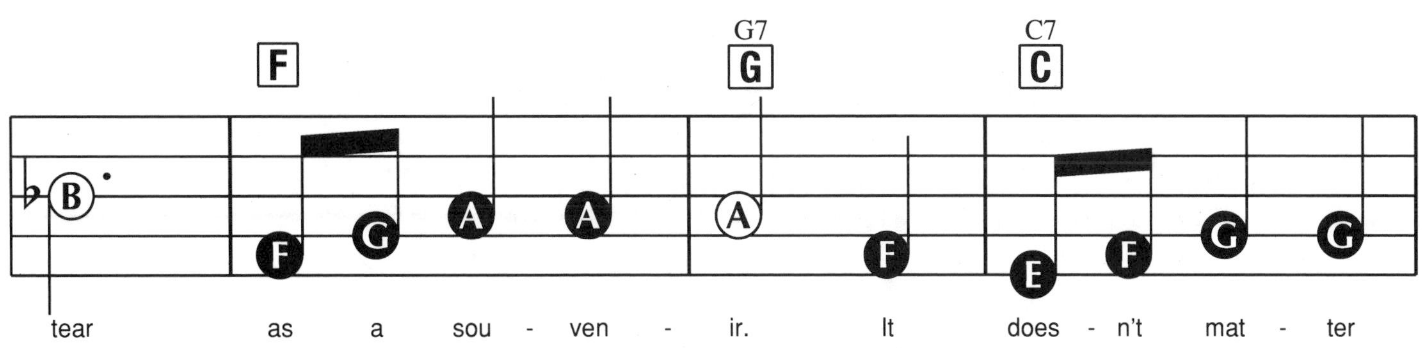
F
G7
G
C7
C
B
F
G
A
A
A
F
E
F
G
G
tear as a sou - ven - ir. It does - n't mat - ter

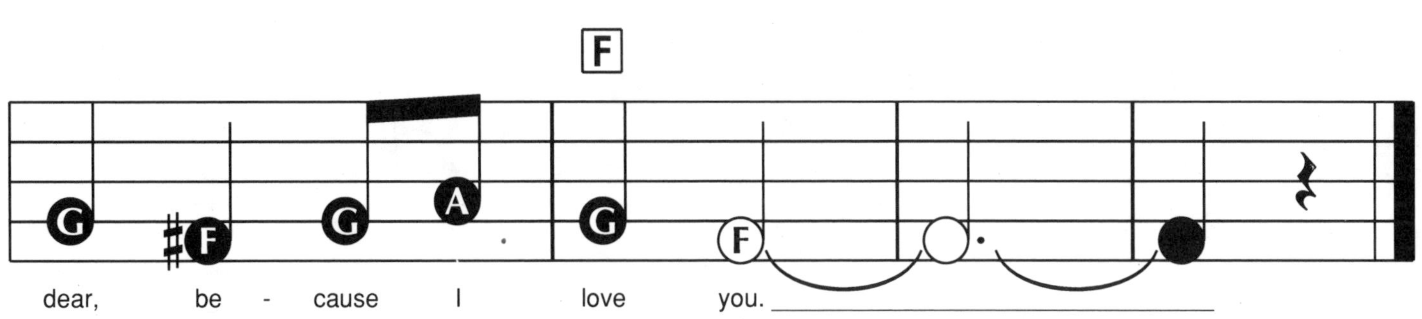
F
G
F
G
A
G
F
dear, be - cause I love you.

Better Luck Next Time

Registration 9
Rhythm: Swing

Words and Music by
Irving Berlin

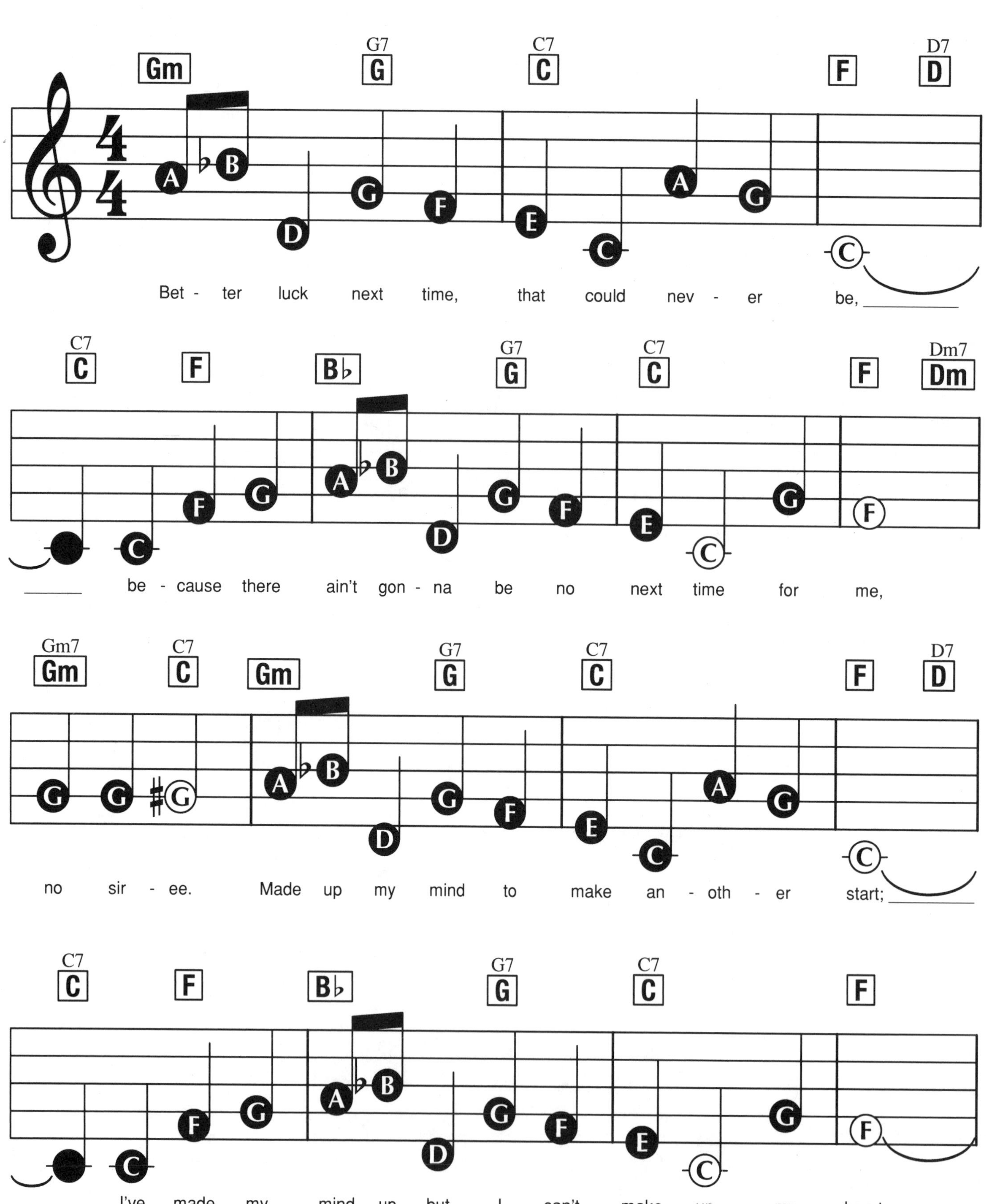

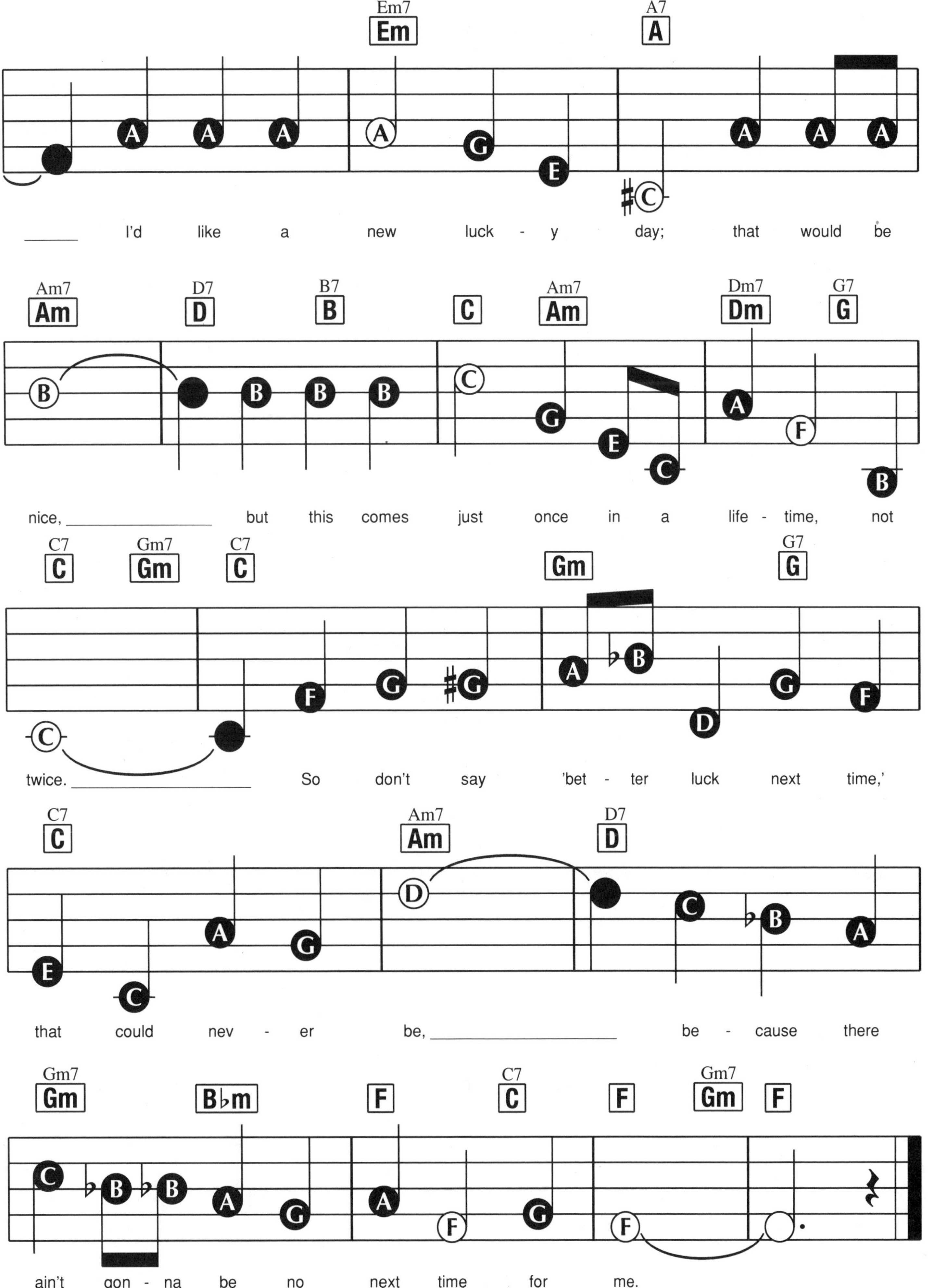
Em7
Em
A7
A
I'd like a new luck - y day; that would be
Am7
Am
D7
D
B7
B
C
Am7
Am
Dm7
Dm
G7
G
nice, but this comes just once in a life - time, not
C7
C
Gm7
Gm
C7
C
Gm
G7
G
twice. So don't say 'bet - ter luck next time,'
C7
C
Am7
Am
D7
D
that could nev - er be, be - cause there
Gm7
Gm
B♭m
F
C7
C
F
Gm7
Gm
F
ain't gon - na be no next time for me.

Blue Skies

Registration 8
Rhythm: Fox Trot or Swing

Words and Music by
Irving Berlin

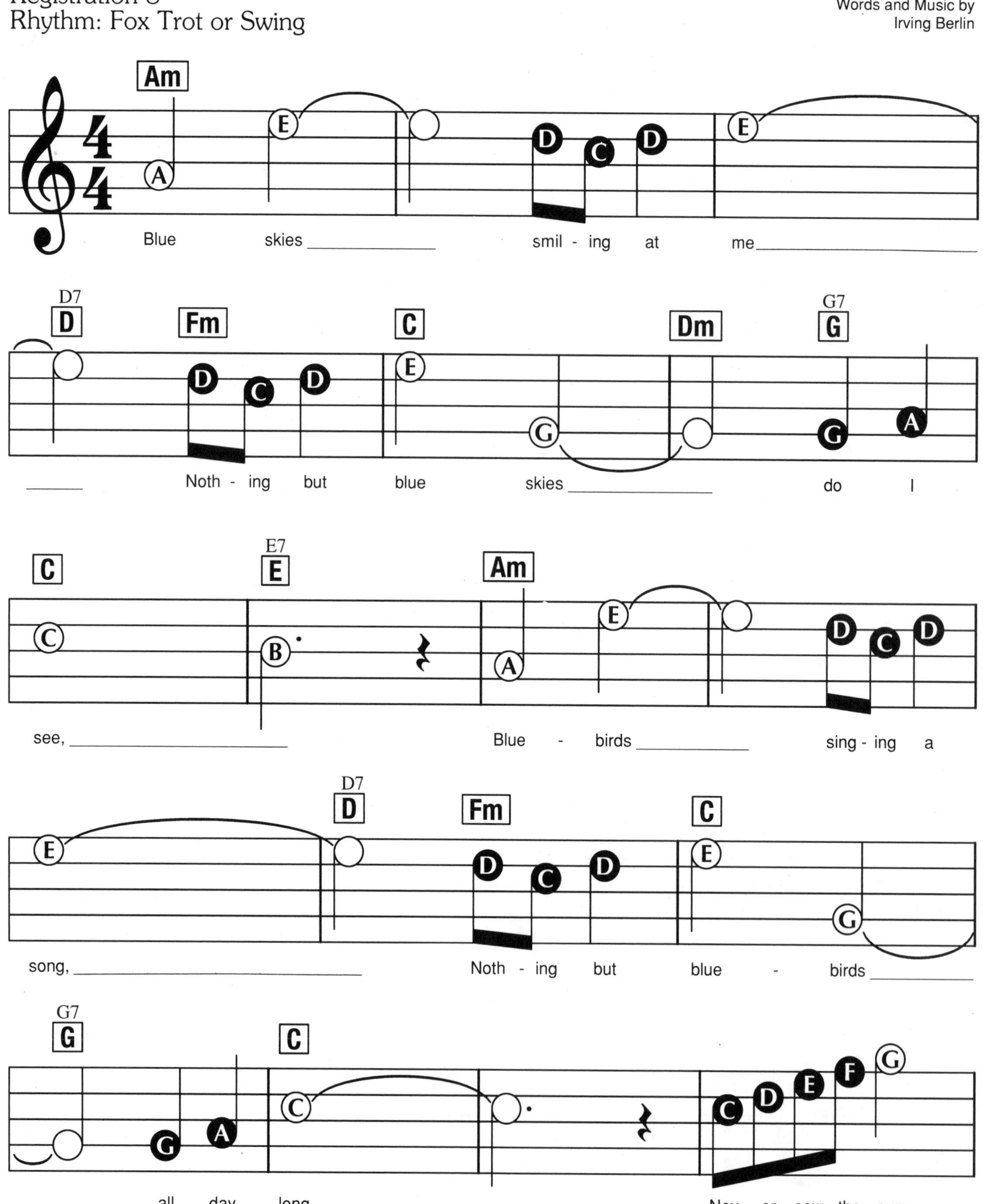

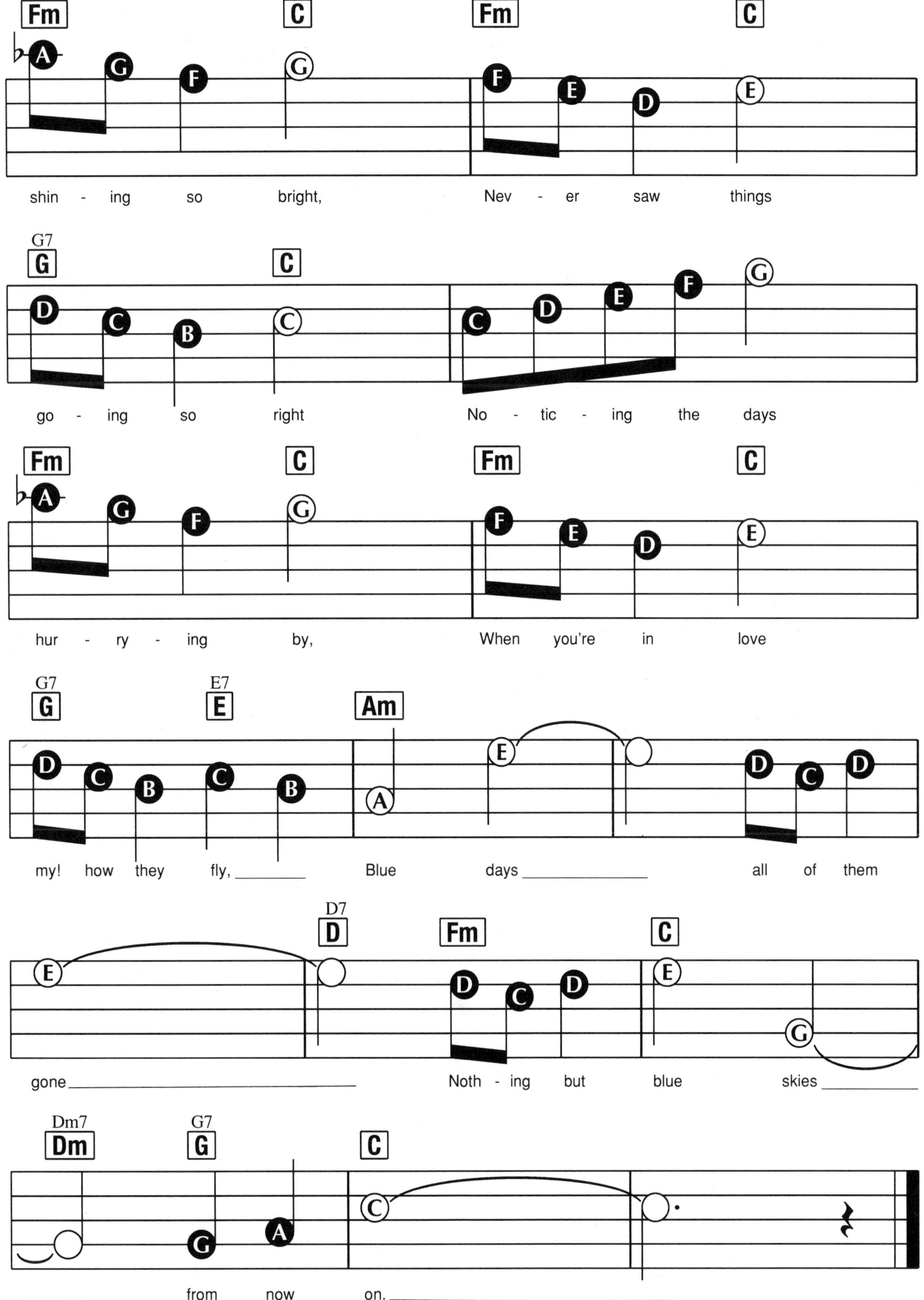
Fm C Fm C
shin - ing so bright, Nev - er saw things
G7 G C
go - ing so right No - tic - ing the days
Fm C Fm C
hur - ry - ing by, When you're in love
G7 G E7 E Am
my! how they fly, Blue days all of them
D7 D Fm C
gone Noth - ing but blue skies
Dm7 Dm G7 G C
from now on.

Change Partners

Registration 2
Rhythm: Swing

Words and Music by
Irving Berlin

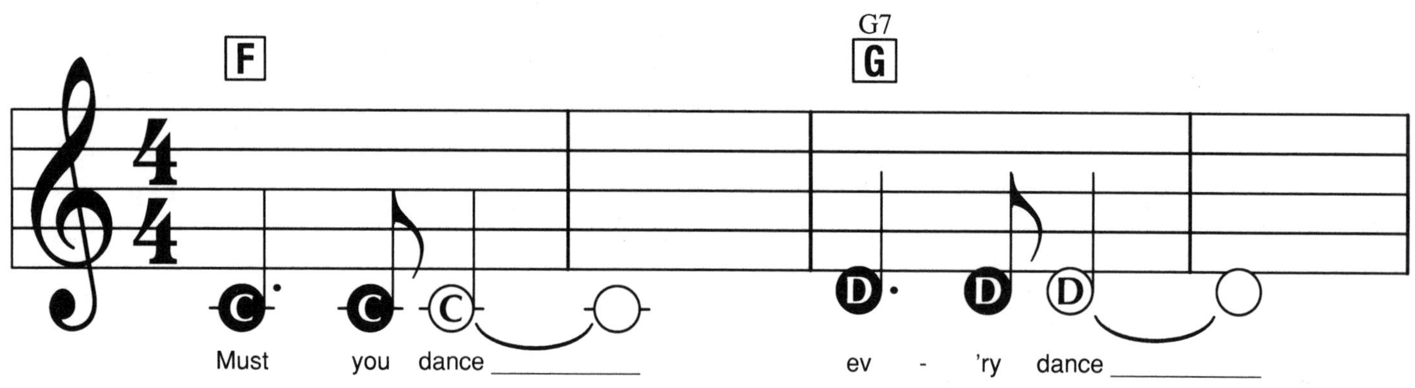

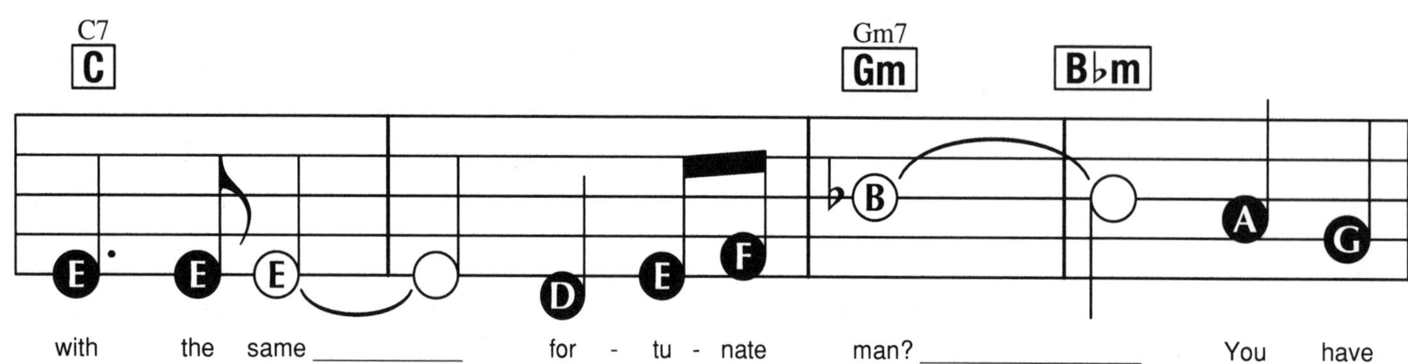

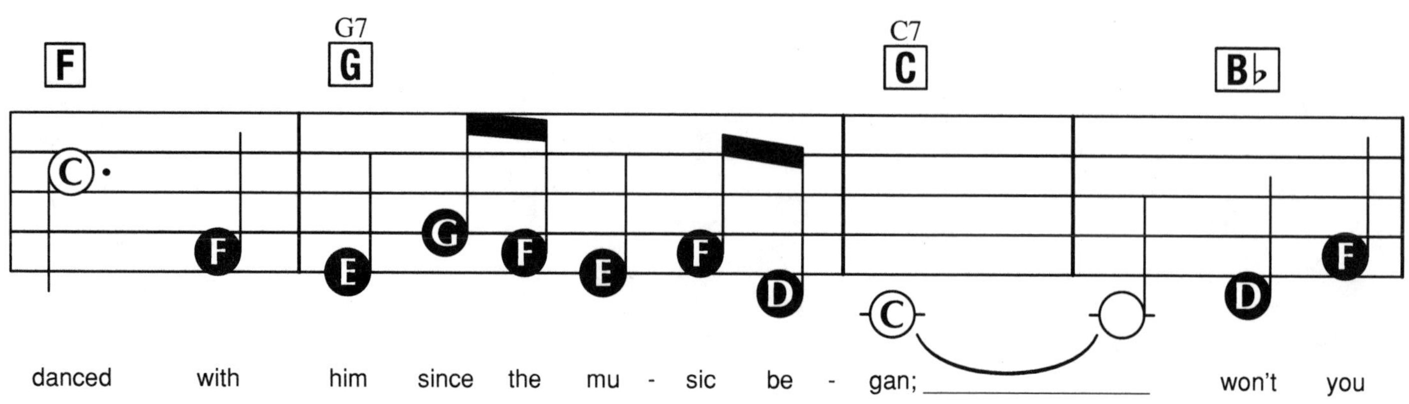

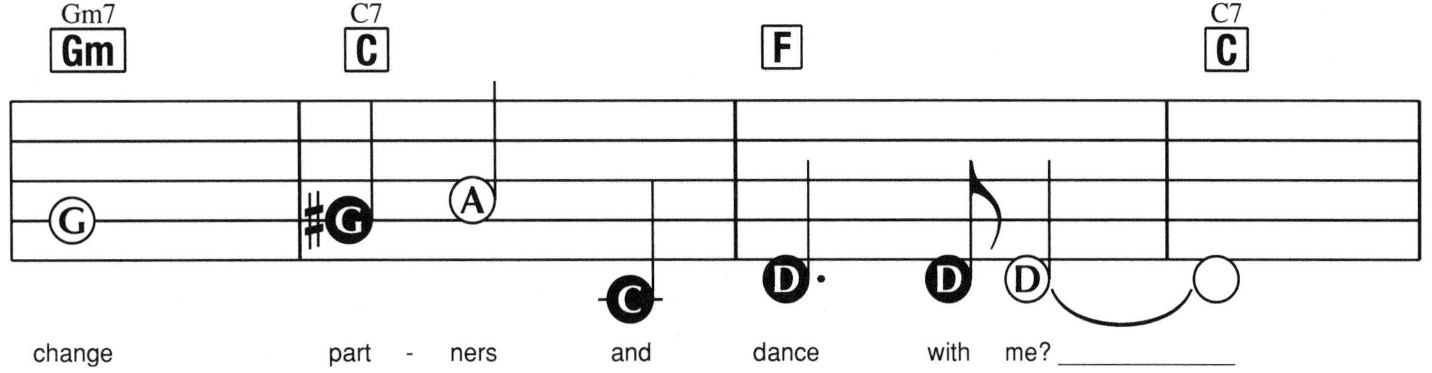
Gm7
Gm
C7
C
F
C7
C
G
G
A
C
D
D
D
change
part - ners
and
dance
with
me?

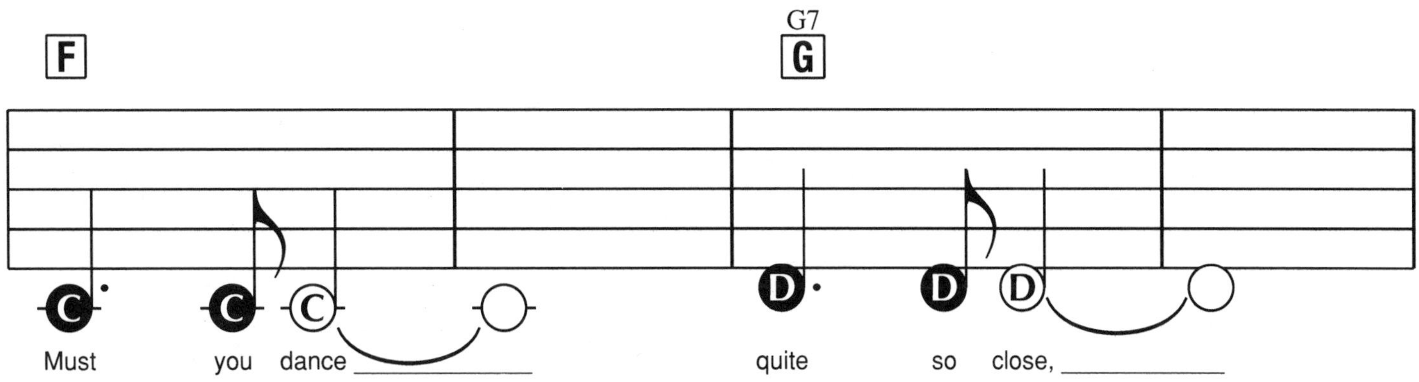
F
G7
G
C
C
C
D
D
D
Must
you
dance
quite
so
close,

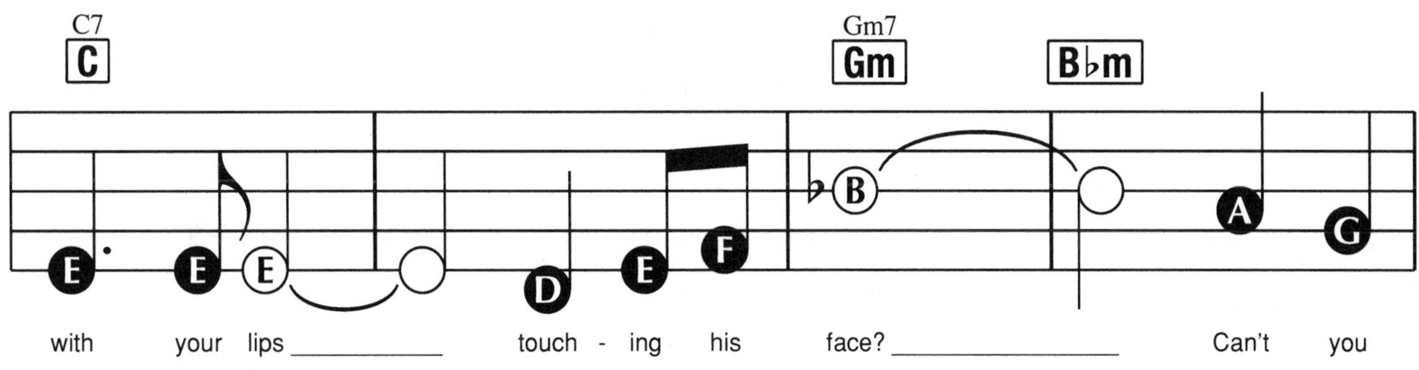
C7
C
Gm7
Gm
B♭m
E
E
E
D
E
F
B
A
G
with
your
lips
touch - ing
his
face?
Can't
you

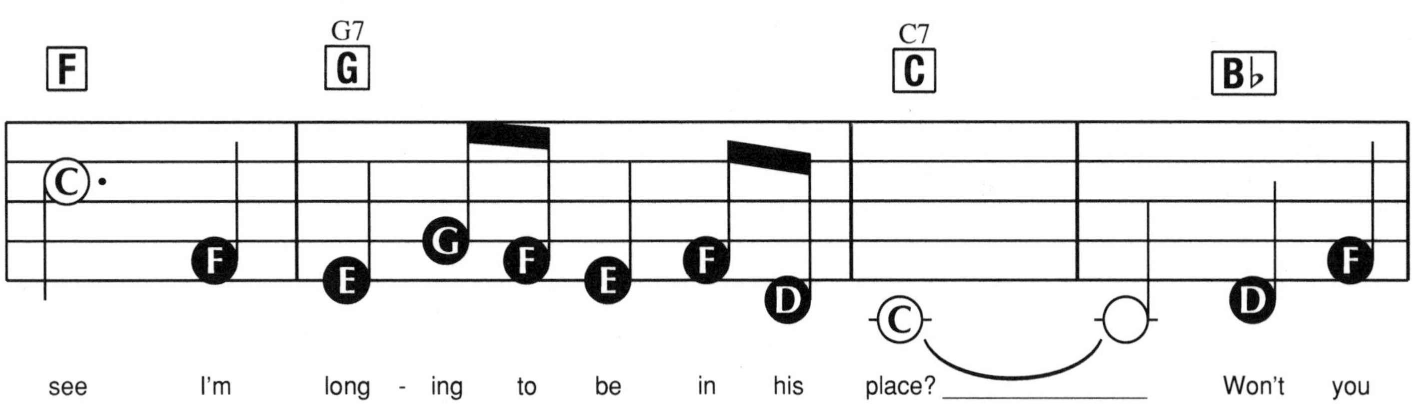
F
G7
G
C7
C
B♭
C
F
E
G
F
E
F
D
C
D
F
see
I'm
long - ing
to
be
in
his
place?
Won't
you

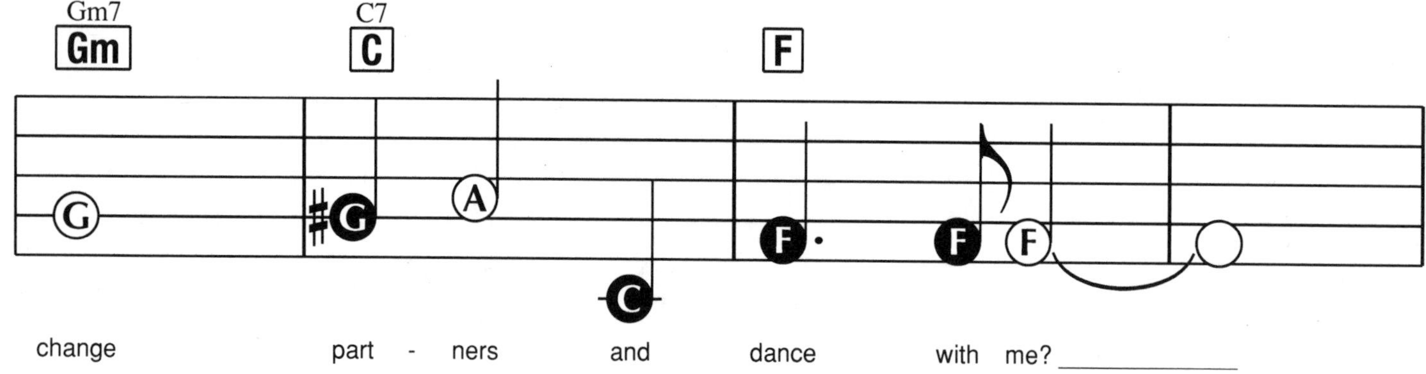
Gm7
Gm
C7
C
F
G
G
A
C
F
F
F
change part - ners and dance with me?

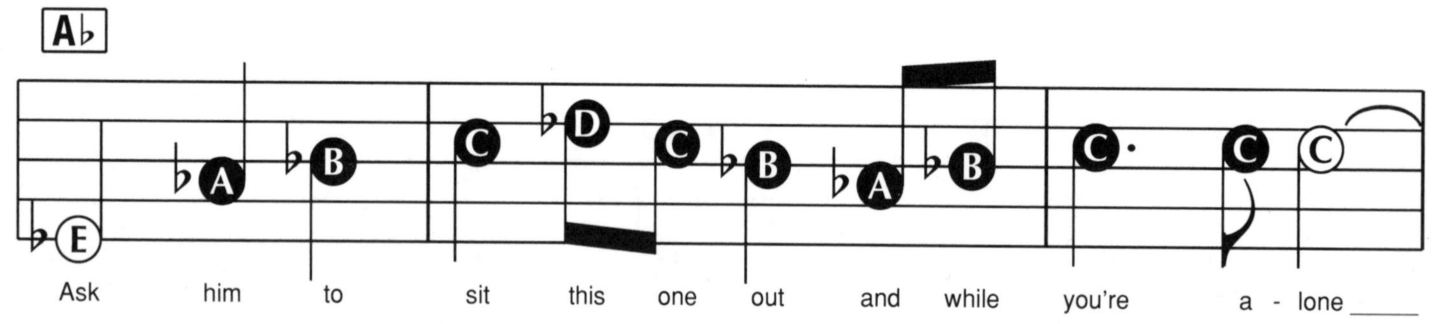
A♭
E
A
B
C
D
C
B
A
B
C
C
C
Ask him to sit this one out and while you're a - lone

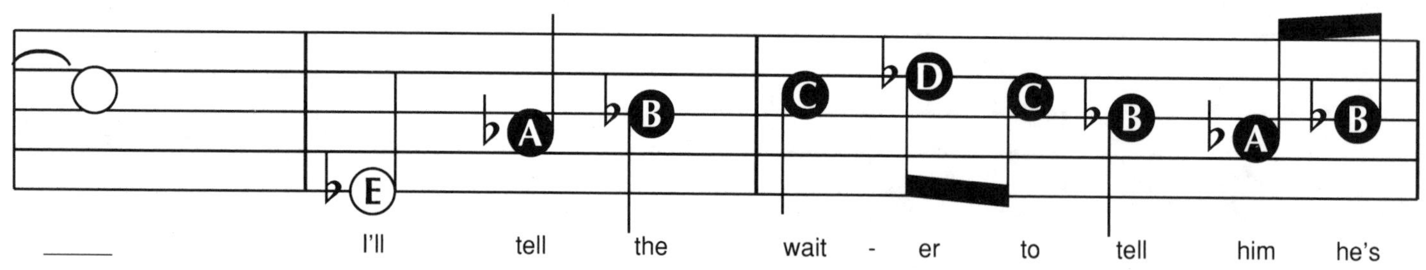
E
A
B
C
D
C
B
A
B
I'll tell the wait - er to tell him he's

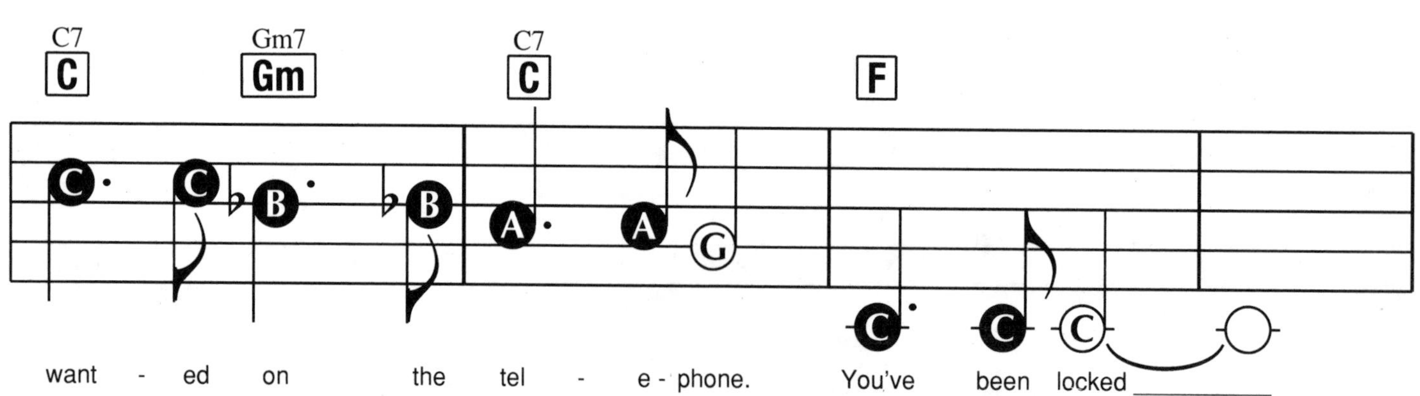
C7
C
Gm7
Gm
C7
C
F
C
C
B
B
A
A
G
C
C
C
want - ed on the tel - e - phone. You've been locked

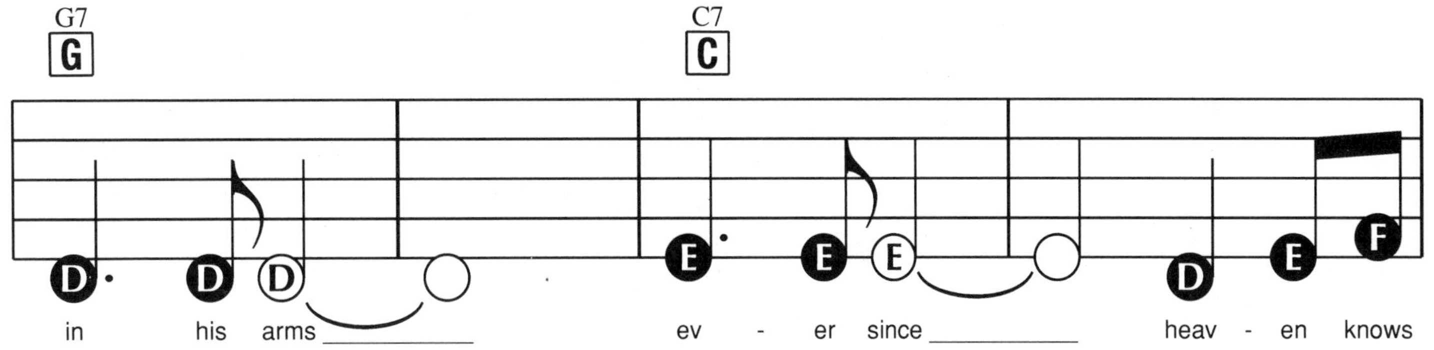
G7
G
C7
C
D D D
E E E
D E F
in his arms
ev - er since
heav - en knows

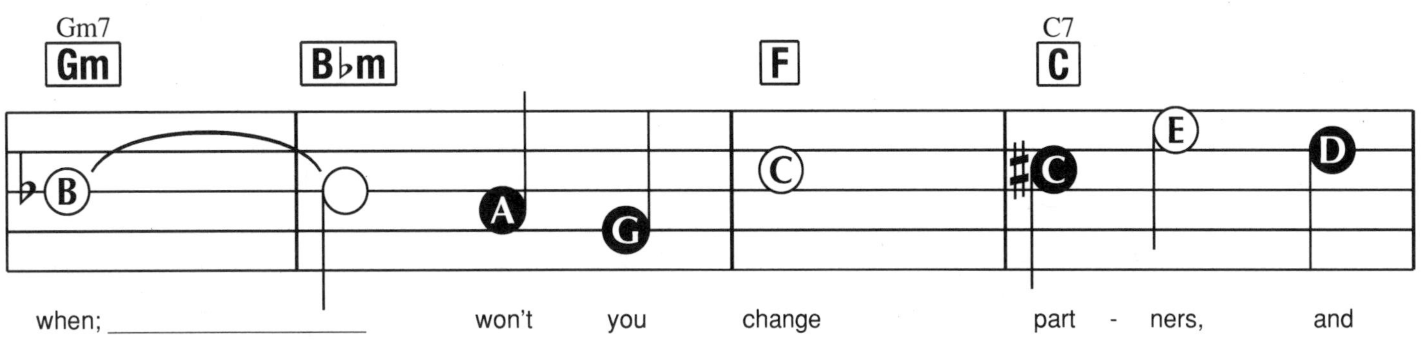
Gm7
Gm
B♭m
F
C7
C
B
A G
C
C E D
when;
won't you change
part - ners, and

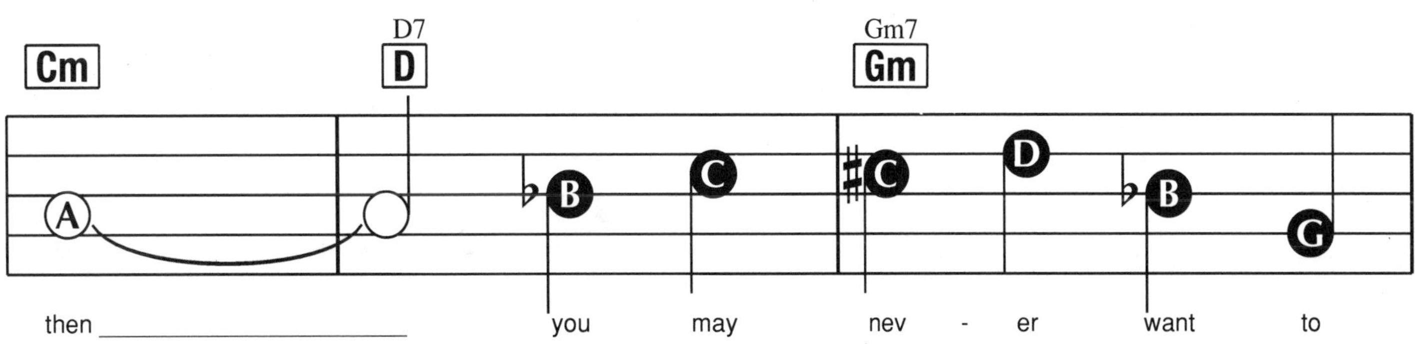
Cm
D7
D
Gm7
Gm
A
B C
C D B G
then
you may
nev - er want to

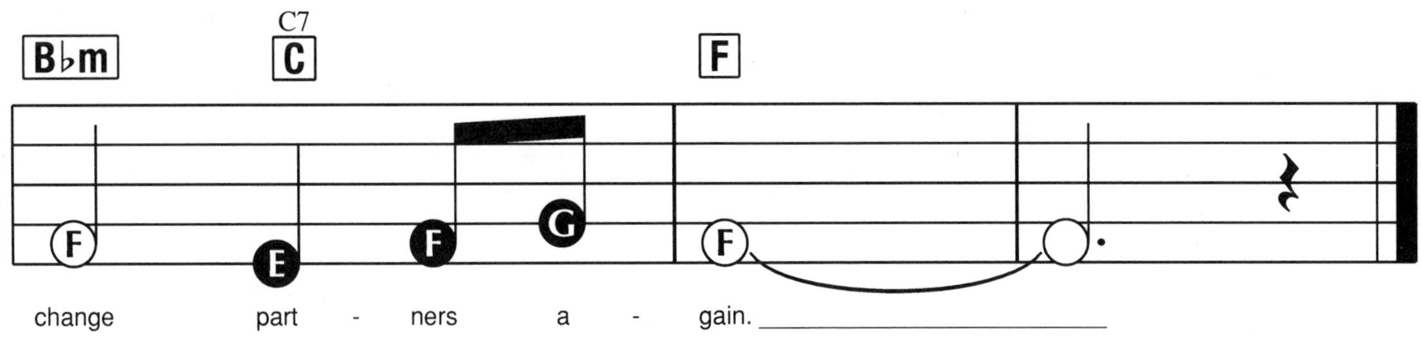
B♭m
C7
C
F
F E F G
F
change part - ners a - gain.

Cheek To Cheek

Registration 2
Rhythm: Fox Trot or Swing

Words and Music by
Irving Berlin

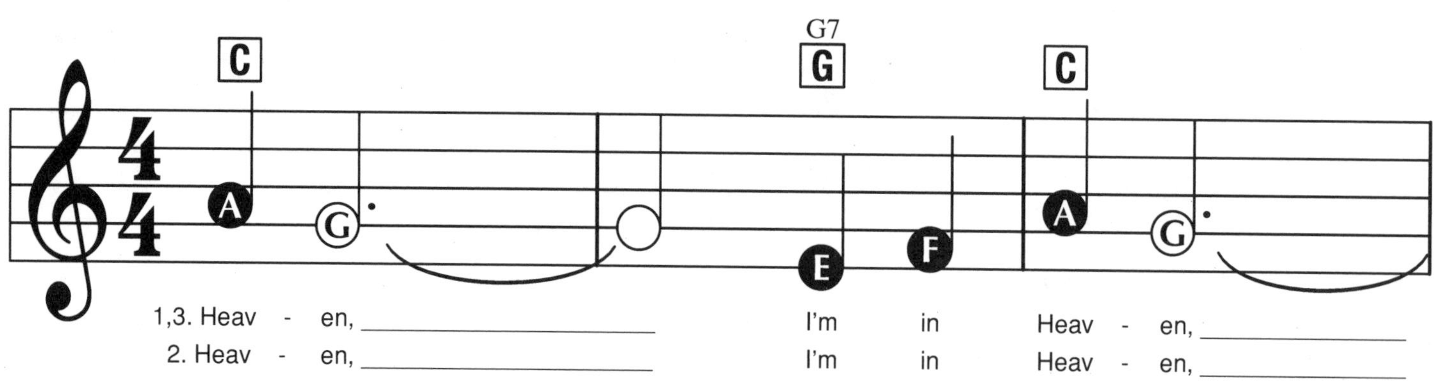

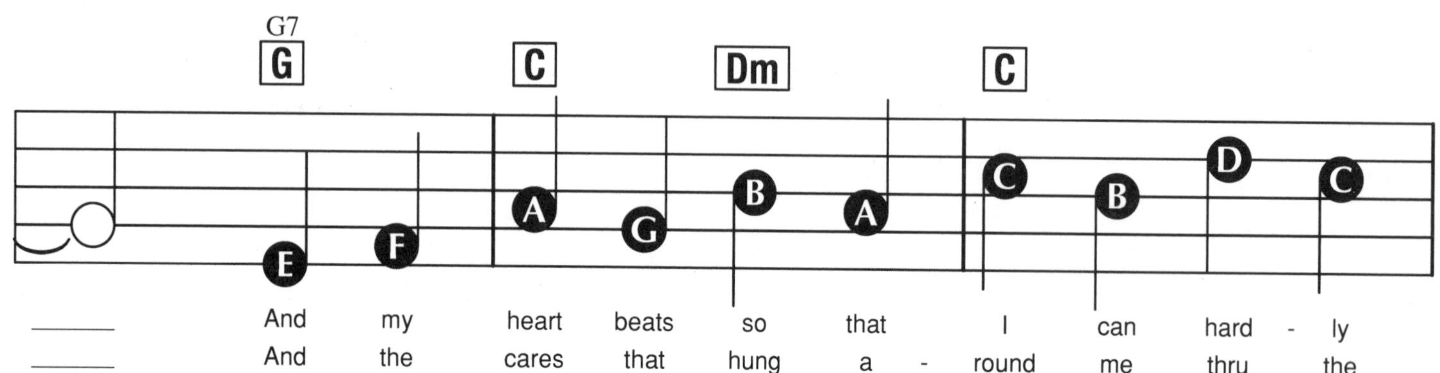

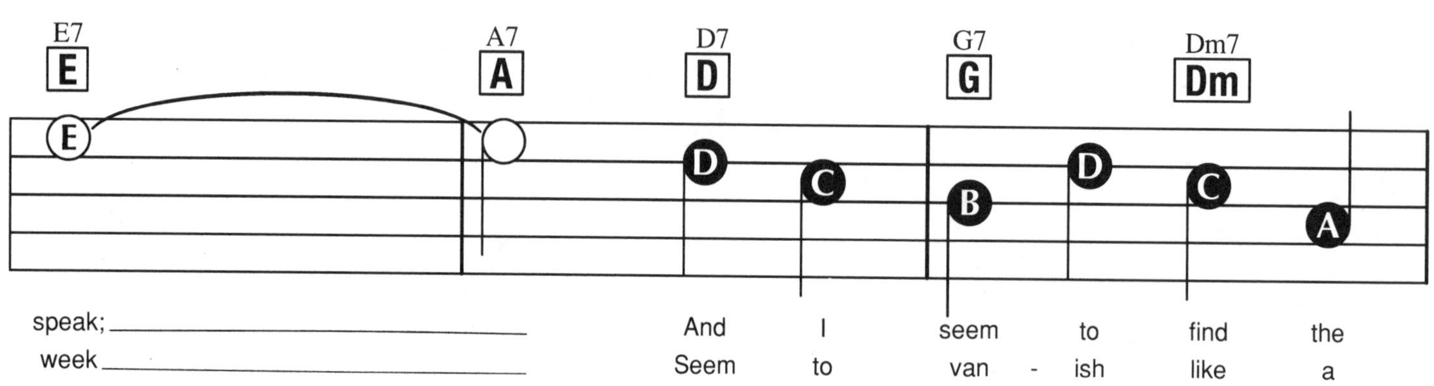

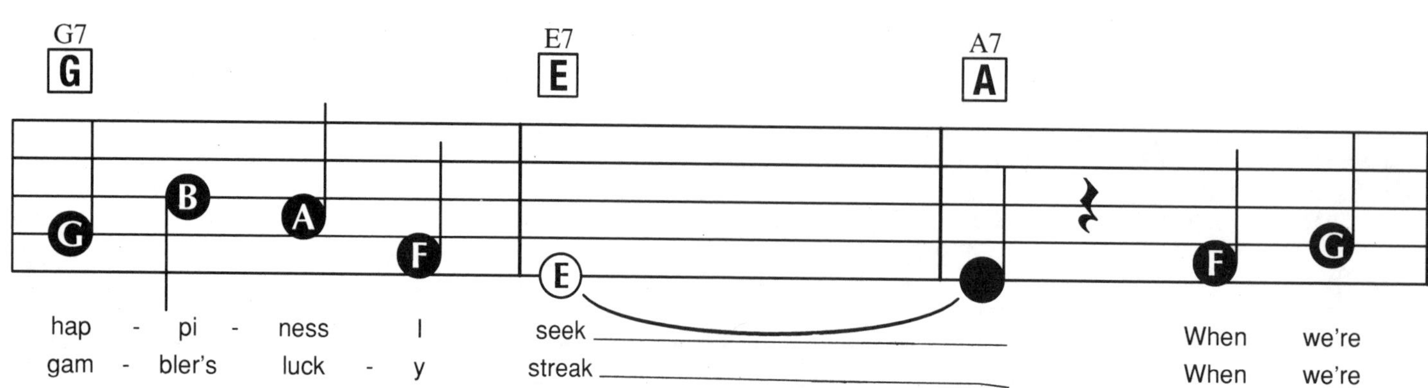

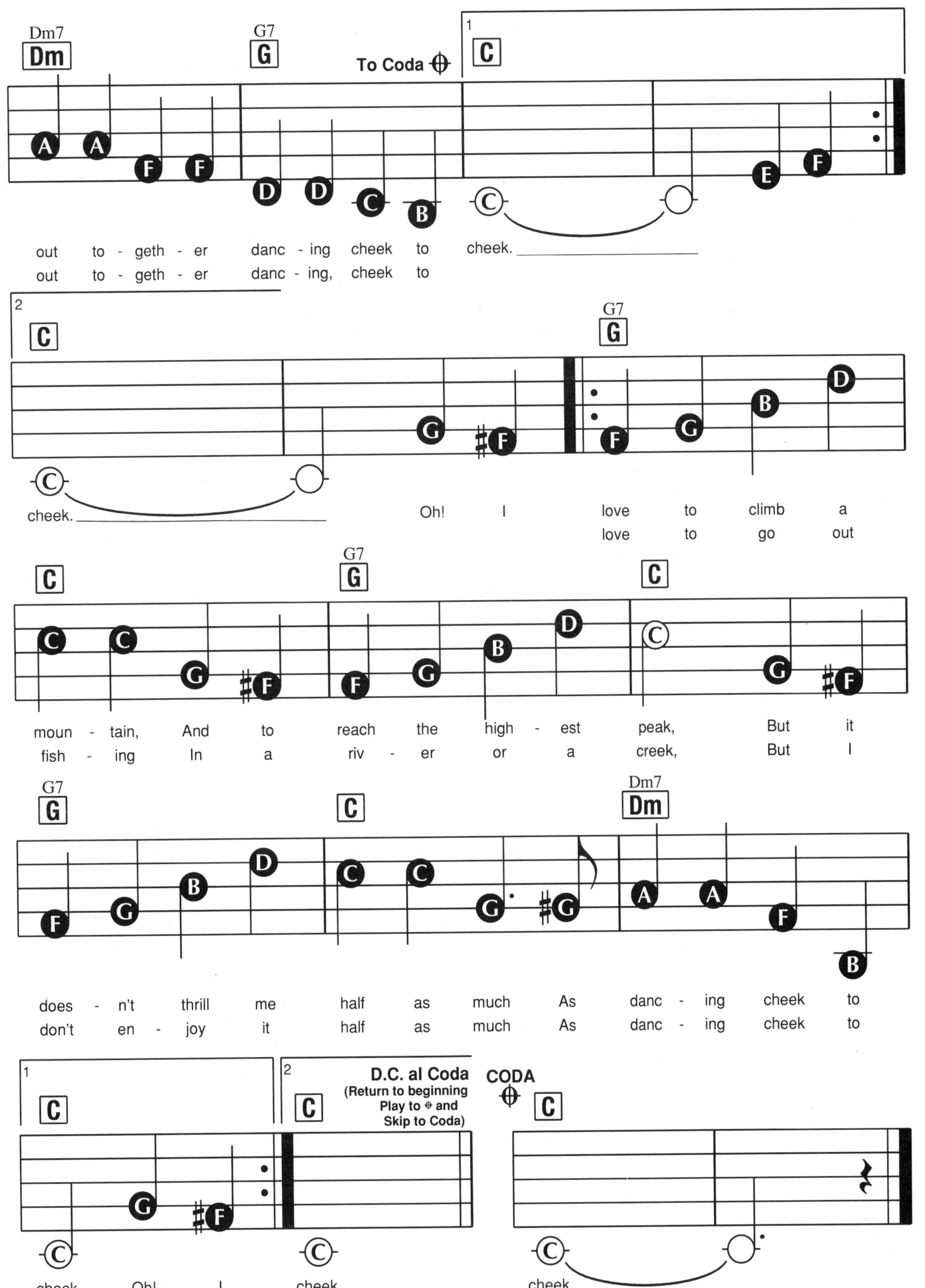

Dm7
Dm
G7
G
To Coda
1
C
out to - geth - er danc - ing cheek to cheek.
out to - geth - er danc - ing, cheek to
2
C
G7
G
cheek. Oh! I love to climb a
love to go out
C
G7
G
C
moun - tain, And to reach the high - est peak, But it
fish - ing In a riv - er or a creek, But I
G7
G
C
Dm7
Dm
does - n't thrill me half as much As danc - ing cheek to
don't en - joy it half as much As danc - ing cheek to
1
C
2
C
D.C. al Coda
(Return to beginning
Play to ⊕ and
Skip to Coda)
CODA
C
cheek. Oh! I cheek. cheek.

Coquette

Registration 2
Rhythm: Waltz

Words and Music by
Irving Berlin

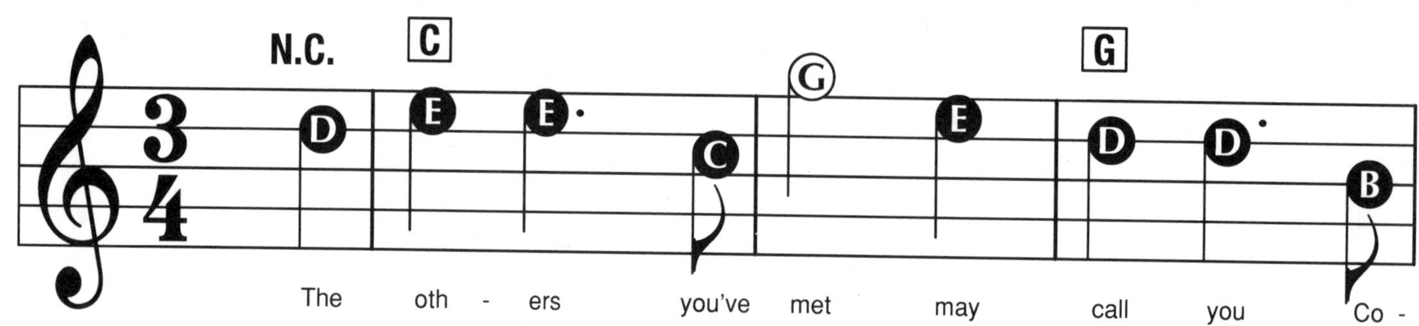

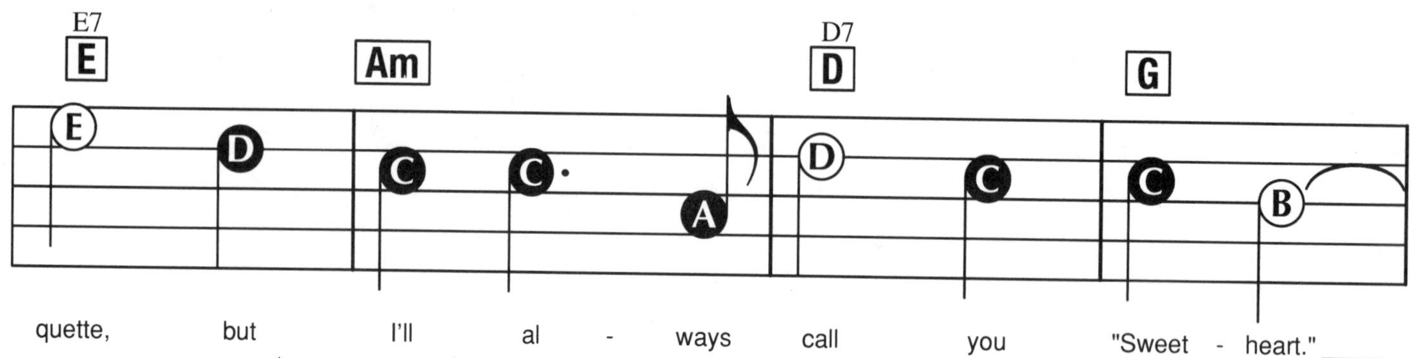

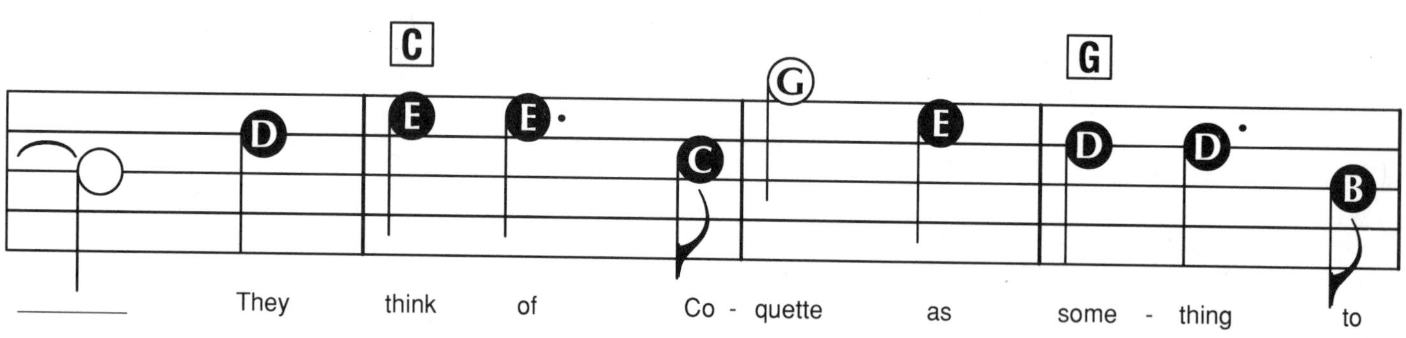

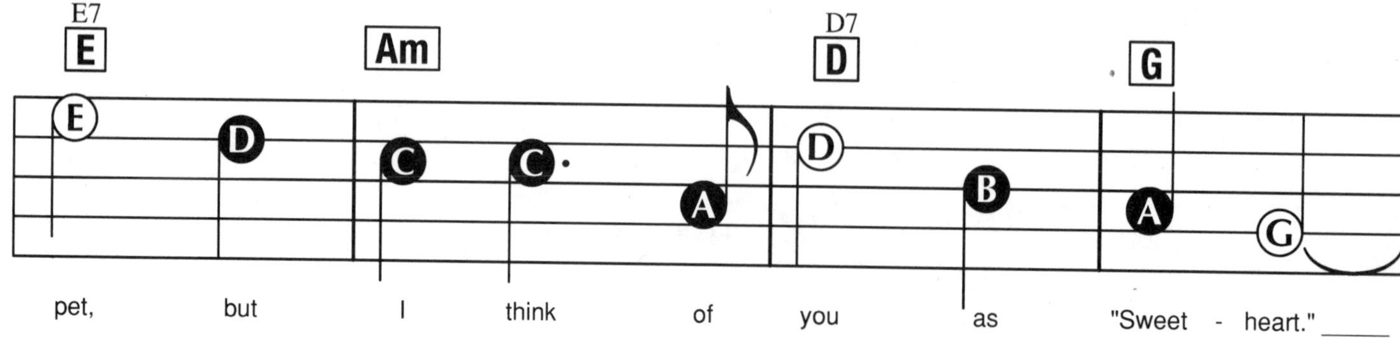

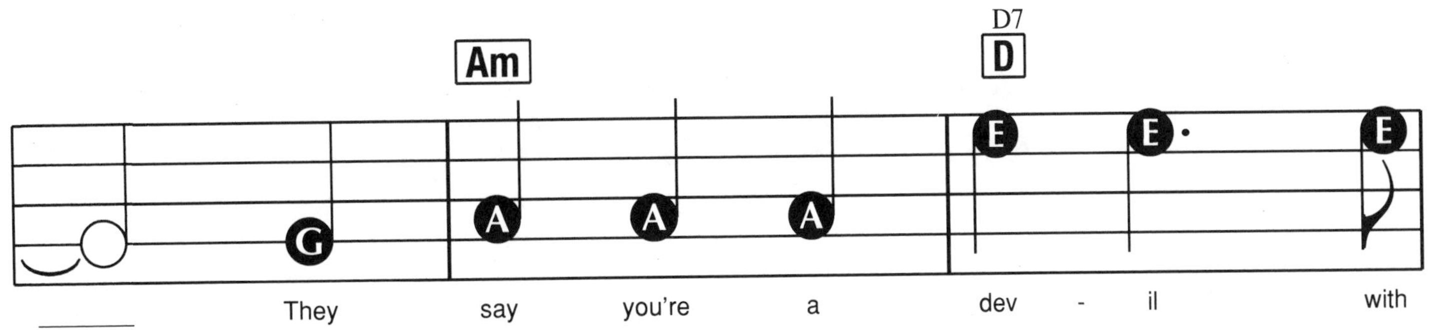
Am
D7
D
They say you're a dev - il with

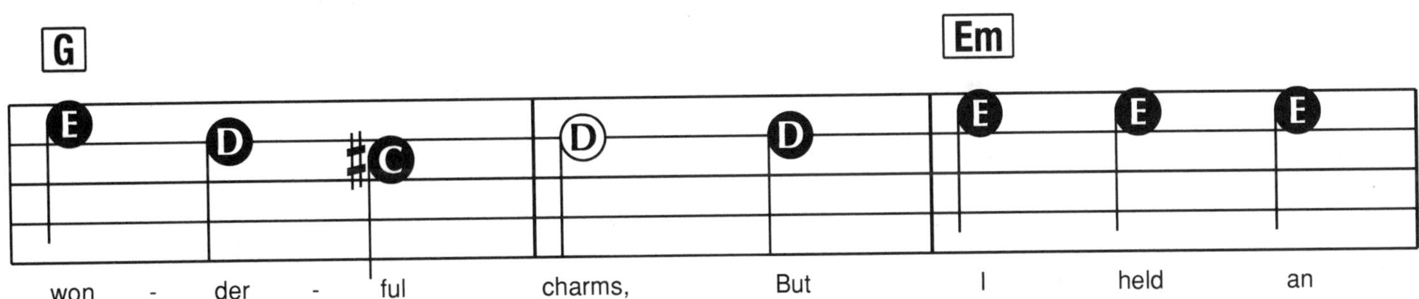
G
Em
won - der - ful charms, But I held an

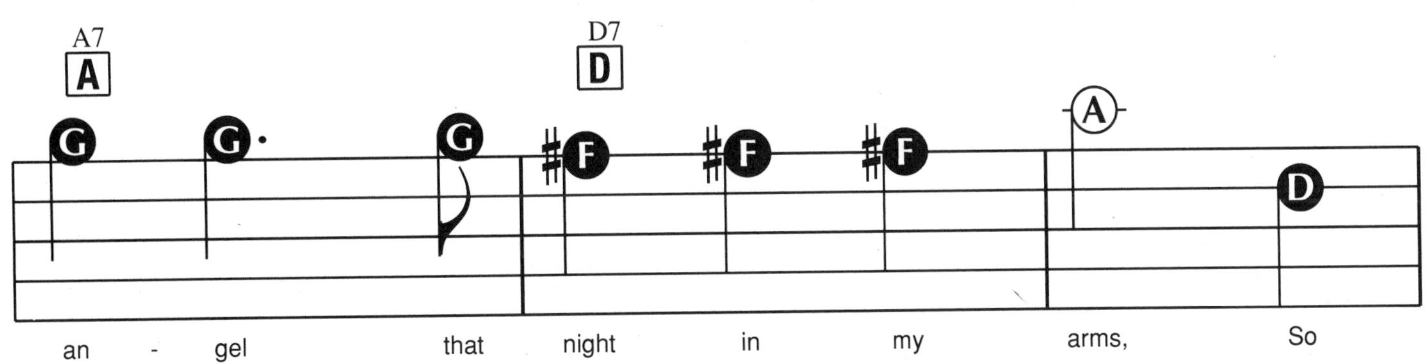
A7
A
D7
D
an - gel that night in my arms, So

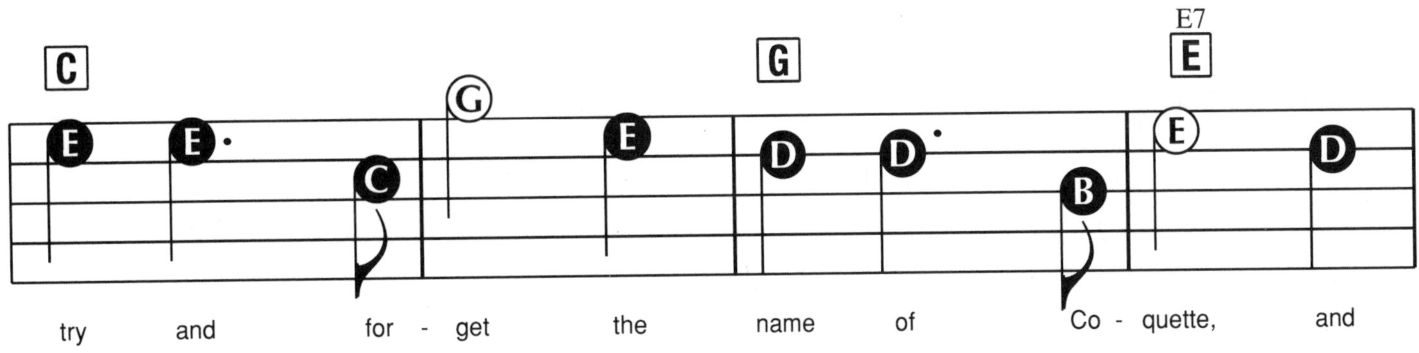
C
G
E7
E
try and for - get the name of Co - quette, and

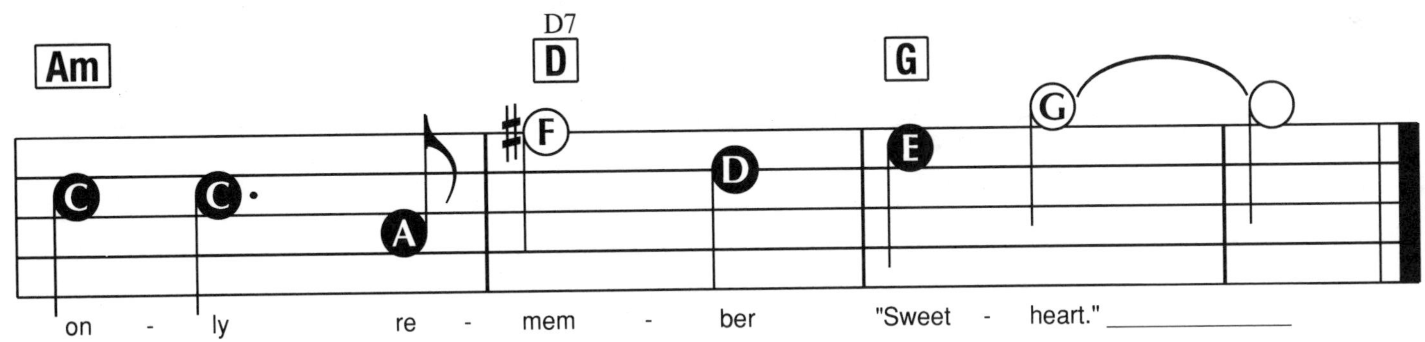
Am
D7
D
G
on - ly re - mem - ber "Sweet - heart."

Count Your Blessings Instead Of Sheep

Registration 4
Rhythm: Swing

Words and Music by
Irving Berlin

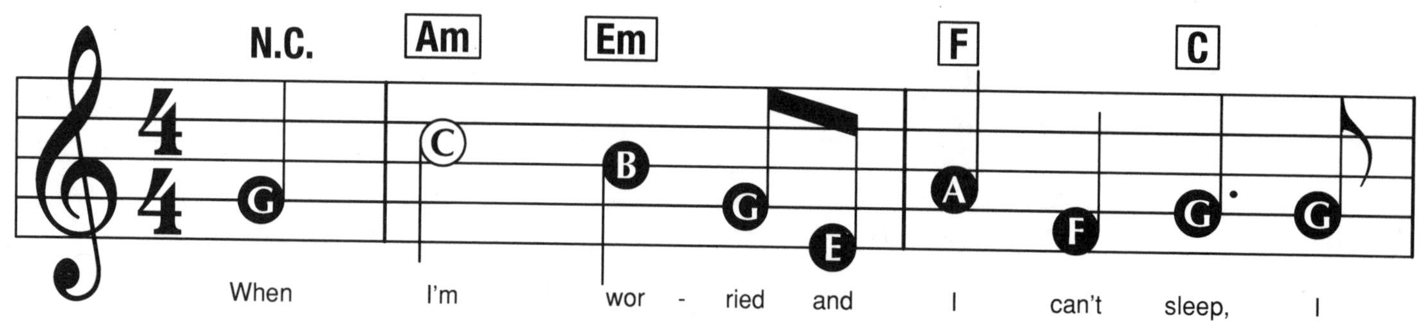

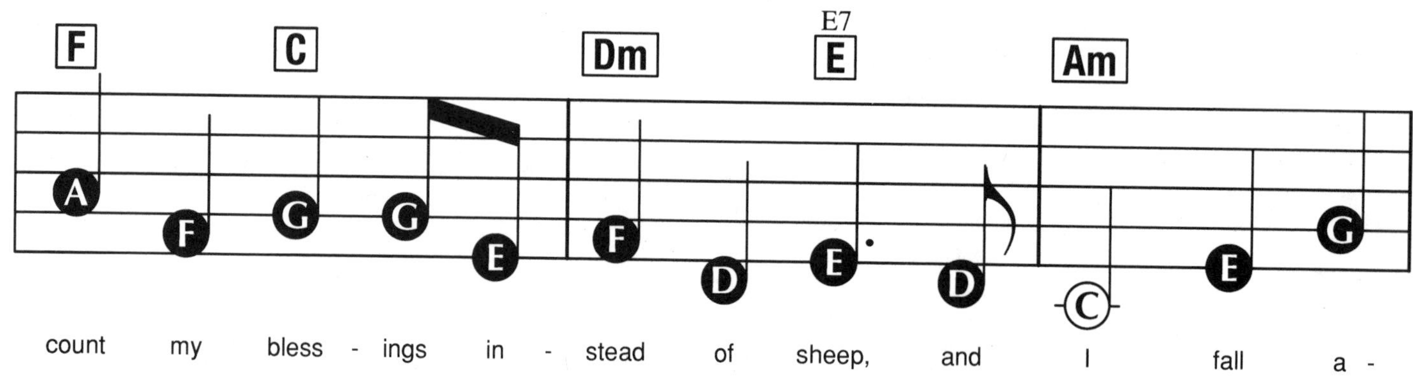

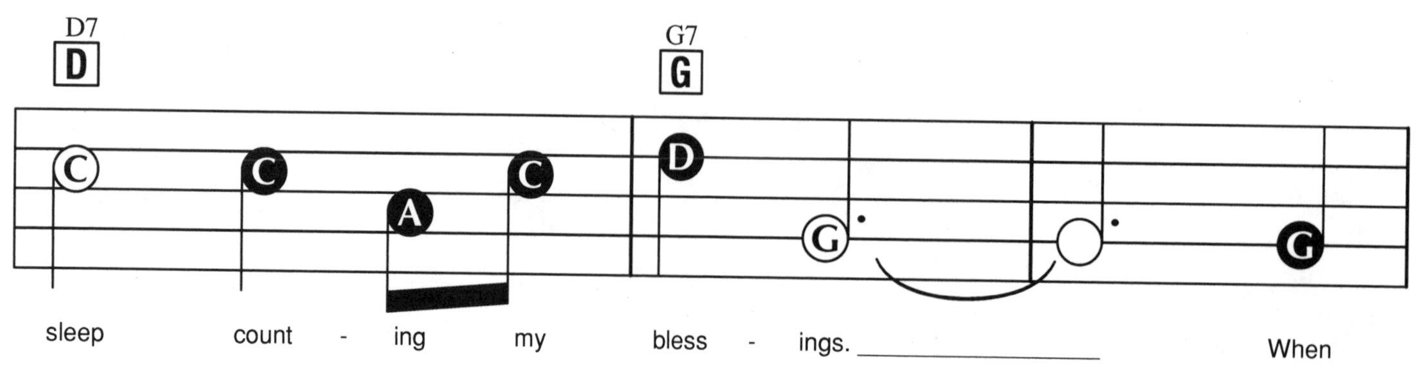

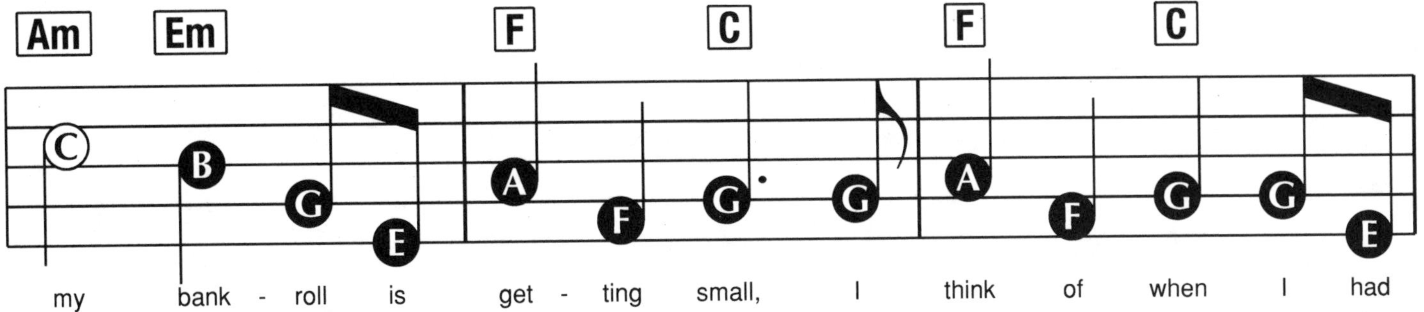
Am
Em
F
C
F
C
C
B
G
E
A
F
G
G
A
F
G
G
E
my bank - roll is get - ting small, I think of when I had

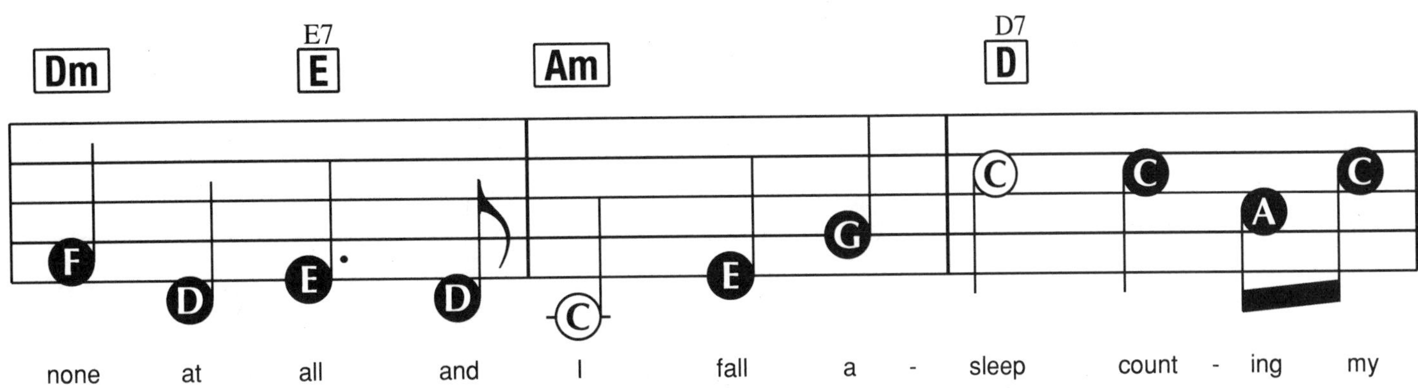
Dm
E7
E
Am
D7
D
F
D
E
D
C
E
G
C
C
A
C
none at all and I fall a - sleep count - ing my

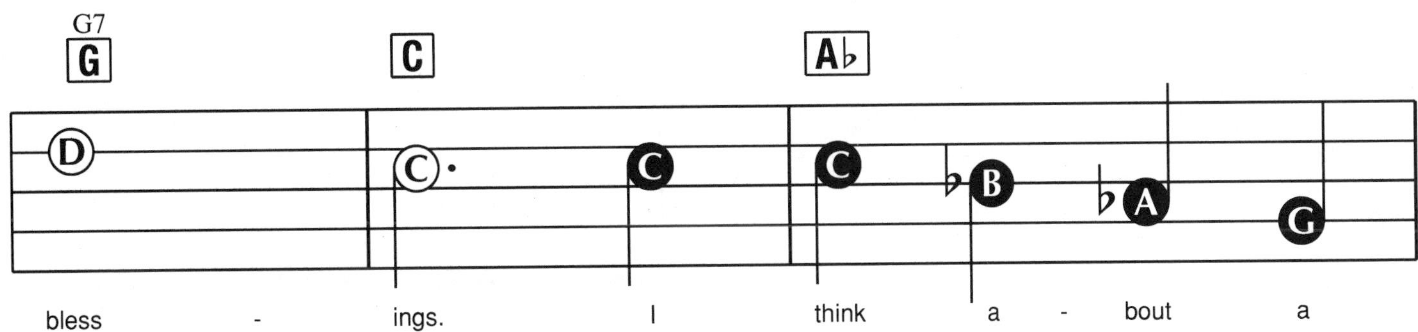
G7
G
C
A♭
D
C
C
C
B
A
G
bless - ings. I think a - bout a

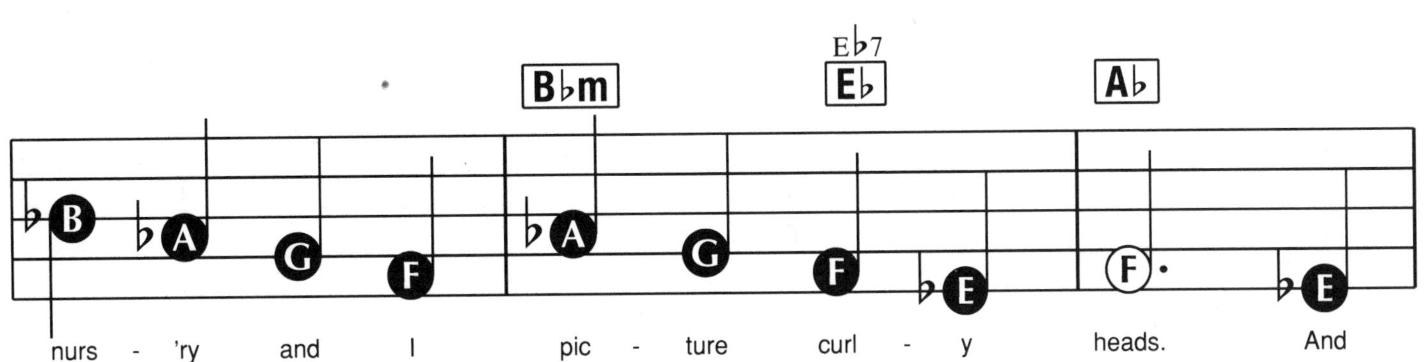
B♭m
E♭7
E♭
A♭
B
A
G
F
A
G
F
E
F
E
nurs - 'ry and I pic - ture curl - y heads. And

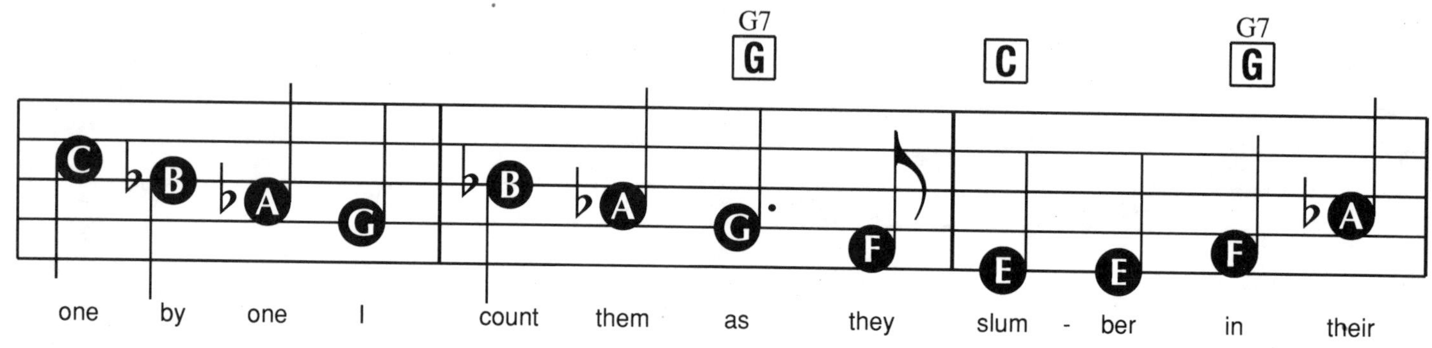
G7
G
C
G7
G
C
B
A
G
B
A
G
F
E
E
F
A
one by one I count them as they slum - ber in their

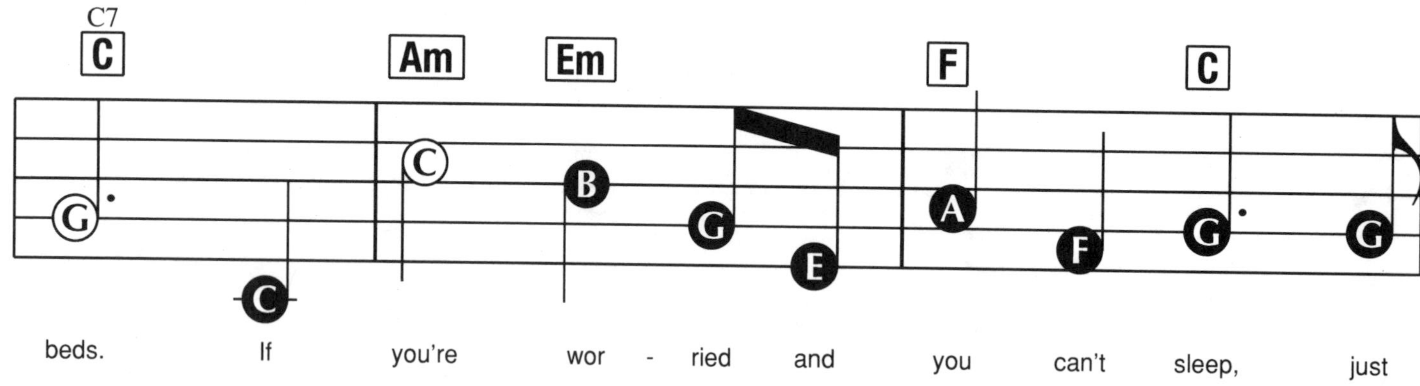
C7
C
Am
Em
F
C
G
C
C
B
G
E
A
F
G
G
beds. If you're wor - ried and you can't sleep, just

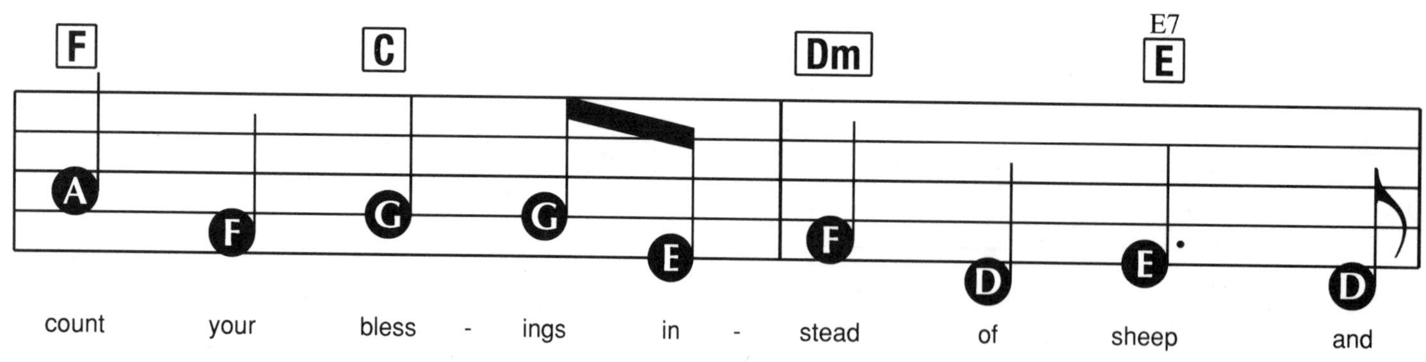
F
C
Dm
E7
E
A
F
G
G
E
F
D
E
D
count your bless - ings in - stead of sheep and

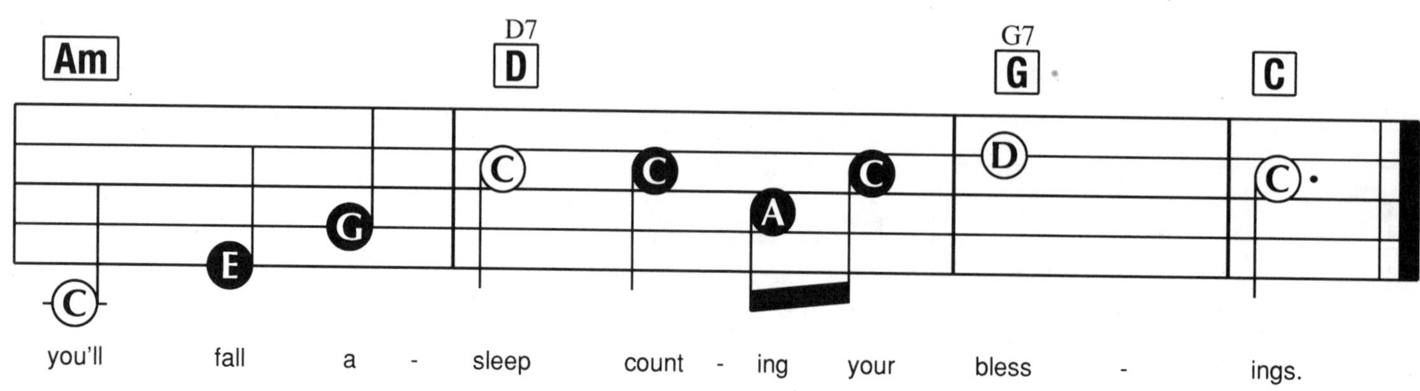
Am
D7
D
G7
G
C
C
E
G
C
C
A
C
D
C
you'll fall a - sleep count - ing your bless - ings.

Anything You Can Do

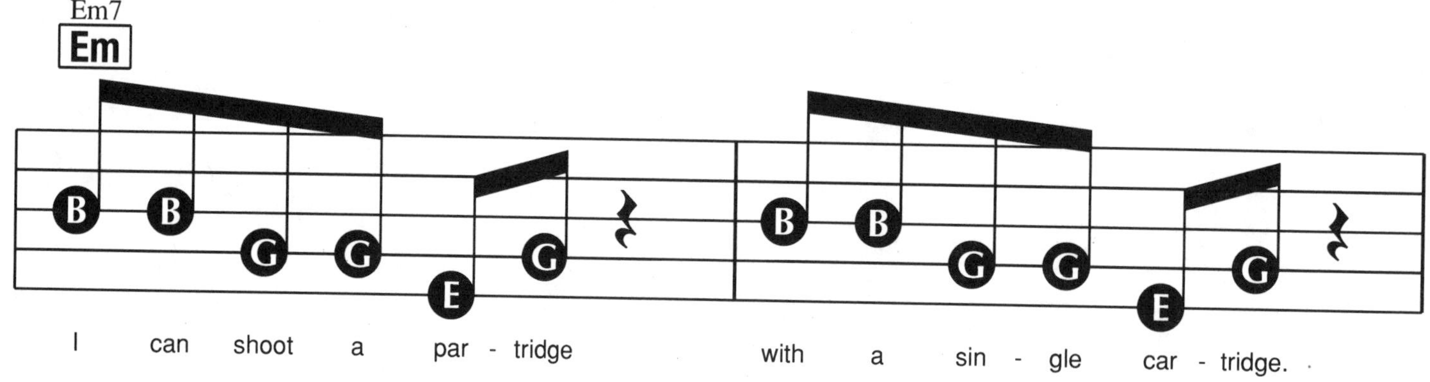
Em7
Em
B B G G E G
B B G G E G
I can shoot a par - tridge with a sin - gle car - tridge.

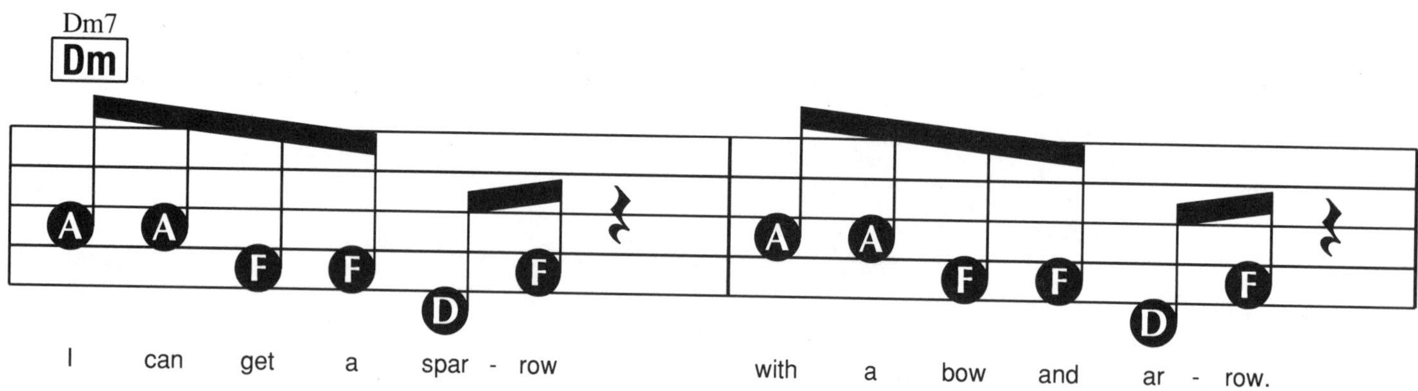
Dm7
Dm
A A F F D F
A A F F D F
I can get a spar - row with a bow and ar - row.

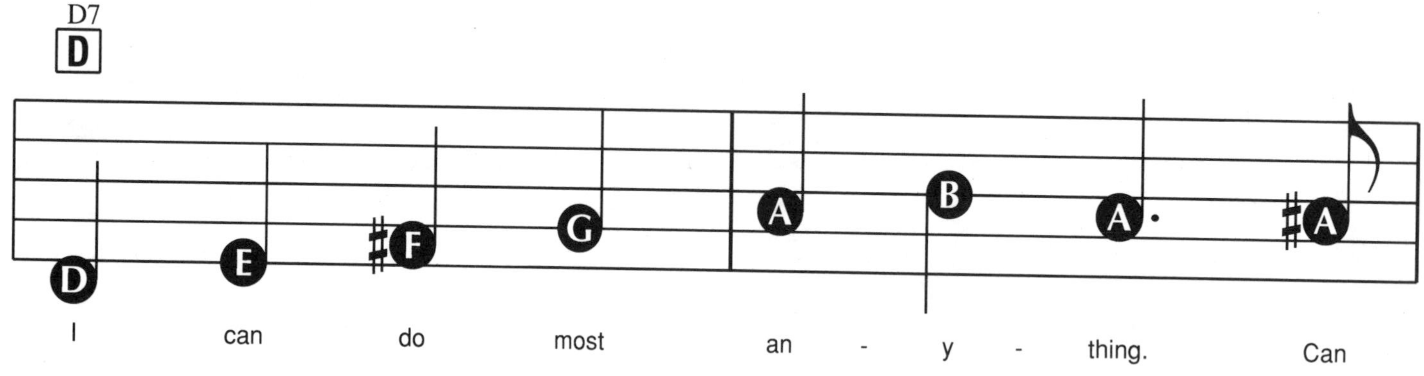
D7
D
D E F G
A B A A
I can do most an - y - thing. Can

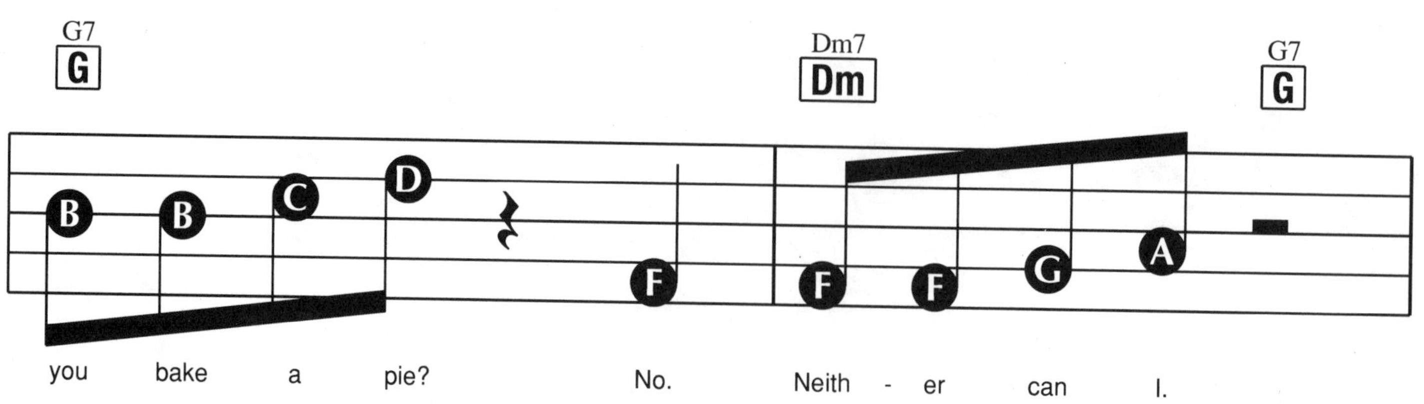
G7
G
Dm7
Dm
G7
G
B B C D F
F F G A
you bake a pie? No. Neith - er can I.

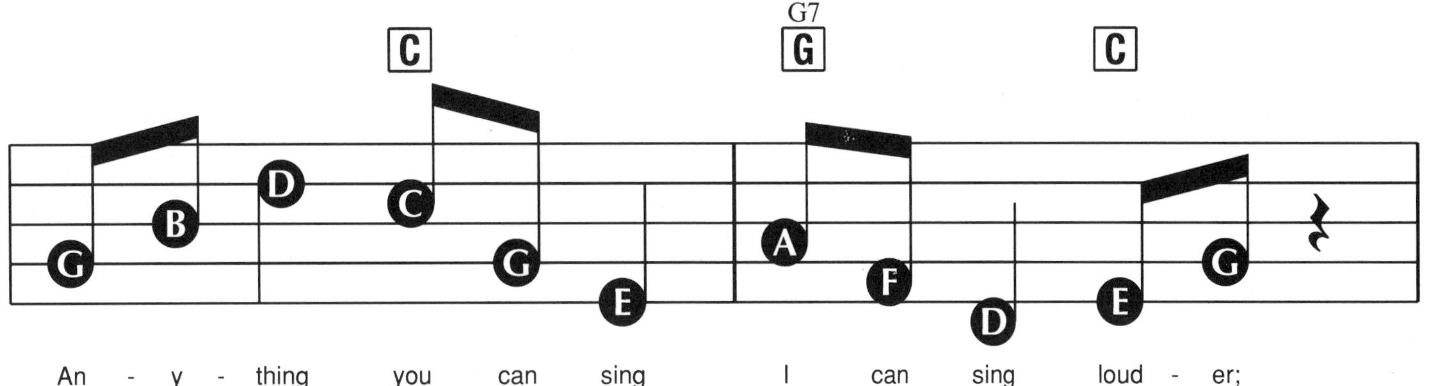
C
G7
G
C
G B D C G E A F D E G
An - y - thing you can sing I can sing loud - er;

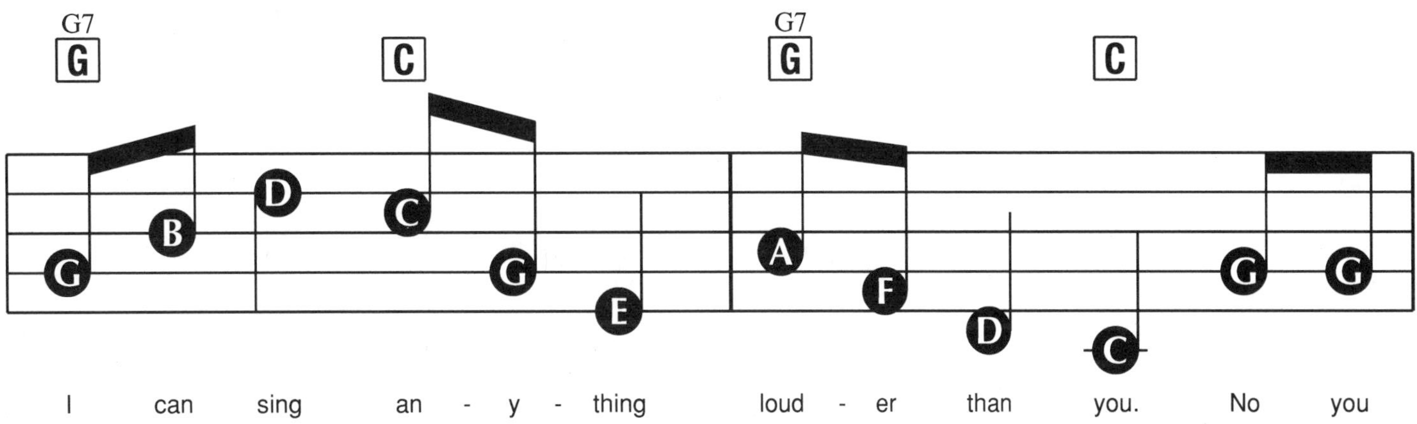
G7
G
C
G7
G
C
G B D C G E A F D C G G
I can sing an - y - thing loud - er than you. No you

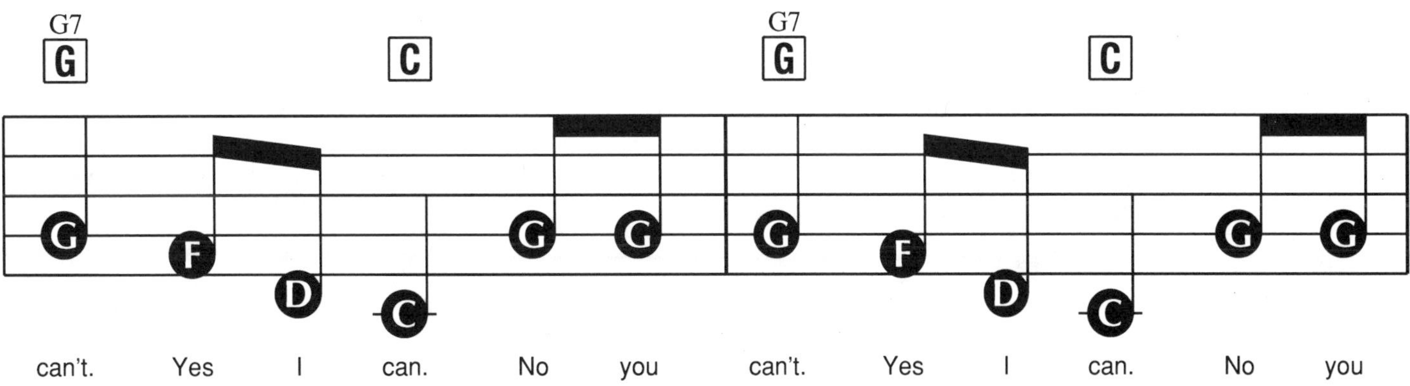
G7
G
C
G7
G
C
G F D C G G G F D C G G
can't. Yes I can. No you can't. Yes I can. No you

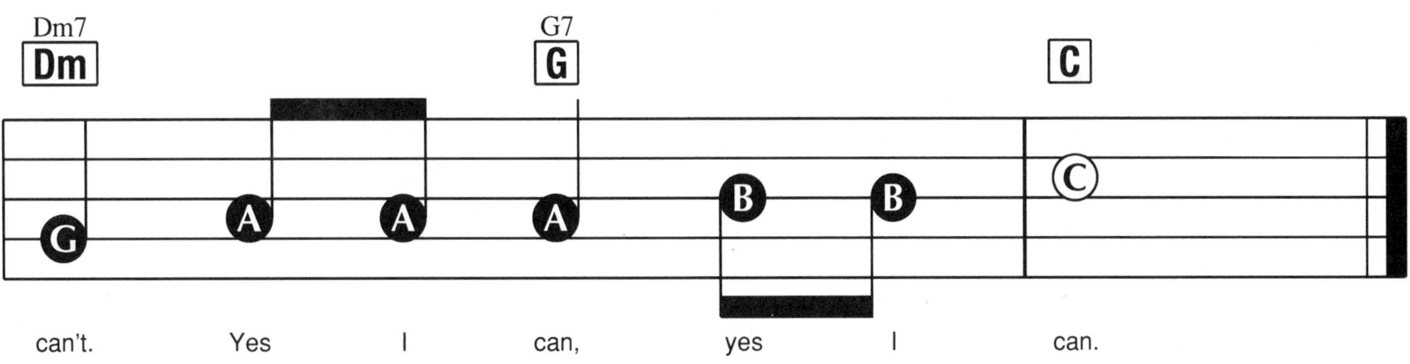
Dm7
Dm
G7
G
C
G A A A B B C
can't. Yes I can, yes I can.

Doin' What Comes Natur'lly

Registration 2
Rhythm: Swing

Words and Music by
Irving Berlin

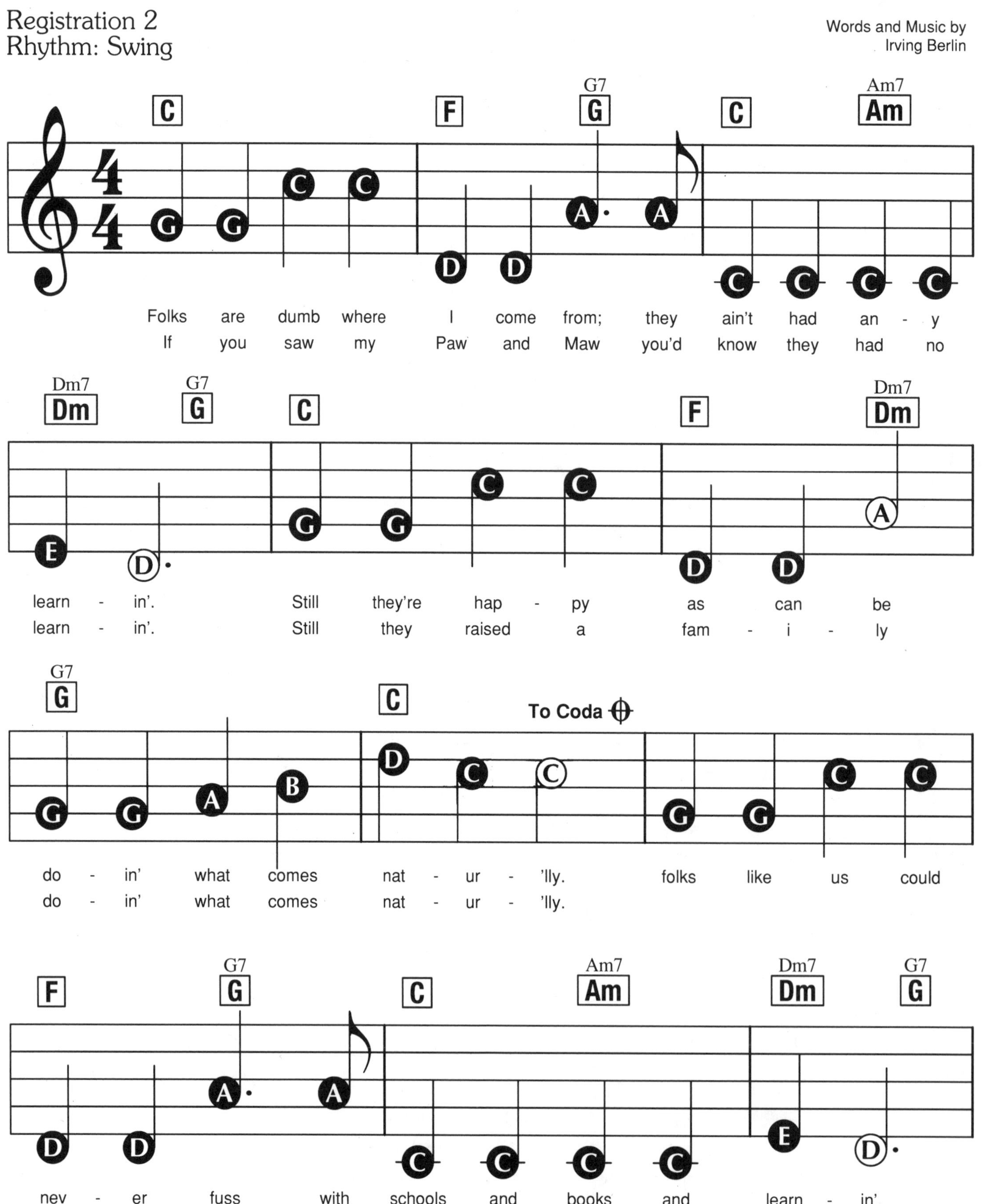

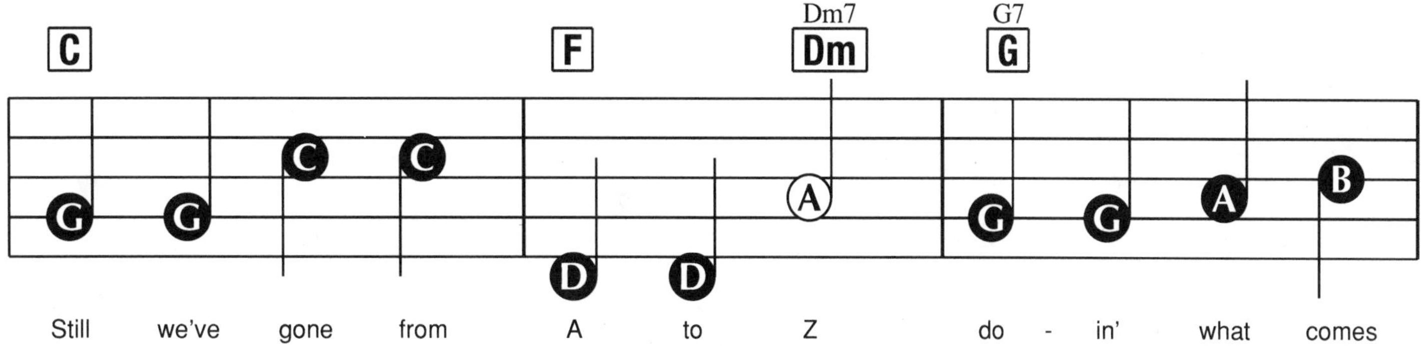
C
F
Dm7
Dm
G7
G
Still we've gone from A to Z do - in' what comes

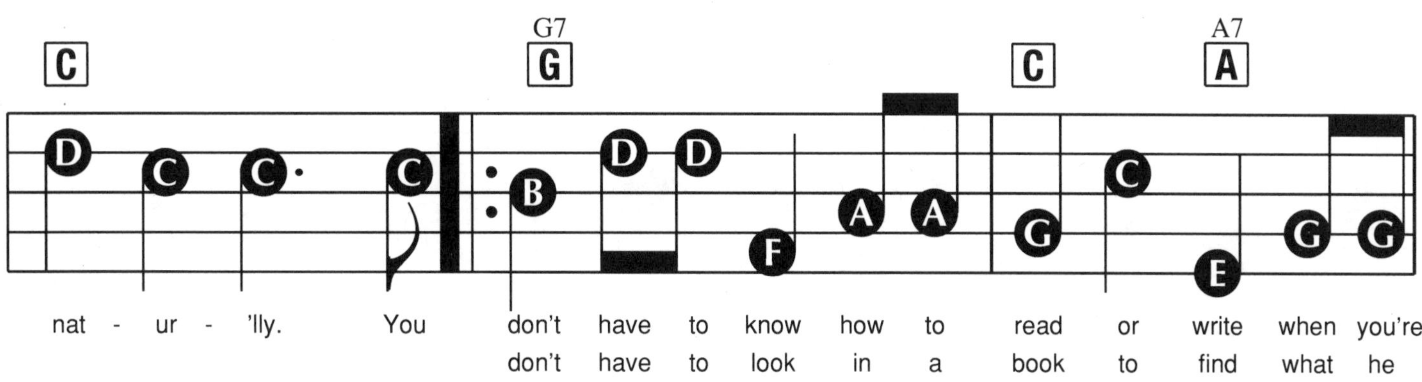
C
G7
G
C
A7
A
nat - ur - 'lly. You don't have to know how to read or write when you're
don't have to look in a book to find what he

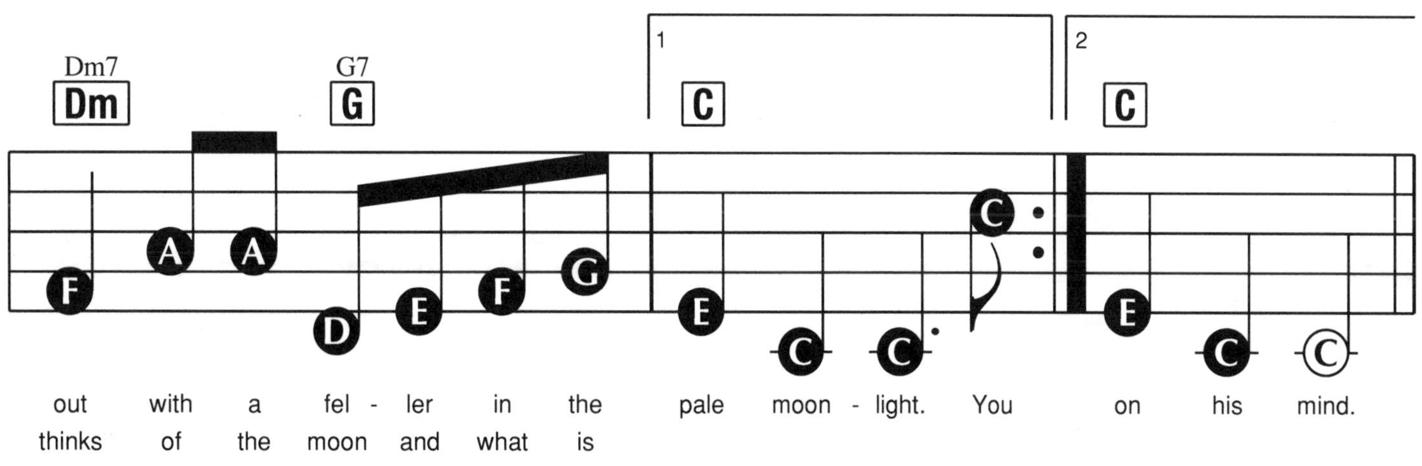
Dm7
Dm
G7
G
1
C
2
C
out with a fel - ler in the pale moon - light. You on his mind.
thinks of the moon and what is

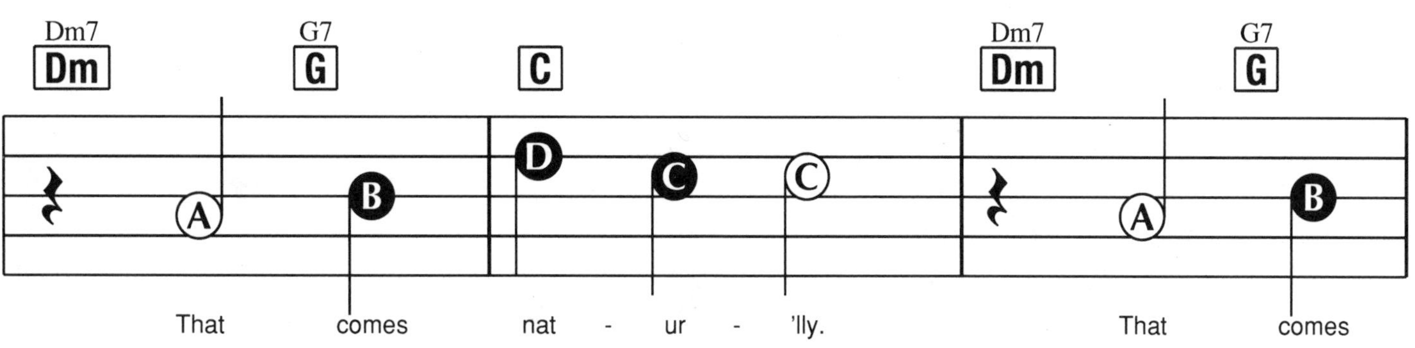
Dm7
Dm
G7
G
C
Dm7
Dm
G7
G
That comes nat - ur - 'lly. That comes

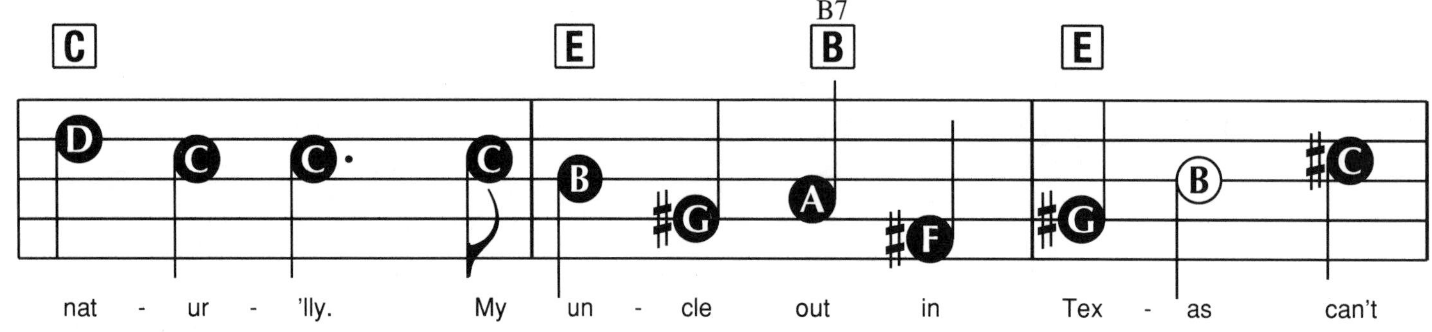
C
E
B7
B
E
D C C C B G A F G B C
nat - ur - 'lly. My un - cle out in Tex - as can't

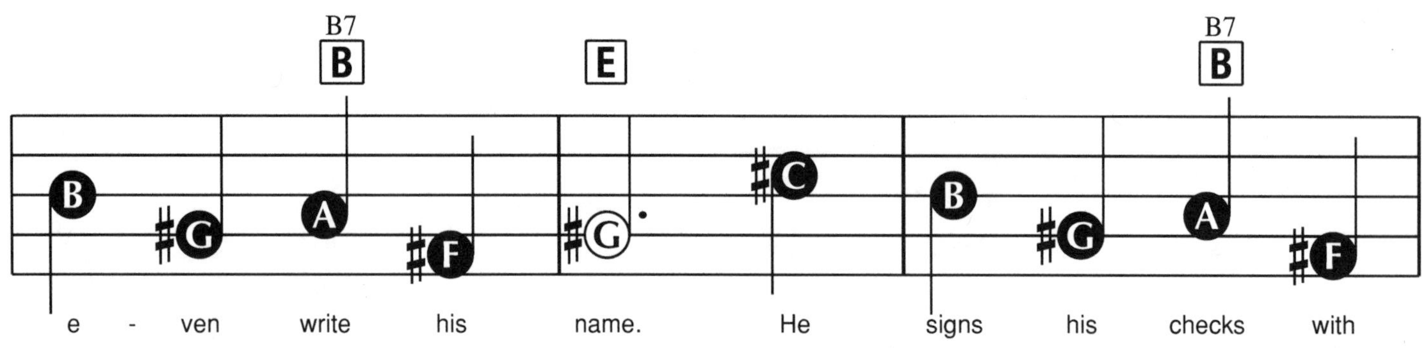
B7
B
E
B7
B
B G A F G C B G A F
e - ven write his name. He signs his checks with

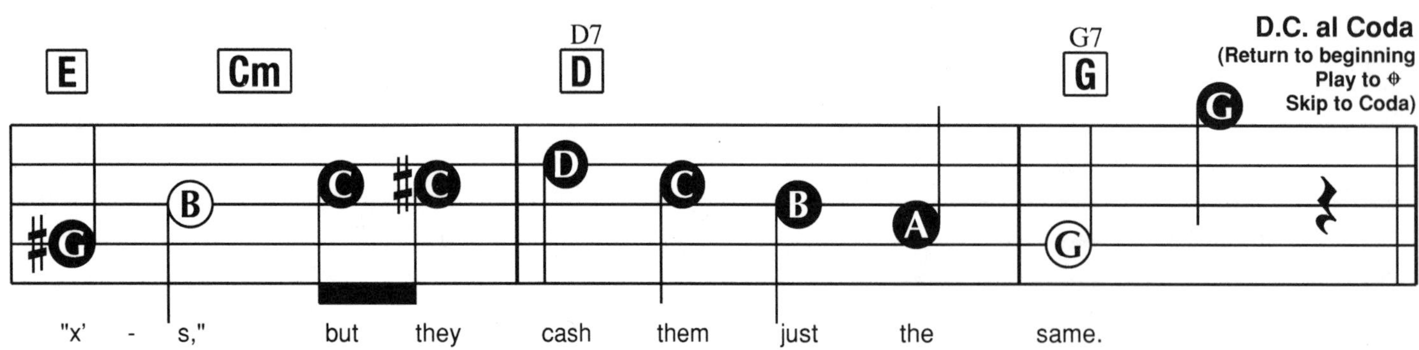
E
Cm
D7
D
G7
G
D.C. al Coda
(Return to beginning
Play to ⊕
Skip to Coda)
G B C C D C B A G G
"x' - s," but they cash them just the same.

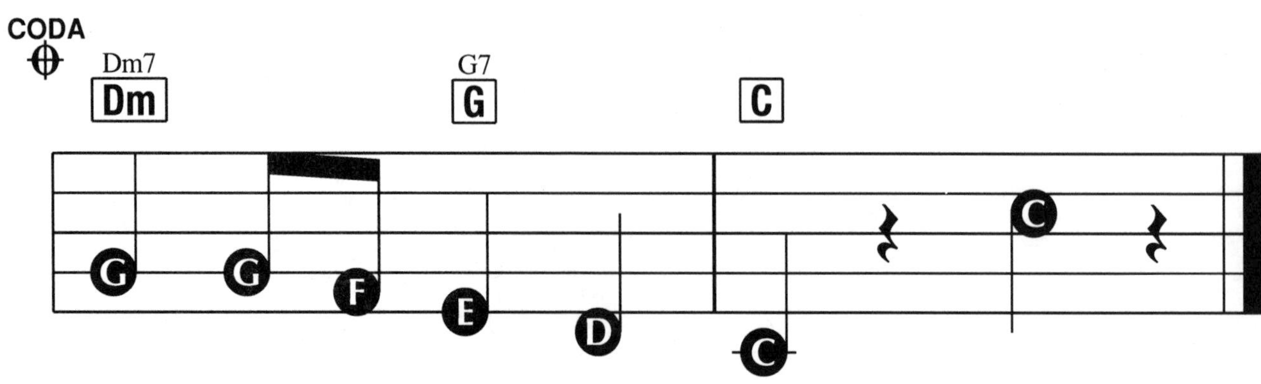
CODA
Dm7
Dm
G7
G
C
G G F E D C C

Everybody's Doin' It Now

Registration 8
Rhythm: Swing

Words and Music by
Irving Berlin

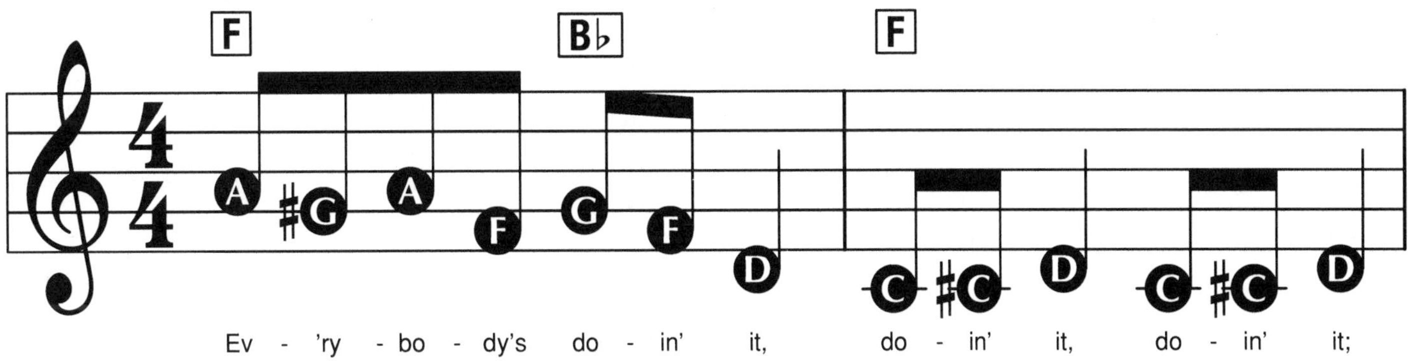

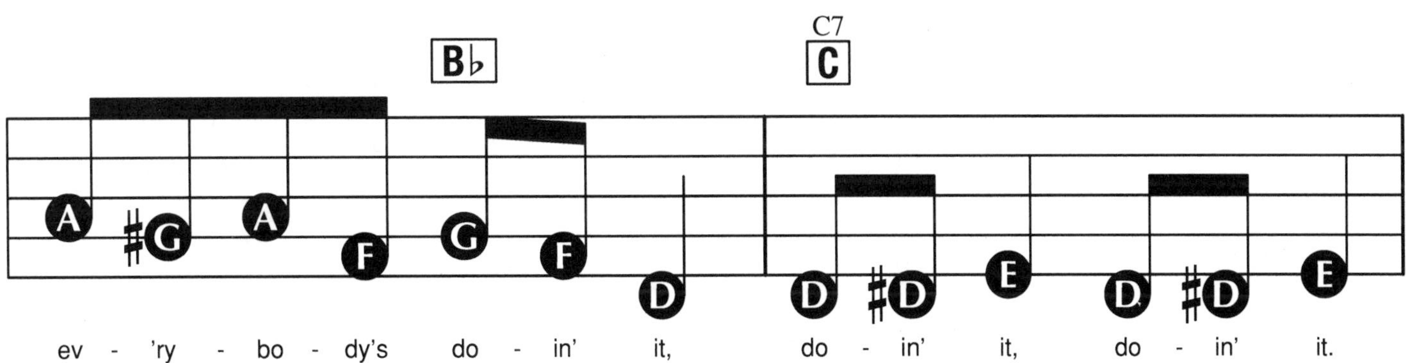

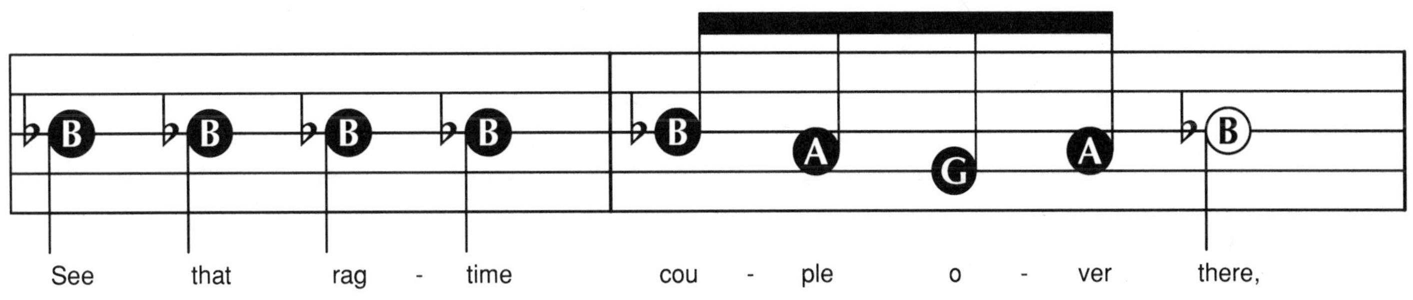

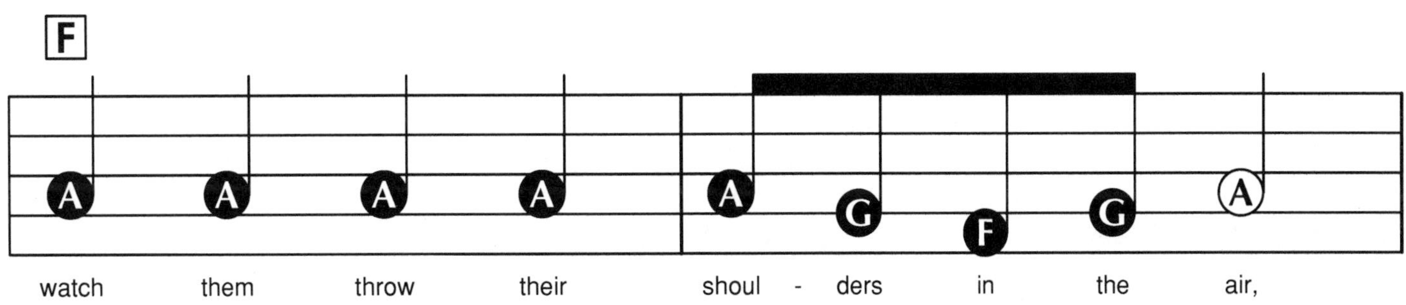

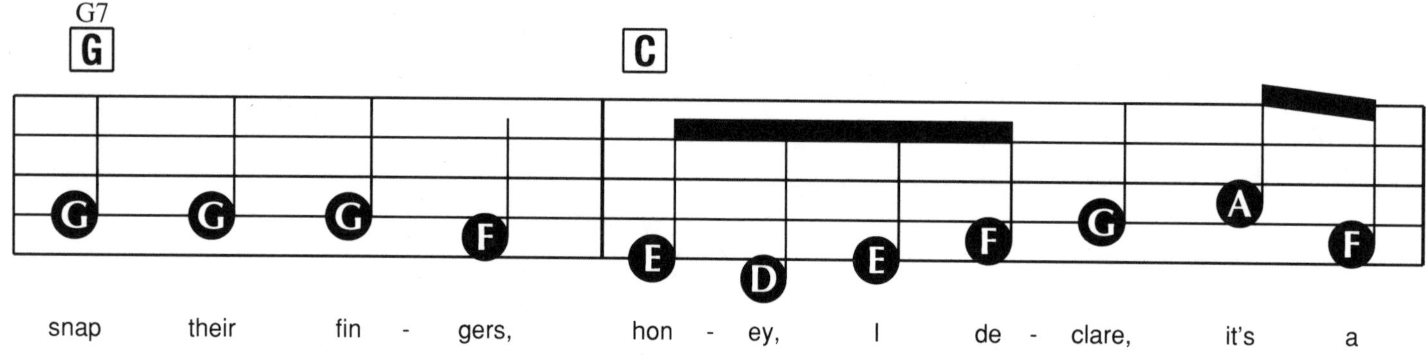
G7
G
C
snap their fin - gers, hon - ey, I de - clare, it's a

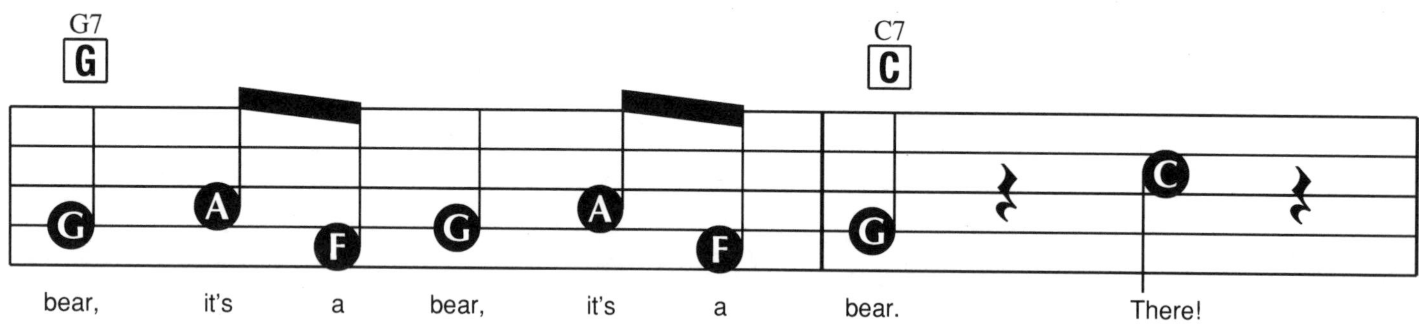
G7
G
C7
C
bear, it's a bear, it's a bear. There!

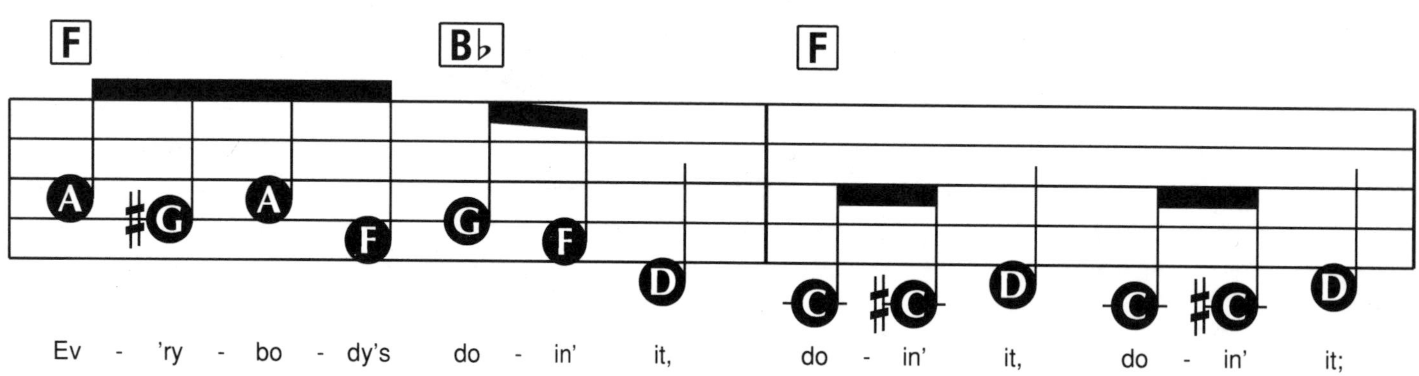
F
B♭
F
Ev - 'ry - bo - dy's do - in' it, do - in' it, do - in' it;

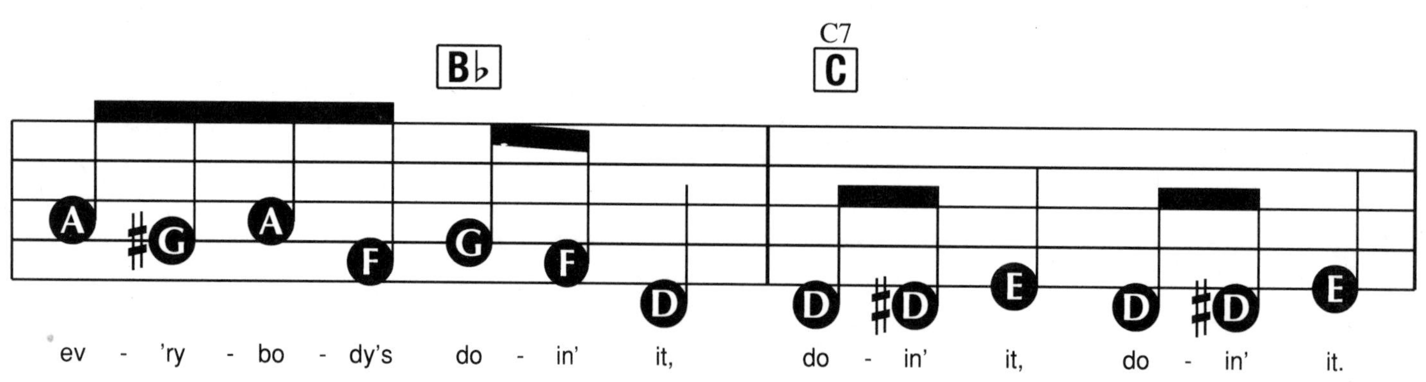
B♭
C7
C
ev - 'ry - bo - dy's do - in' it, do - in' it, do - in' it.

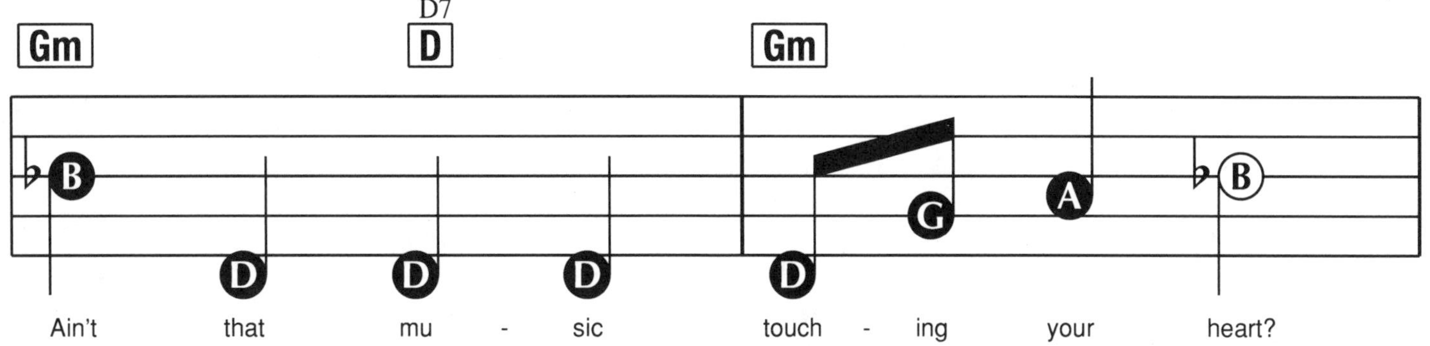
Gm
D7
D
Gm
B
D
D
D
D
G
A
B
Ain't that mu - sic touch - ing your heart?

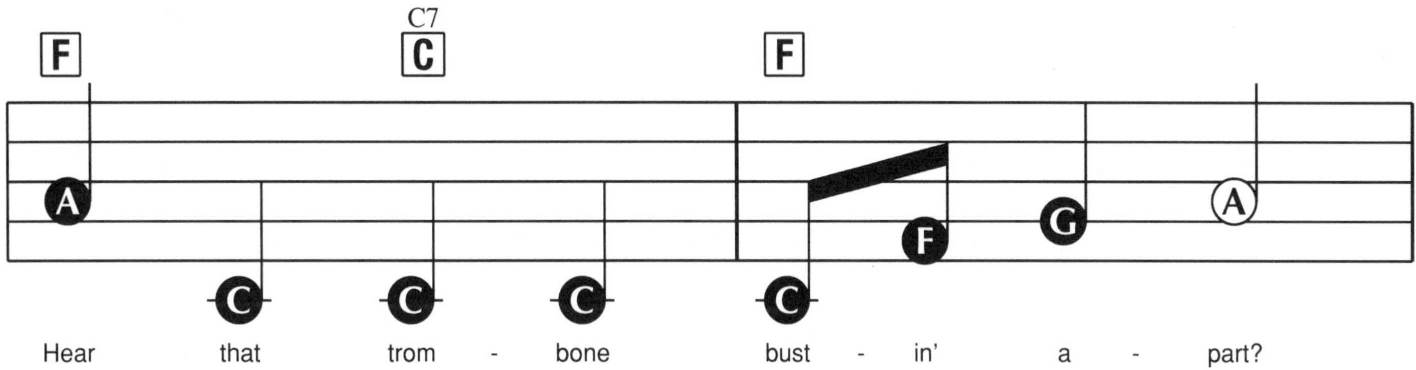
F
C7
C
F
A
C
C
C
C
F
G
A
Hear that trom - bone bust - in' a - part?

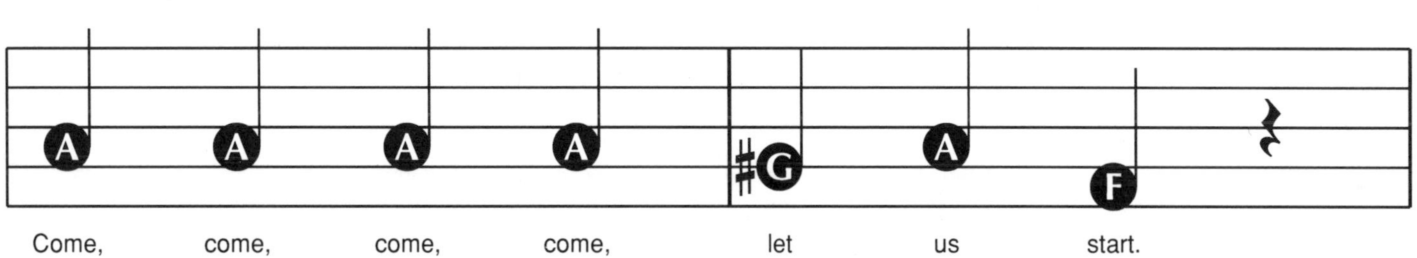
A
A
A
A
G
A
F
Come, come, come, come, let us start.

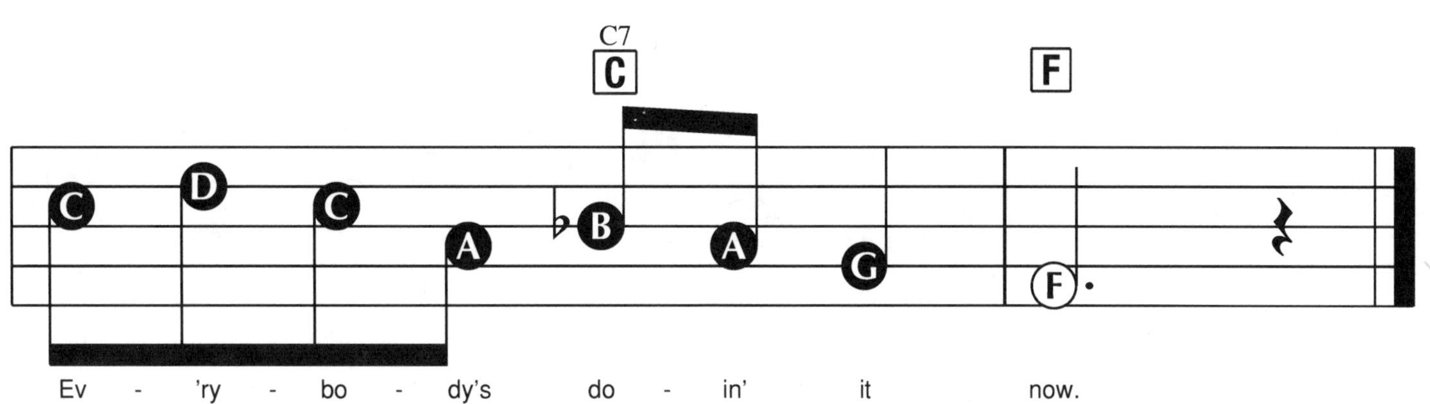
C7
C
F
C
D
C
A
B
A
G
F
Ev - 'ry - bo - dy's do - in' it now.

Easter Parade

Registration 5
Rhythm: Fox Trot or Ballad

Words and Music by
Irving Berlin

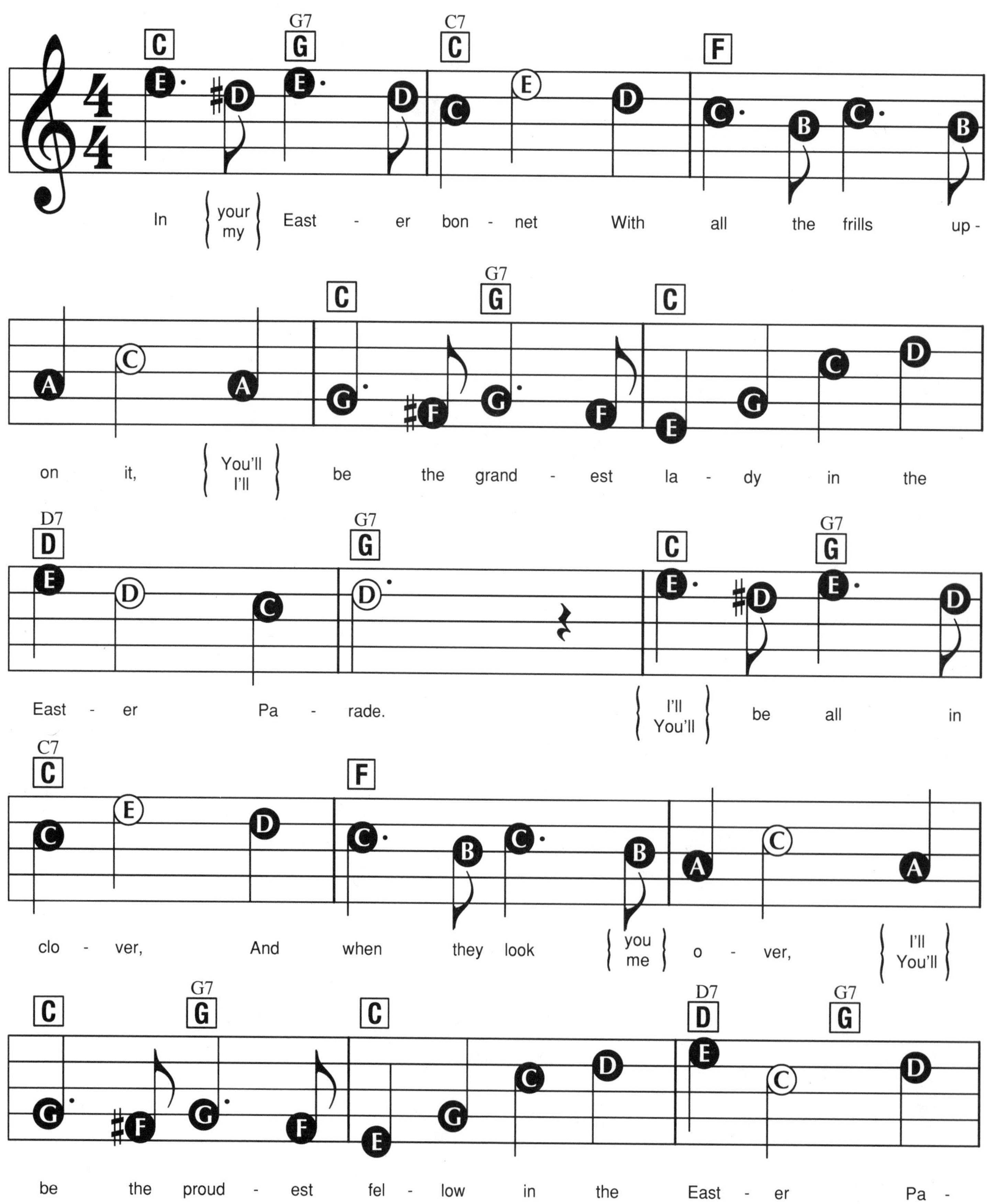

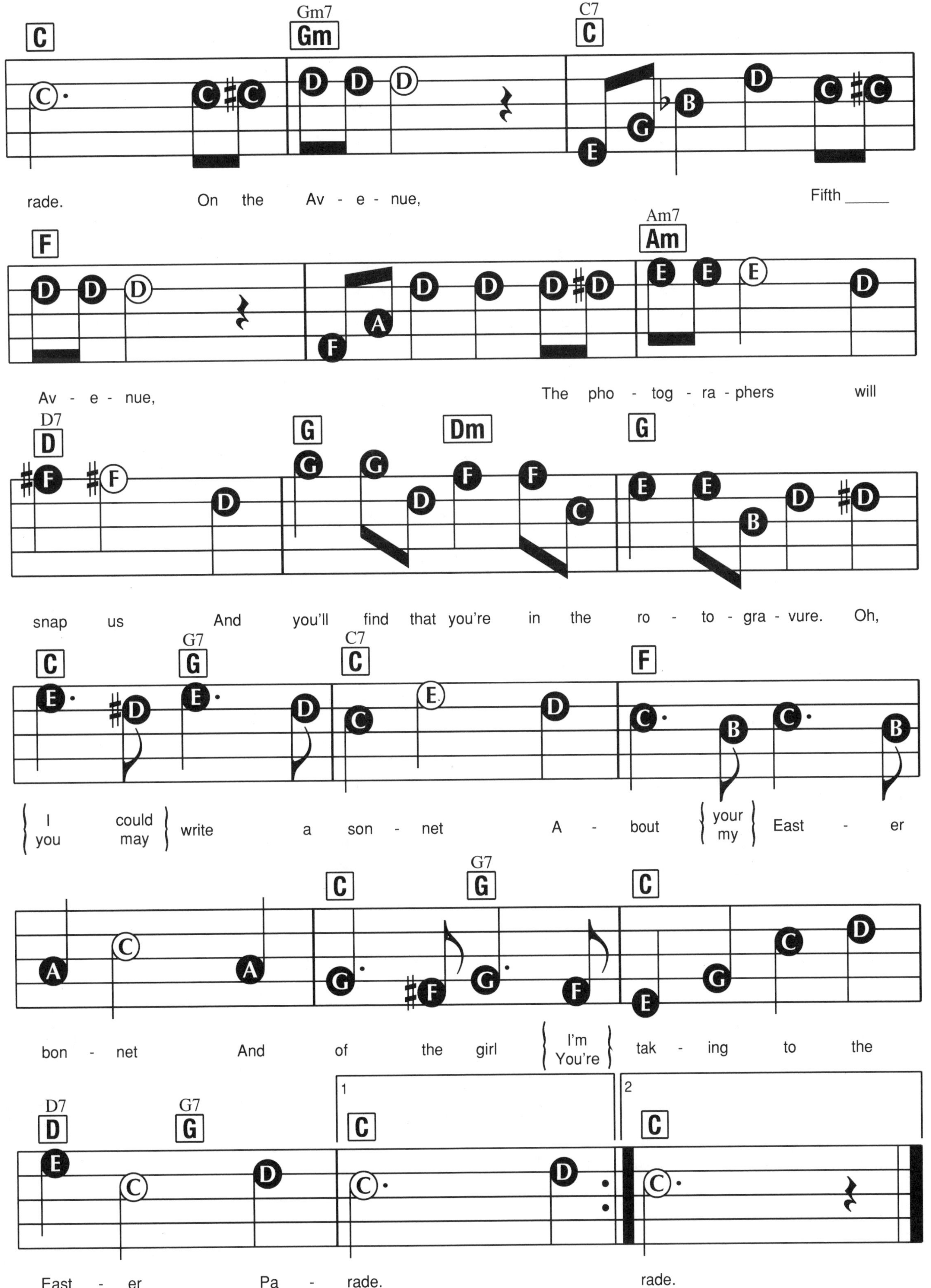
C Gm7 Gm C7 C
rade. On the Av - e - nue, Fifth
F Am7 Am
Av - e - nue, The pho - tog - ra - phers will
D7 D G Dm G
snap us And you'll find that you're in the ro - to - gra - vure. Oh,
C G7 G C7 C F
I could / you may write a son - net A - bout your / my East - er
C G7 G C
bon - net And of the girl I'm / You're tak - ing to the
D7 D G7 G 1 C 2 C
East - er Pa - rade. rade.

A Fella With An Umbrella

Registration 4
Rhythm: Swing

Words and Music by Irving Berlin

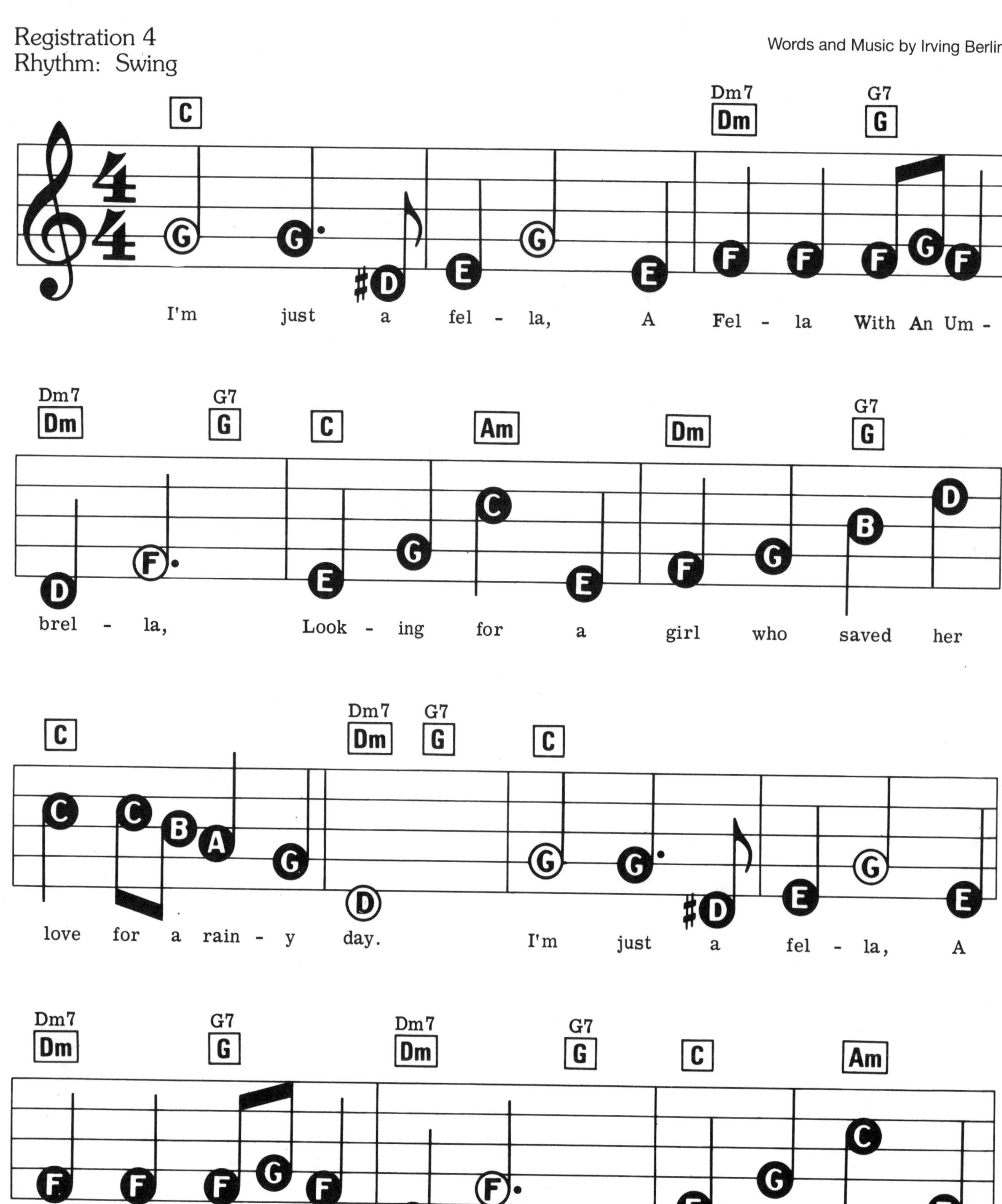

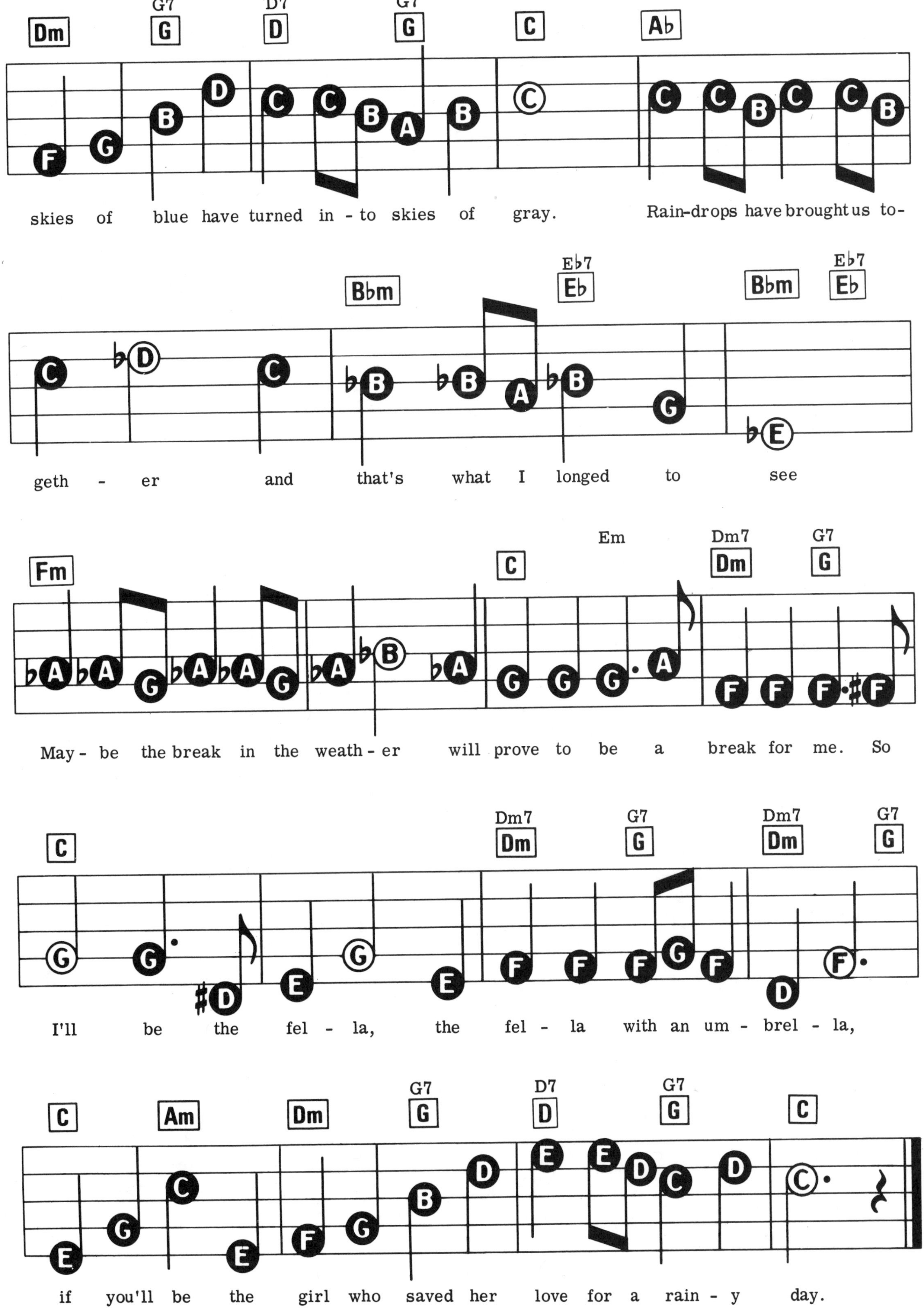

Dm G7 G D7 D G7 G C Ab

skies of blue have turned in - to skies of gray. Rain-drops have brought us to-

Bbm Eb7 Eb Bbm Eb7 Eb

geth - er and that's what I longed to see

Fm C Em Dm7 Dm G7 G

May - be the break in the weath - er will prove to be a break for me. So

C Dm7 Dm G7 G Dm7 Dm G7 G

I'll be the fel - la, the fel - la with an um - brel - la,

C Am Dm G7 G D7 D G7 G C

if you'll be the girl who saved her love for a rain - y day.

Fools Fall In Love

Registration 10
Rhythm: Swing

Words and Music by
Irving Berlin

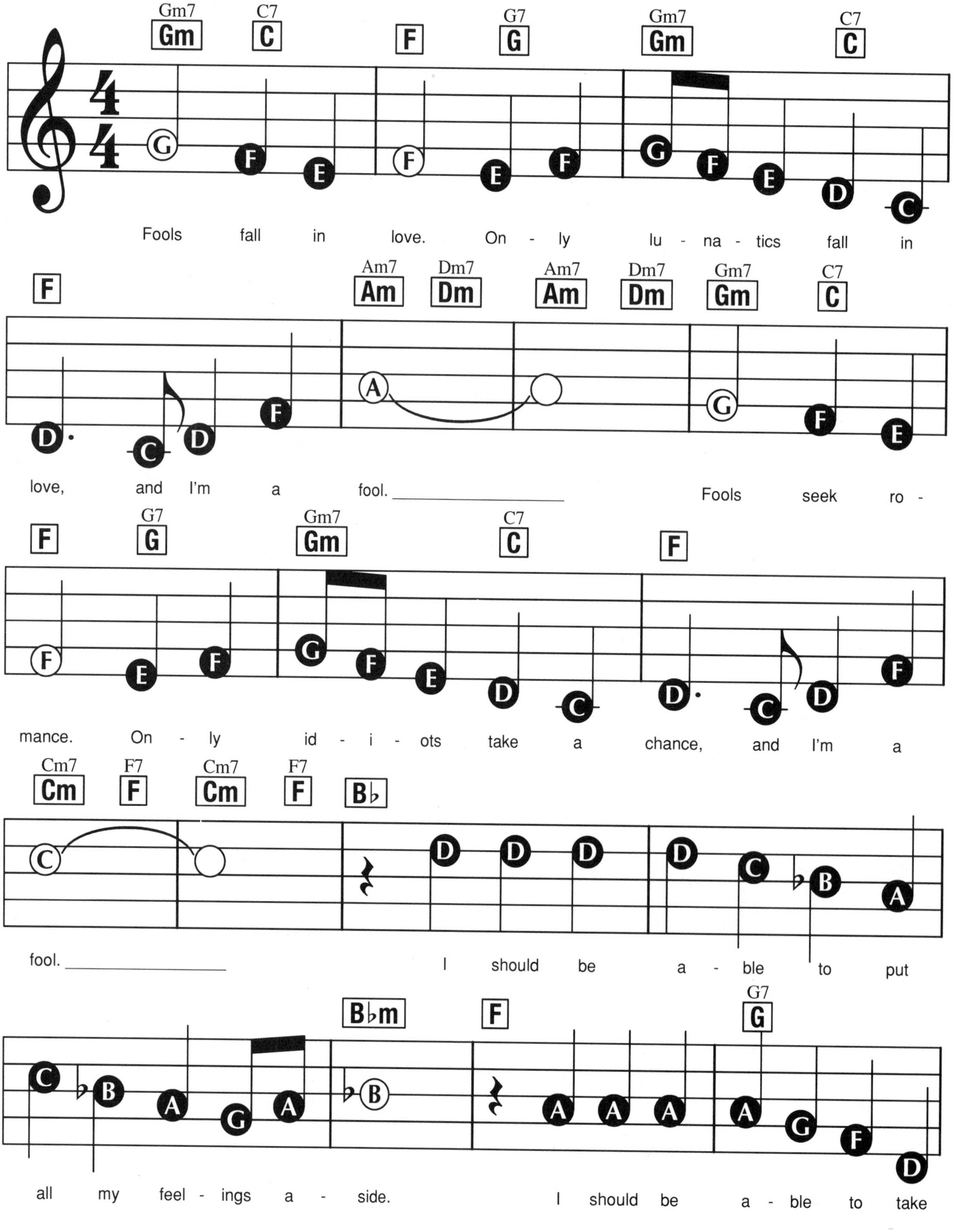
Gm7 Gm C7 C F G7 G Gm7 Gm C7 C
Fools fall in love. On - ly lu - na - tics fall in
F Am7 Am Dm7 Dm Am7 Am Dm7 Dm Gm7 Gm C7 C
love, and I'm a fool. Fools seek ro -
F G7 G Gm7 Gm C7 C F
mance. On - ly id - i - ots take a chance, and I'm a
Cm7 Cm F7 F Cm7 Cm F7 F B♭
fool. I should be a - ble to put
B♭m F G7 G
all my feel - ings a - side. I should be a - ble to take

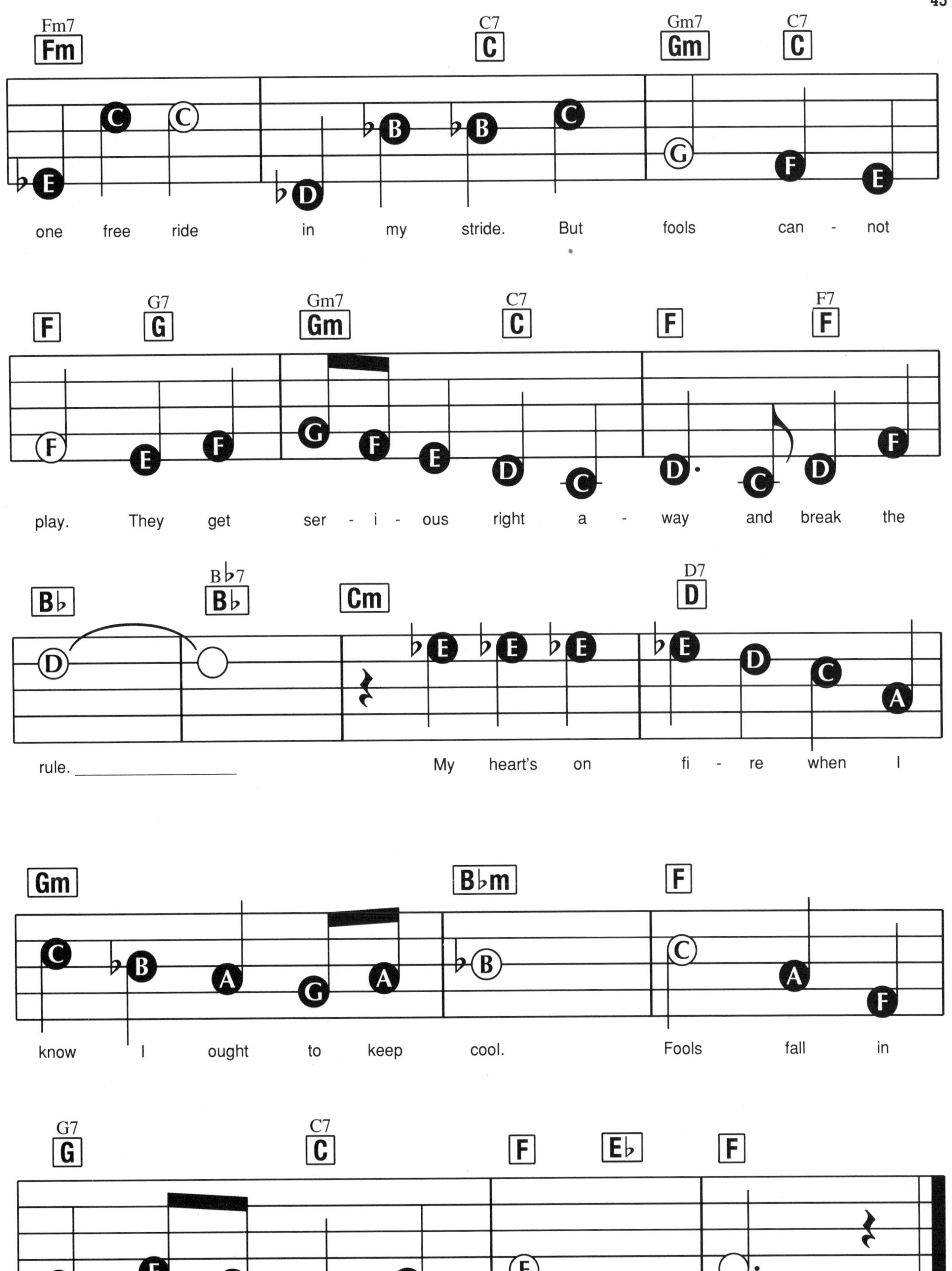
Fm7 Fm C7 C Gm7 Gm C7 C
one free ride in my stride. But fools can - not
F G7 G Gm7 Gm C7 C F F7 F
play. They get ser - i - ous right a - way and break the
B♭ B♭7 B♭ Cm D7 D
rule. My heart's on fi - re when I
Gm B♭m F
know I ought to keep cool. Fools fall in
G7 G C7 C F E♭ F
love and I'm such a fool.

The Girl That I Marry

Registration 2

Words and Music by Irving Berlin

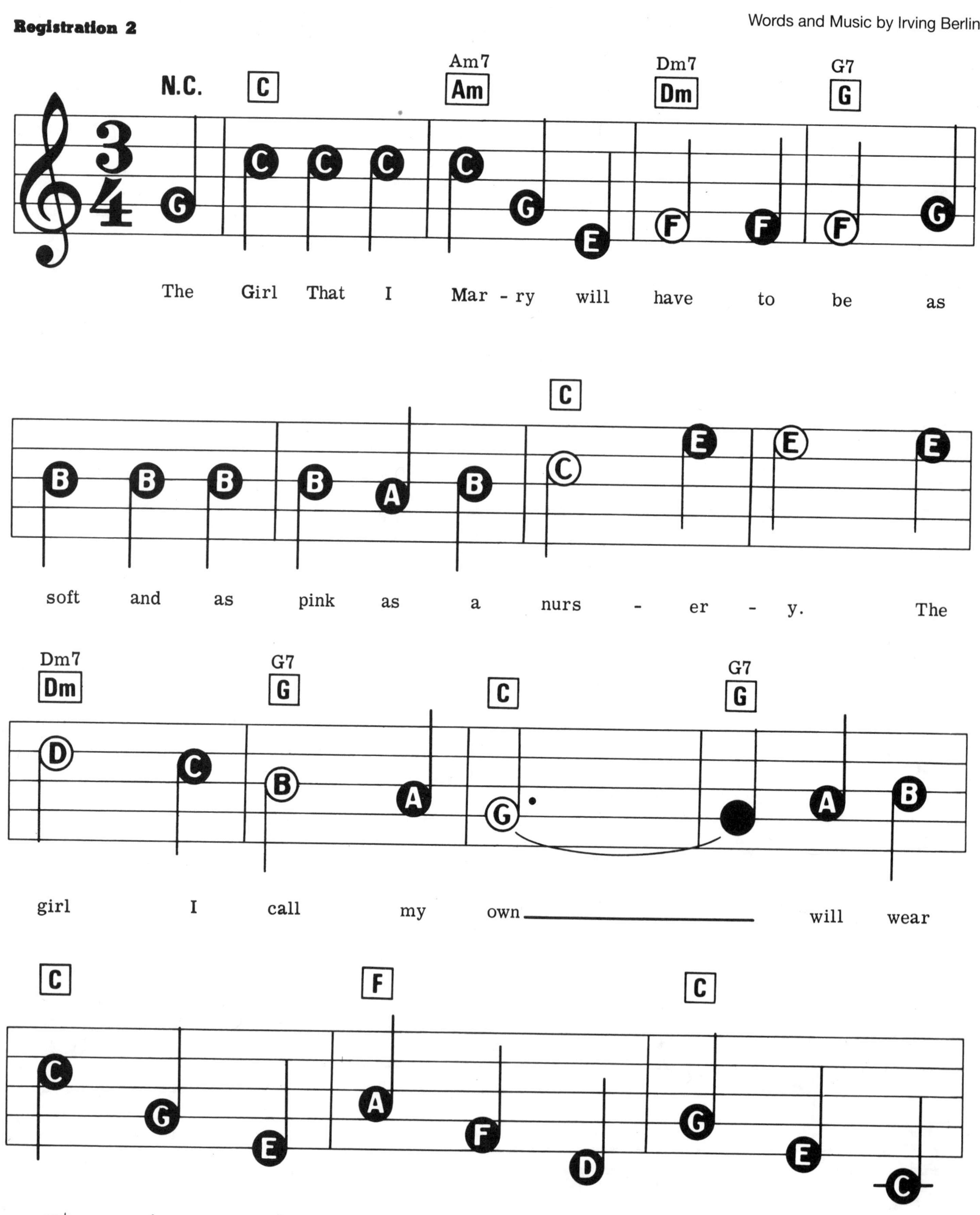

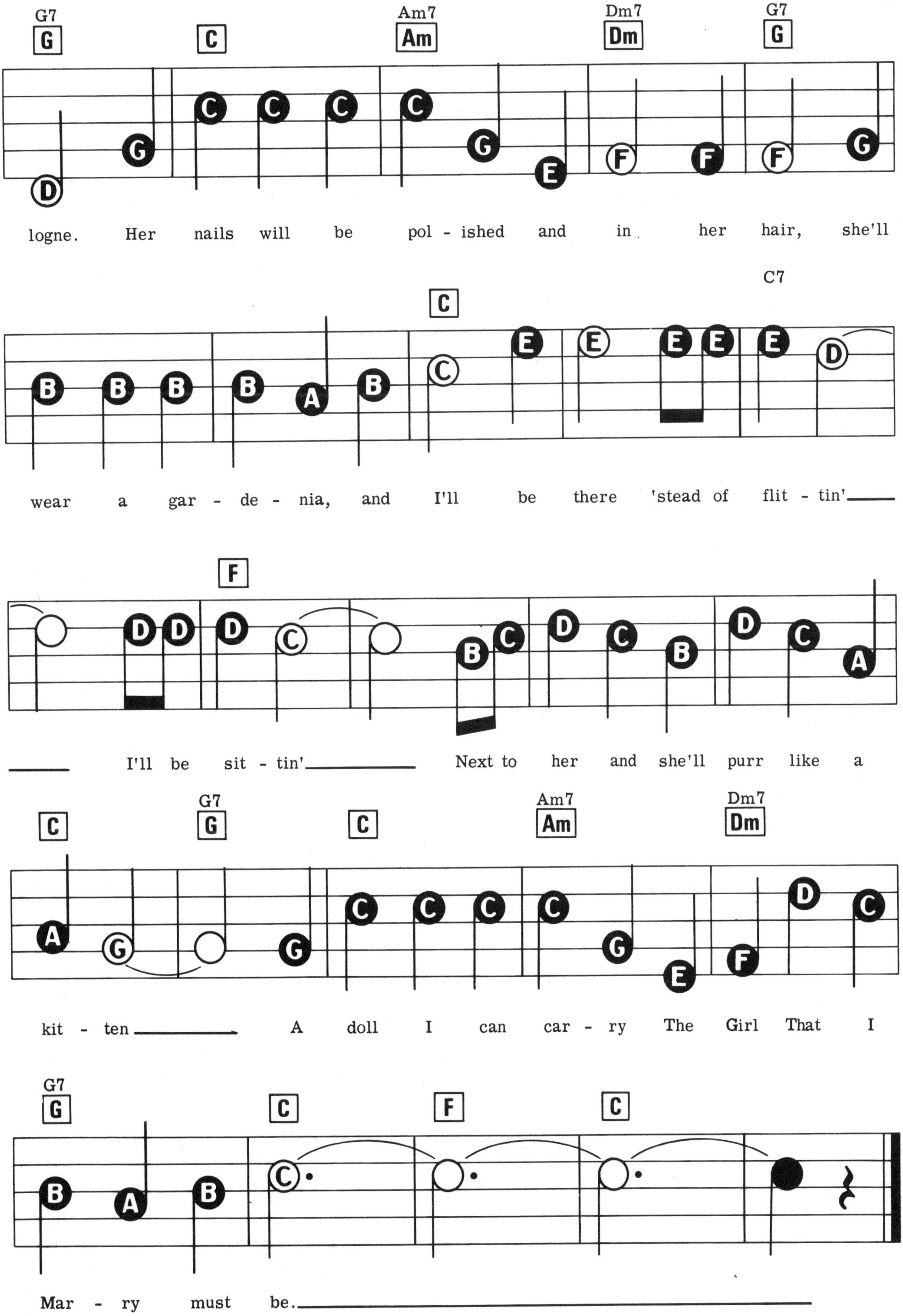

G7 G | C | Am7 Am | Dm7 Dm | G7 G

logne. Her nails will be pol - ished and in her hair, she'll

C | C7

wear a gar - de - nia, and I'll be there 'stead of flit - tin'

F

I'll be sit - tin' Next to her and she'll purr like a

C | G7 G | C | Am7 Am | Dm7 Dm

kit - ten A doll I can car - ry The Girl That I

G7 G | C | F | C

Mar - ry must be.

God Bless America

Registration 3
Rhythm: Fox Trot or Swing

Words and Music by Irving Berlin

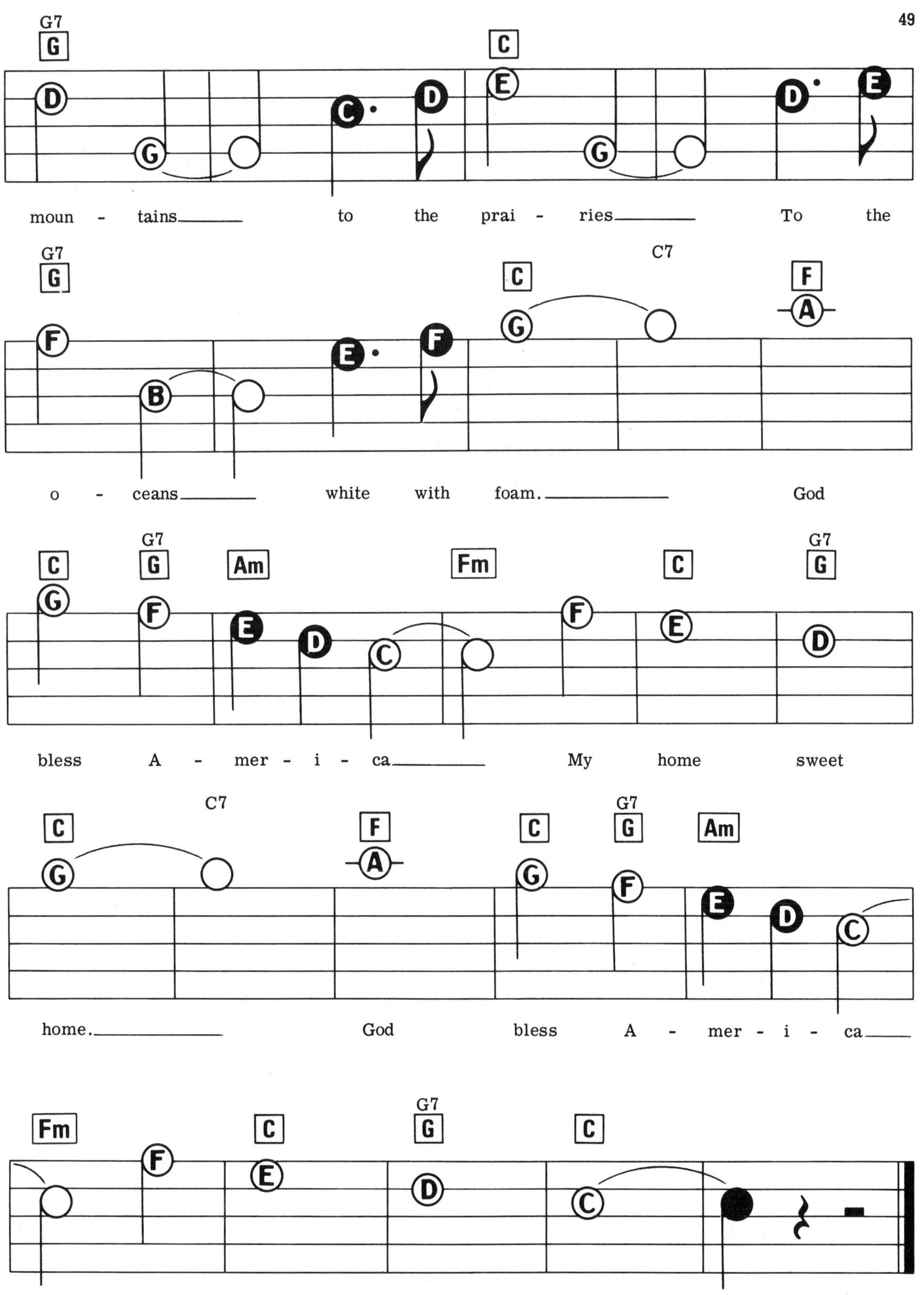
G7 G C C7 F Fm Am
mountains to the prairies To the
oceans white with foam. God
bless America My home sweet
home. God bless America
My home sweet home.

Give Me Your Tired, Your Poor

Registration 1
Rhythm: March

Words by Emma Lazarus: The New Colossus
Music by Irving Berlin

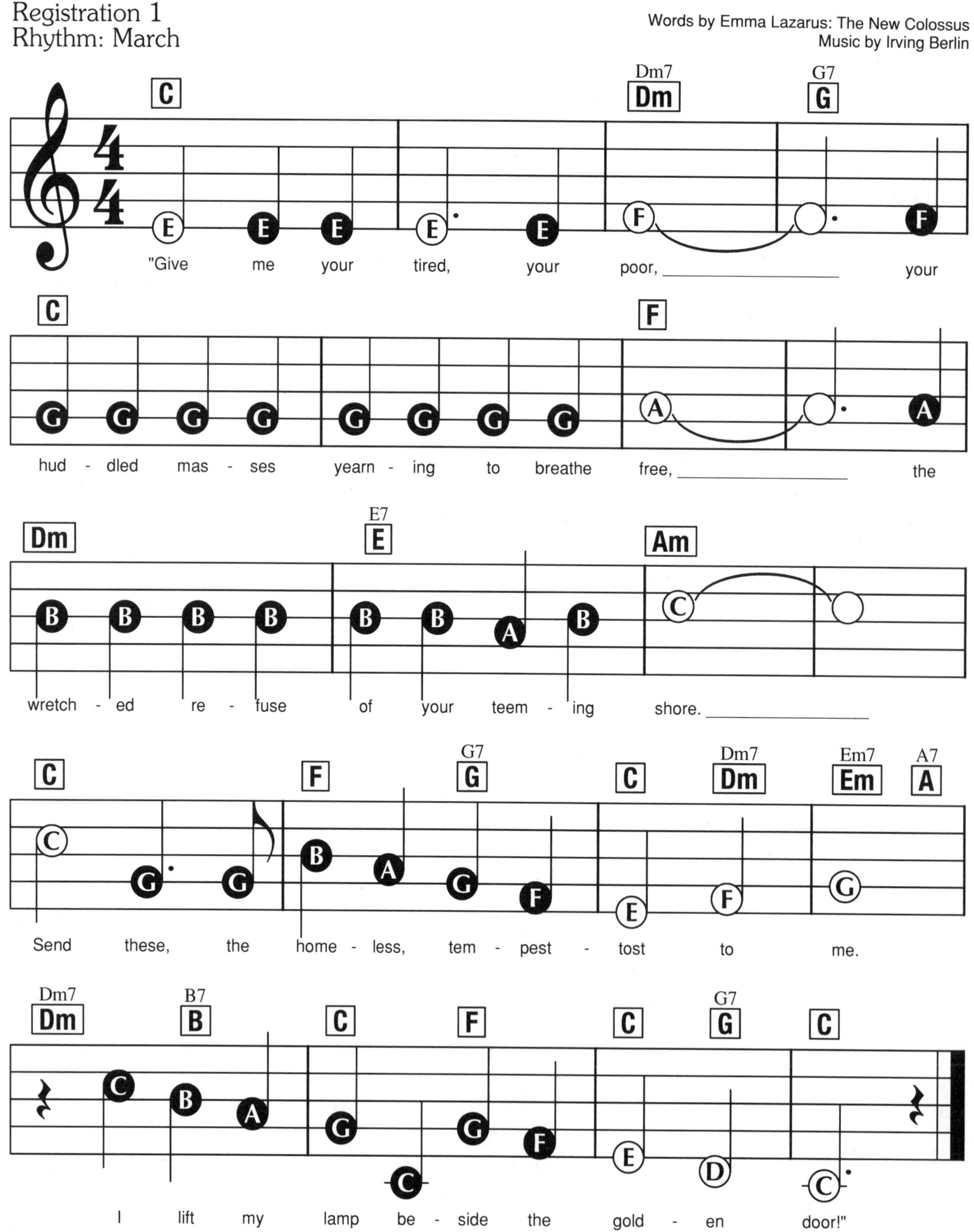

Heat Wave

Registration 4
Rhythm: Latin

Words and Music by
Irving Berlin

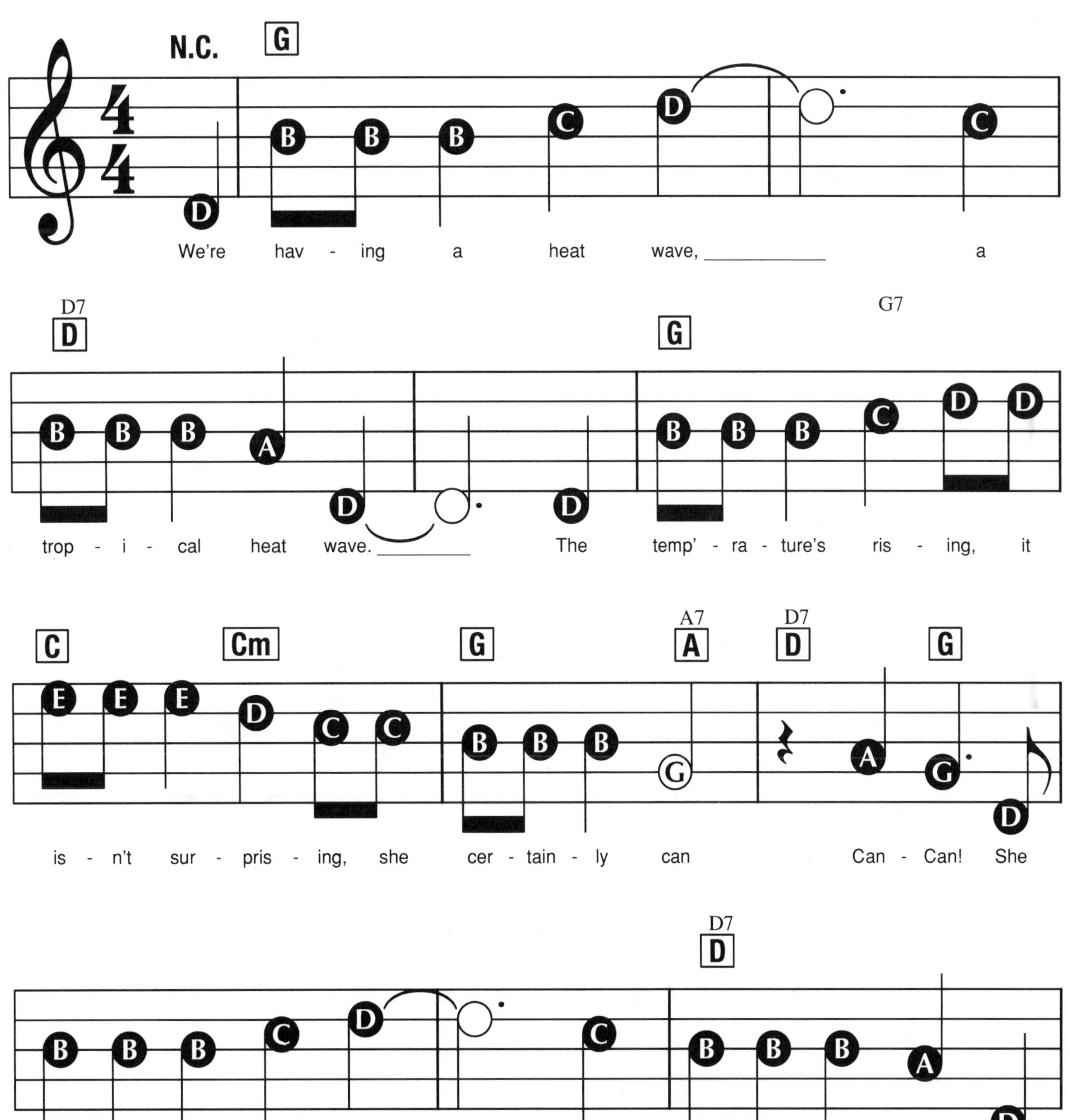

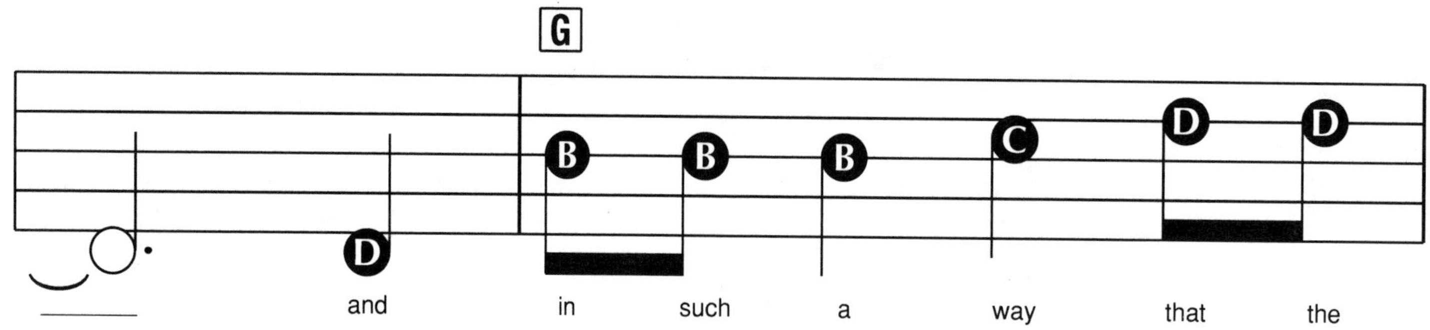
G
D
B
B
B
C
D
D
and
in
such
a
way
that
the

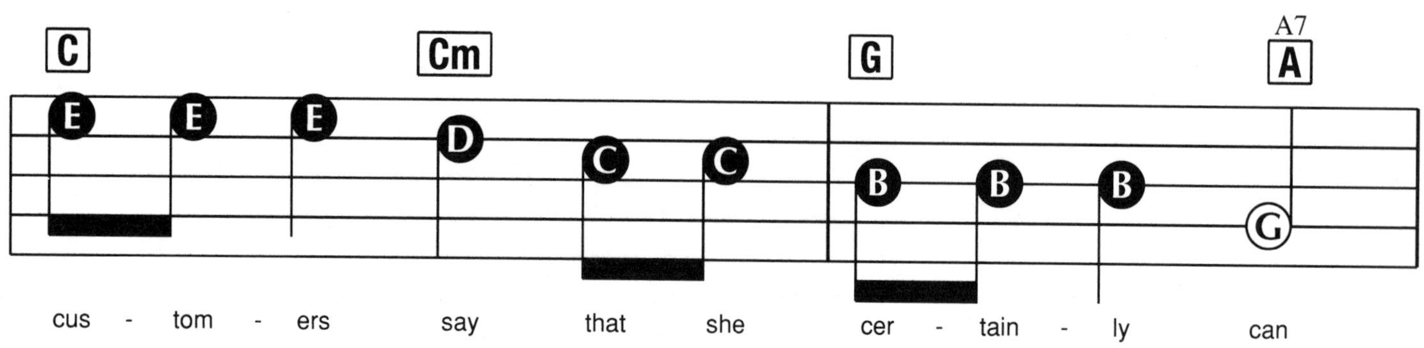
C
Cm
G
A7
A
E
E
E
D
C
C
B
B
B
G
cus - tom - ers
say
that
she
cer - tain - ly
can

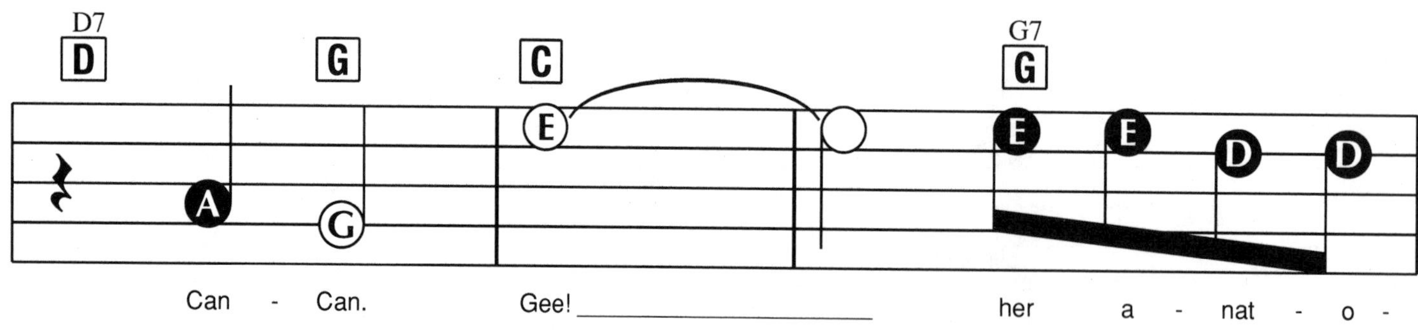
D7
D
G
C
G7
G
A
G
E
E
E
D
D
Can - Can.
Gee!
her
a - nat - o -

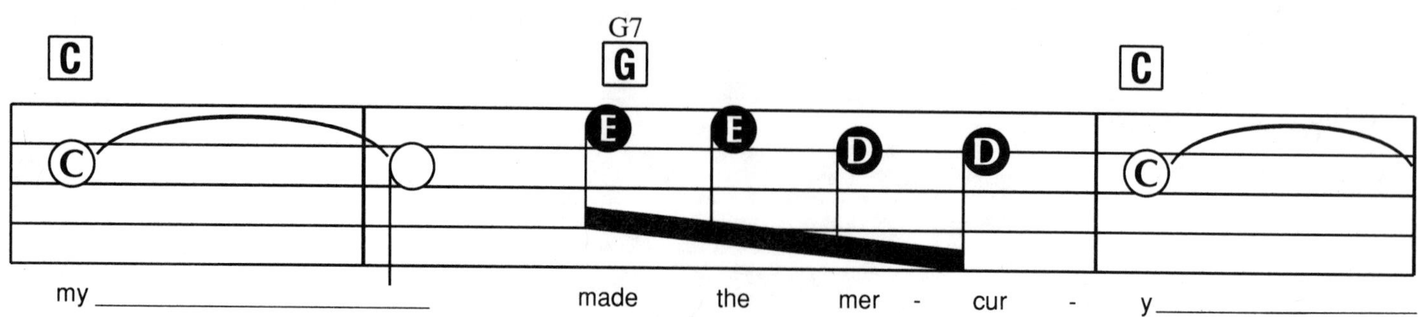
C
G7
G
C
C
E
E
D
D
C
my
made
the
mer - cur - y

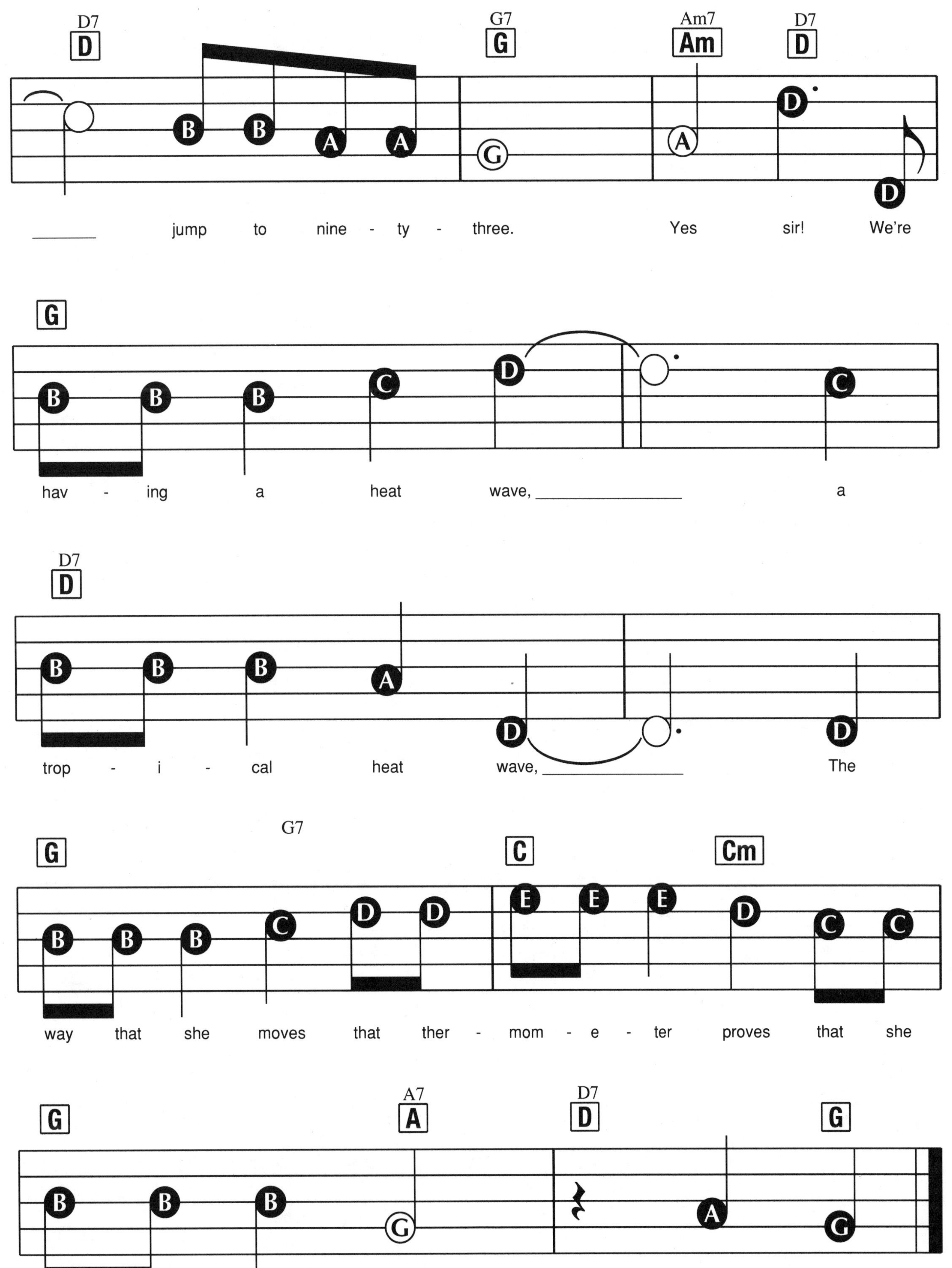
D7
D
G7
G
Am7
Am
D7
D
B
B
A
A
G
A
D
D
jump to nine - ty - three.
Yes sir! We're
G
B B B C D C
hav - ing a heat wave,
a
D7
D
B B B A D D
trop - i - cal heat wave,
The
G
G7
C
Cm
B B B C D D E E E D C C
way that she moves that ther - mom - e - ter proves that she
G
A7
A
D7
D
G
B B B G A G
cer - tain - ly can
Can - Can.

Happy Holiday

Registration 4
Rhythm: Fox Trot or Ballad

Words and Music by
Irving Berlin

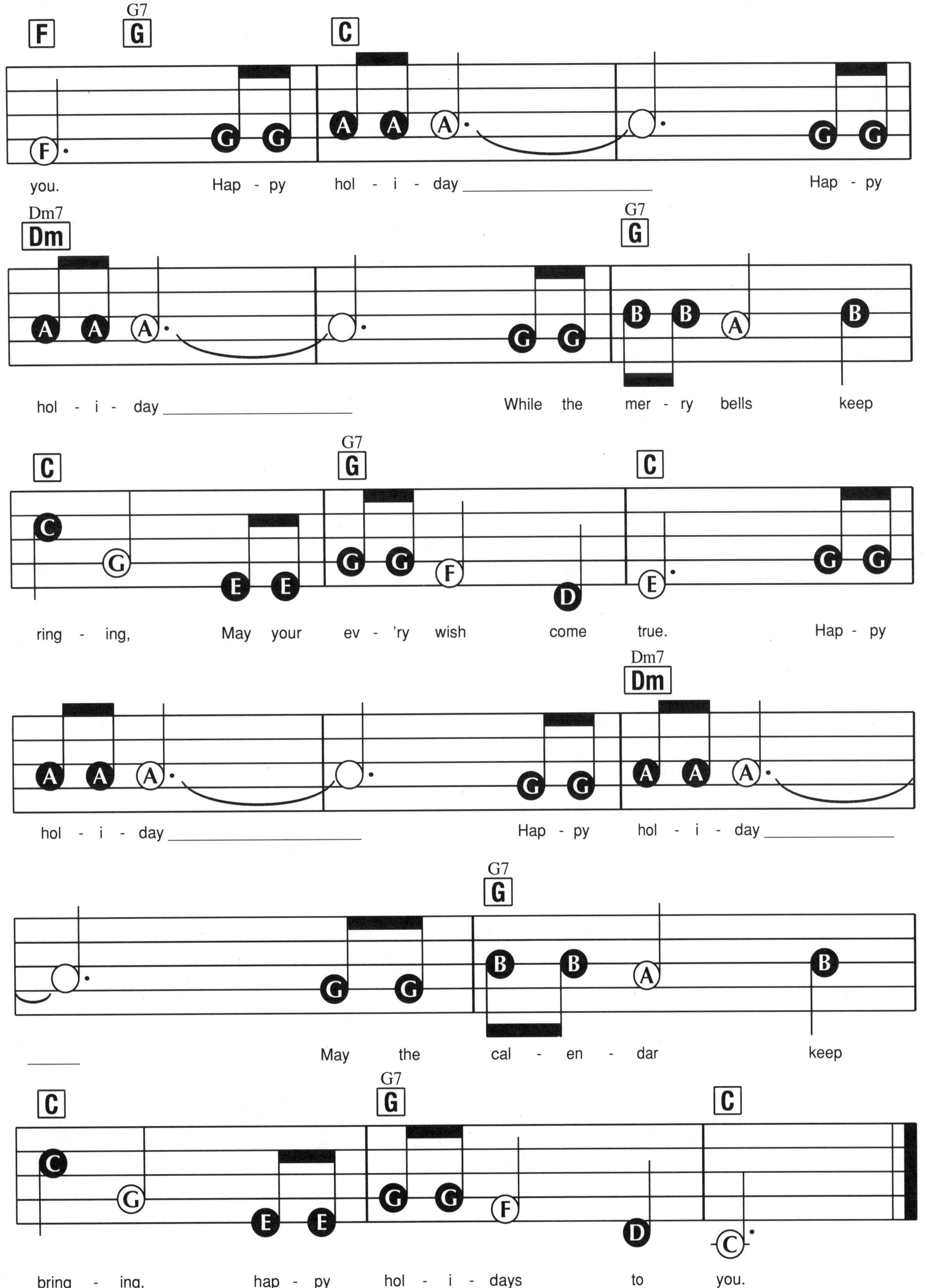
F G7 G C
you. Hap - py hol - i - day Hap - py
Dm7 Dm G7 G
hol - i - day While the mer - ry bells keep
C G7 G C
ring - ing, May your ev - 'ry wish come true. Hap - py
Dm7 Dm
hol - i - day Hap - py hol - i - day
G7 G
May the cal - en - dar keep
C G7 G C
bring - ing, hap - py hol - i - days to you.

How Deep Is The Ocean
(How High Is The Sky)

Registration 4
Rhythm: Fox Trot or Swing

Words and Music by
Irving Berlin

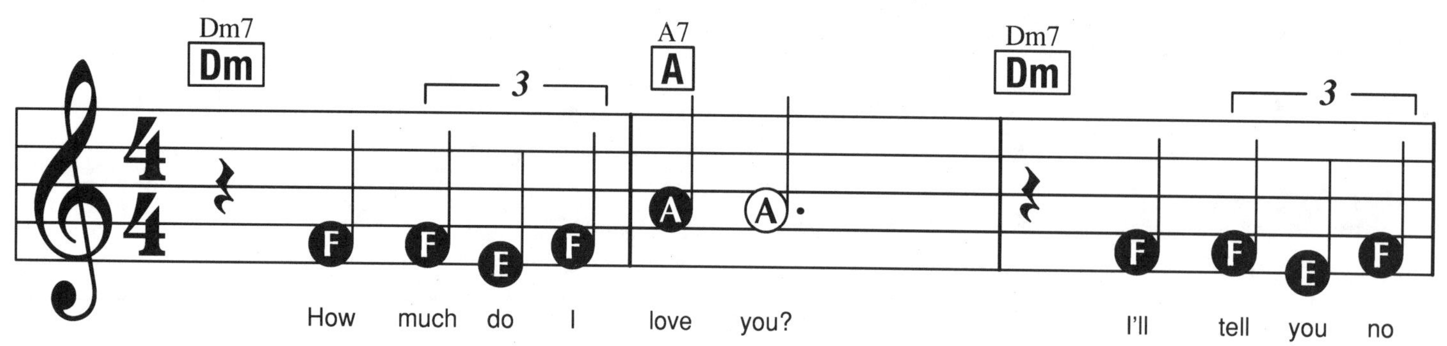

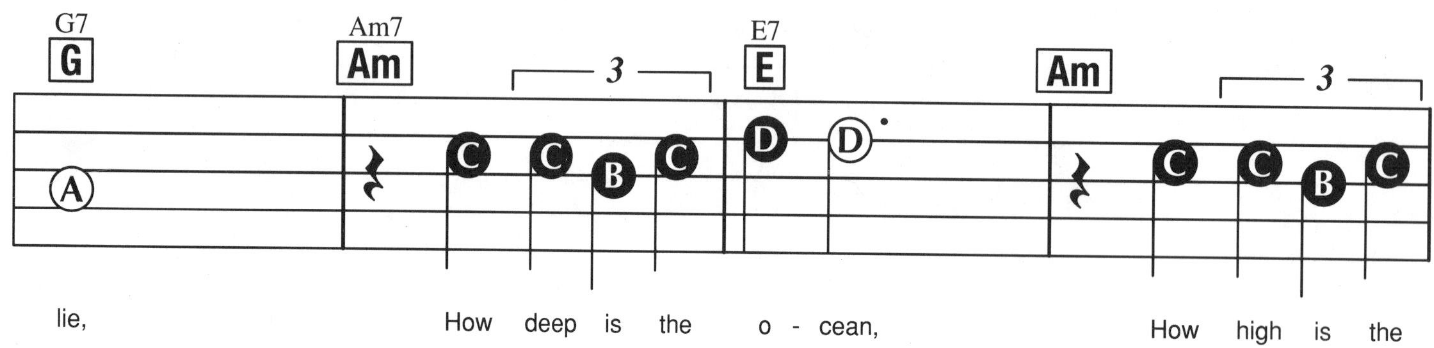

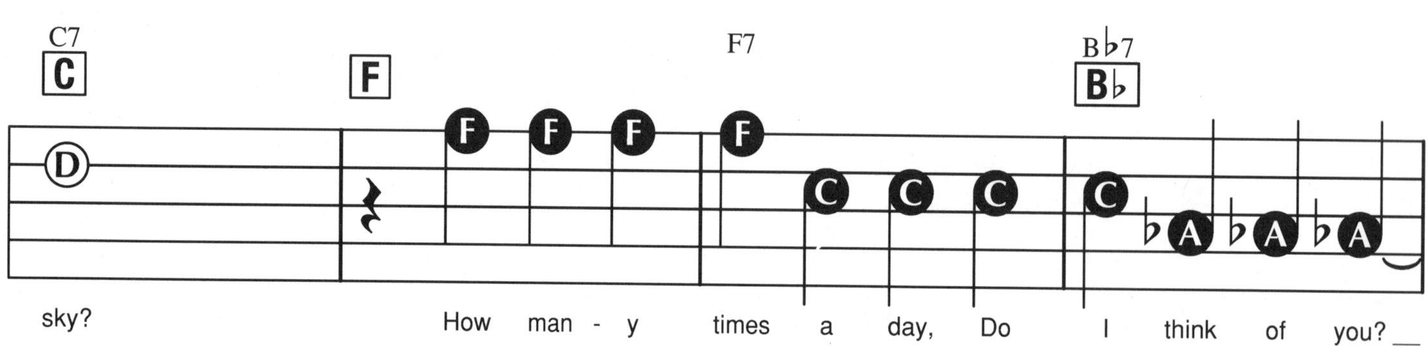

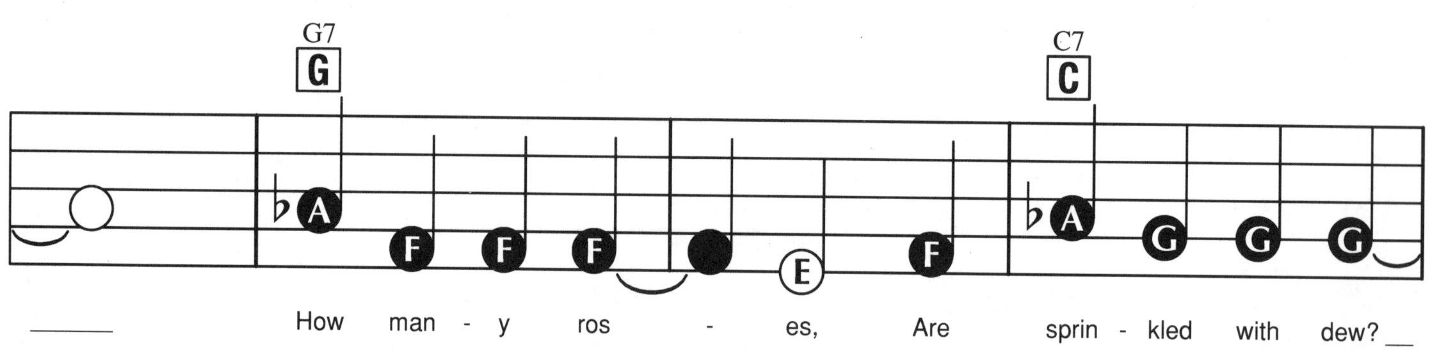

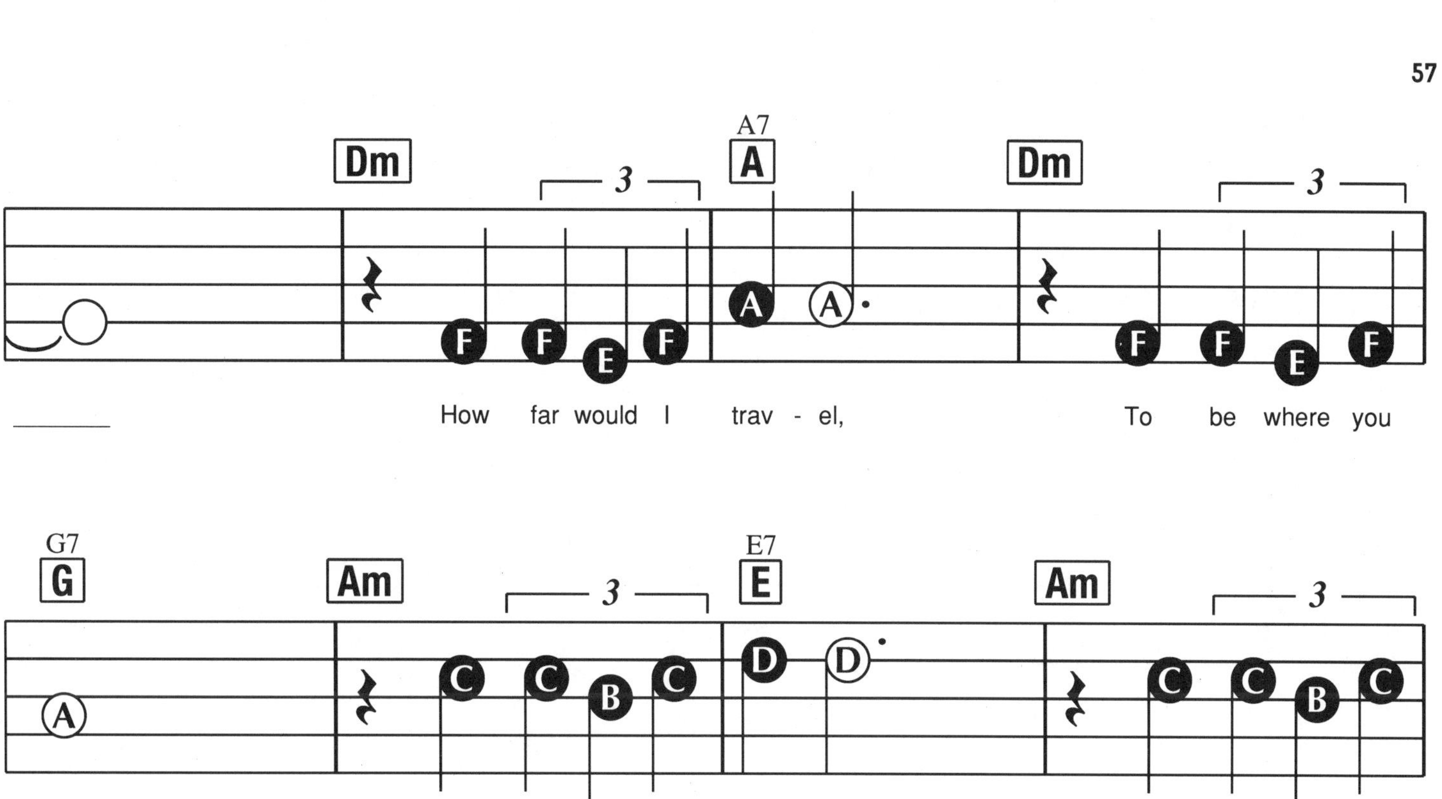
Dm A7 A Dm
How far would I trav - el,
To be where you
G7 G Am E7 E Am
are?
How far is the jour - ney,
From here to a

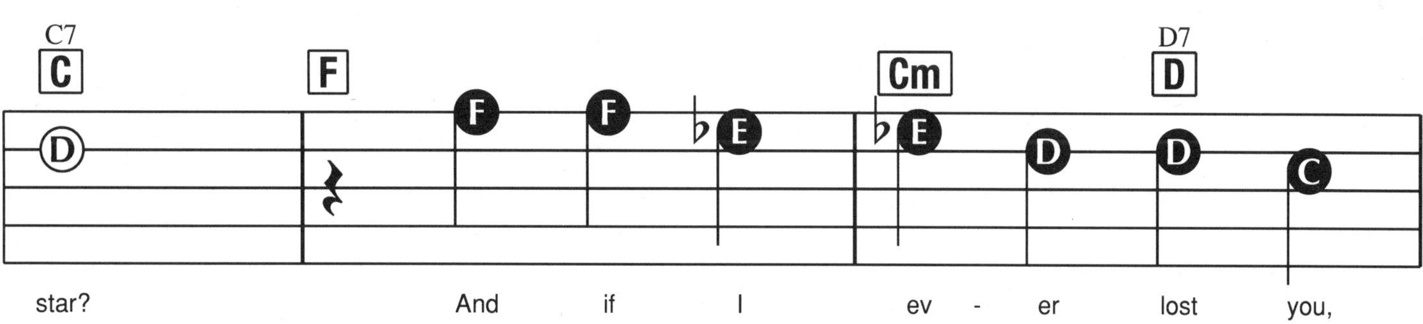
C7 C F Cm D7 D
star?
And if I ev - er lost you,

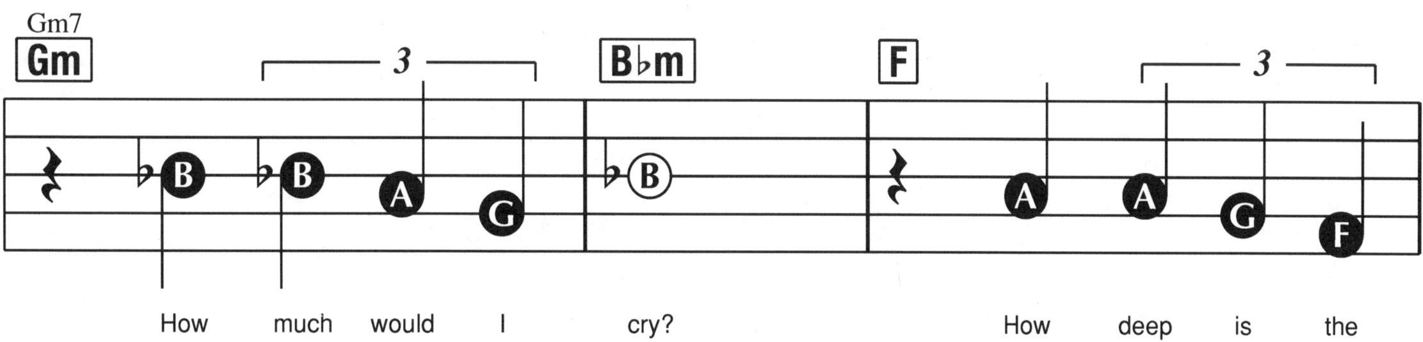
Gm7 Gm B♭m F
How much would I cry?
How deep is the

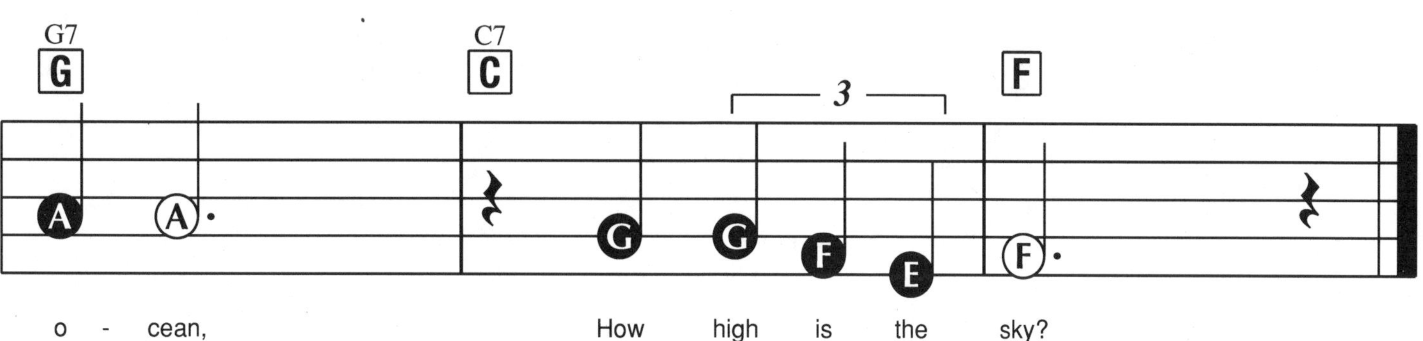
G7 G C7 C F
o - cean,
How high is the sky?

How's Chances?

Registration 4
Rhythm: Swing

Words and Music by
Irving Berlin

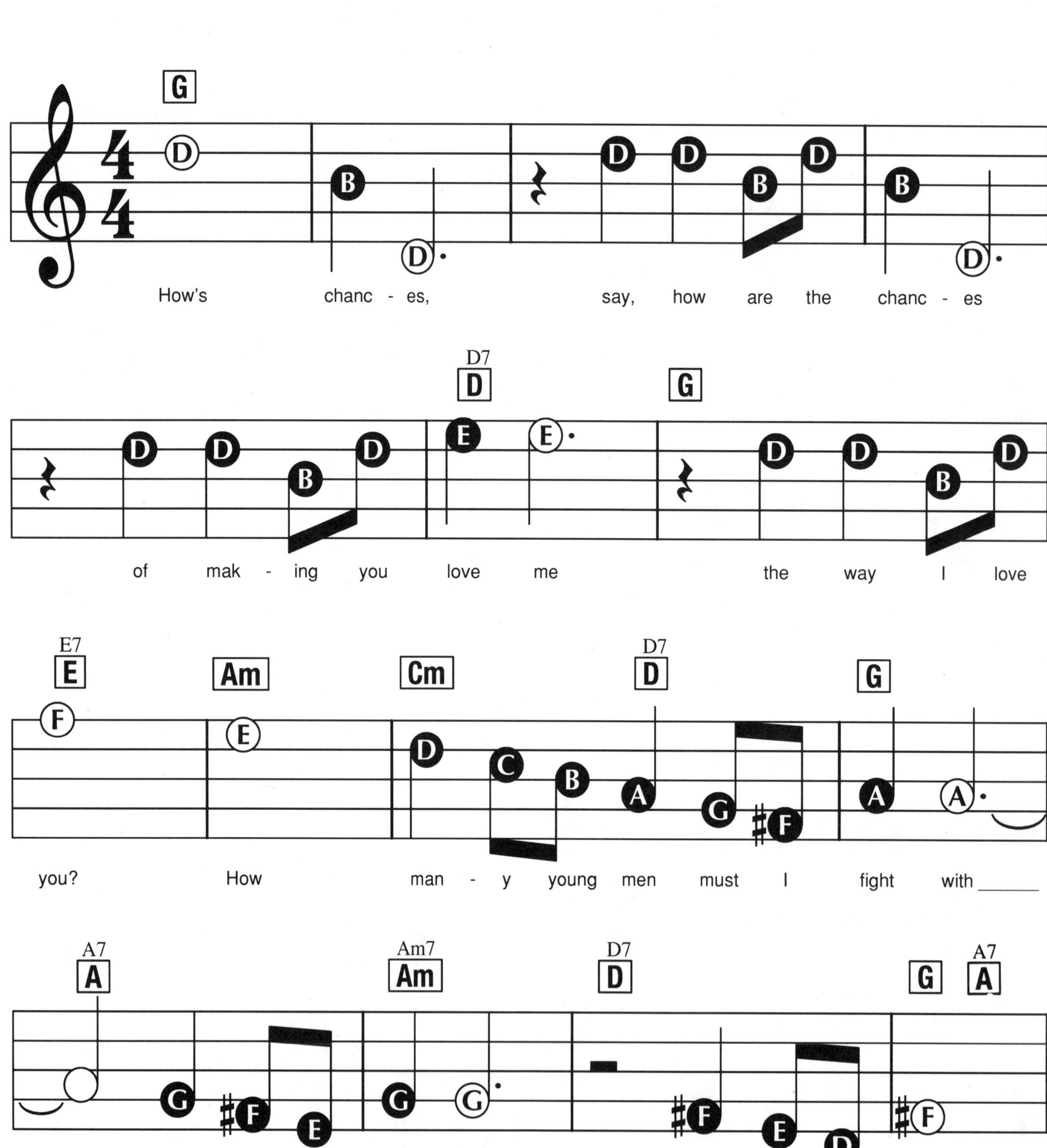

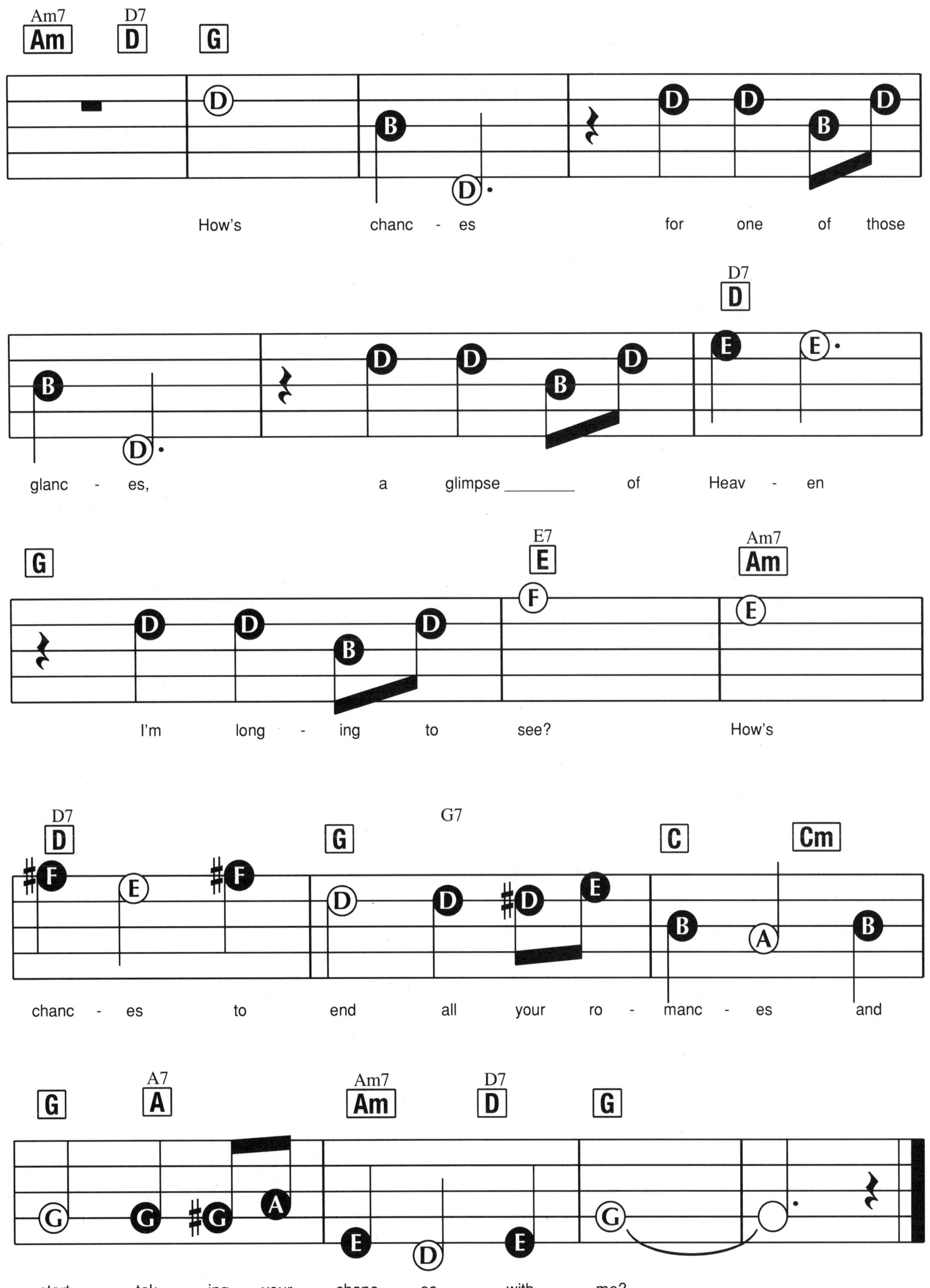
Am7 Am D7 D G
How's chanc - es for one of those
glanc - es, a glimpse ________ of Heav - en
D7 D
G E7 E Am7 Am
I'm long - ing to see? How's
D7 D G G7 C Cm
chanc - es to end all your ro - manc - es and
G A7 A Am7 Am D7 D G
start tak - ing your chanc - es with me? ________________

I Got Lost In His Arms

Registration 10
Rhythm: Swing

Words and Music by
Irving Berlin

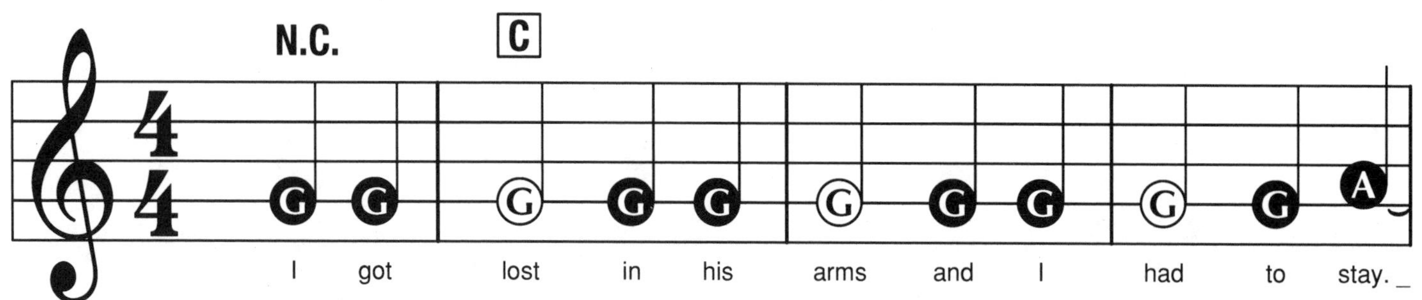

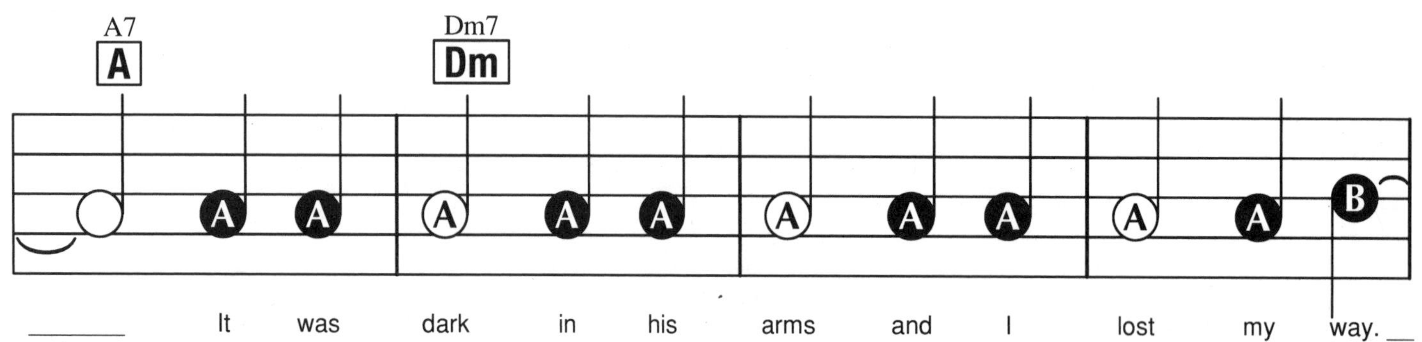

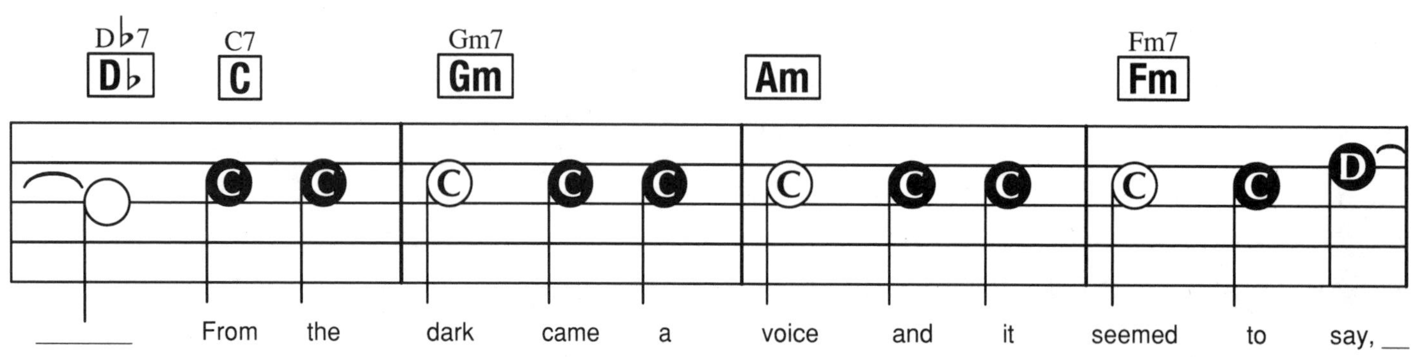

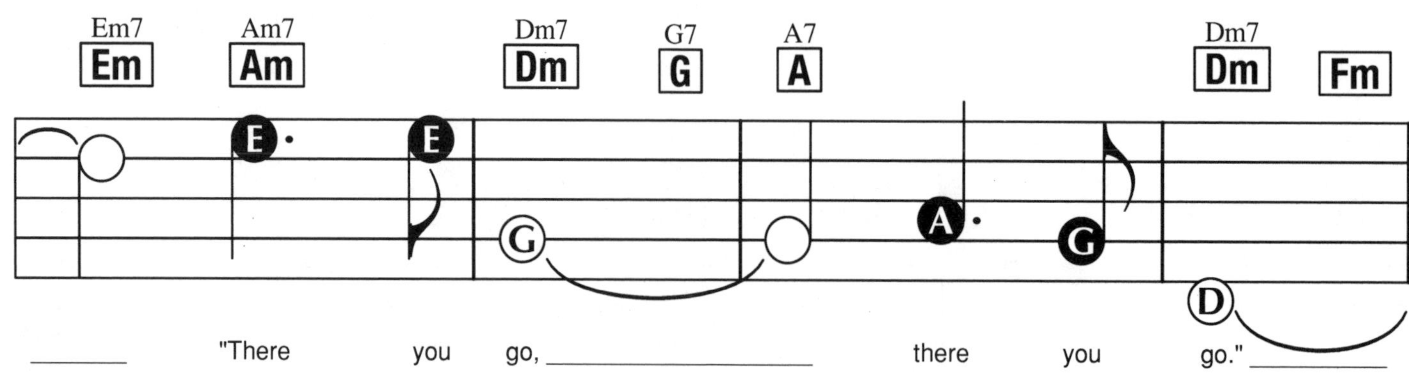

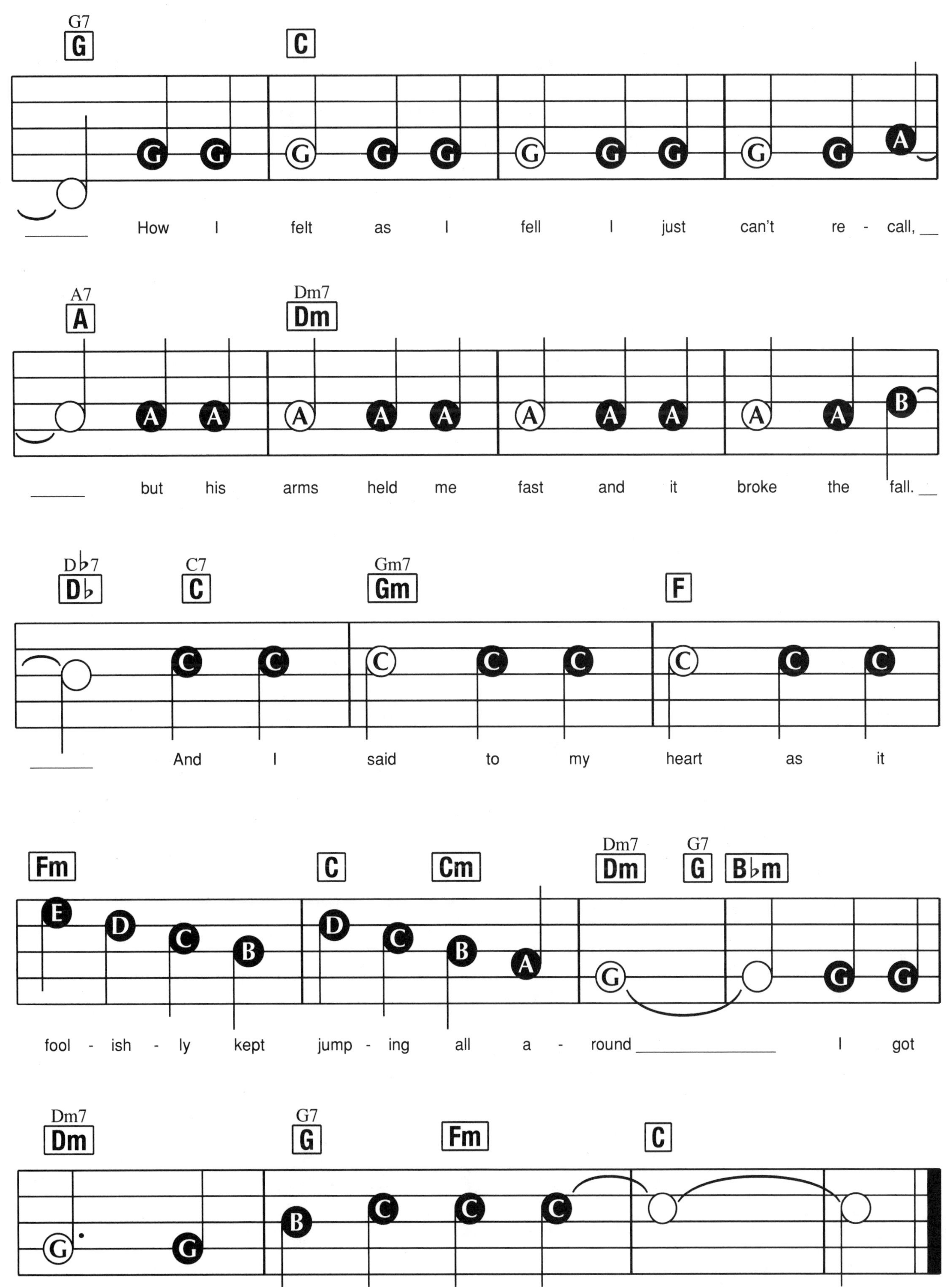
G7 G C
How I felt as I fell I just can't re - call,
A7 A Dm7 Dm
but his arms held me fast and it broke the fall.
D♭7 D♭ C7 C Gm7 Gm F
And I said to my heart as it
Fm C Cm Dm7 Dm G7 G B♭m
fool - ish - ly kept jump - ing all a - round I got
Dm7 Dm G7 G Fm C
lost but look what I found.

I Got The Sun In The Morning

Registration 7
Rhythm: Swing

Words and Music by
Irving Berlin

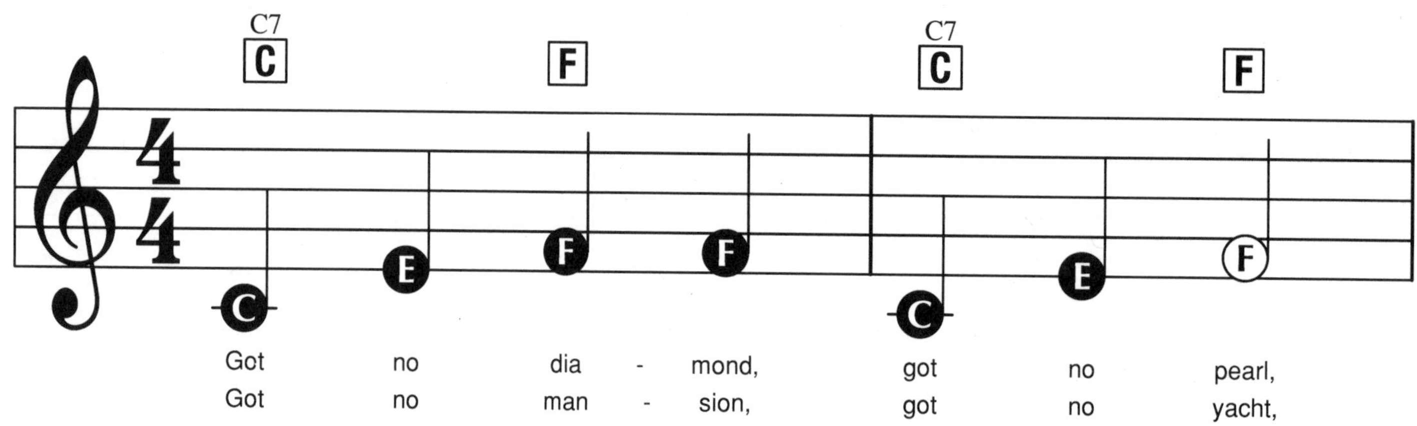

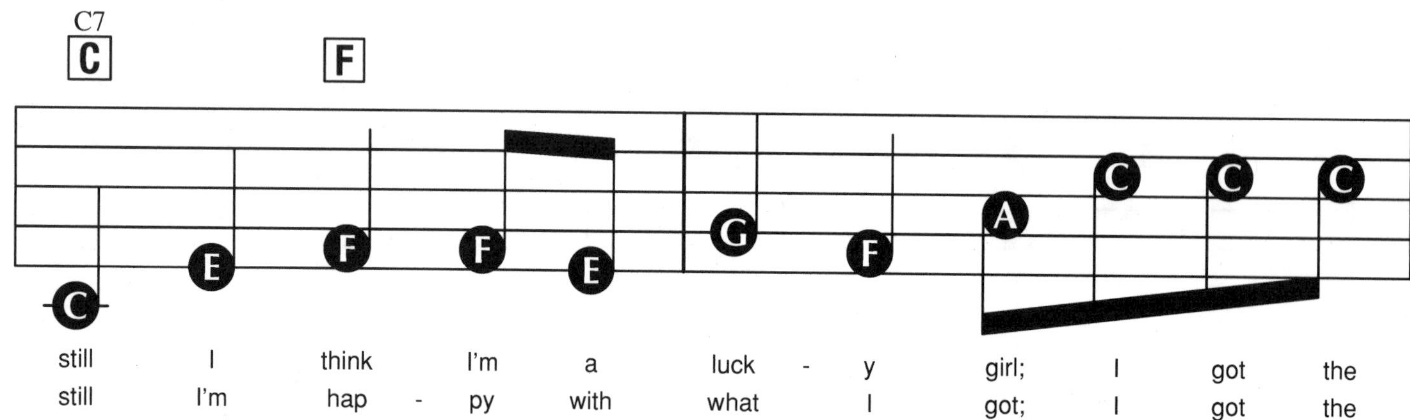

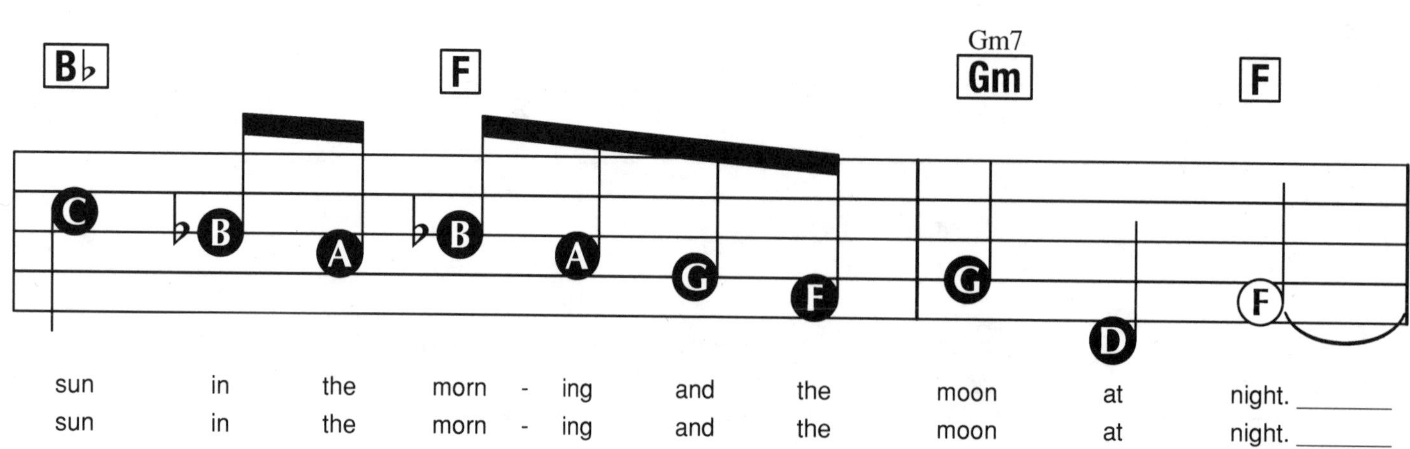

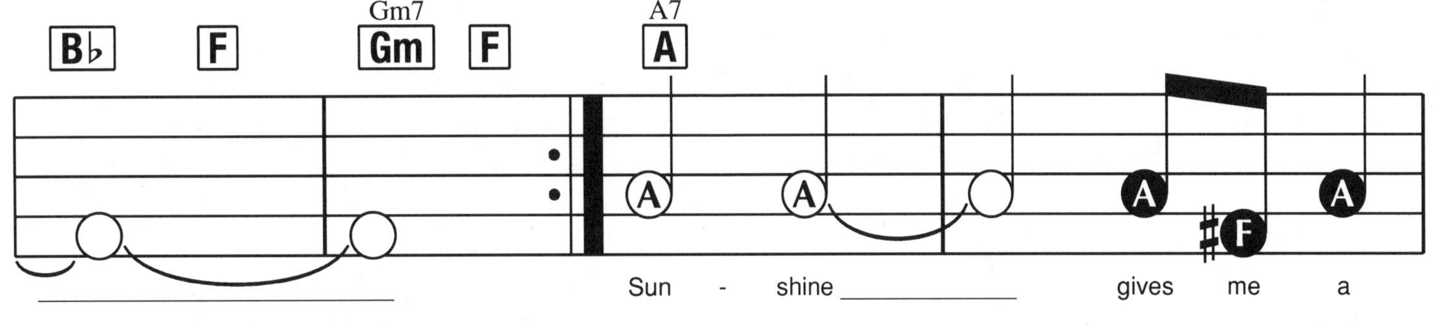
B♭
F
Gm7
Gm
F
A7
A
Sun - shine gives me a

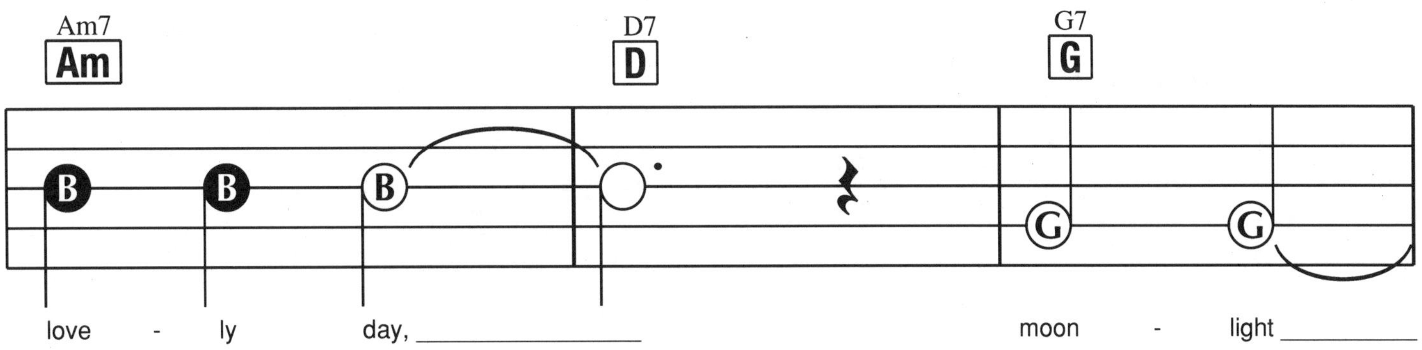
Am7
Am
D7
D
G7
G
love - ly day,
moon - light

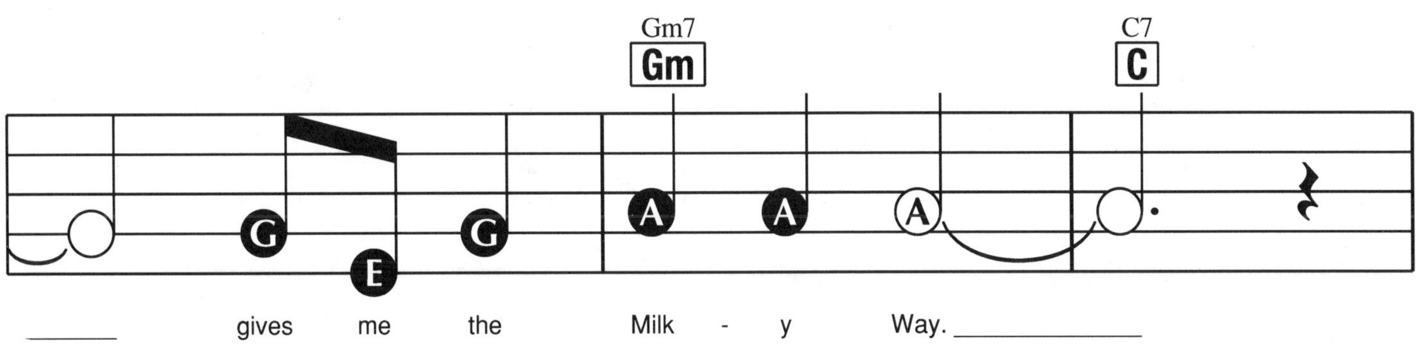
Gm7
Gm
C7
C
gives me the
Milk - y Way.

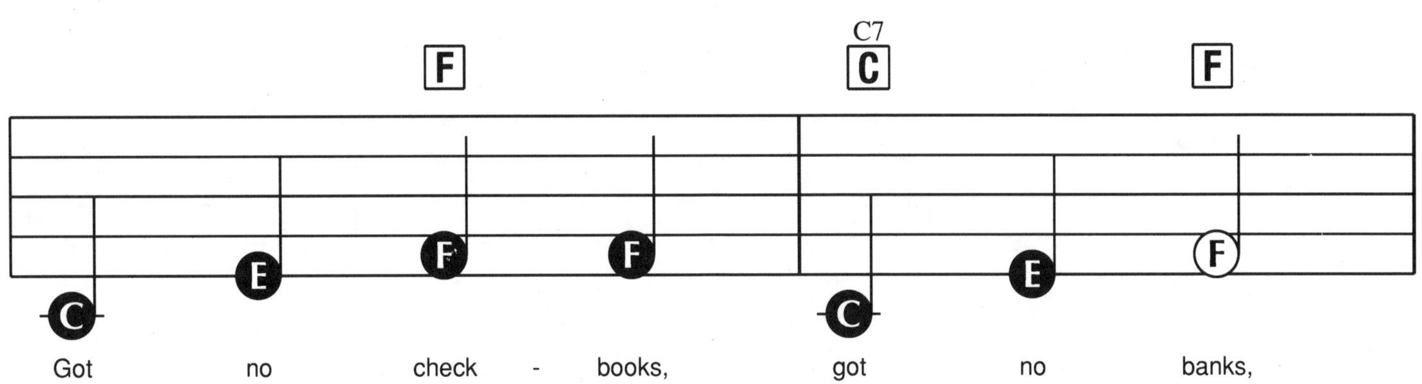
F
C7
C
F
Got no check - books, got no banks,

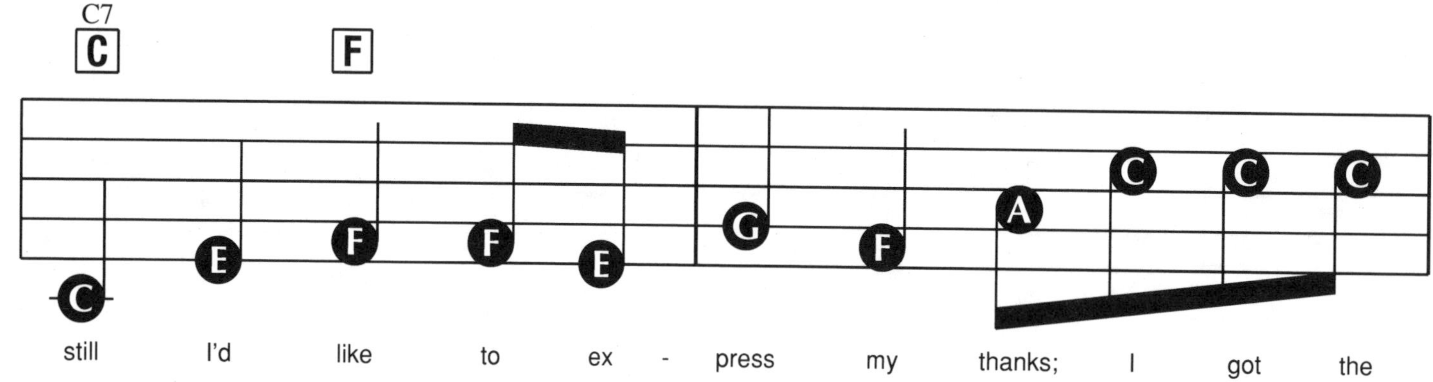
C7
C
F
C
E
F
F
E
G
F
A
C
C
C
still I'd like to ex - press my thanks; I got the

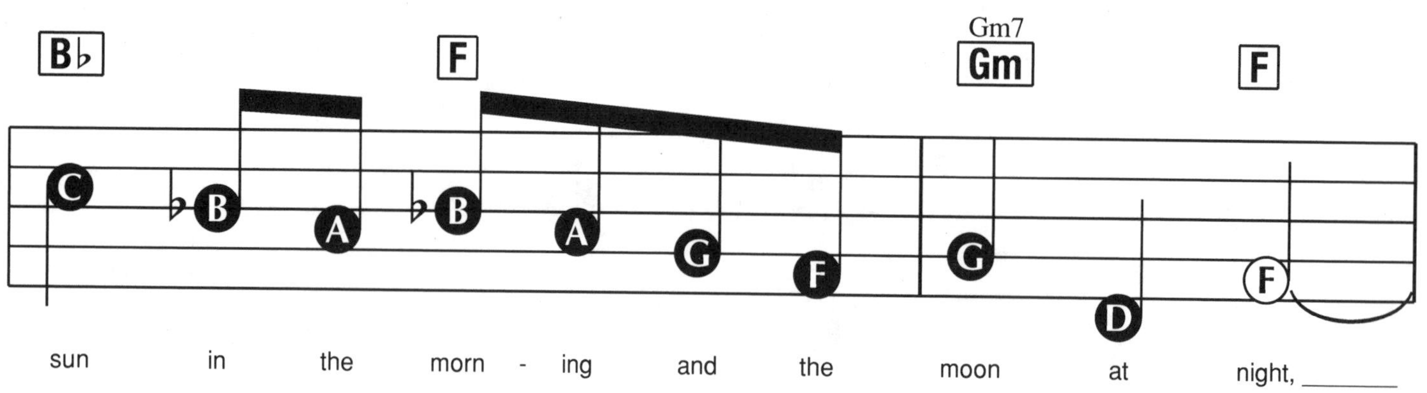
B♭
F
Gm7
Gm
F
C
B
A
B
A
G
F
G
D
F
sun in the morn - ing and the moon at night,

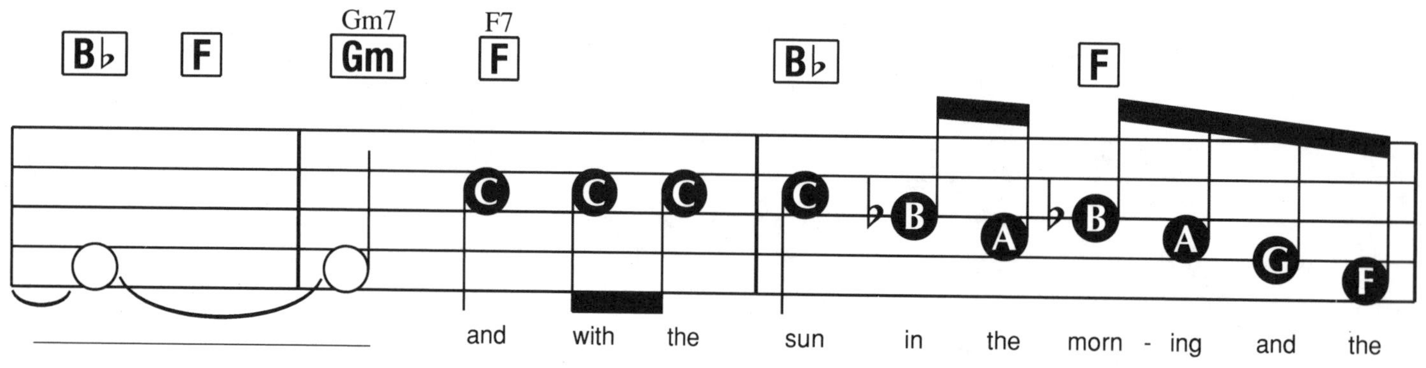
B♭
F
Gm7
Gm
F7
F
B♭
F
C
C
C
C
B
A
B
A
G
F
and with the sun in the morn - ing and the

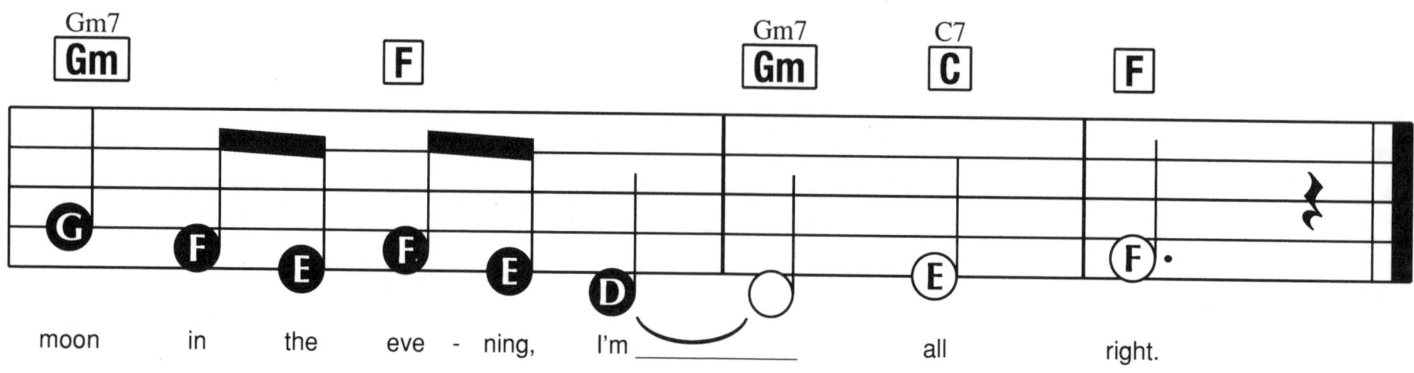
Gm7
Gm
F
Gm7
Gm
C7
C
F
G
F
E
F
E
D
E
F
moon in the eve - ning, I'm all right.

I Love A Piano

Registration 8
Rhythm: Swing

Words and Music by
Irving Berlin

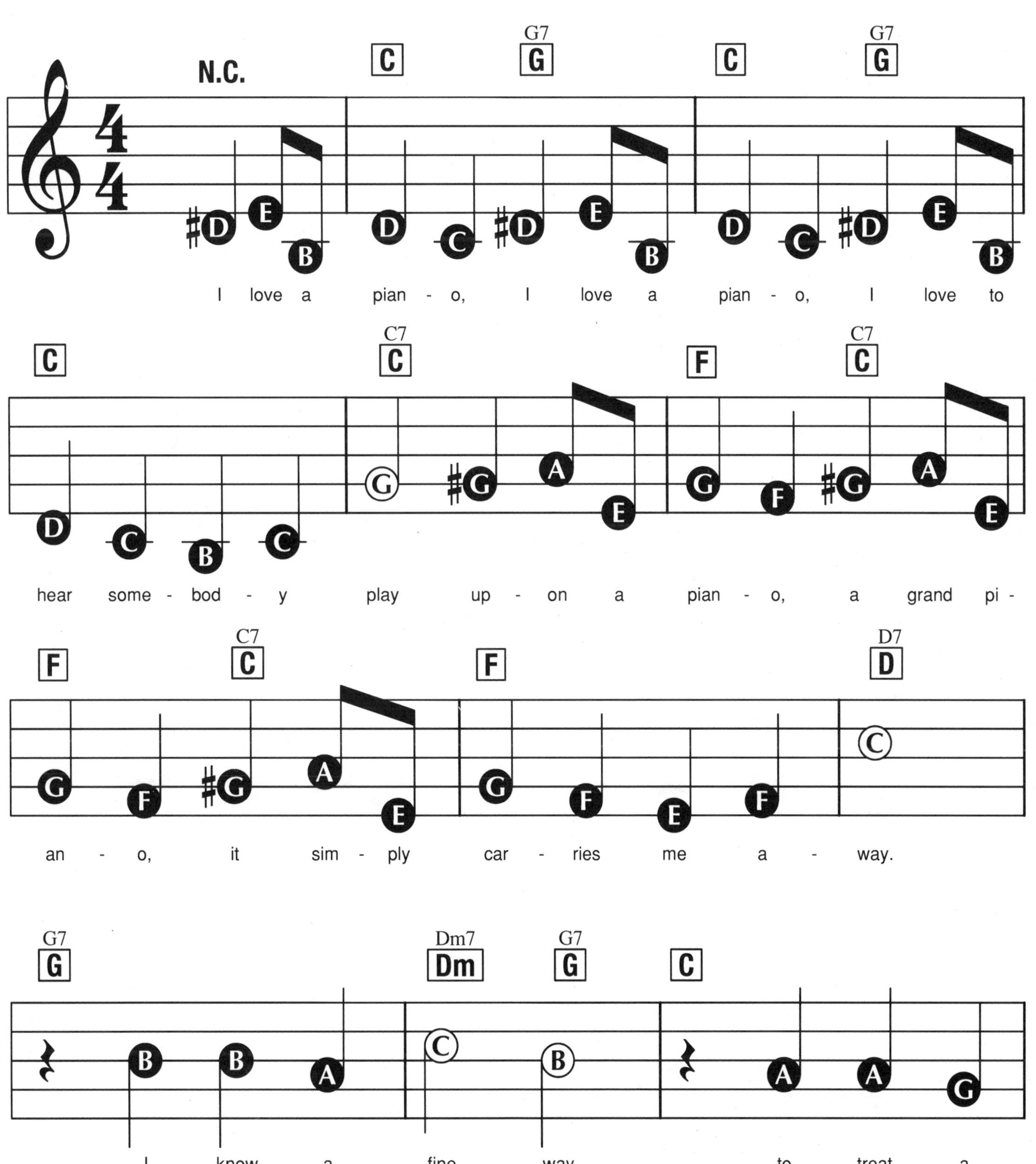

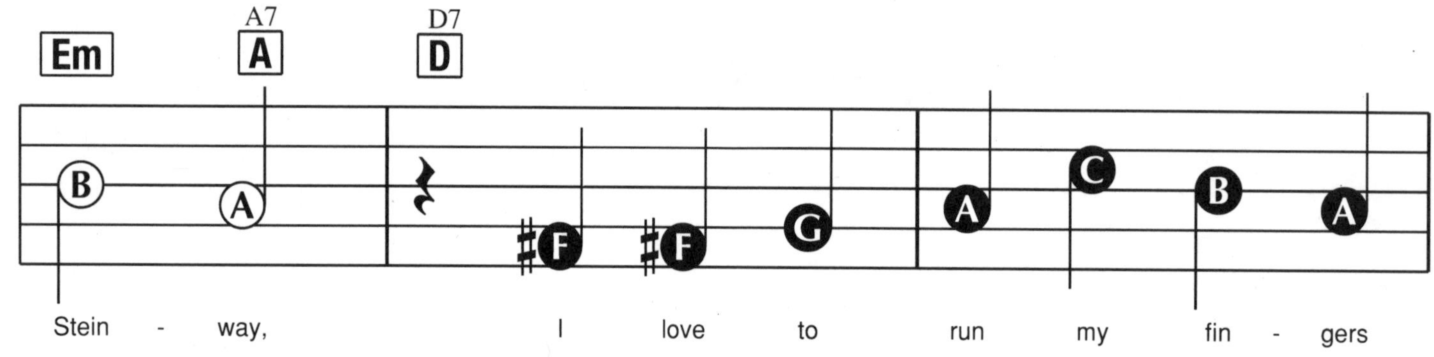
Em
A7
A
D7
D
Stein - way, I love to run my fin - gers

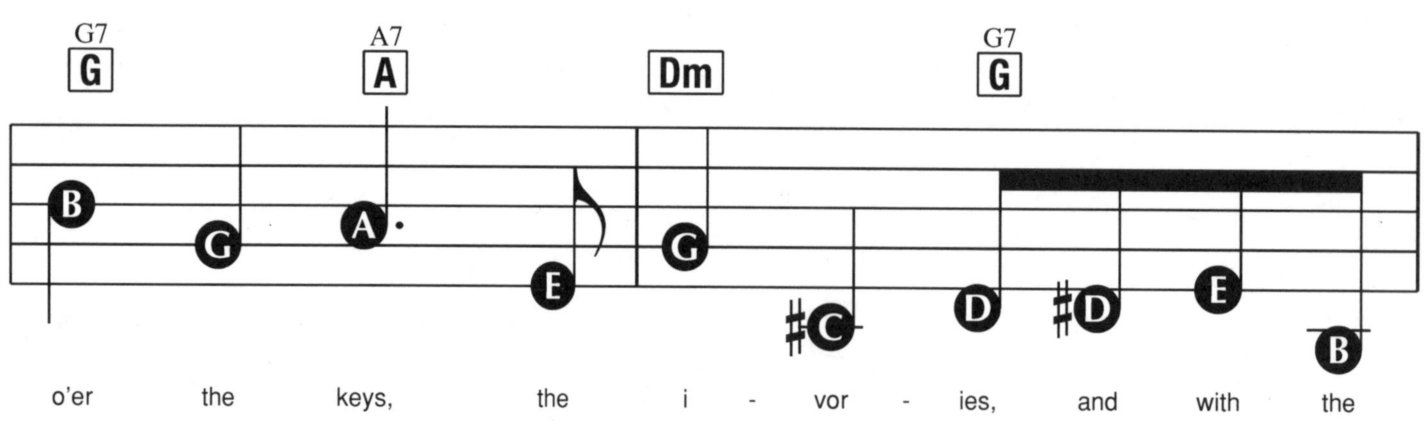
G7
G
A7
A
Dm
G7
G
o'er the keys, the i - vor - ies, and with the

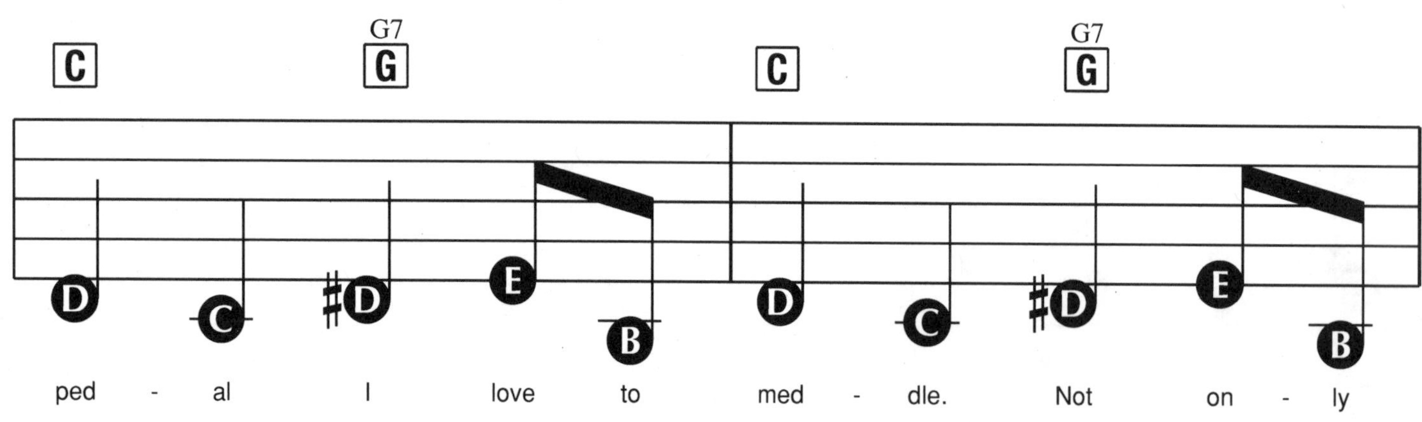
C
G7
G
C
G7
G
ped - al I love to med - dle. Not on - ly

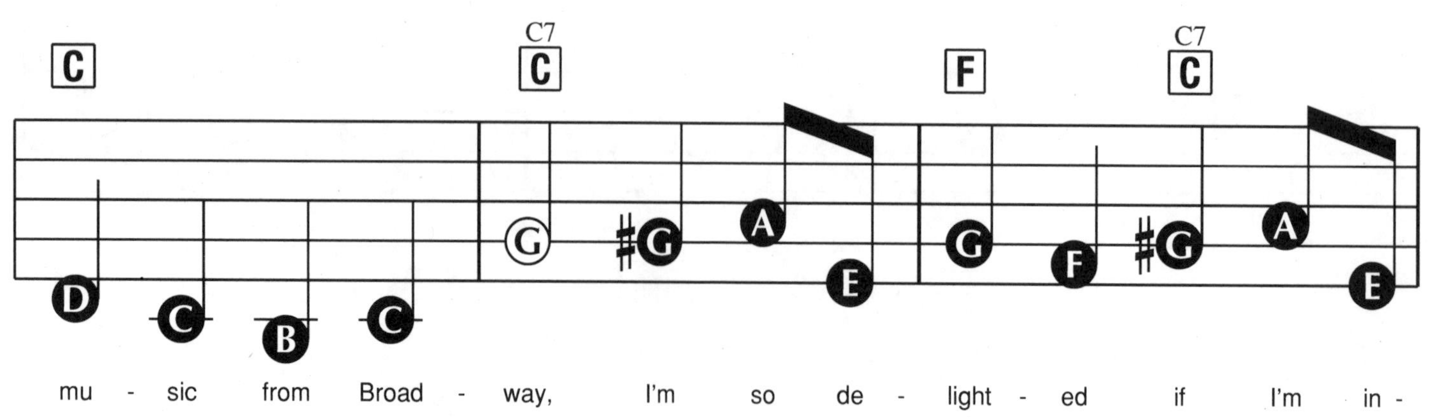
C
C7
C
F
C7
C
mu - sic from Broad - way, I'm so de - light - ed if I'm in -

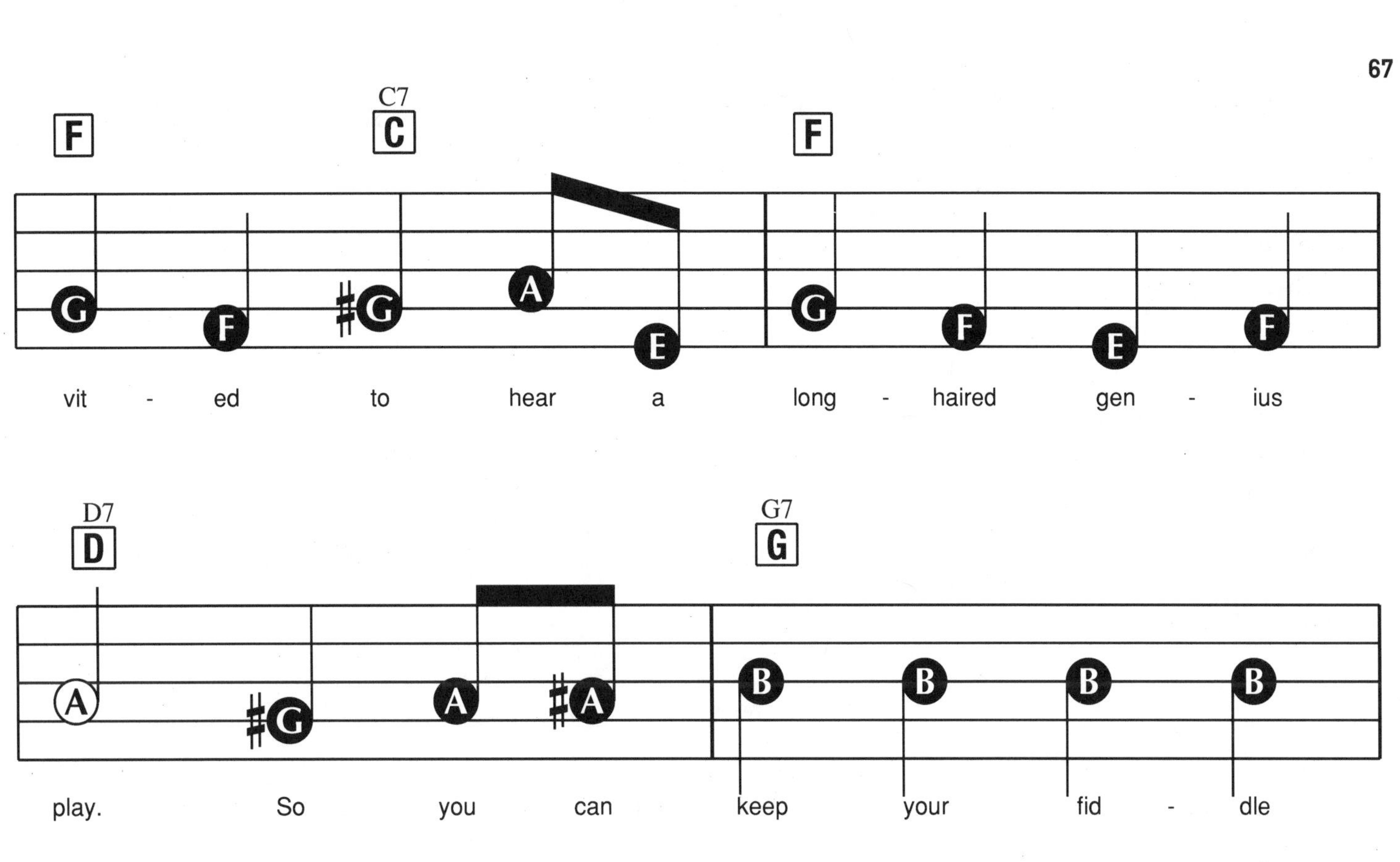
F
C7
C
F
vit - ed to hear a long - haired gen - ius
D7
D
G7
G
play. So you can keep your fid - dle

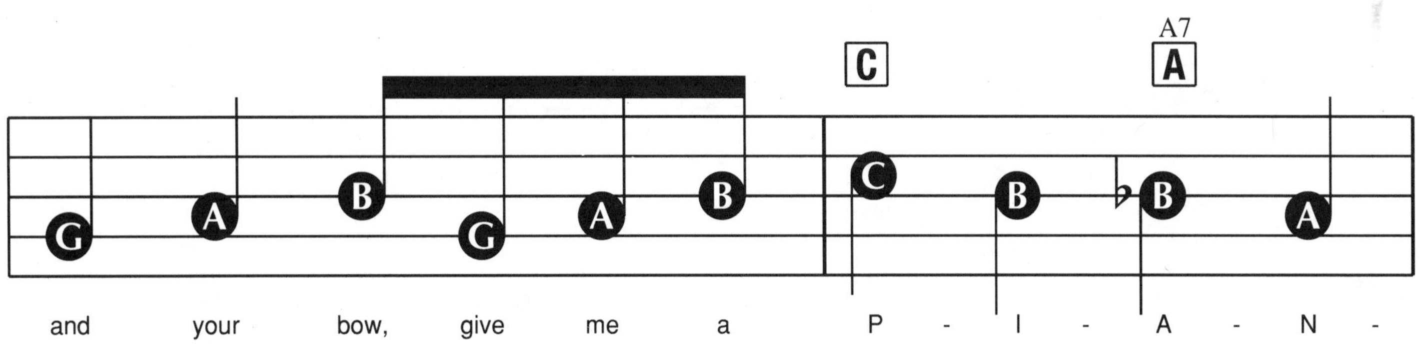
C
A7
A
and your bow, give me a P - I - A - N -

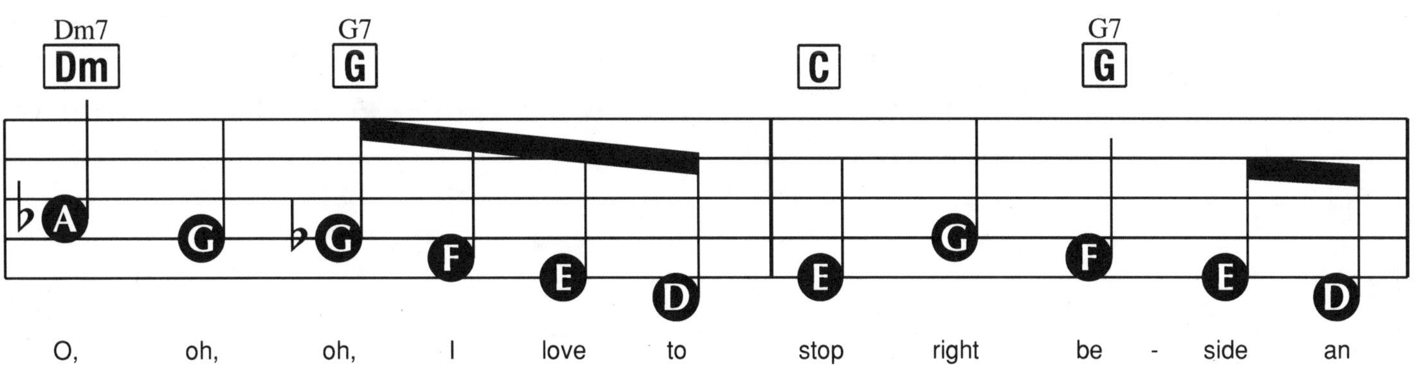
Dm7
Dm
G7
G
C
G7
G
O, oh, oh, I love to stop right be - side an

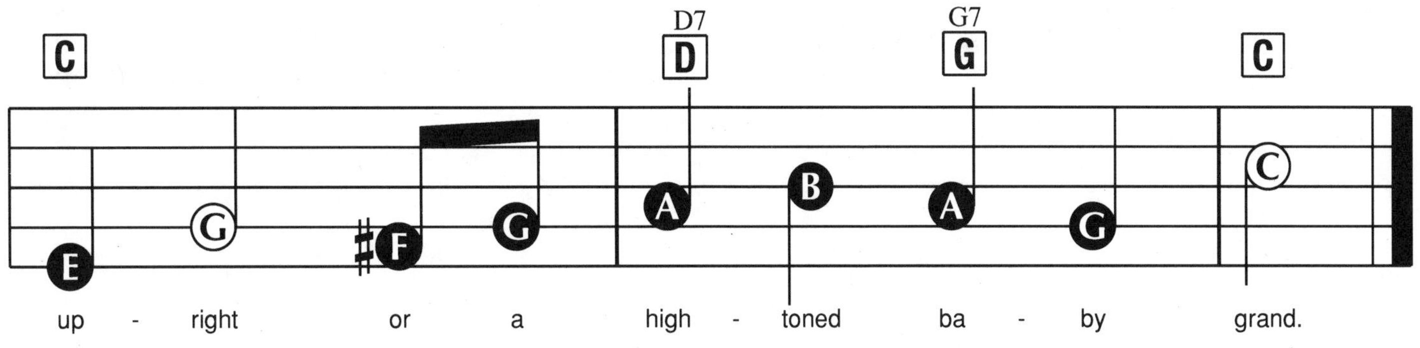
C
D7
D
G7
G
C
up - right or a high - toned ba - by grand.

I Poured My Heart Into A Song

Registration 8
Rhythm: Swing

Words and Music by
Irving Berlin

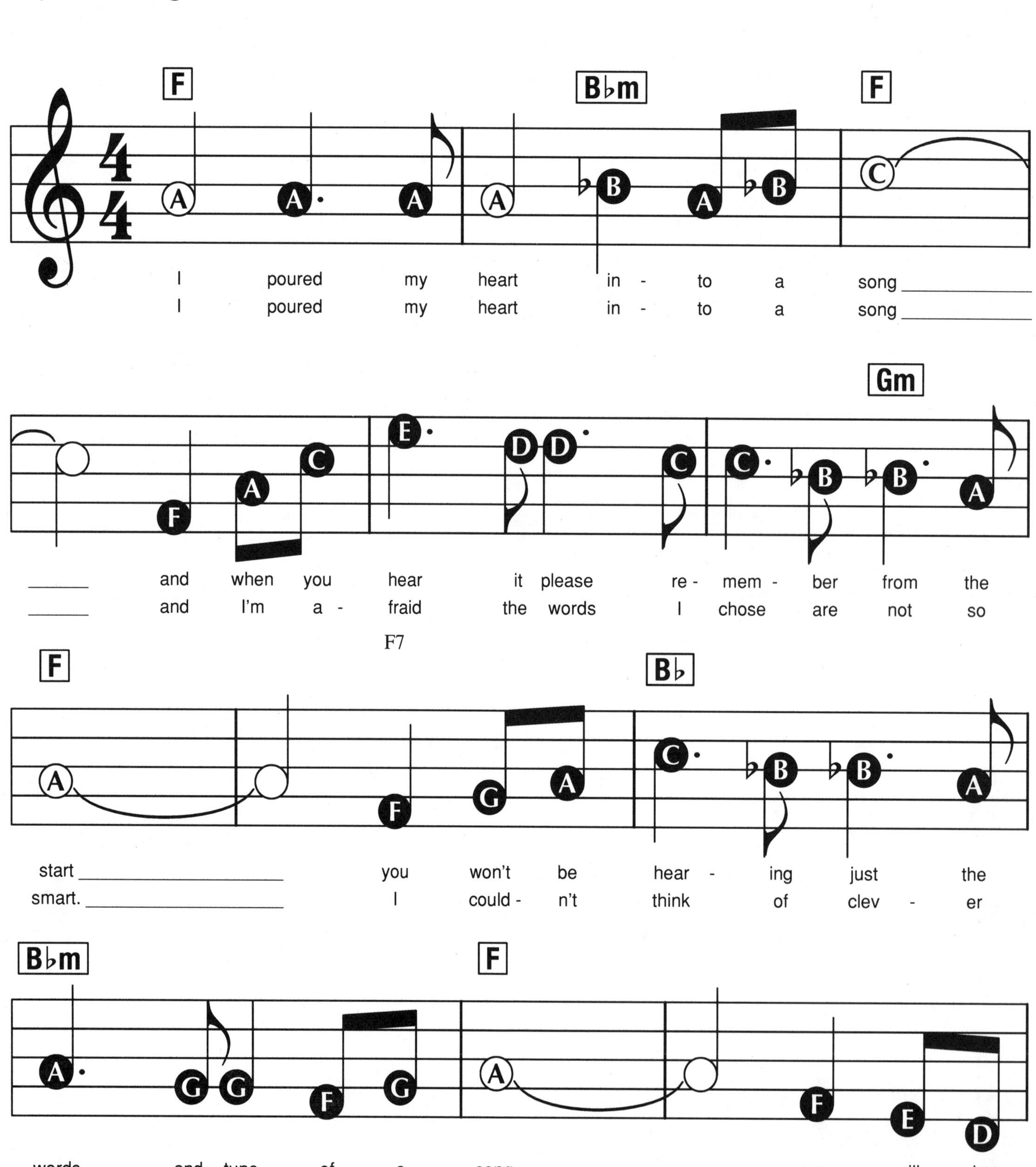

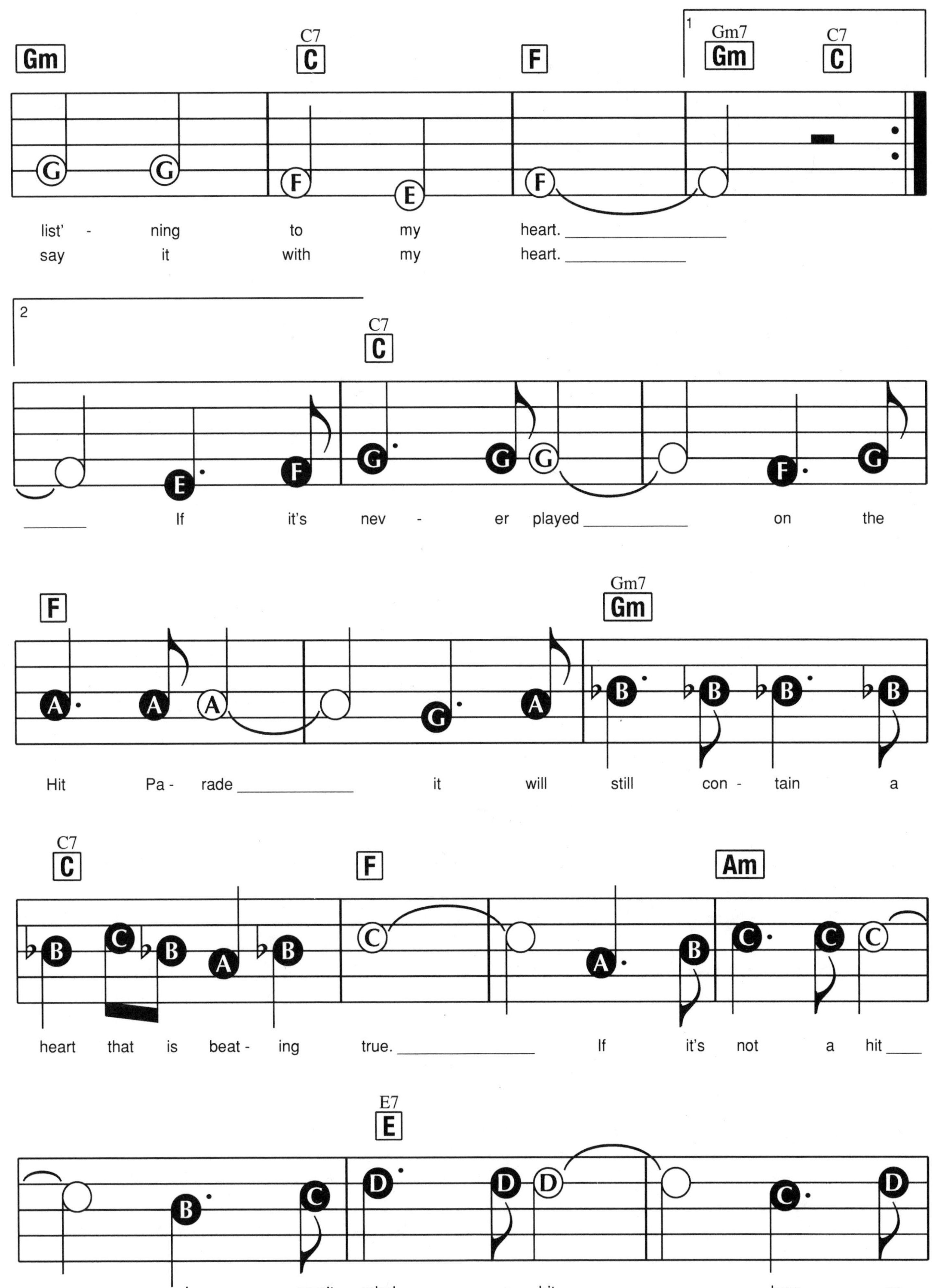
Gm C7 C F 1 Gm7 Gm C7 C
G G F E F
list' - ning to my heart.
say it with my heart.
2 C7 C
E F G G G F G
If it's nev - er played on the
F Gm7 Gm
A A A G A B B B B
Hit Pa - rade it will still con - tain a
C7 C F Am
B C B A B C A B C C C
heart that is beat - ing true. If it's not a hit
E7 E
B C D D D C D
I won't mind a bit, long as

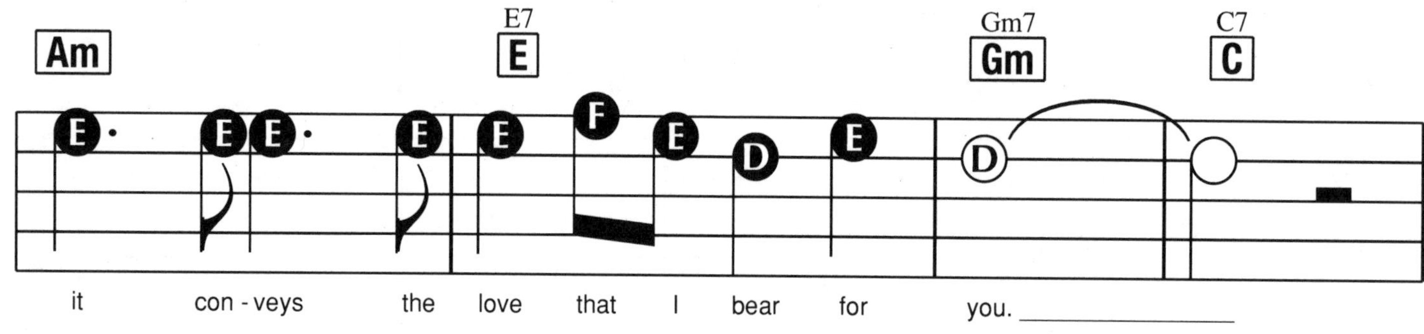
Am
E7
E
Gm7
Gm
C7
C
E E E E E F E D E D
it con - veys the love that I bear for you.

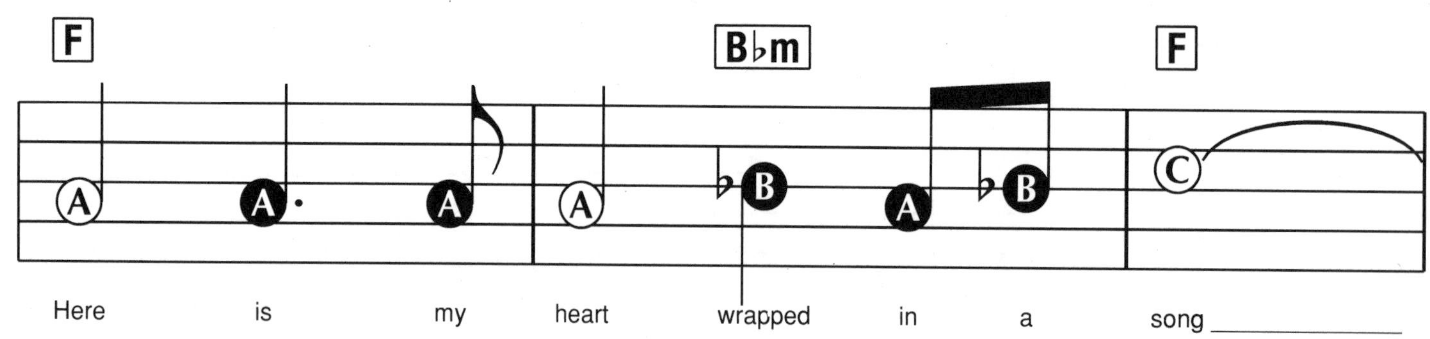
F
B♭m
F
A A A A B A B C
Here is my heart wrapped in a song

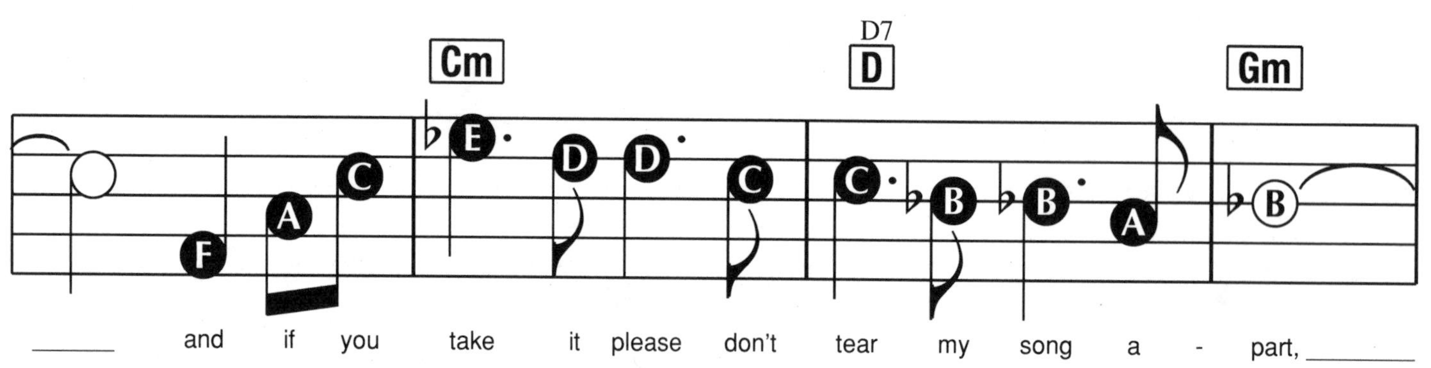
Cm
D7
D
Gm
F A C E D D C C B B A B
and if you take it please don't tear my song a - part,

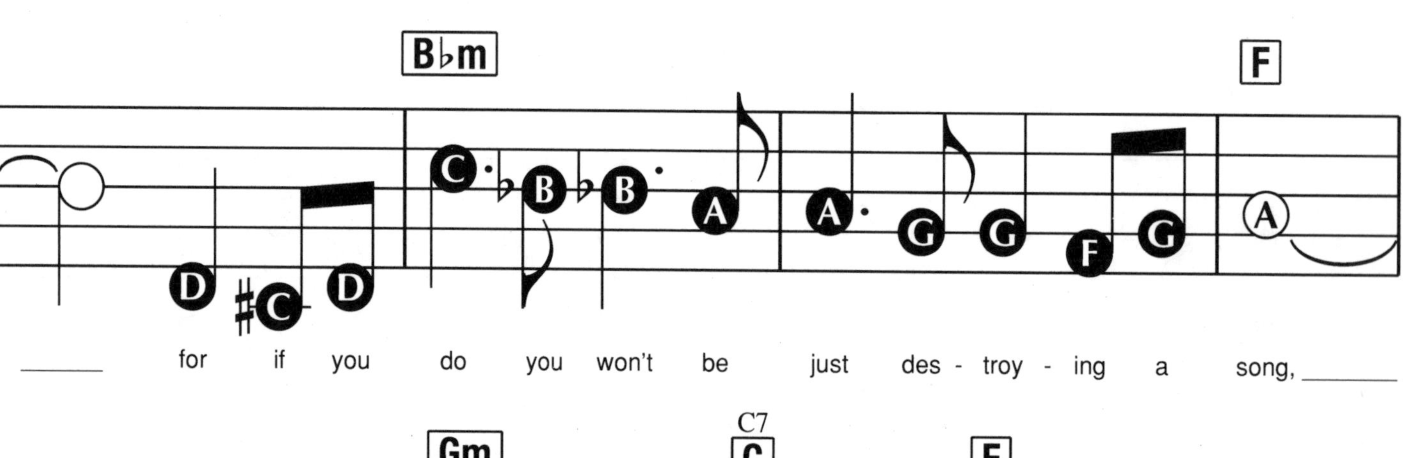
B♭m
F
D C D C B B A A G G F G A
for if you do you won't be just des - troy - ing a song,

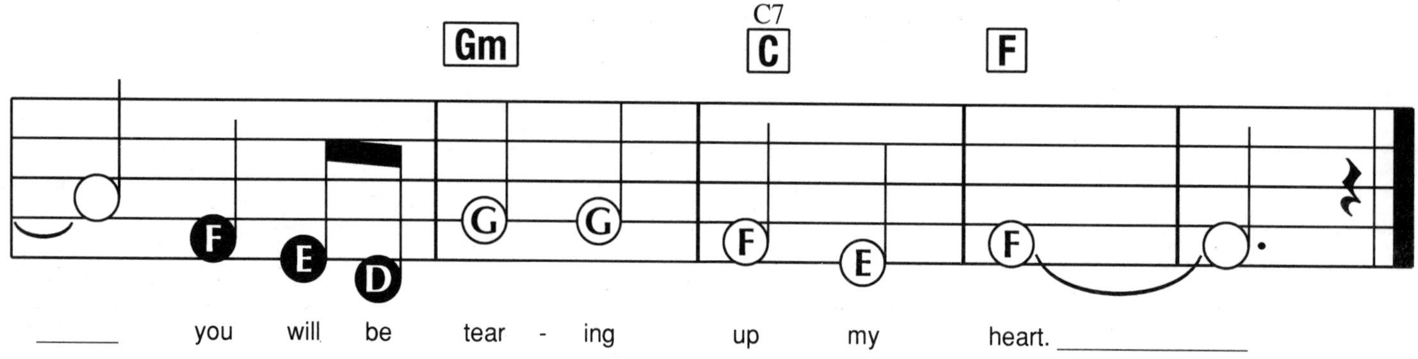
Gm
C7
C
F
F E D G G F E F
you will be tear - ing up my heart.

Isn't This A Lovely Day (To Be Caught In The Rain?)

Registration 10
Rhythm: Swing

Words and Music by
Irving Berlin

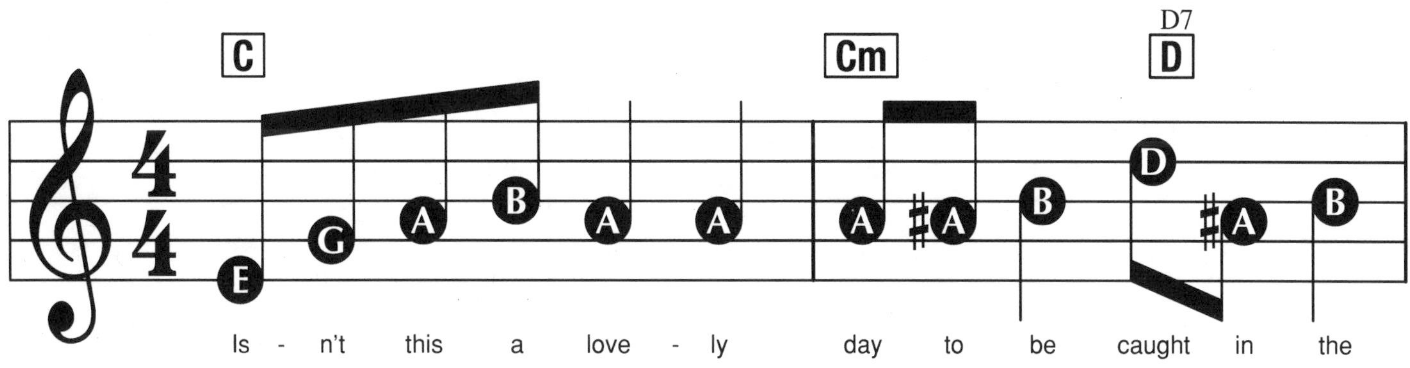

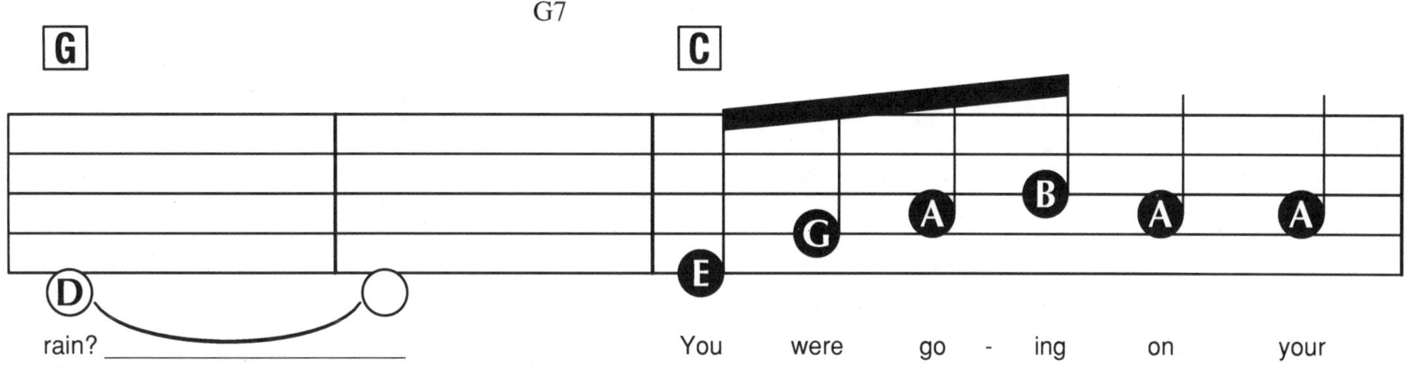

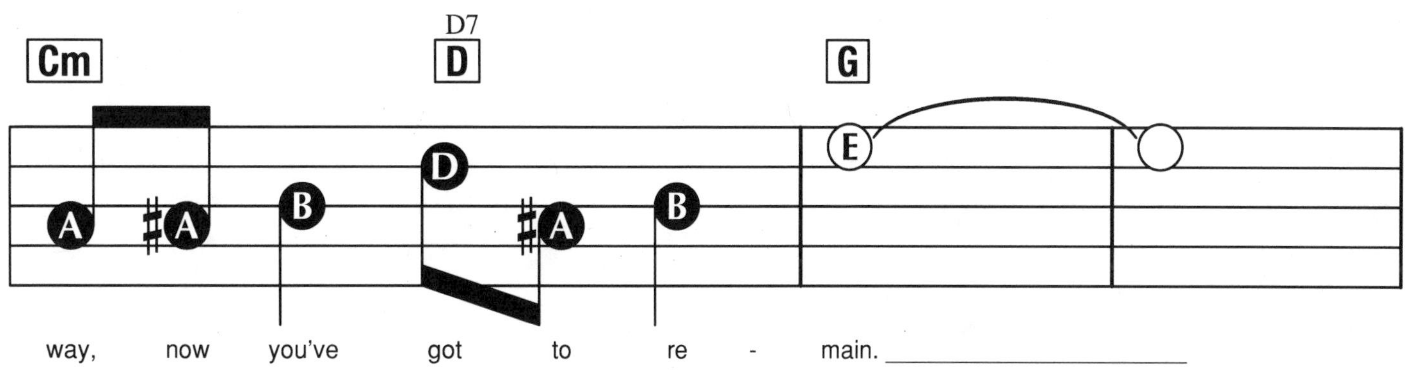

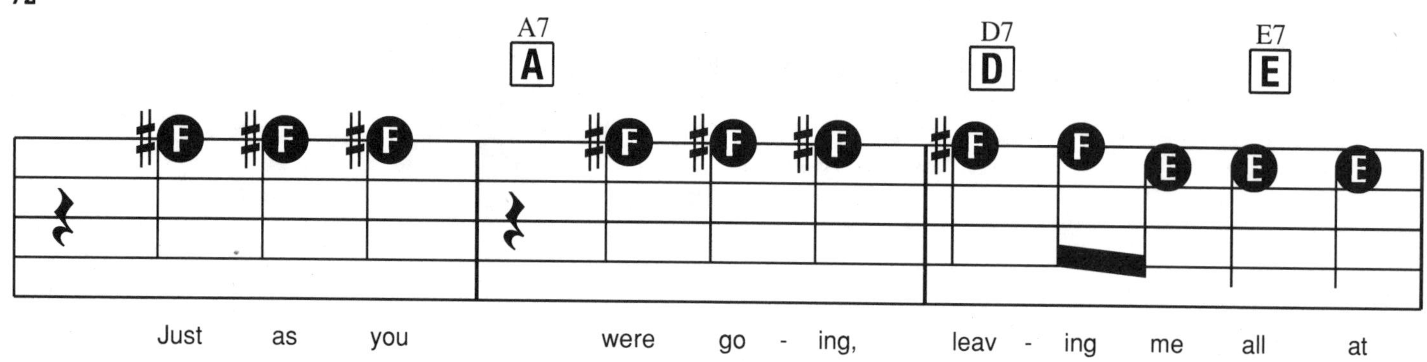
A7
A
D7
D
E7
E
#F #F #F #F #F #F #F F E E E
Just as you were go - ing, leav - ing me all at

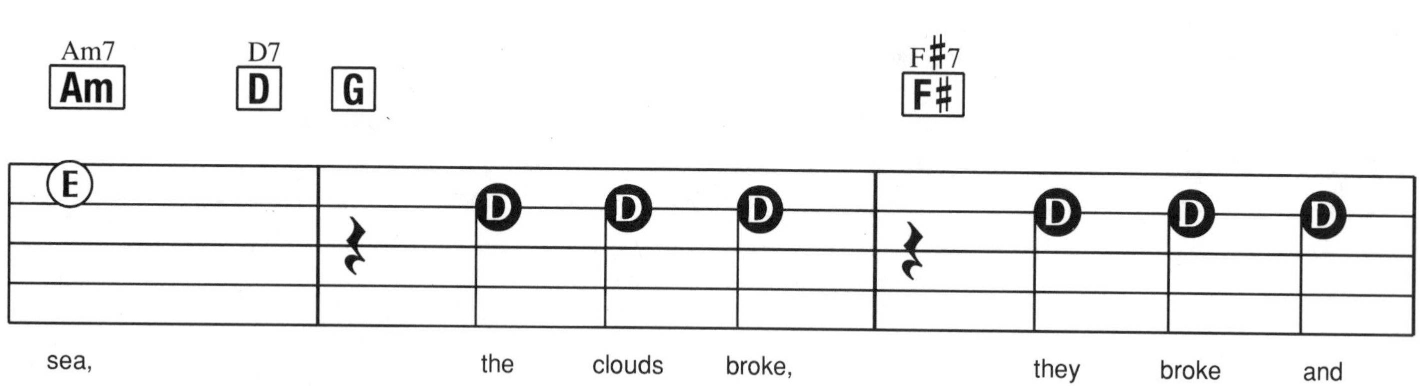
Am7
Am
D7
D
G
F#7
F#
E D D D D D D
sea, the clouds broke, they broke and

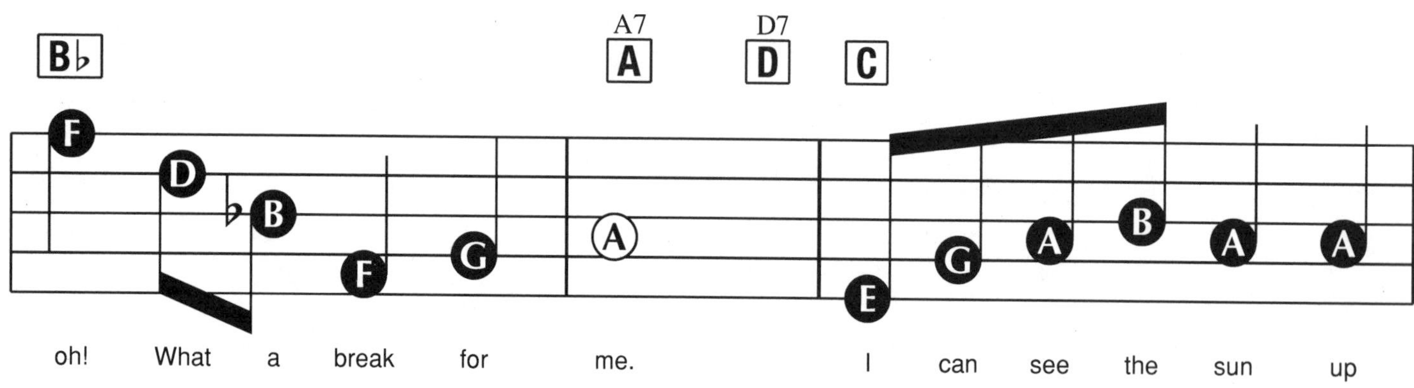
B♭
A7
A
D7
D
C
F D B F G A E G A B A A
oh! What a break for me. I can see the sun up

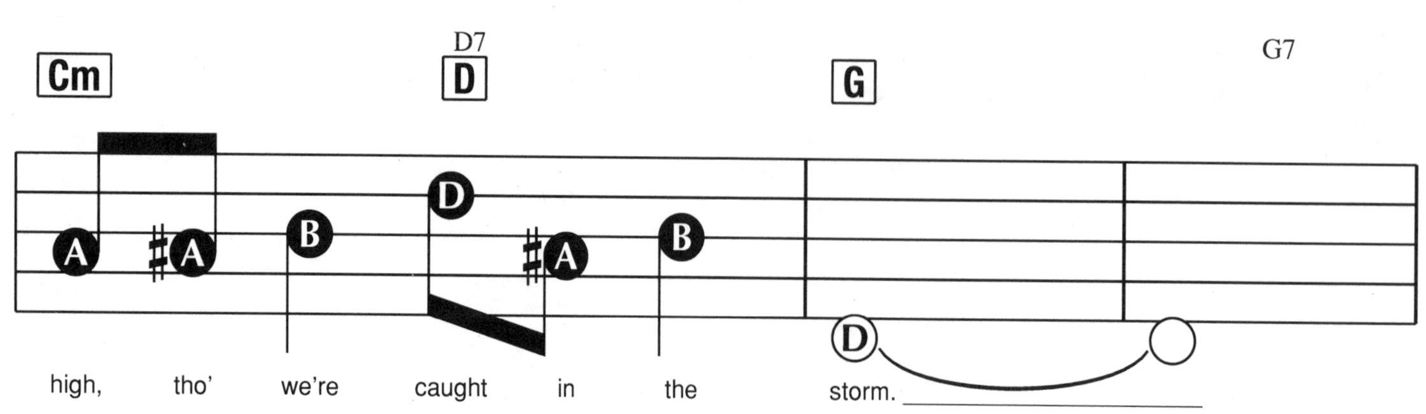
Cm
D7
D
G
G7
A #A B D #A B D
high, tho' we're caught in the storm.

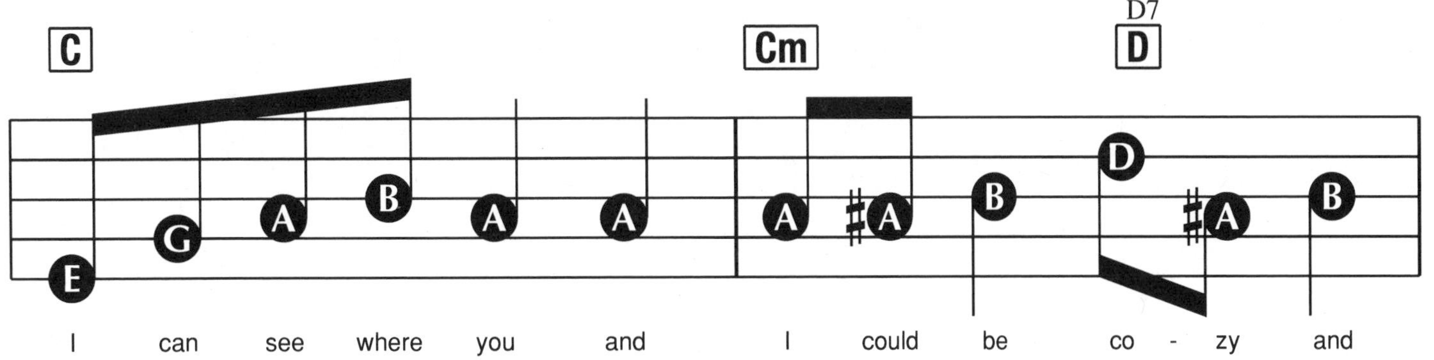
C
Cm
D7
D
I can see where you and
I could be co - zy and

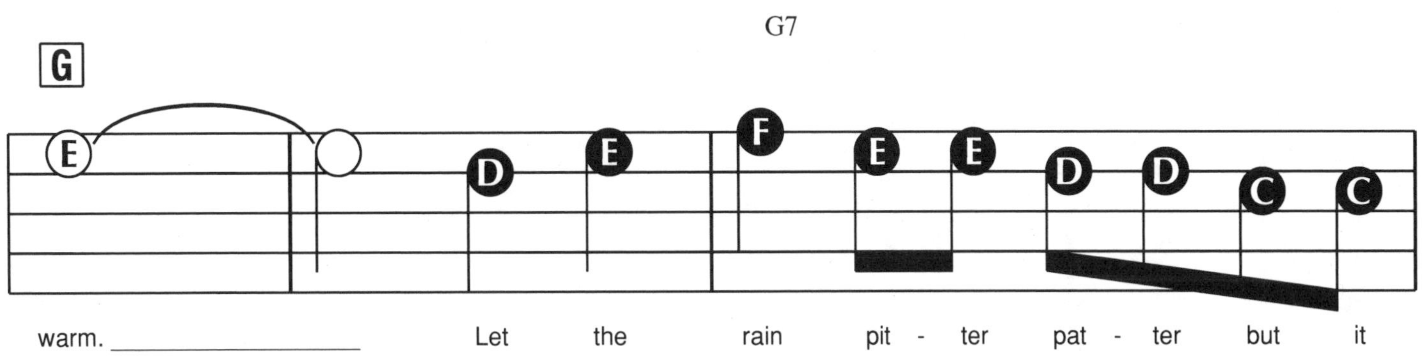
G
G7
warm.
Let the rain pit - ter pat - ter but it

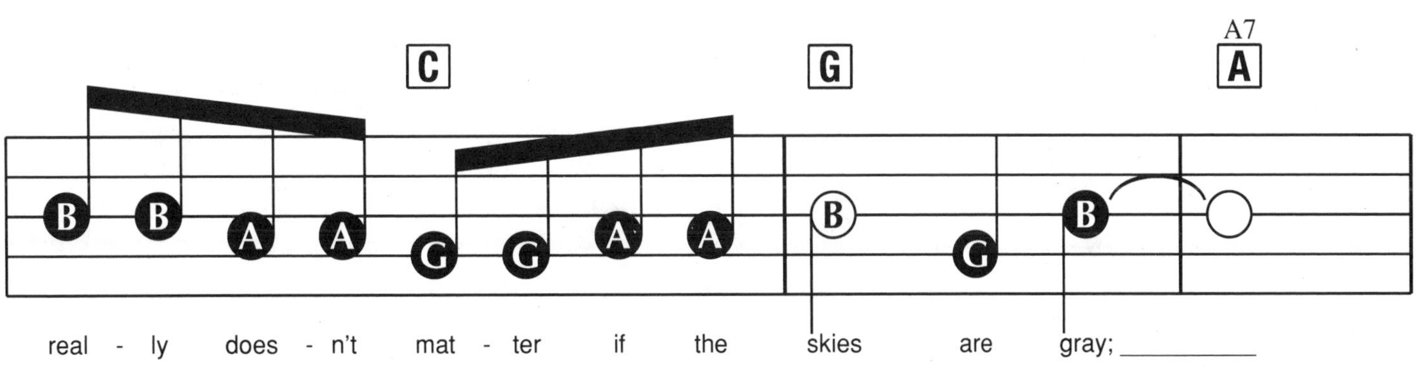
C
G
A7
A
real - ly does - n't mat - ter if the skies are gray;

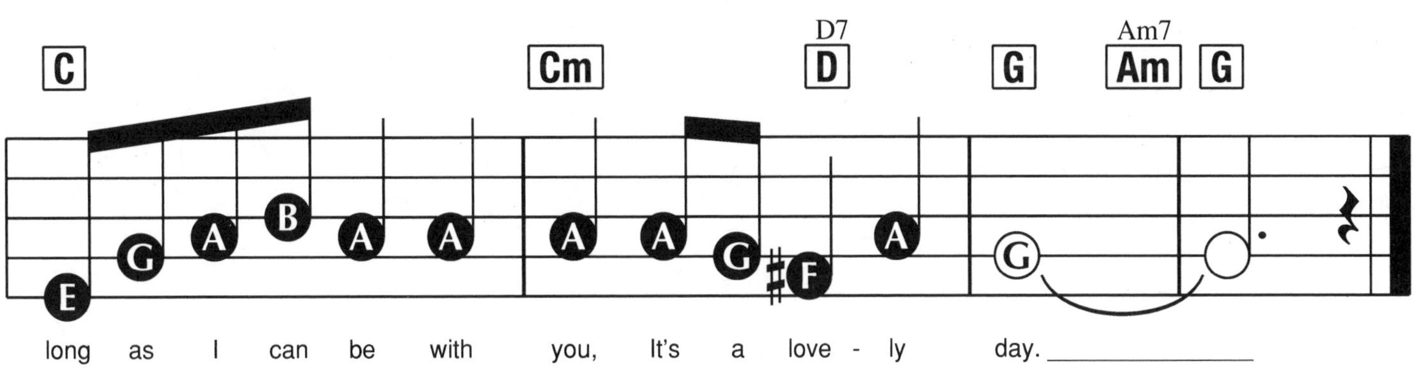
C
Cm
D7
D
G
Am7
Am
G
long as I can be with you, It's a love - ly day.

I Want To Go Back To Michigan

(Down On The Farm)

Registration 2
Rhythm: Swing

Words and Music by
Irving Berlin

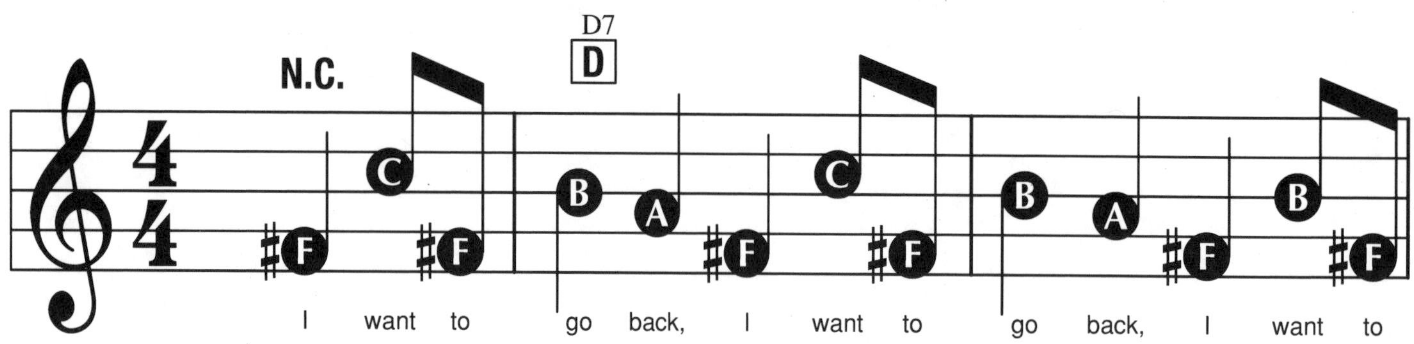

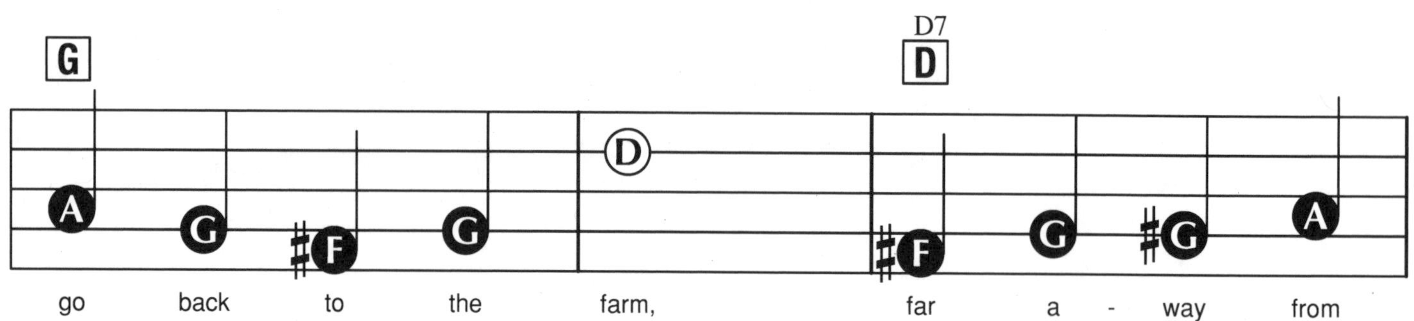

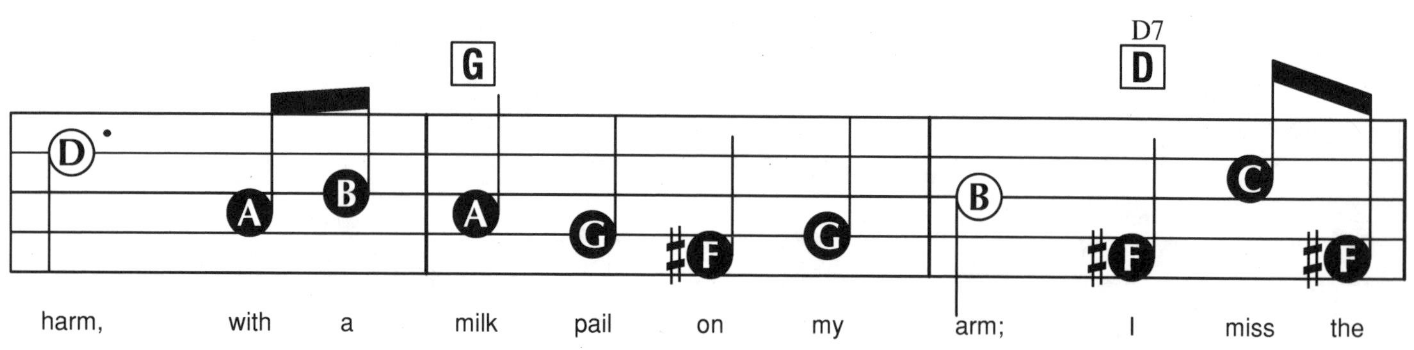

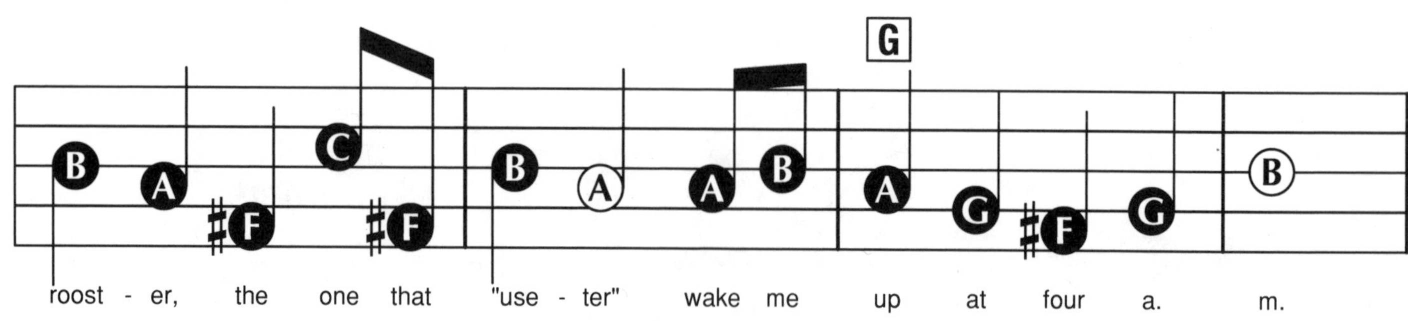

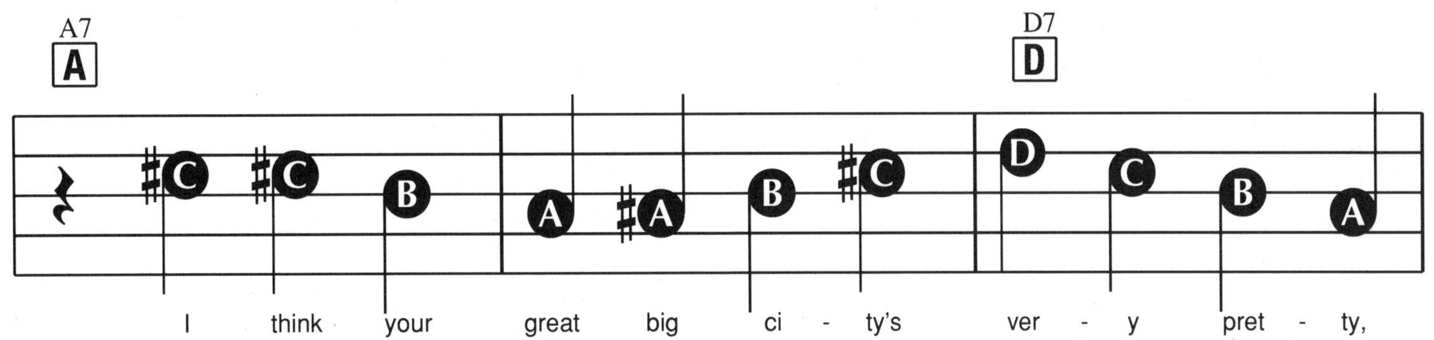
A7
A
D7
D
I think your great big ci - ty's ver - y pret - ty,

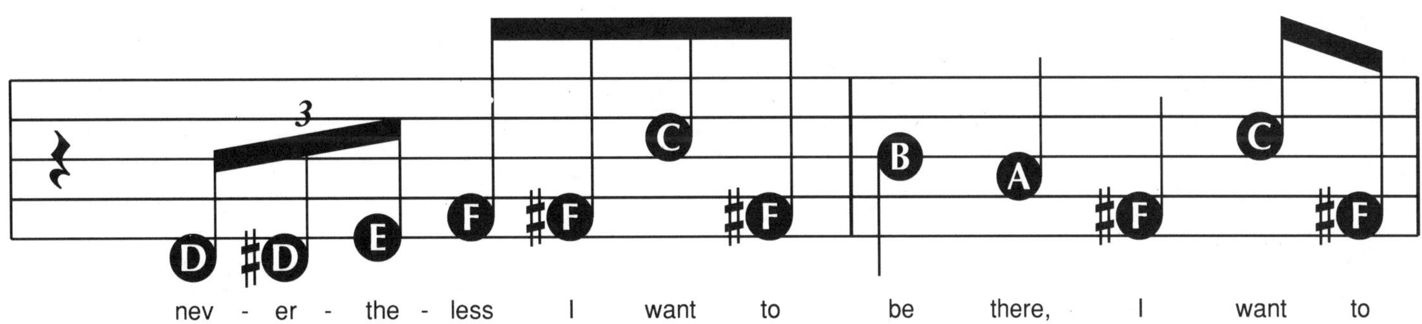
3
nev - er - the - less I want to be there, I want to

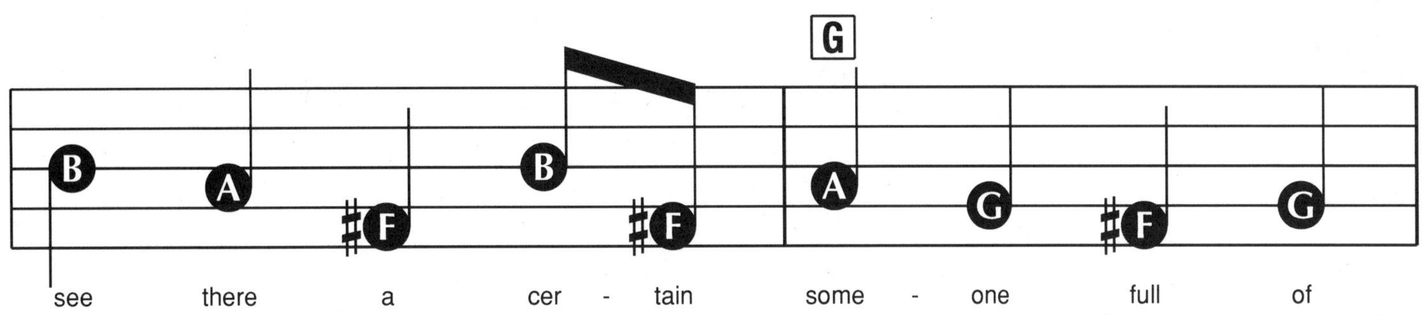
G
see there a cer - tain some - one full of

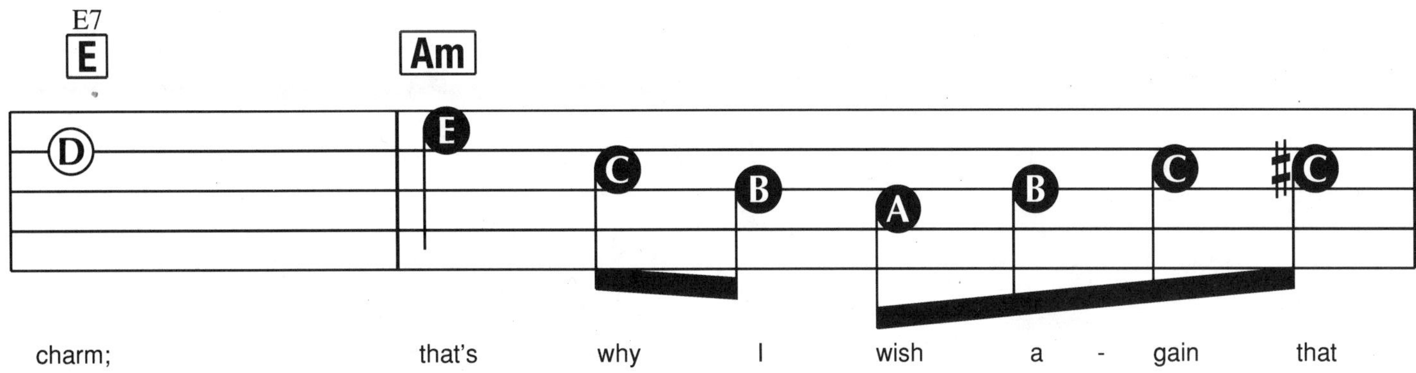
E7
E
Am
charm; that's why I wish a - gain that

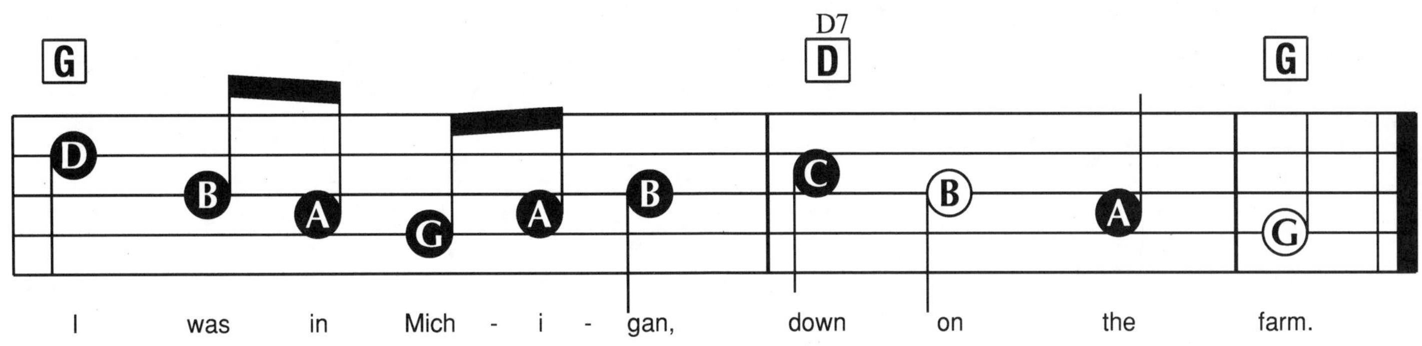
G
D7
D
G
I was in Mich - i - gan, down on the farm.

I'm Playing With Fire

Registration 9
Rhythm: Swing

Words and Music by
Irving Berlin

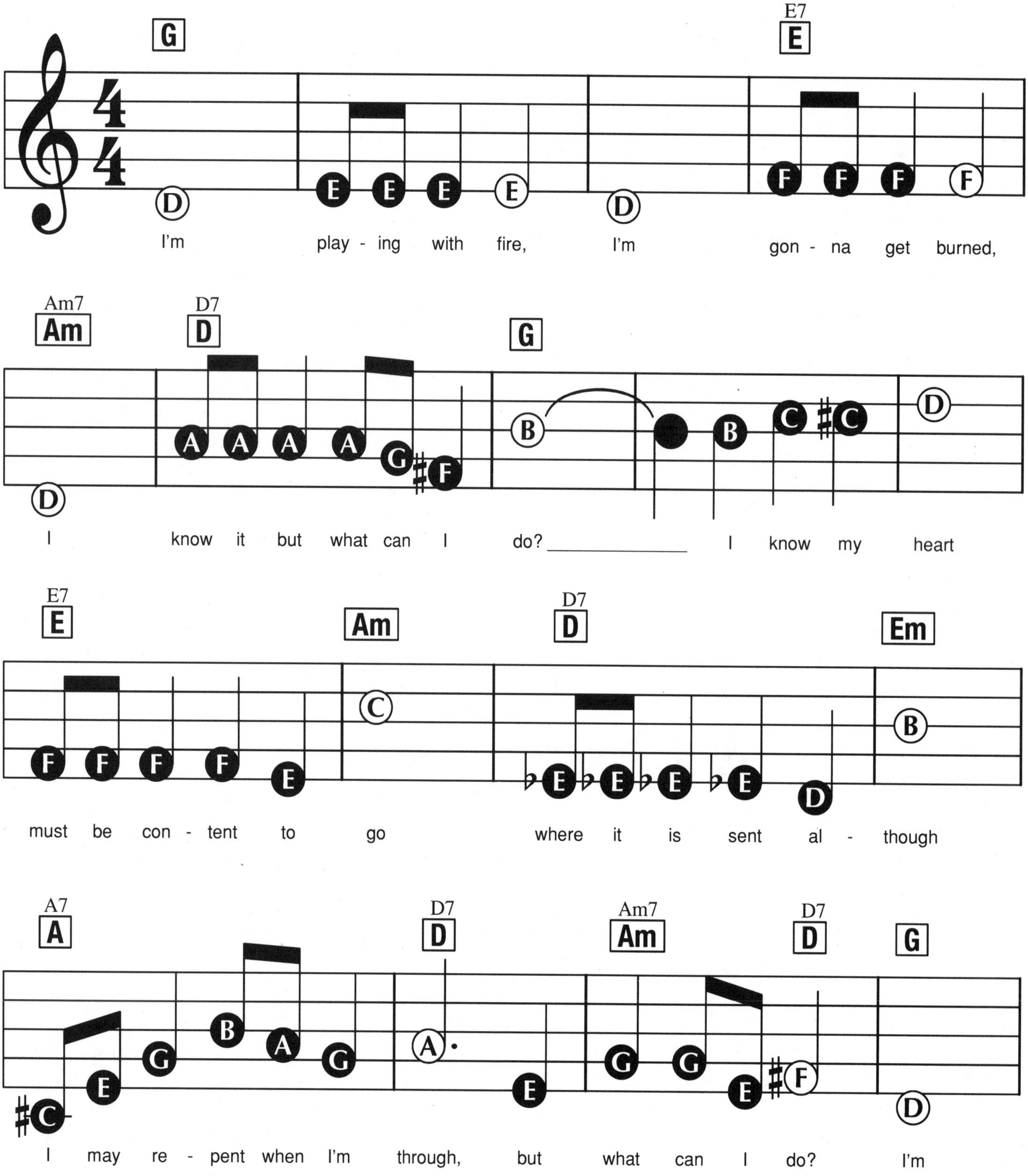
G E7 E
I'm playing - ing with fire, I'm gon - na get burned,
Am7 Am D7 D G
I know it but what can I do? I know my heart
E7 E Am D7 D Em
must be con - tent to go where it is sent al - though
A7 A D7 D Am7 Am D7 D G
I may re - pent when I'm through, but what can I do? I'm

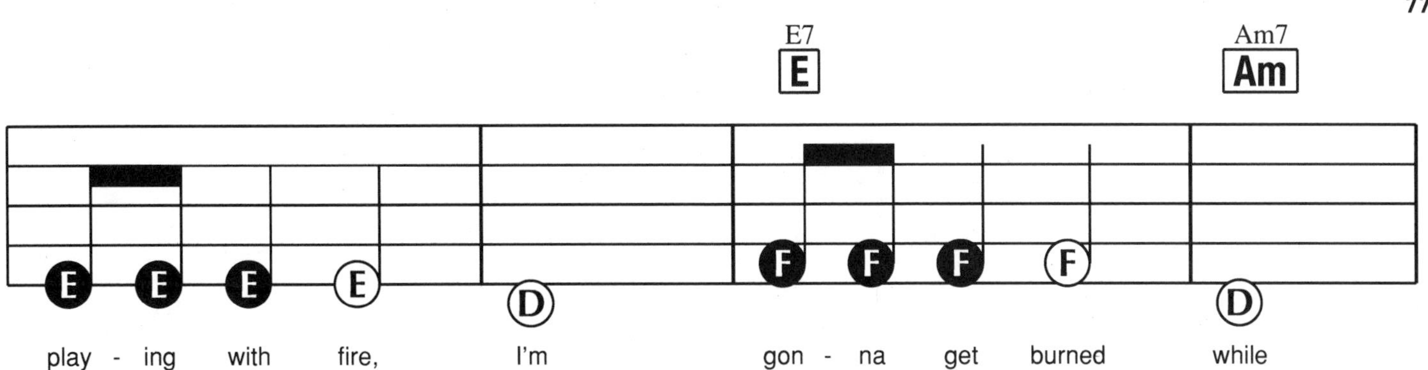
E7
E
Am7
Am
E E E E D F F F F D
play - ing with fire, I'm gon - na get burned while

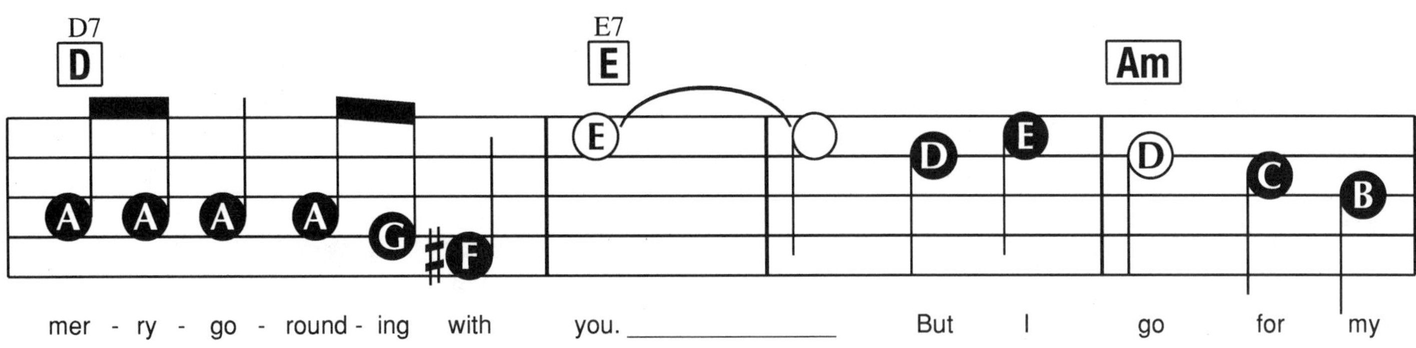
D7
D
E7
E
Am
A A A A G F E D E D C B
mer - ry - go - round - ing with you. But I go for my

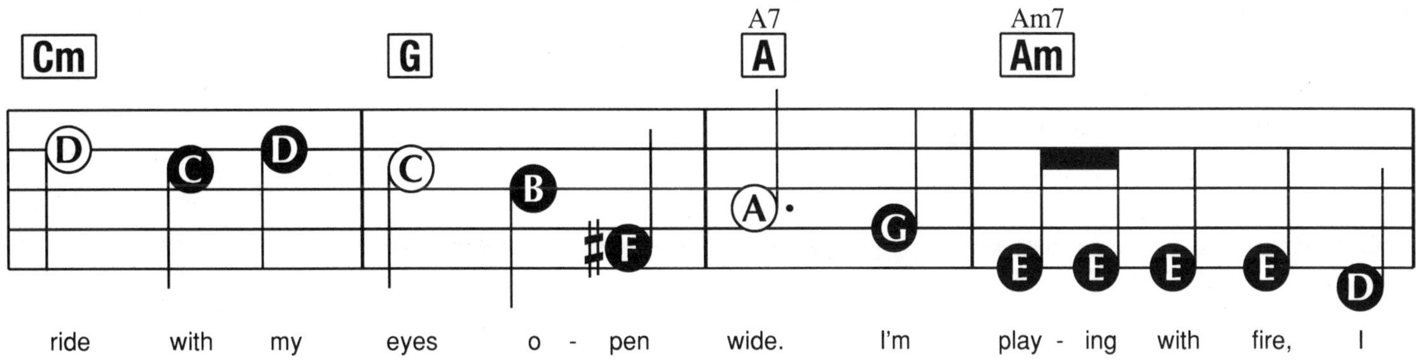
Cm
G
A7
A
Am7
Am
D C D C B F A G E E E E D
ride with my eyes o - pen wide. I'm play - ing with fire, I

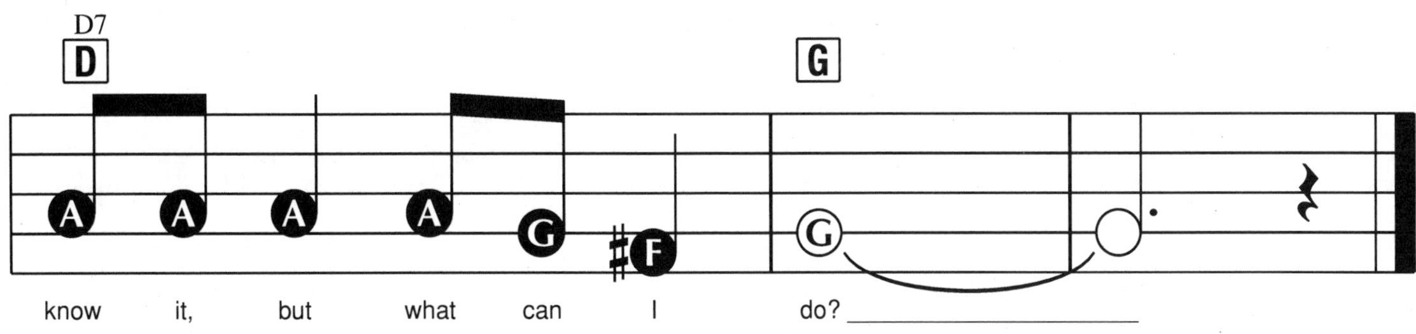
D7
D
G
A A A A G F G
know it, but what can I do?

I'm Putting All My Eggs In One Basket

Registration 2
Rhythm: Swing

Words and Music by
Irving Berlin

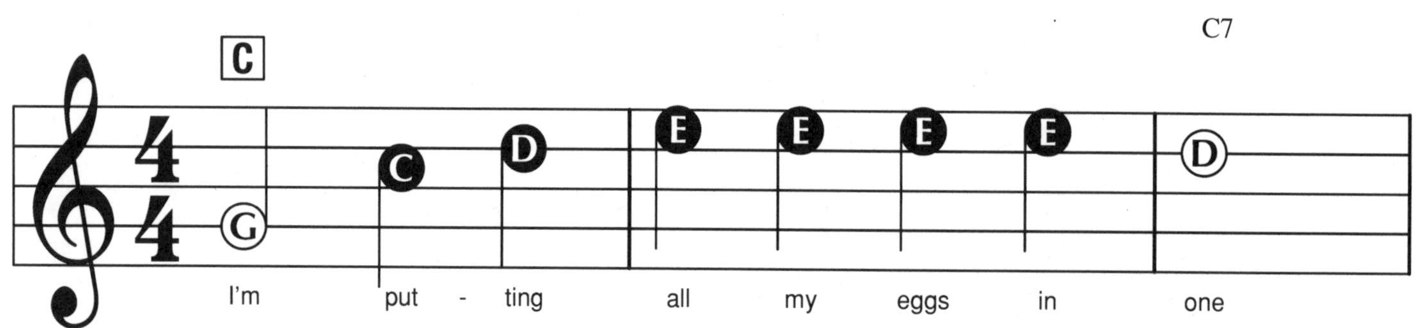

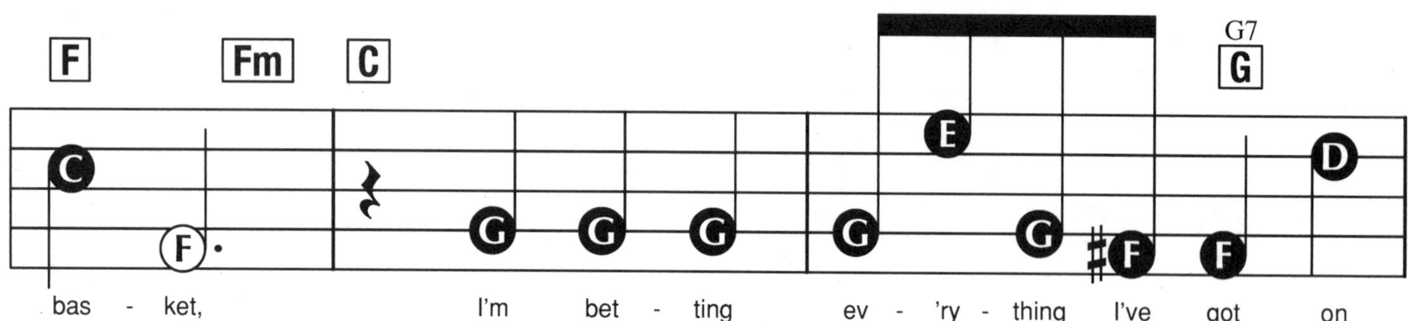

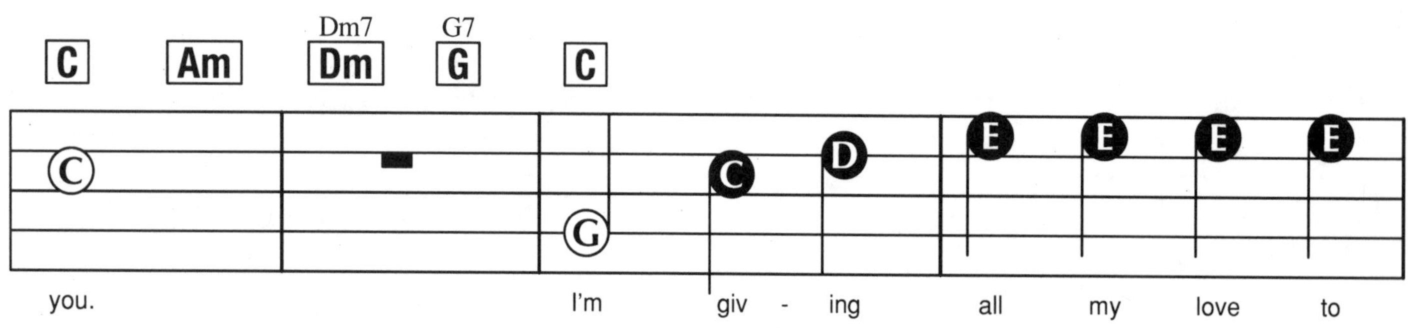

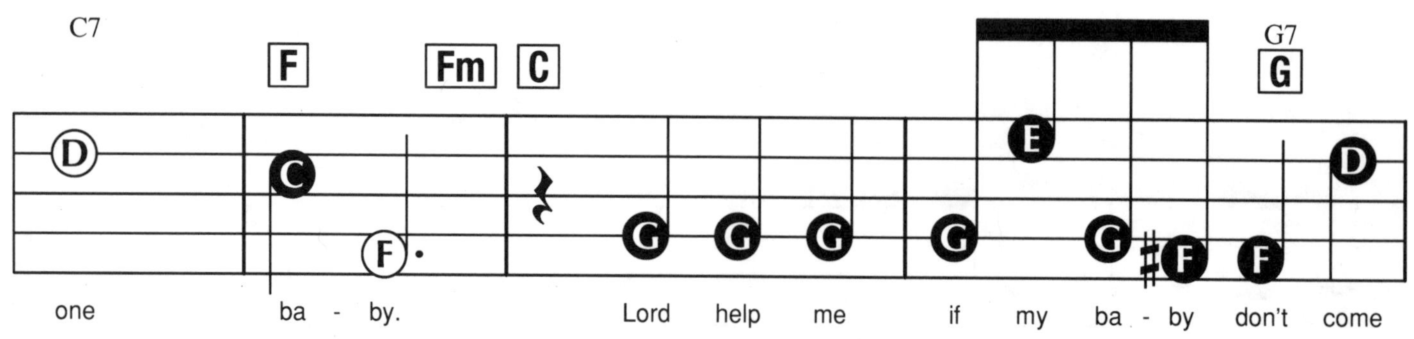

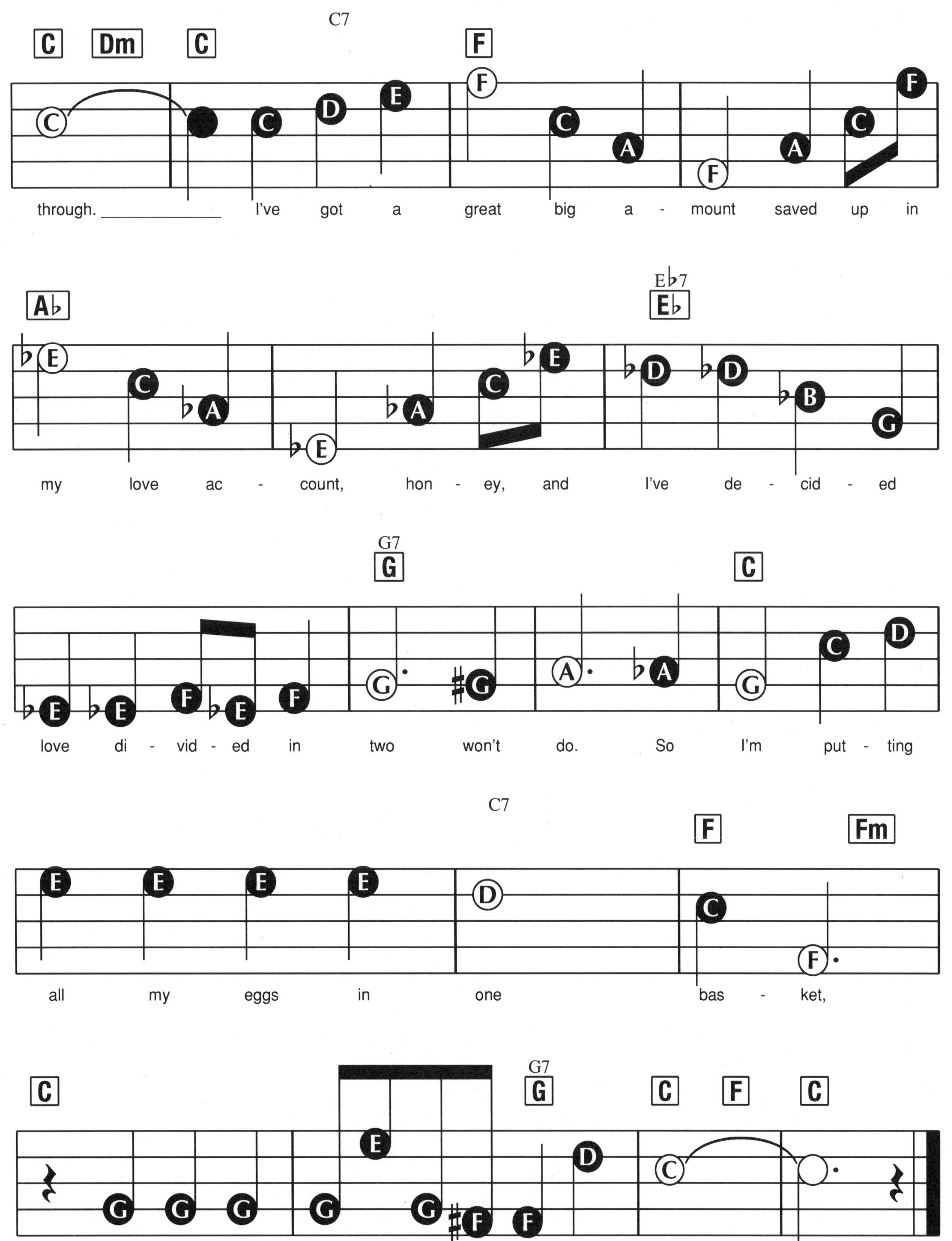
C7
C
Dm
C
F
C
D
E
F
C
A
F
A
C
F
through.
I've
got
a
great
big
a
-
mount
saved
up
in
E♭7
A♭
E♭
E
C
A
E
A
C
E
D
D
B
G
my
love
ac
-
count,
hon
-
ey,
and
I've
de
-
cid
-
ed
G7
G
C
E
E
F
E
F
G
G
A
A
G
C
D
love
di
-
vid
-
ed
in
two
won't
do.
So
I'm
put
-
ting
C7
F
Fm
E
E
E
E
D
C
F
all
my
eggs
in
one
bas
-
ket,
C
G7
G
C
F
C
G
G
G
G
E
G
F
F
D
C
I'm
bet
-
ting
ev
-
'ry
-
thing
I've
got
on
you.

It's A Lovely Day Tomorrow

Registration 9
Rhythm: Swing

Words and Music by
Irving Berlin

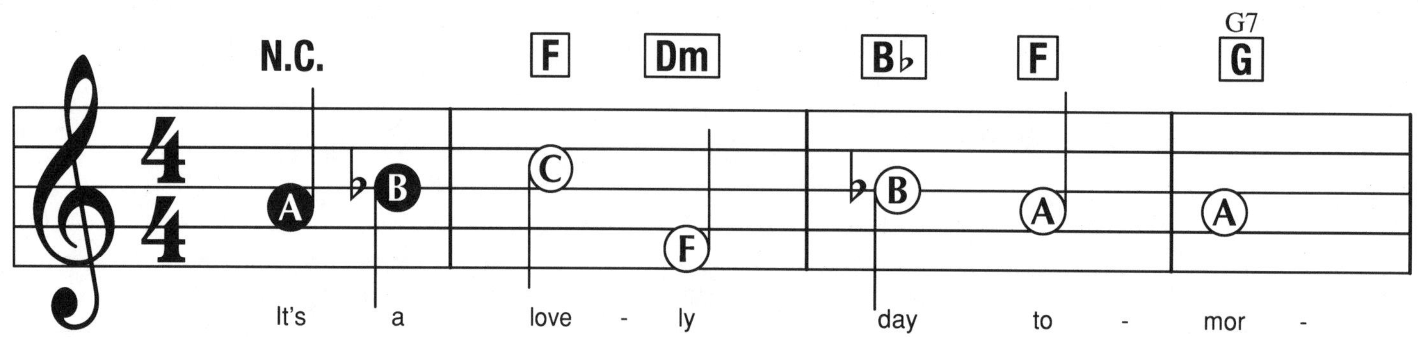

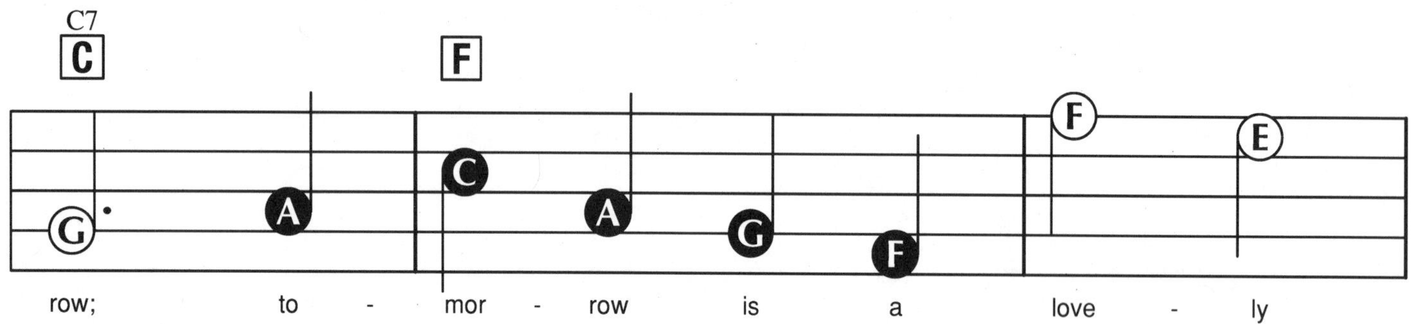

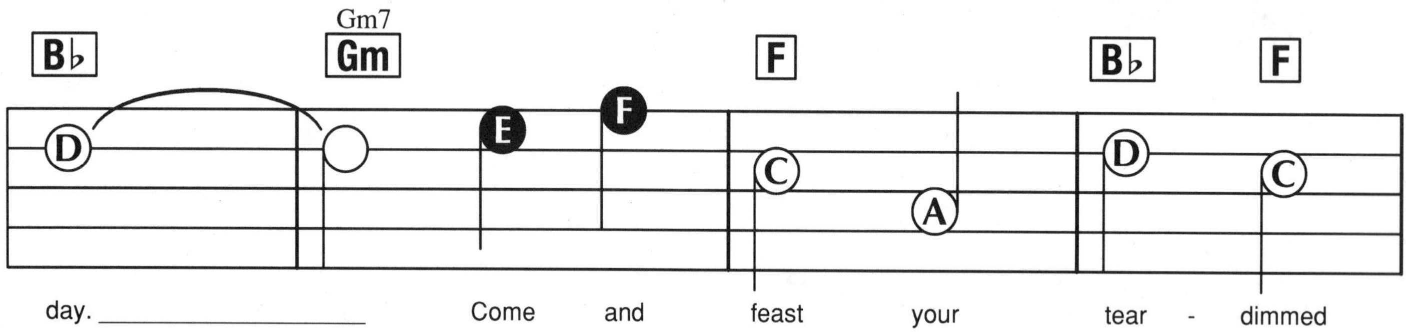

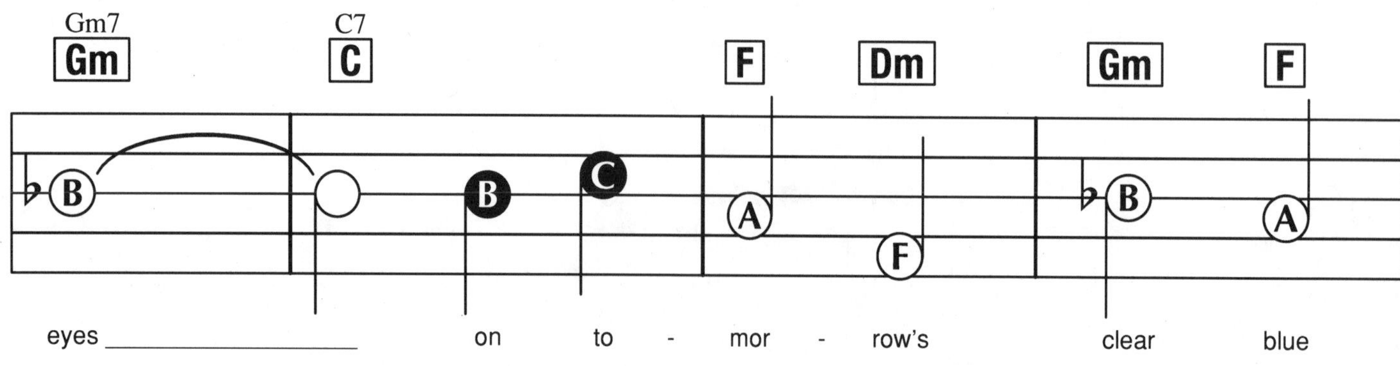

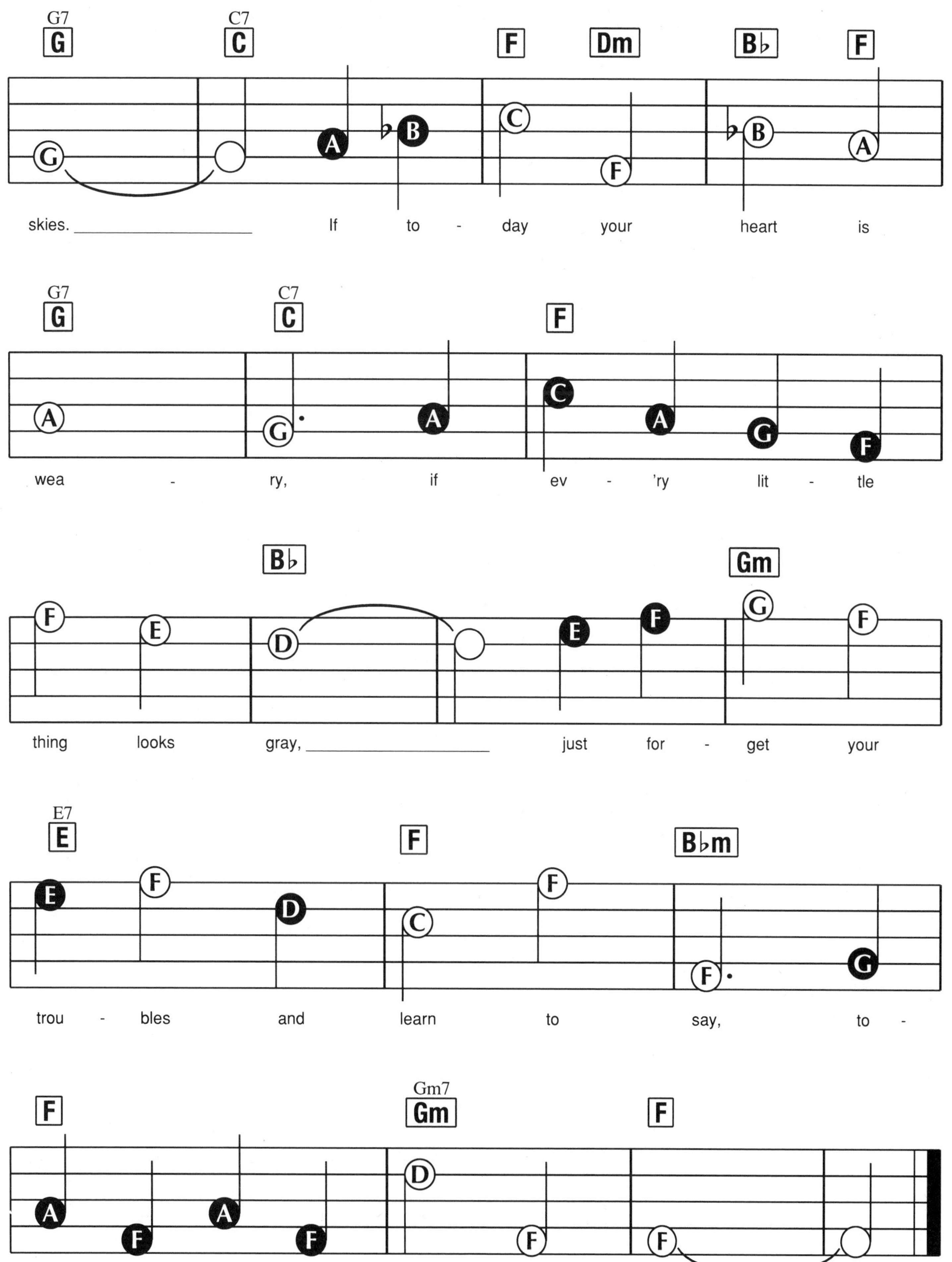
G7
G
C7
C
F
Dm
B♭
F
skies.
If to - day your heart is
G7
G
C7
C
F
wea - ry, if ev - 'ry lit - tle
B♭
Gm
thing looks gray,
just for - get your
E7
E
F
B♭m
trou - bles and learn to say, to -
F
Gm7
Gm
F
mor - row is a love - ly day.

I've Got My Love To Keep Me Warm

Registration 4
Rhythm: Fox Trot or Swing

Words and Music by
Irving Berlin

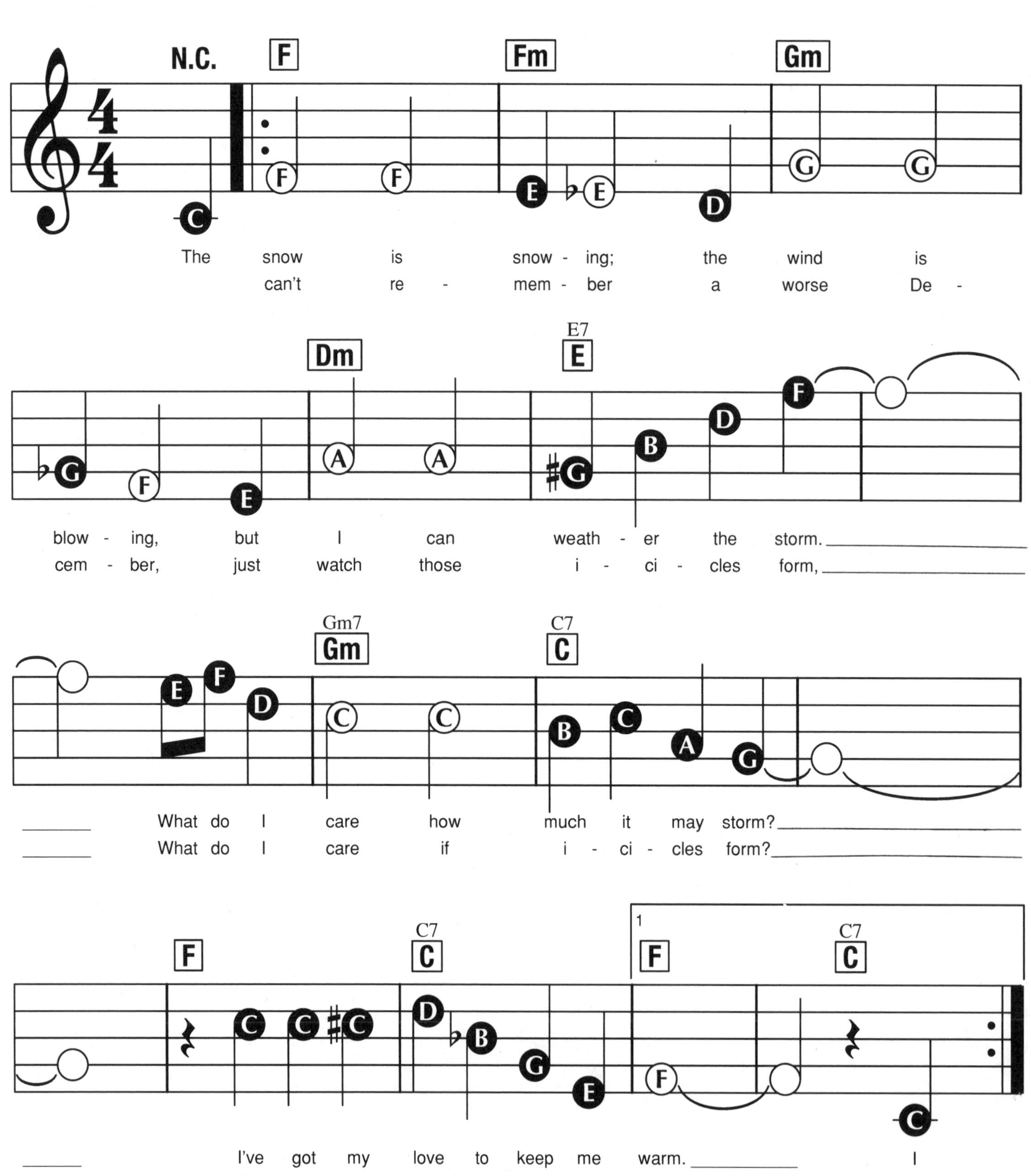

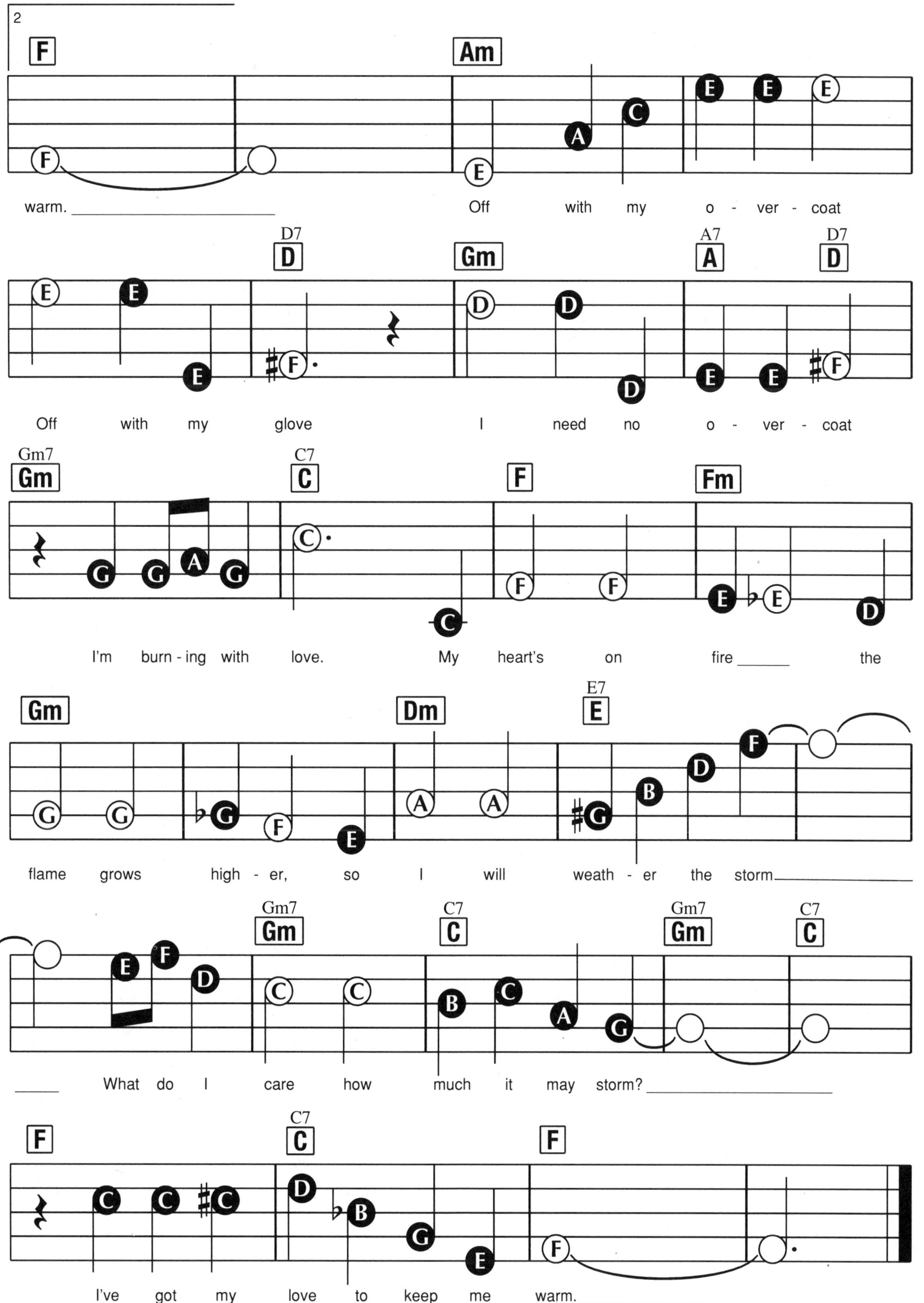
2
F Am
warm. Off with my o - ver - coat
D7 Gm A7 D7
D Gm A D
Off with my glove I need no o - ver - coat
Gm7 C7
Gm C F Fm
I'm burn - ing with love. My heart's on fire the
E7
Gm Dm E
flame grows high - er, so I will weath - er the storm
Gm7 C7 Gm7 C7
Gm C Gm C
What do I care how much it may storm?
C7
F C F
I've got my love to keep me warm.

It's A Lovely Day Today

Registration 8
Rhythm: Swing

Words and Music by
Irving Berlin

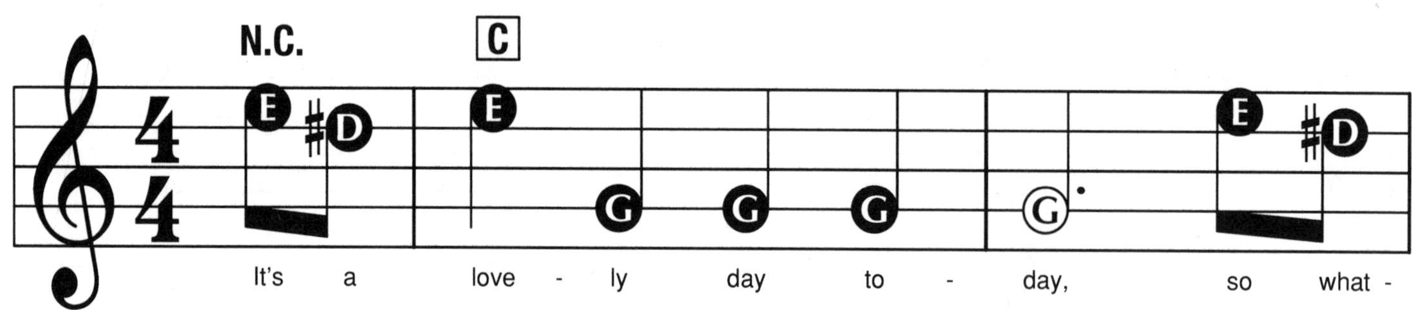

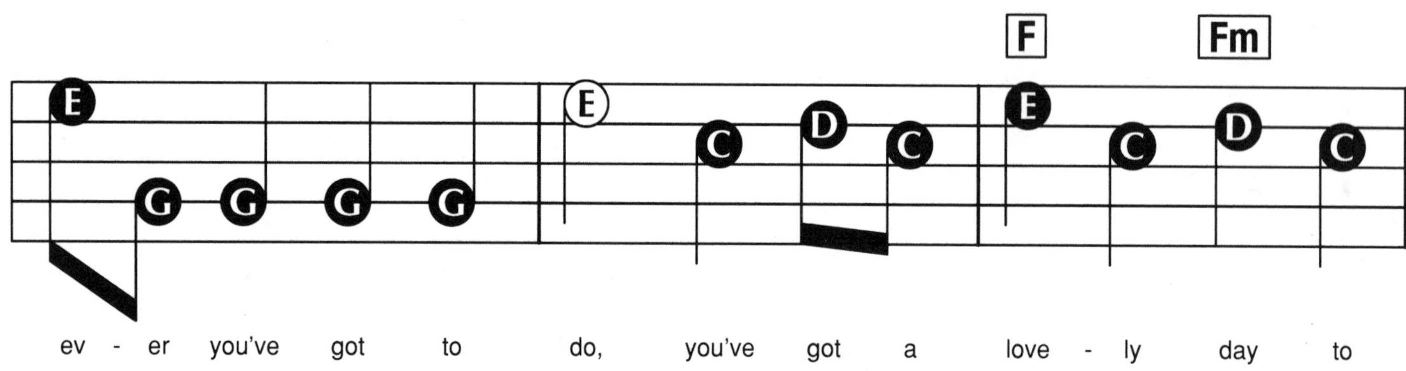

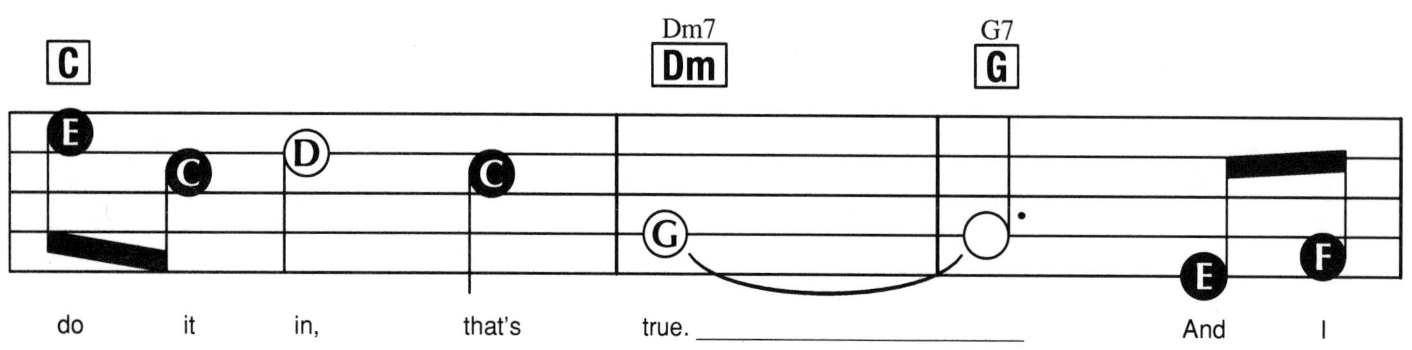

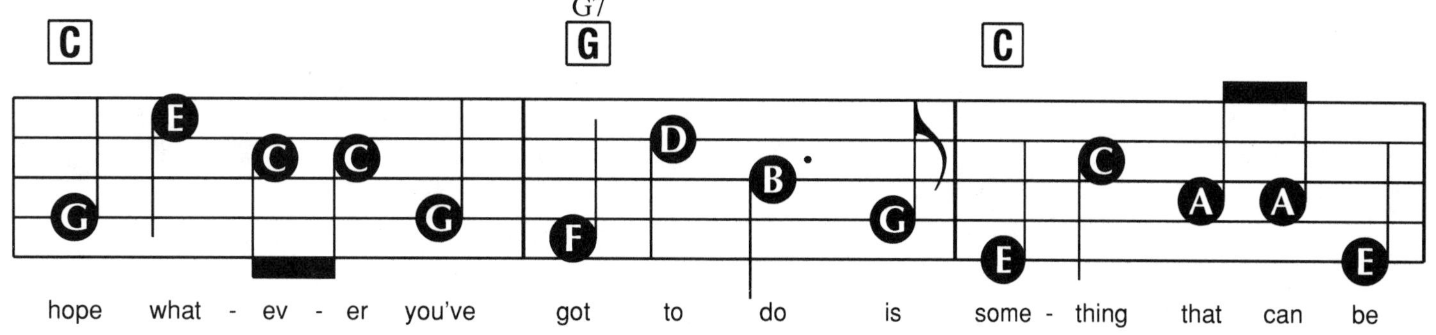
C
G7
G
C
hope what - ev - er you've got to do is some - thing that can be

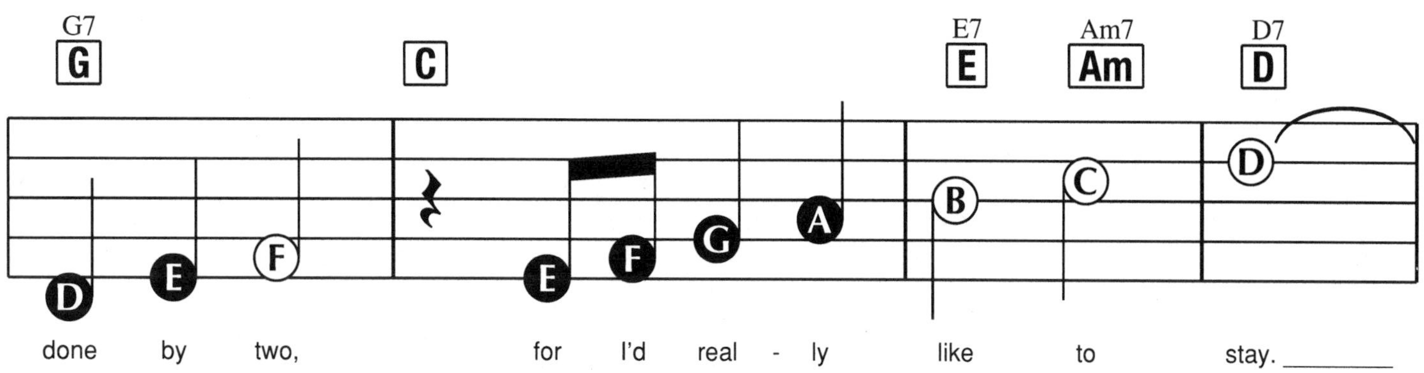
G7
G
C
E7
E
Am7
Am
D7
D
done by two, for I'd real - ly like to stay.

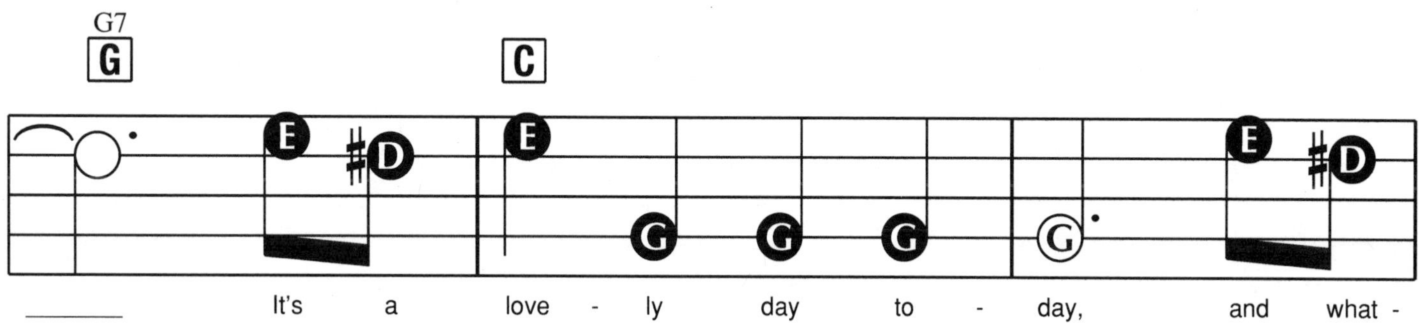
G7
G
C
It's a love - ly day to - day, and what -

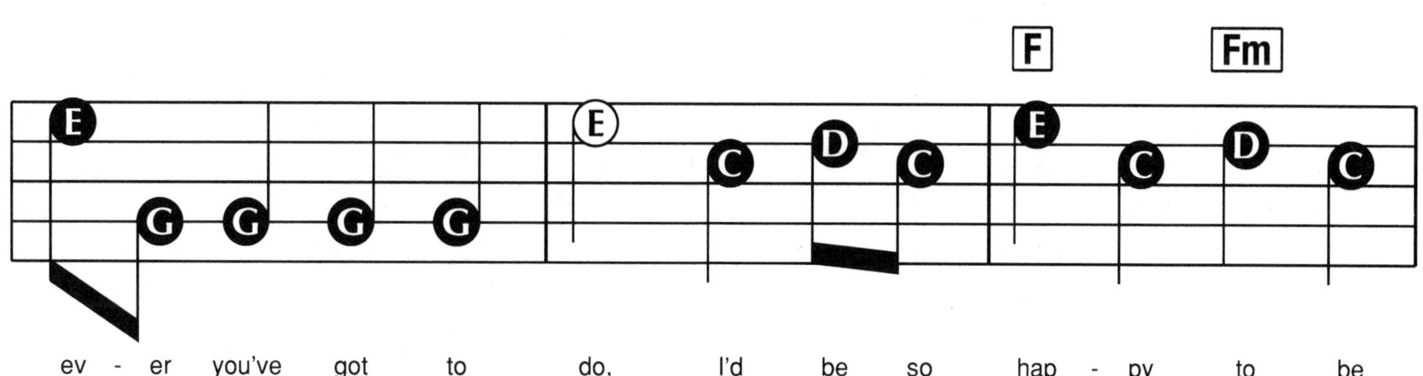
F
Fm
ev - er you've got to do, I'd be so hap - py to be

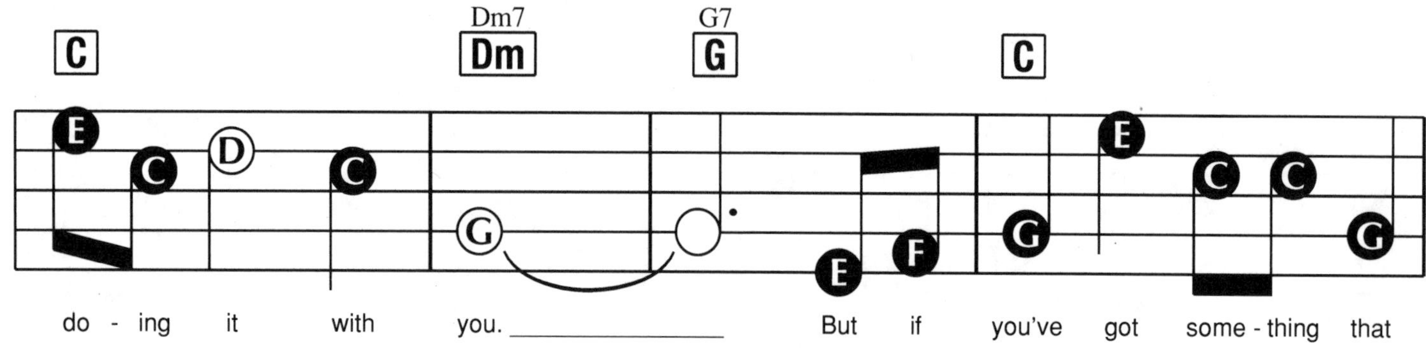
C
Dm7
Dm
G7
G
C
E C D C G E F G E C C G
do - ing it with you. But if you've got some - thing that

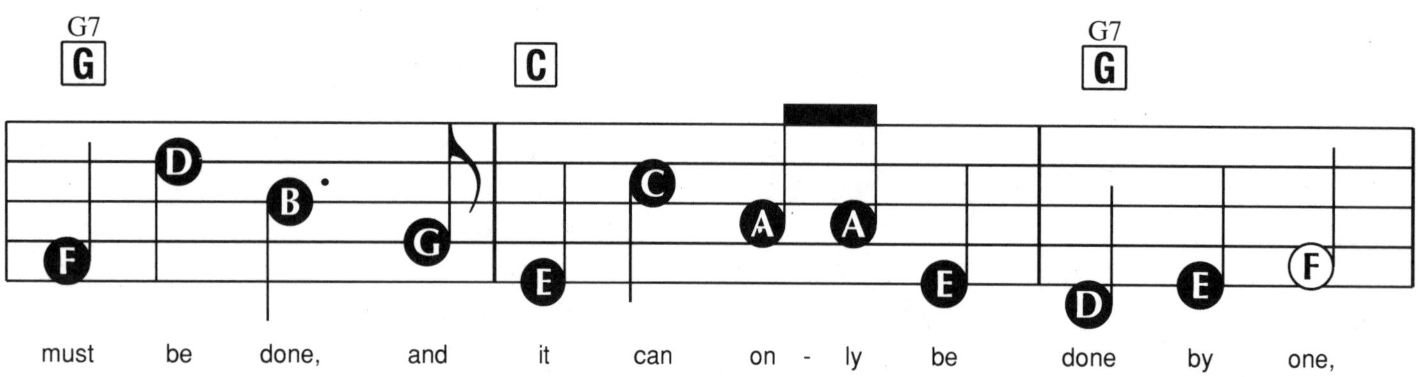
G7
G
C
G7
G
F D B G E C A A E D E F
must be done, and it can on - ly be done by one,

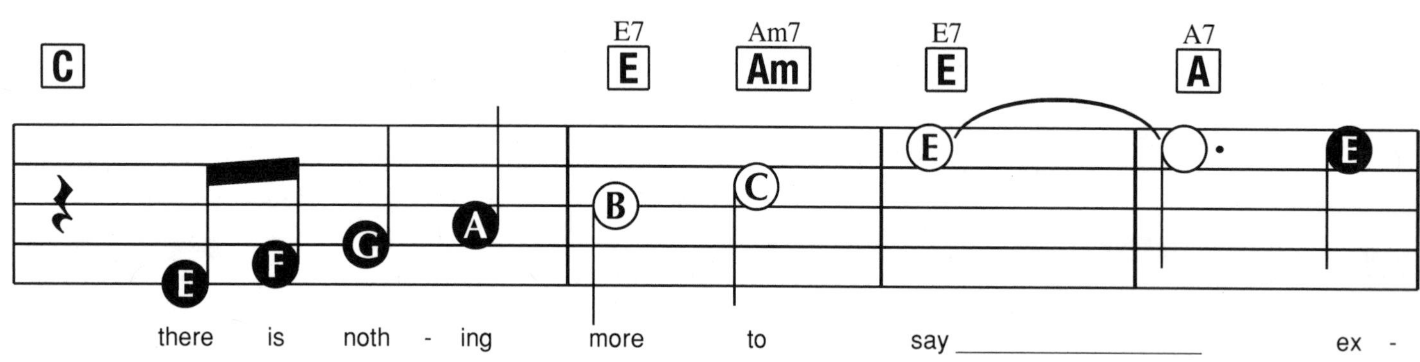
C
E7
E
Am7
Am
E7
E
A7
A
E F G A B C E E
there is noth - ing more to say ex -

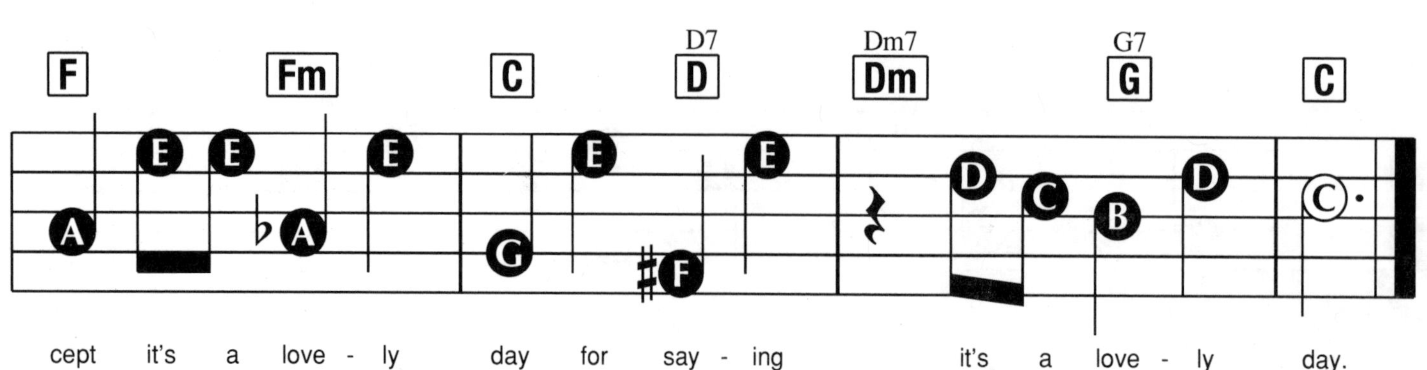
F
Fm
C
D7
D
Dm7
Dm
G7
G
C
A E E A E G E F E D C B D C
cept it's a love - ly day for say - ing it's a love - ly day.

Let Yourself Go

Registration 4
Rhythm: Swing

Words and Music by
Irving Berlin

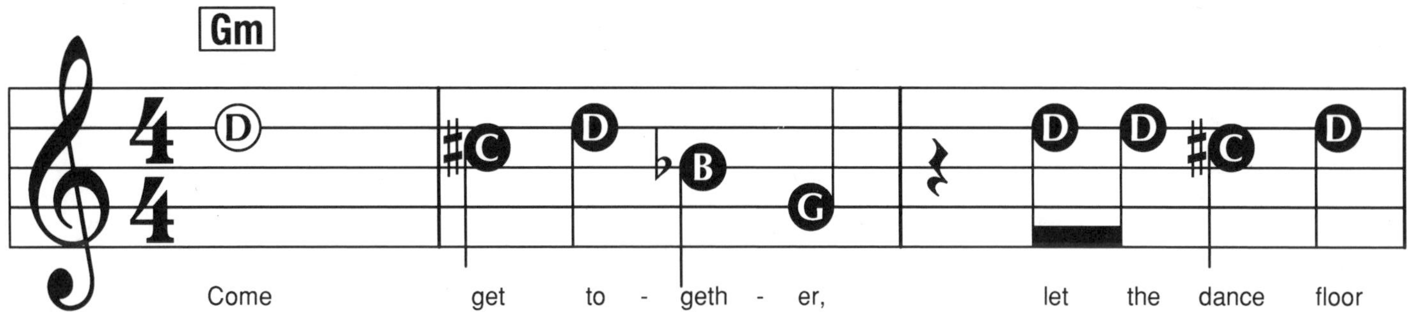

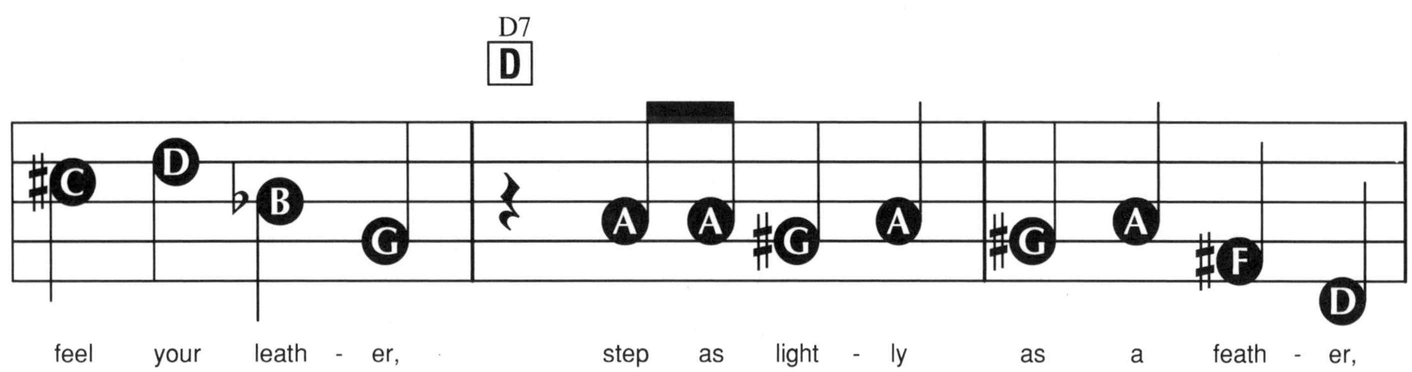

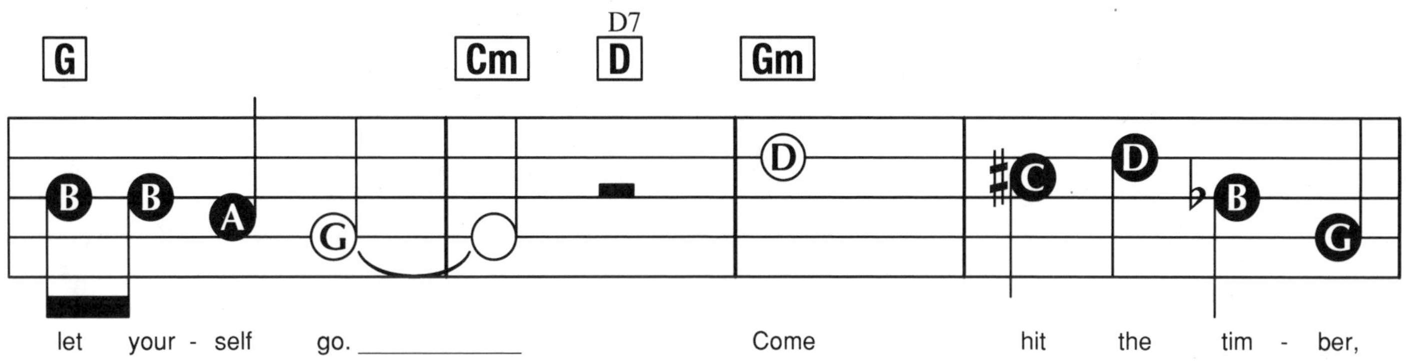

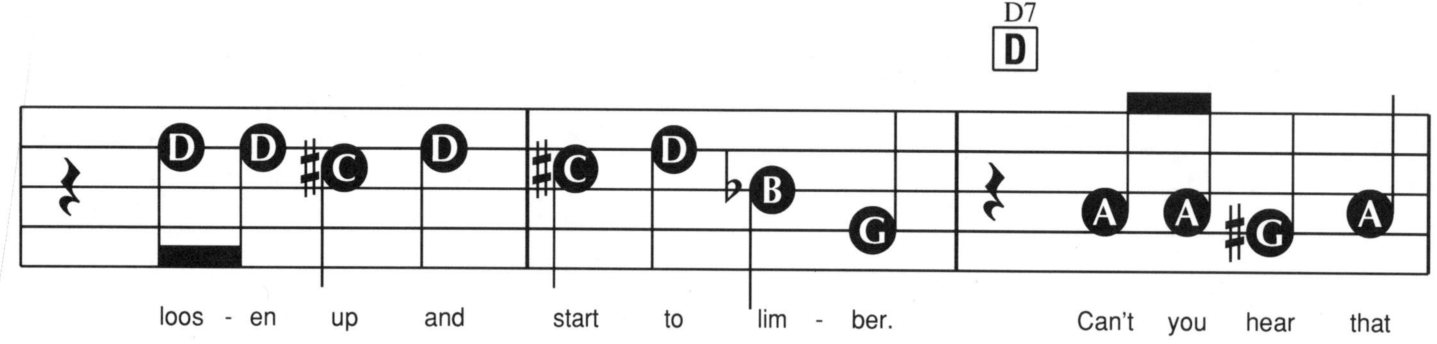
D7
D
D D C D C D B G A A G A
loos - en up and start to lim - ber. Can't you hear that

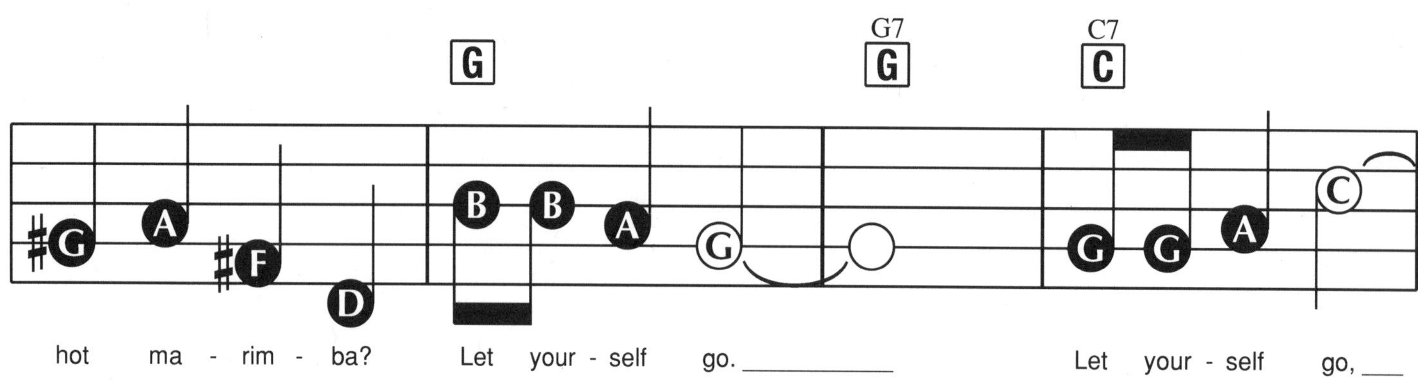
G
G7
G
C7
C
G A F D B B A G G G A C
hot ma - rim - ba? Let your - self go. Let your - self go,

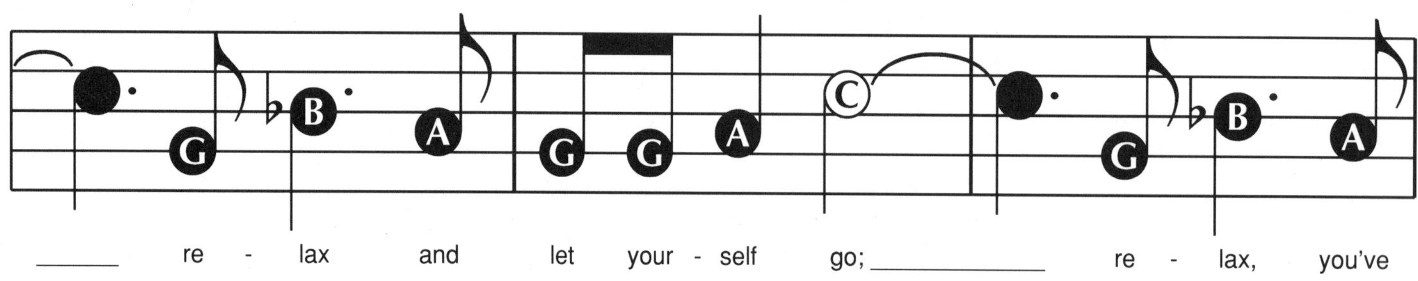
G B A G G A C G B A
re - lax and let your - self go; re - lax, you've

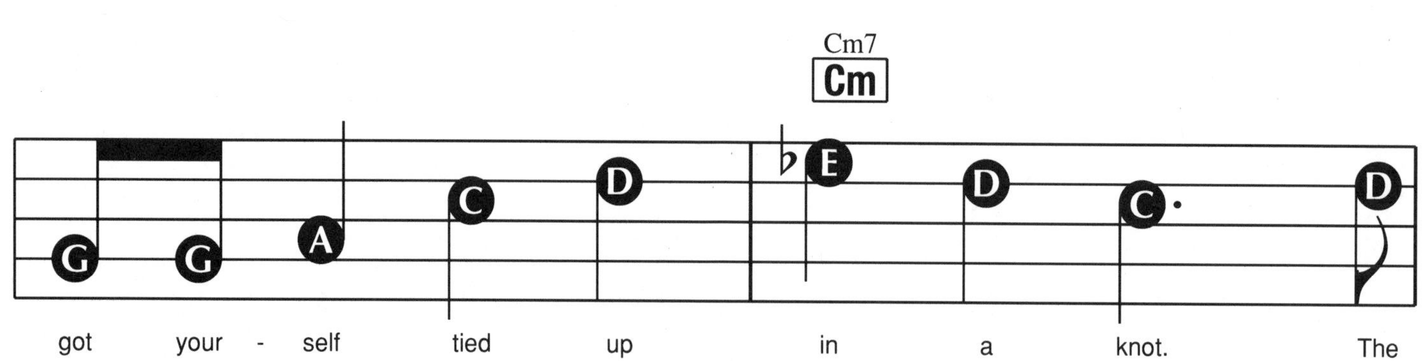
Cm7
Cm
G G A C D E D C D
got your - self tied up in a knot. The

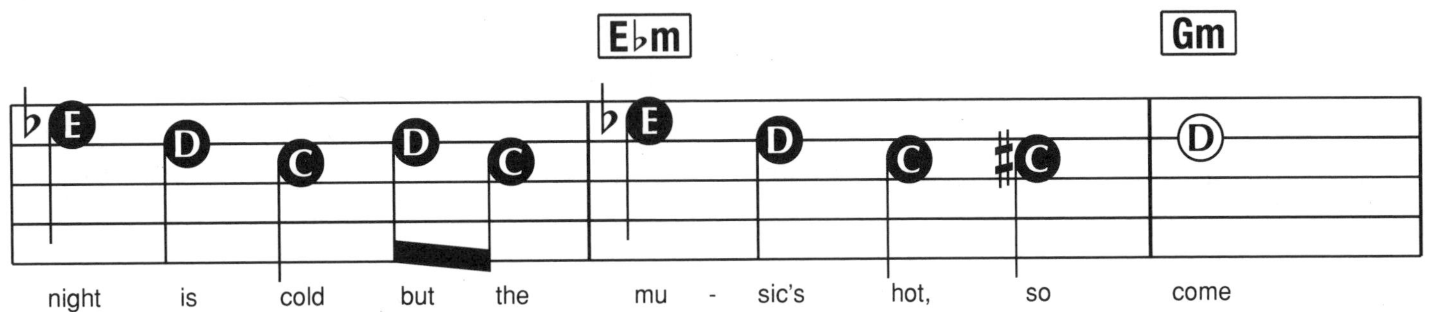
E♭m
Gm
night is cold but the mu - sic's hot, so come

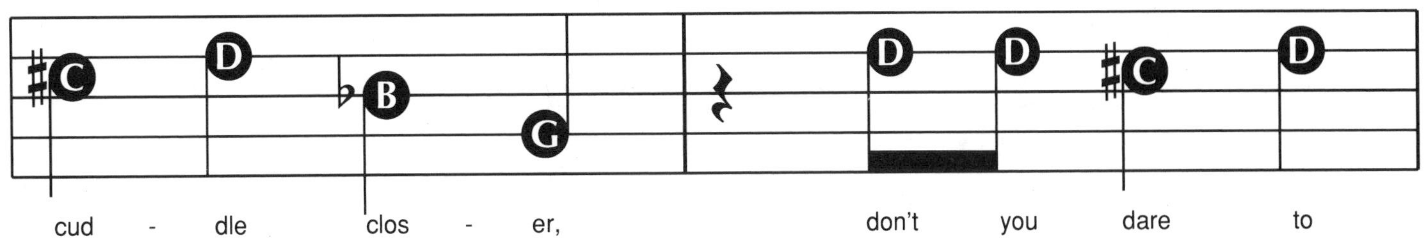
cud - dle clos - er, don't you dare to

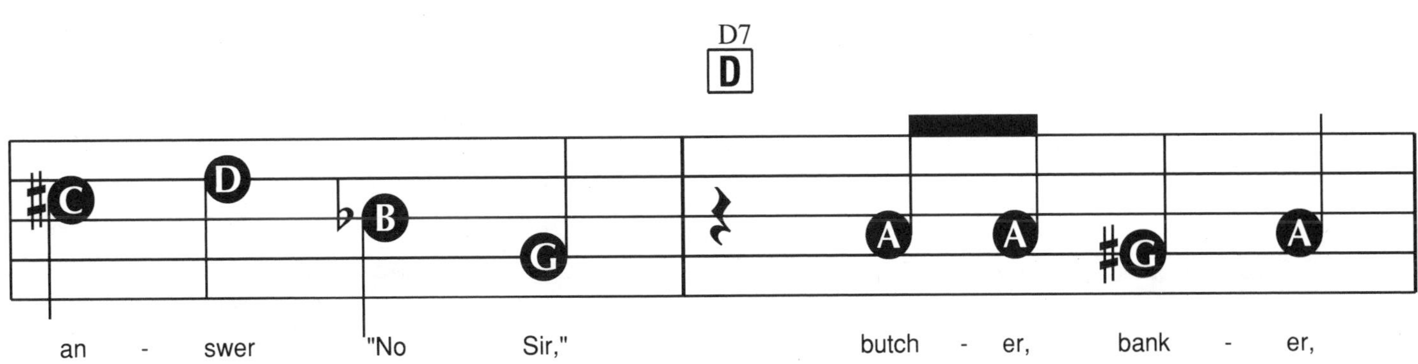
D7
D
an - swer "No Sir," butch - er, bank - er,

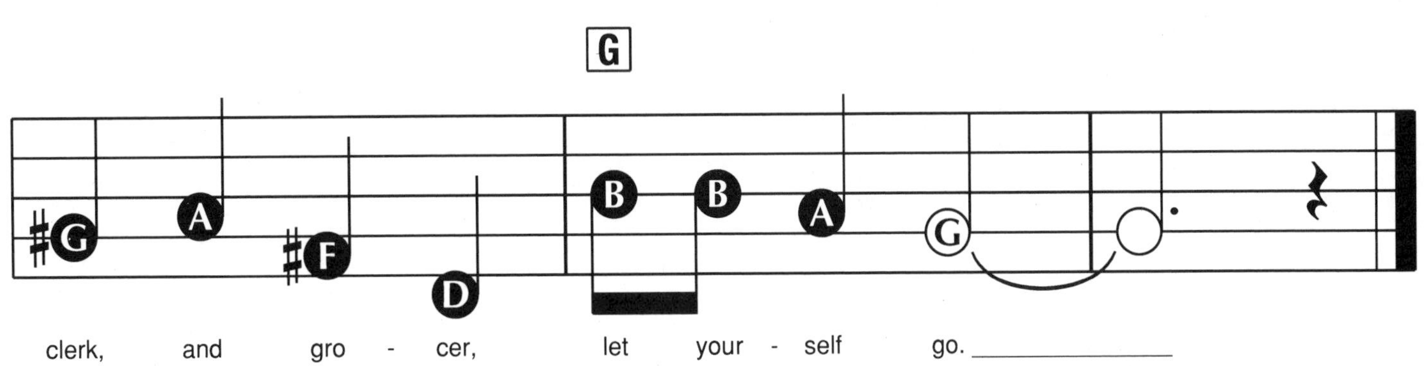
G
clerk, and gro - cer, let your - self go.

Lady Of The Evening

Registration 9
Rhythm: Latin

Words and Music by
Irving Berlin

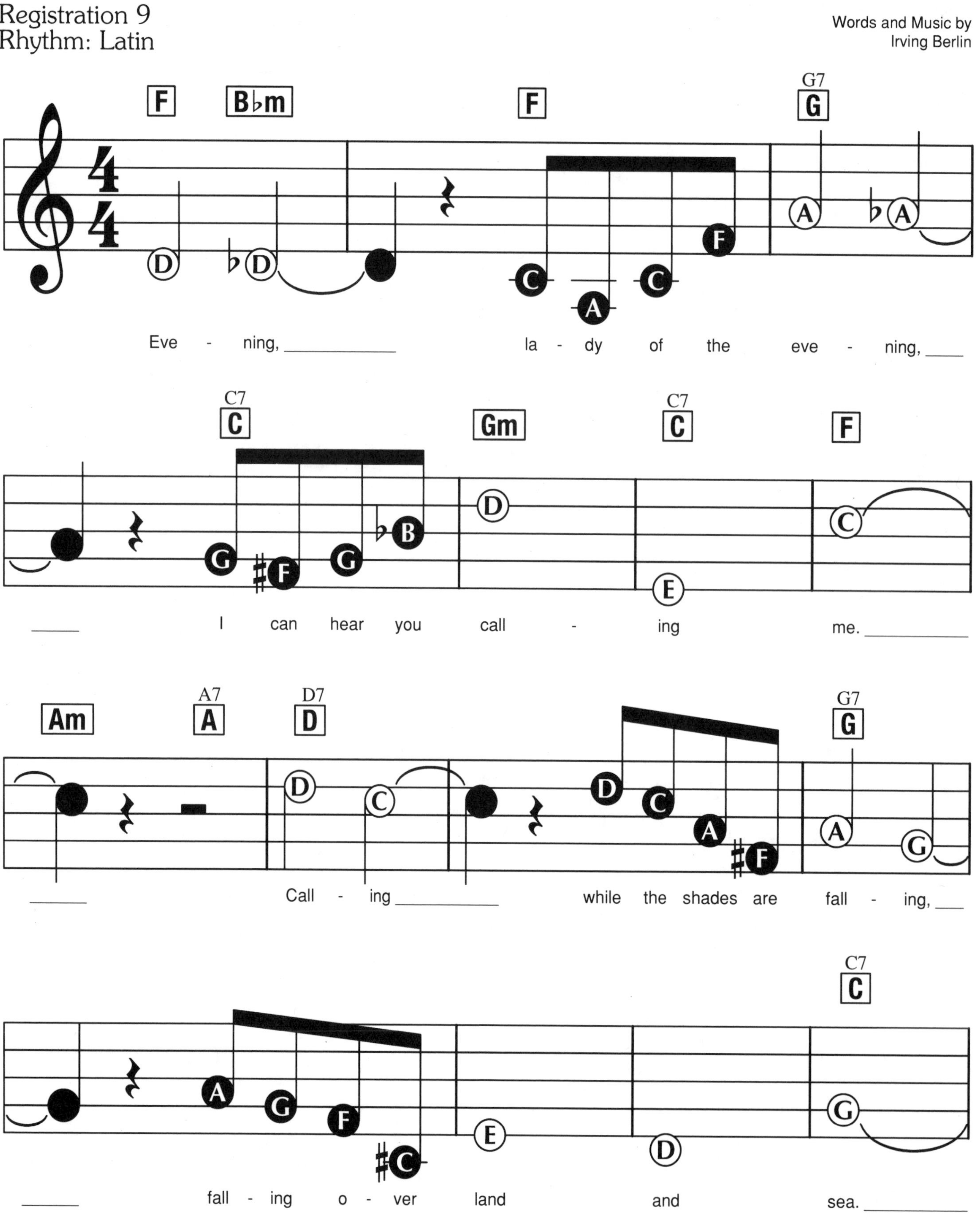

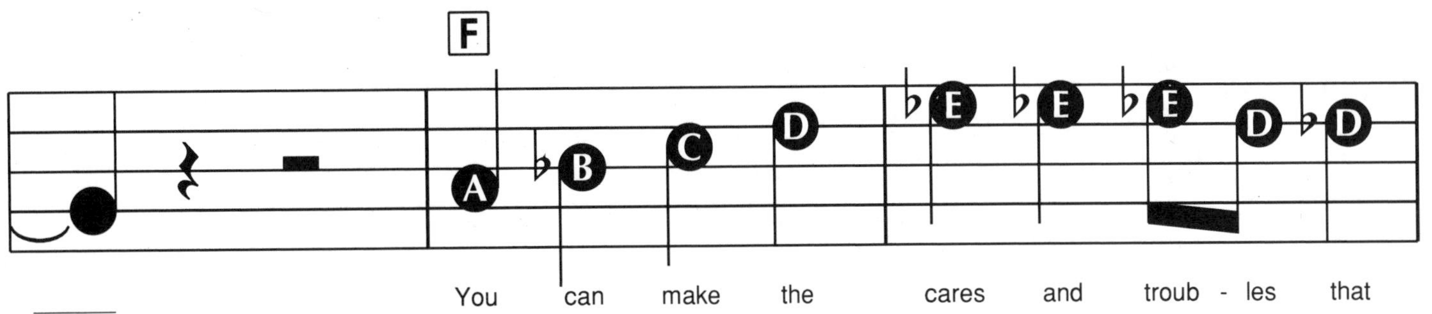
F
A
B
C
D
E
E
E
D
D
You can make the cares and troub - les that

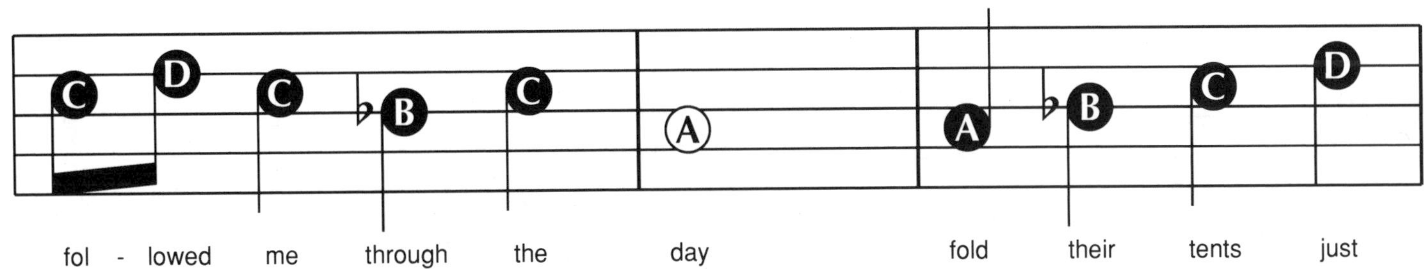
C
D
C
B
C
A
A
B
C
D
fol - lowed me through the day fold their tents just

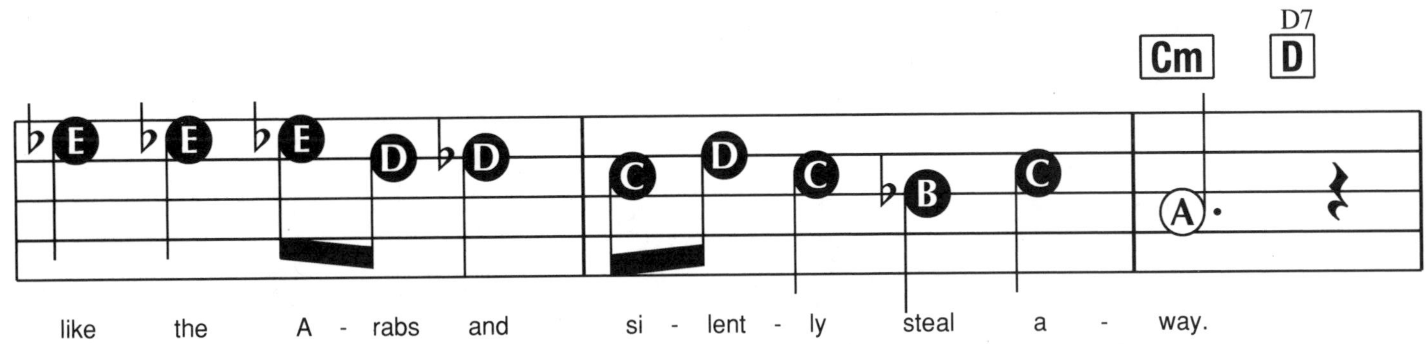
Cm
D7
D
E
E
E
D
D
C
D
C
B
C
A
like the A - rabs and si - lent - ly steal a - way.

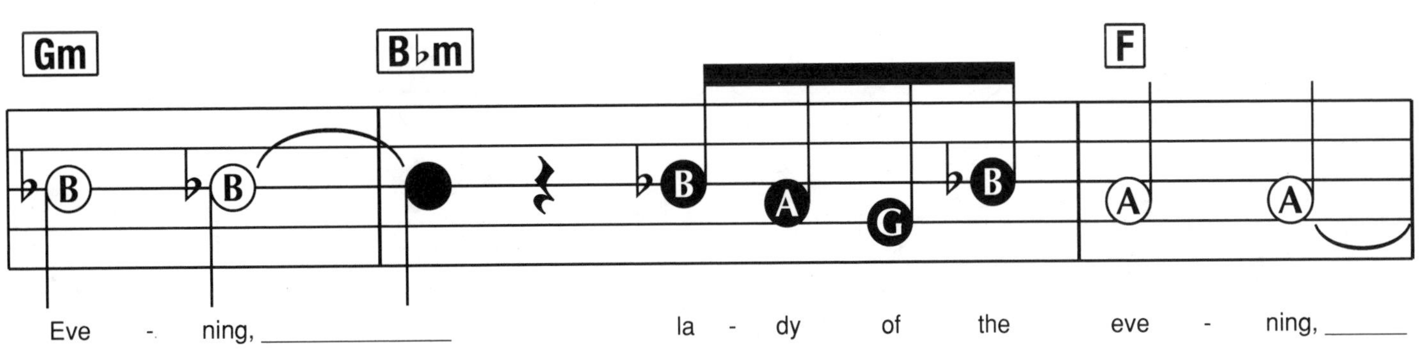
Gm
B♭m
F
B
B
B
A
G
B
A
A
Eve - ning, lady of the eve - ning,

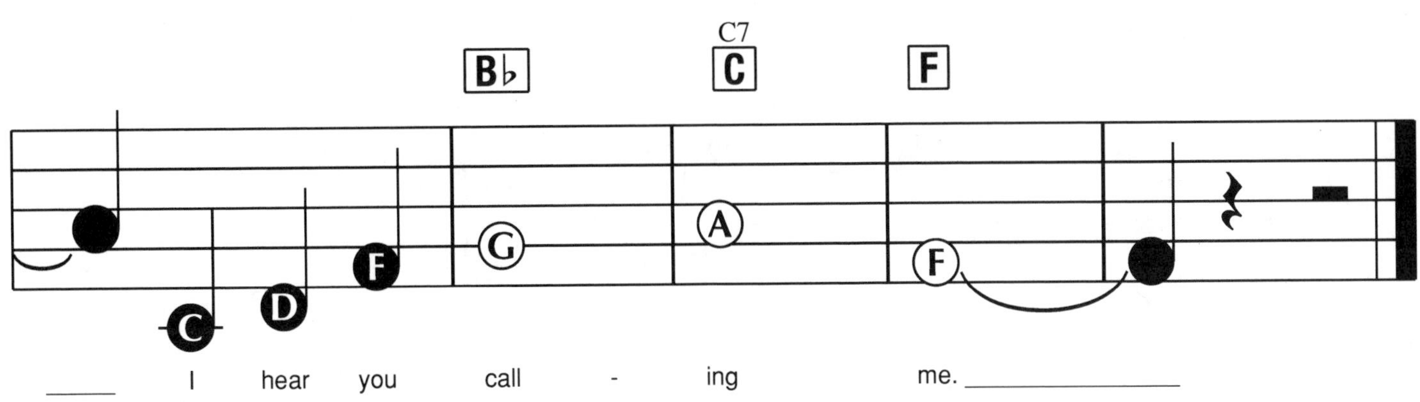
B♭
C7
C
F
C
D
F
G
A
F
I hear you call - ing me.

Let Me Sing And I'm Happy

Registration 2
Rhythm: Swing

Words and Music by
Irving Berlin

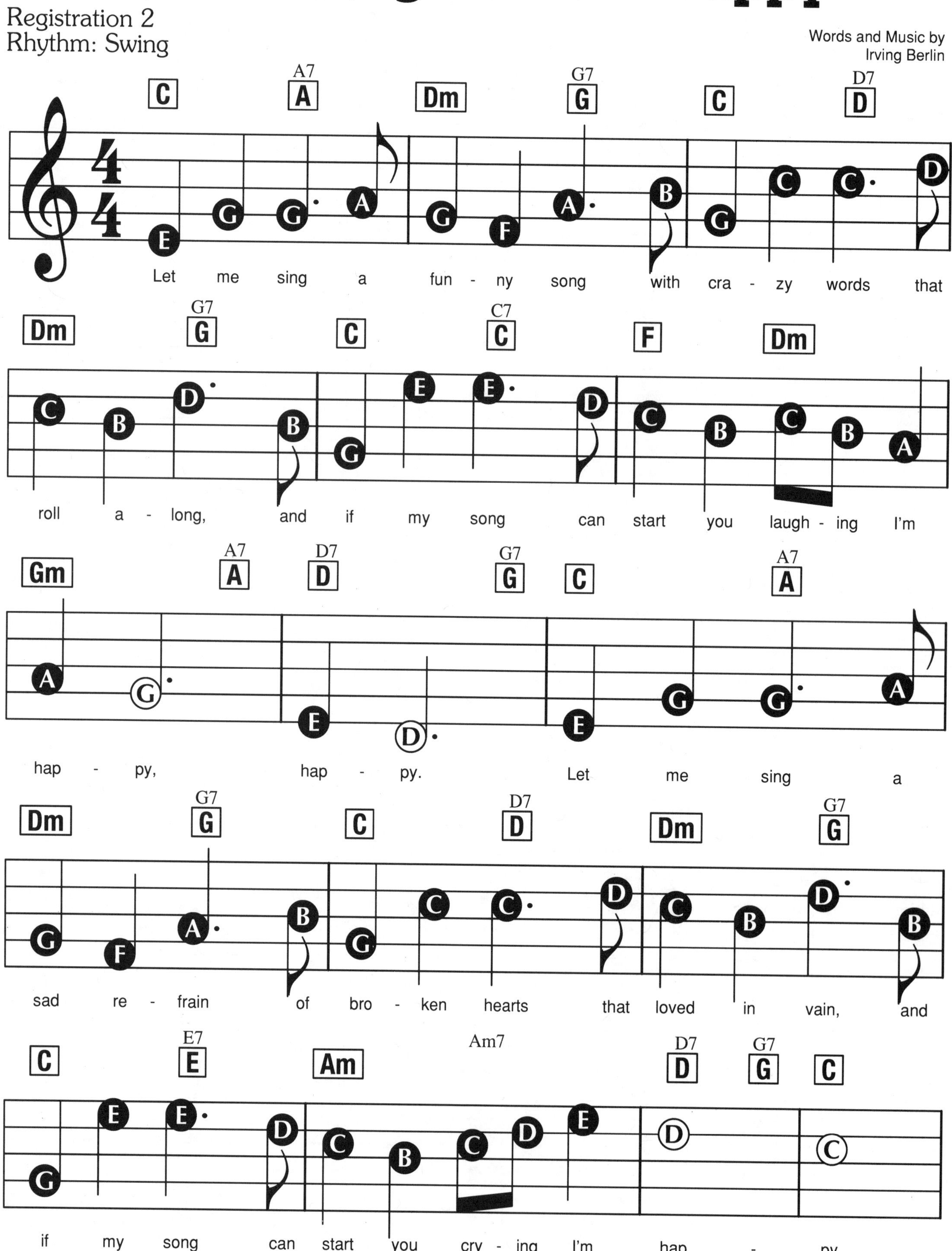

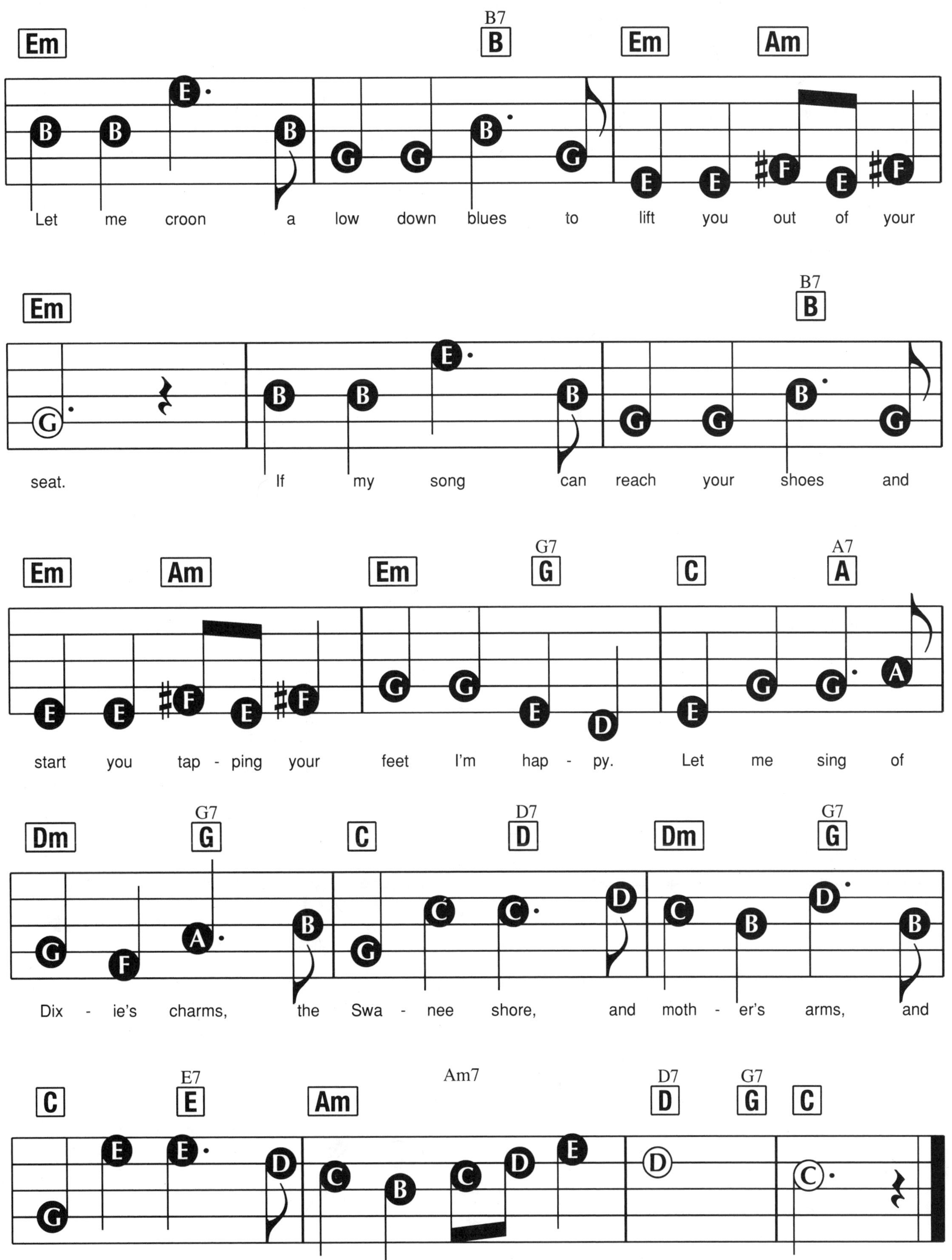

Em B7 B Em Am
Let me croon a low down blues to lift you out of your
Em B7 B
seat. If my song can reach your shoes and
Em Am Em G7 G C A7 A
start you tap - ping your feet I'm hap - py. Let me sing of
Dm G7 G C D7 D Dm G7 G
Dix - ie's charms, the Swa - nee shore, and moth - er's arms, and
C E7 E Am Am7 D7 D G7 G C
if my song can make you home - sick I'm hap - py.

Let's Face The Music And Dance

Registration 3
Rhythm: Swing

Words and Music by
Irving Berlin

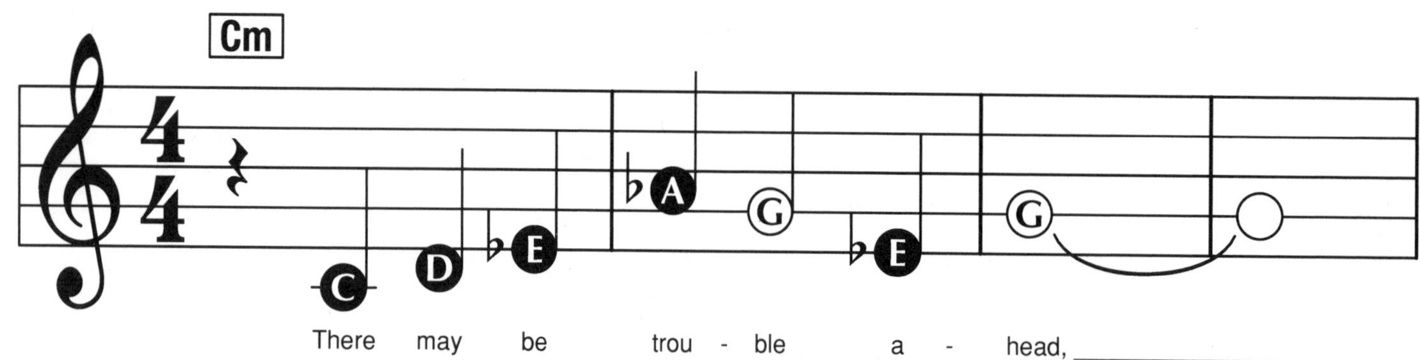

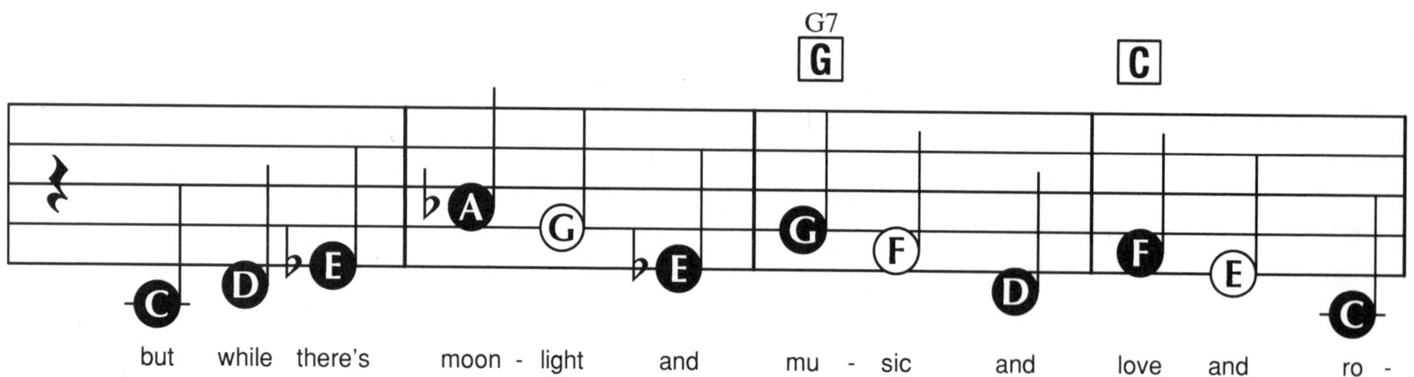

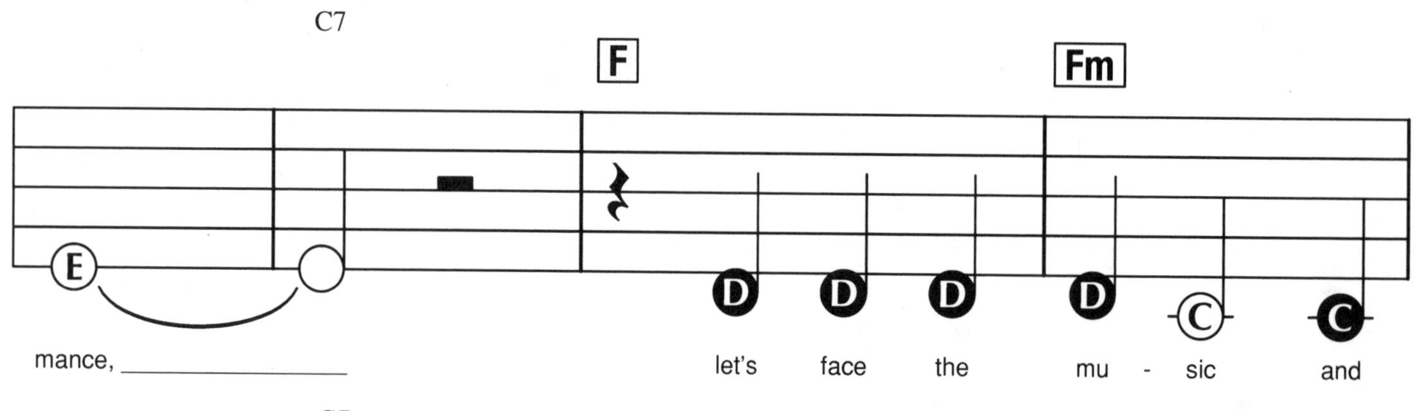

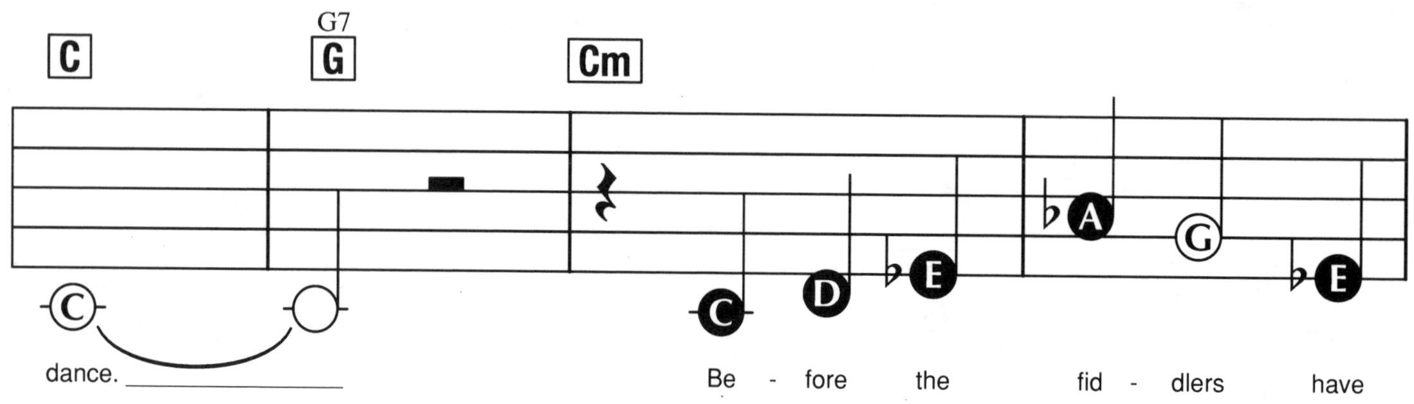

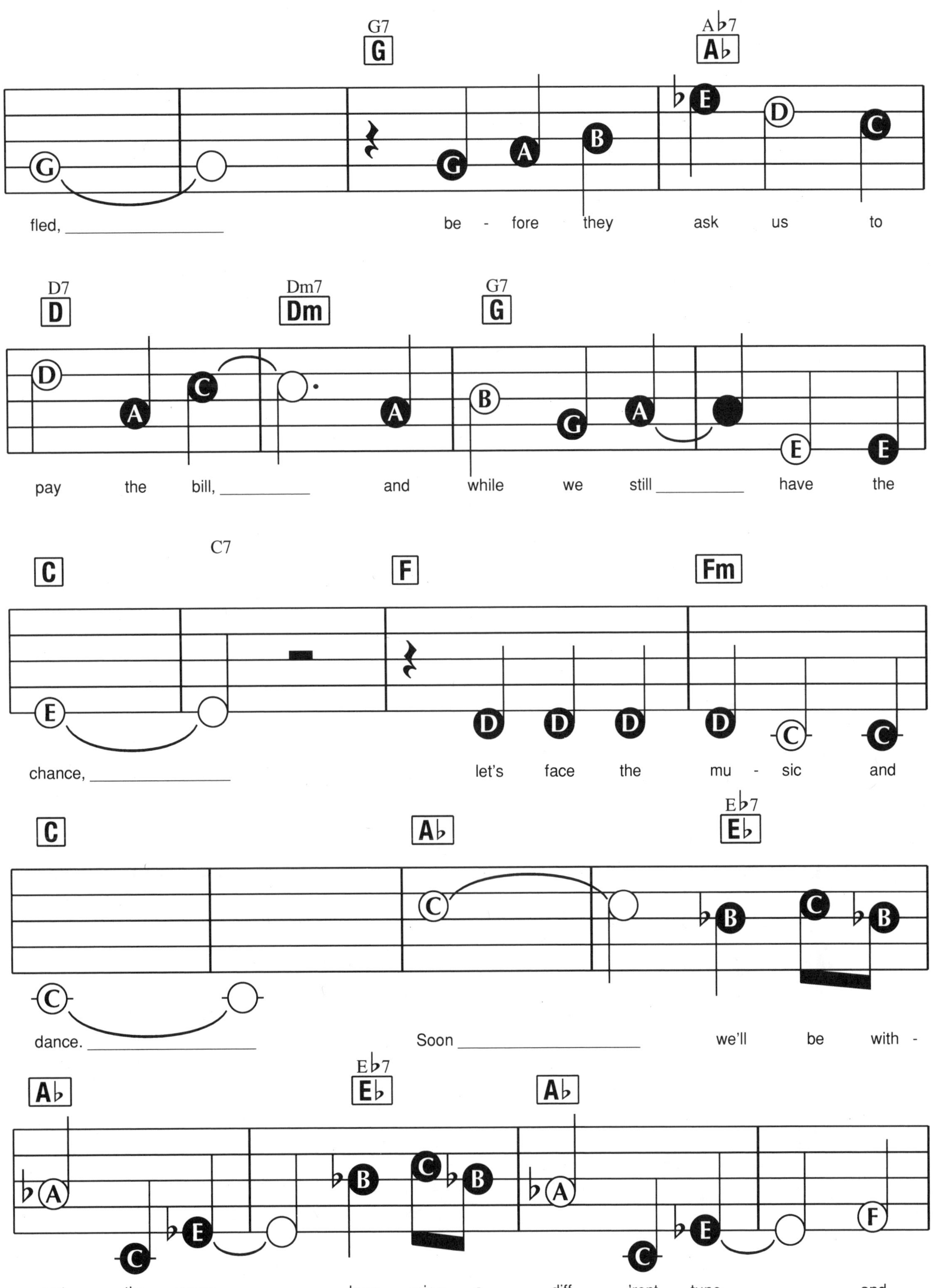
G7 G
A♭7 A♭
fled, ___ be - fore they ask us to
D7 D
Dm7 Dm
G7 G
pay the bill, ___ and while we still ___ have the
C
C7
F
Fm
chance, ___ let's face the mu - sic and
C
A♭
E♭7 E♭
dance. ___ Soon ___ we'll be with -
A♭
E♭7 E♭
A♭
out the moon, ___ hum - ming a diff - 'rent tune ___ and

G7 G Cm
then, there may be tear - drops to
shed. So while there's moon - light and
G7 G C C7
mu - sic and love and ro - mance,
F Fm C D7 D
let's face the mu - sic and dance, dance,
C Dm7 Dm G7 G 1 C G7 G 2 C Fm C
let's face the mu - sic and dance. dance.

Let's Have Another Cup O' Coffee

Registration 5
Rhythm: Swing

Words and Music by
Irving Berlin

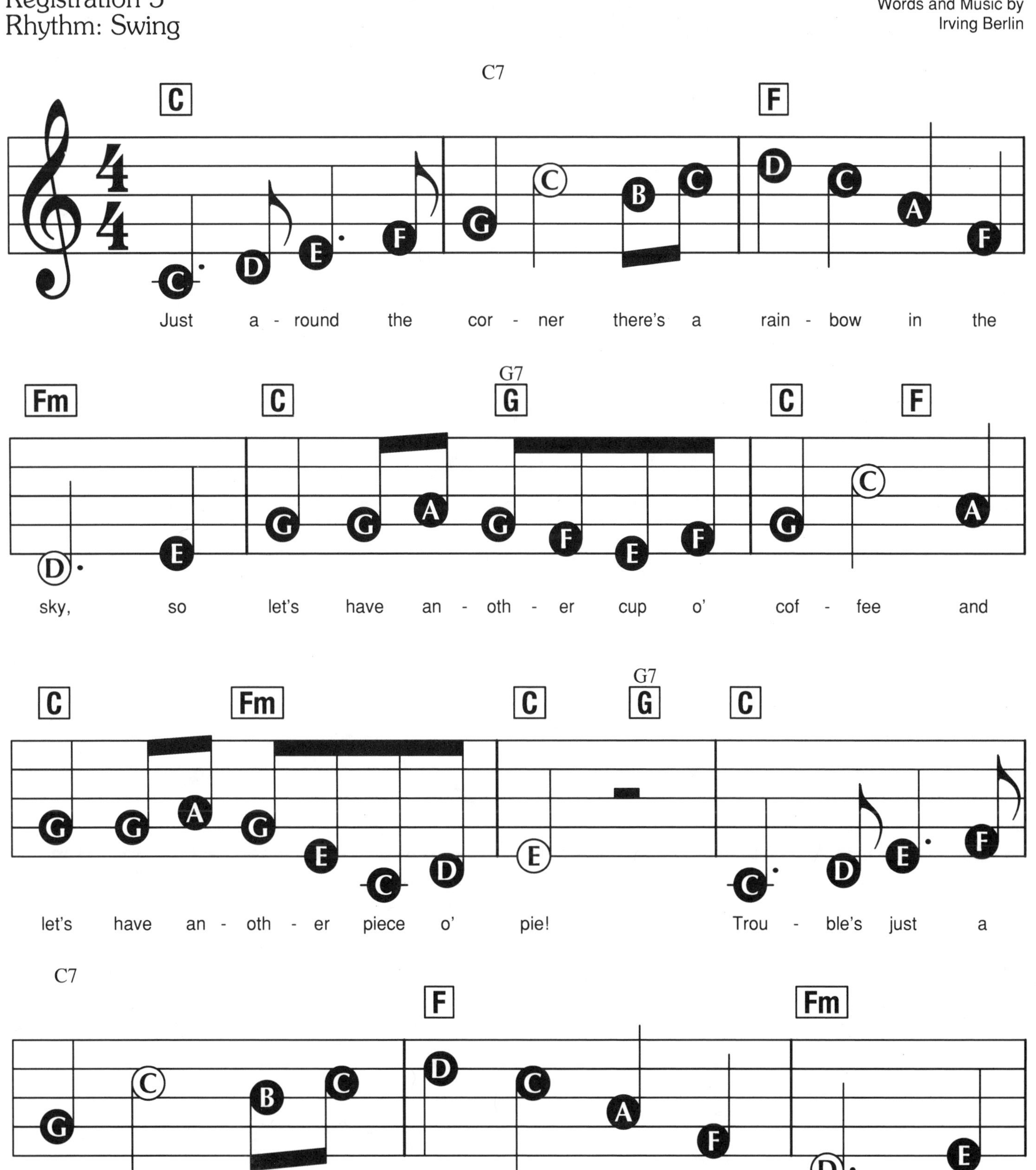

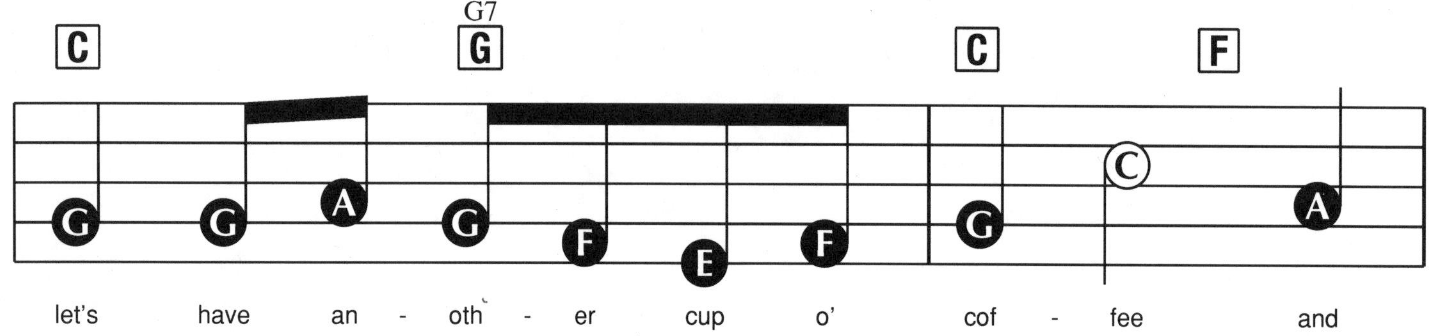
G7
C
G
C
F
G G A G F E F G C A
let's have an - oth - er cup o' cof - fee and

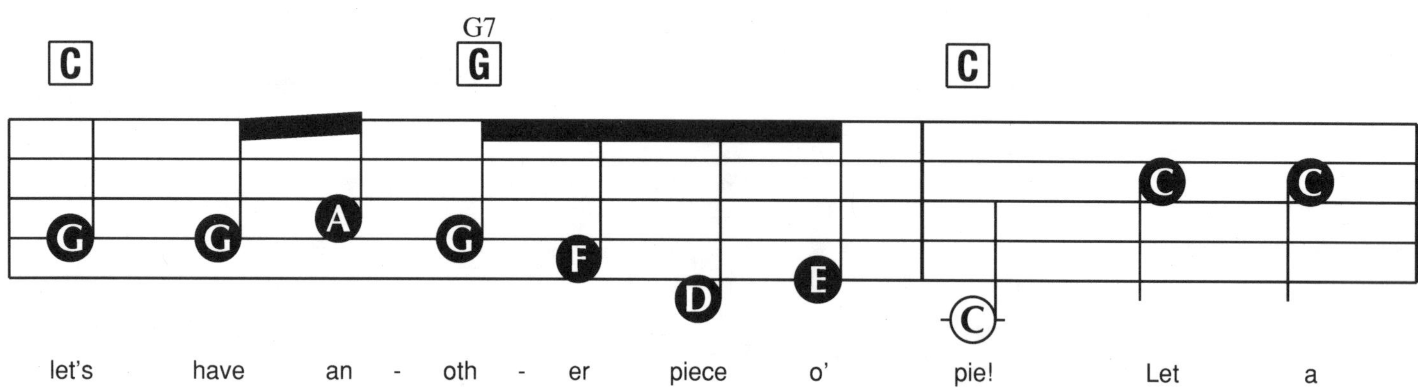
G7
C
G
C
G G A G F D E C C C
let's have an - oth - er piece o' pie! Let a

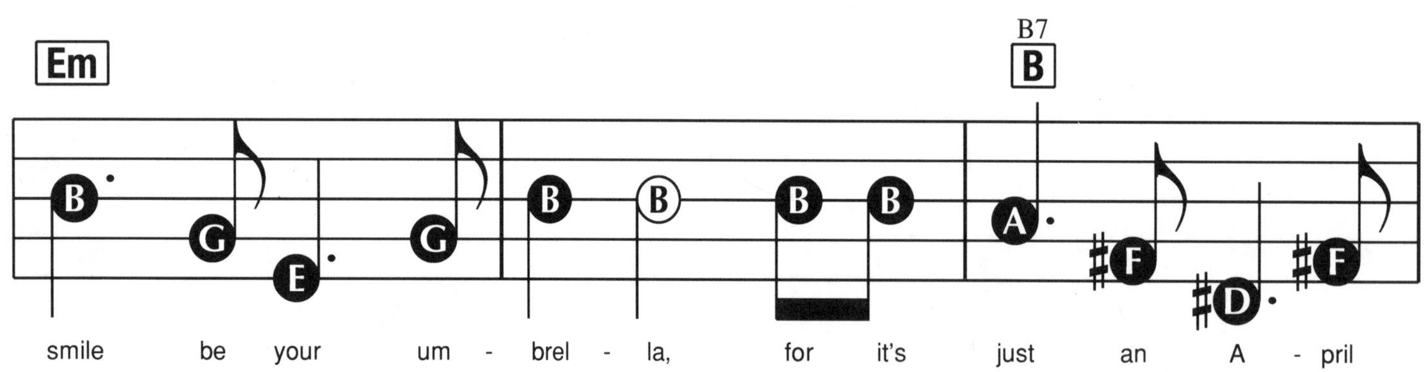
B7
Em
B
B G E G B B B B A F D F
smile be your um - brel - la, for it's just an A - pril

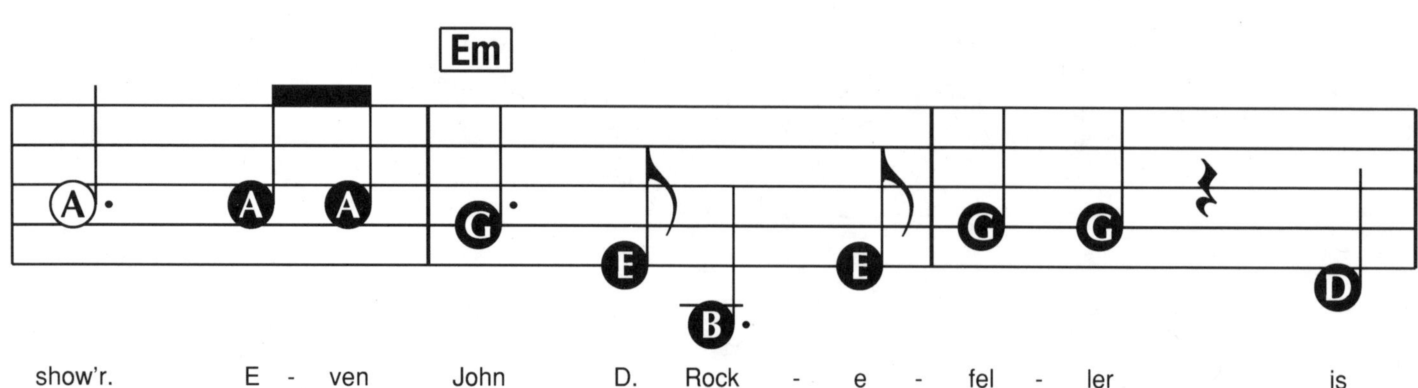
Em
A A A G E B E G G D
show'r. E - ven John D. Rock - e - fel - ler is

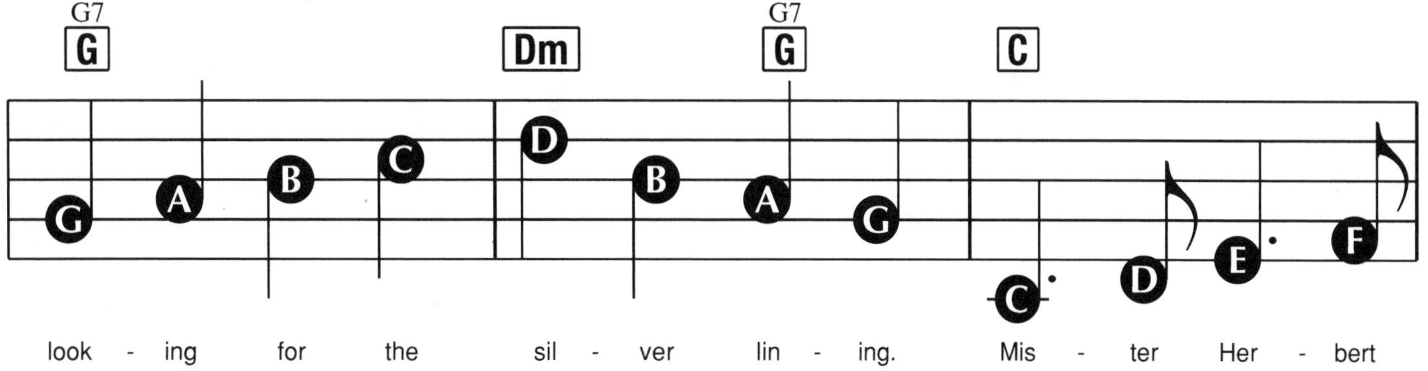
G7
G
Dm
G7
G
C
G A B C D B A G C D E F
look - ing for the sil - ver lin - ing. Mis - ter Her - bert

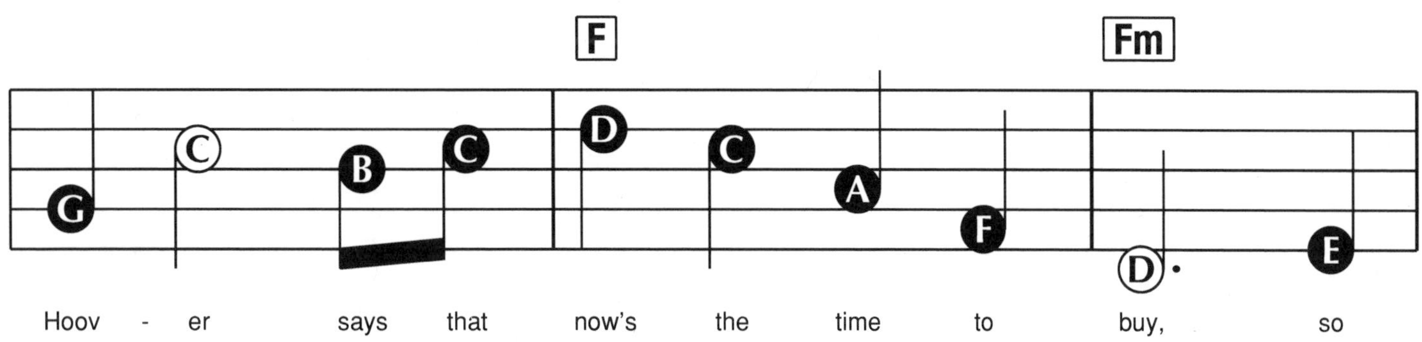
F
Fm
G C B C D C A F D E
Hoov - er says that now's the time to buy, so

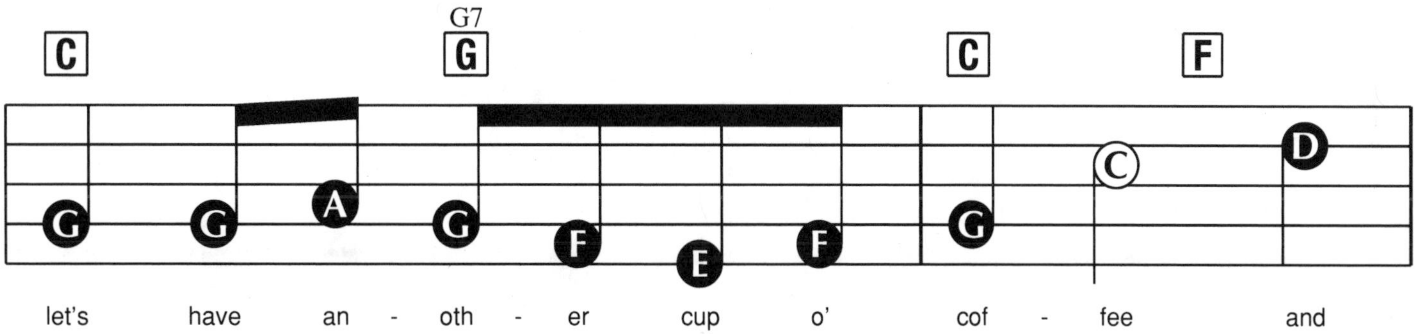
C
G7
G
C
F
G G A G F E F G C D
let's have an - oth - er cup o' cof - fee and

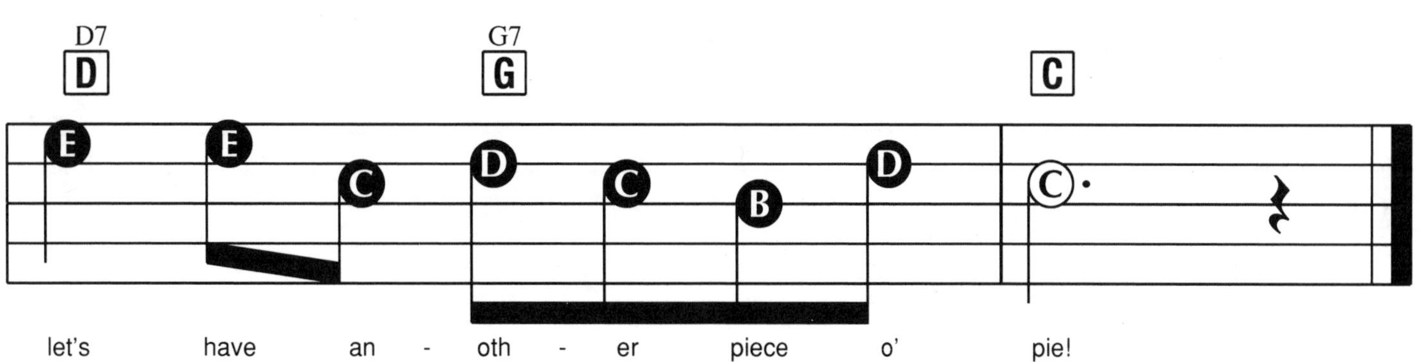
D7
D
G7
G
C
E E C D C B D C
let's have an - oth - er piece o' pie!

Let's Take An Old-Fashioned Walk

Registration 1
Rhythm: Waltz

Words and Music by
Irving Berlin

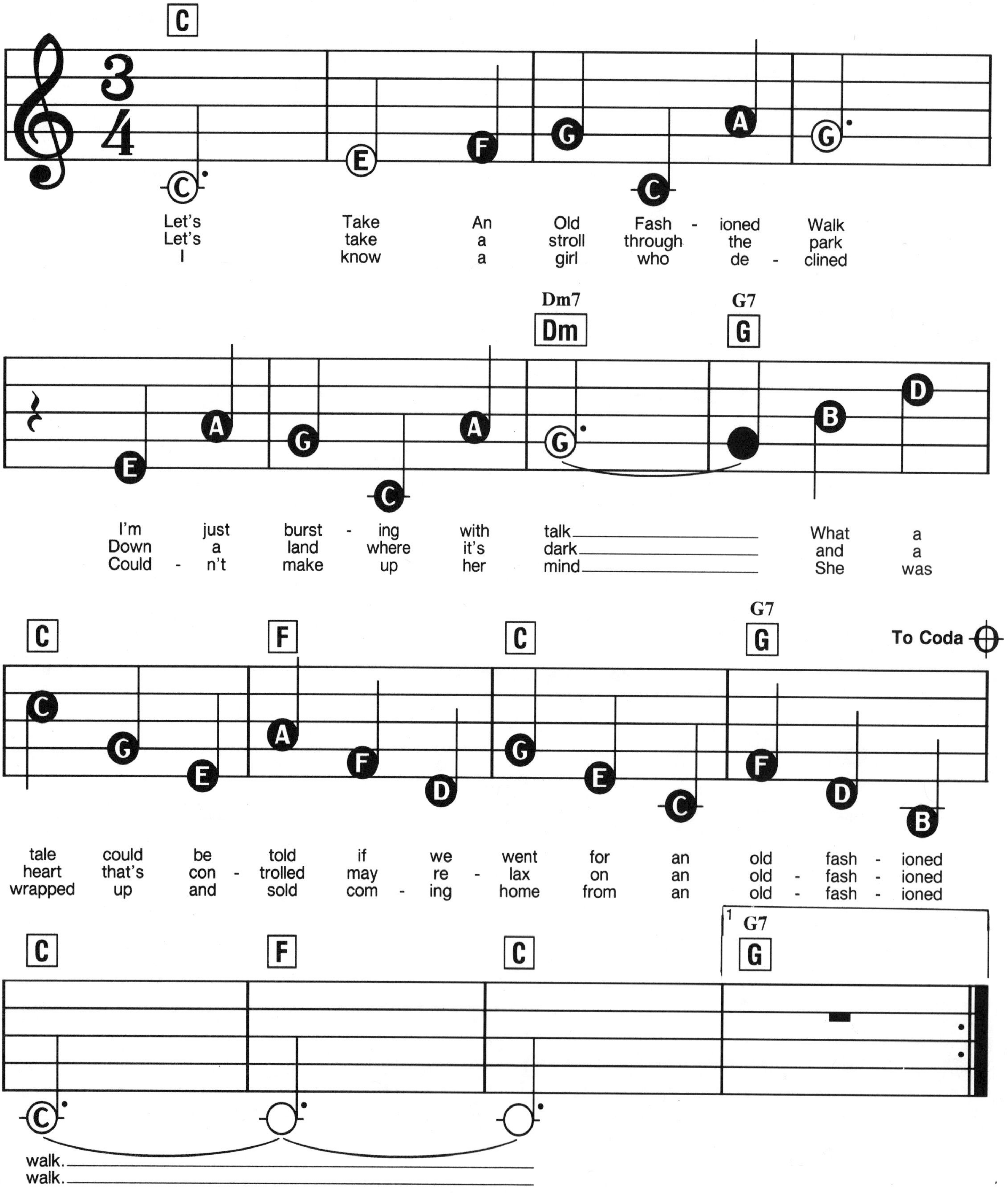

C

Let's Take An Old Fash - ioned Walk
Let's take a stroll through the park
I know a girl who de - clined

Dm7 Dm G7 G

I'm just burst - ing with talk
Down a land where it's dark
Could - n't make up her mind

What a
and a
She was

C F C G7 G To Coda

tale could be told if we went for an old fash - ioned
heart that's con - trolled may re - lax on an old - fash - ioned
wrapped up and sold com - ing home from an old - fash - ioned

C F C 1 G7 G

walk.
walk.

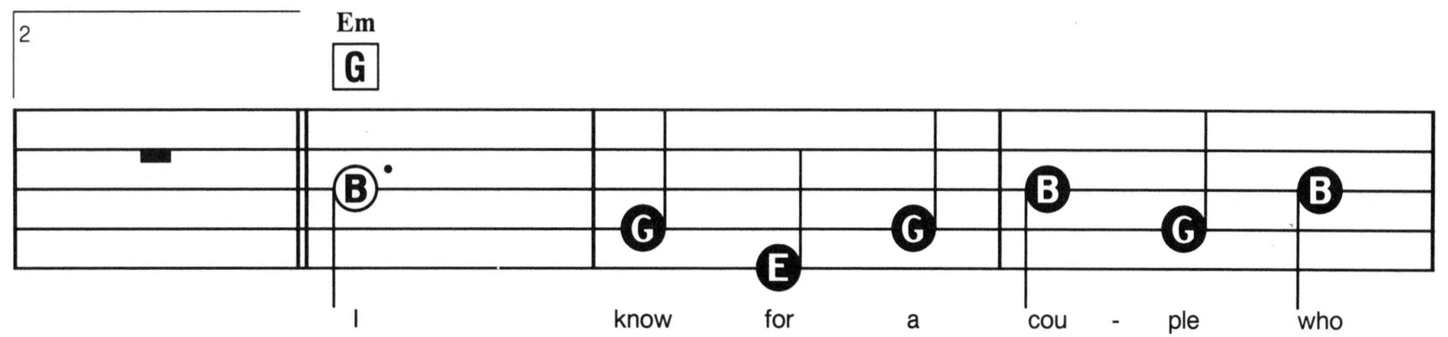
2
Em
G
B
G
E
G
G
B
G
B
I know for a cou - ple who

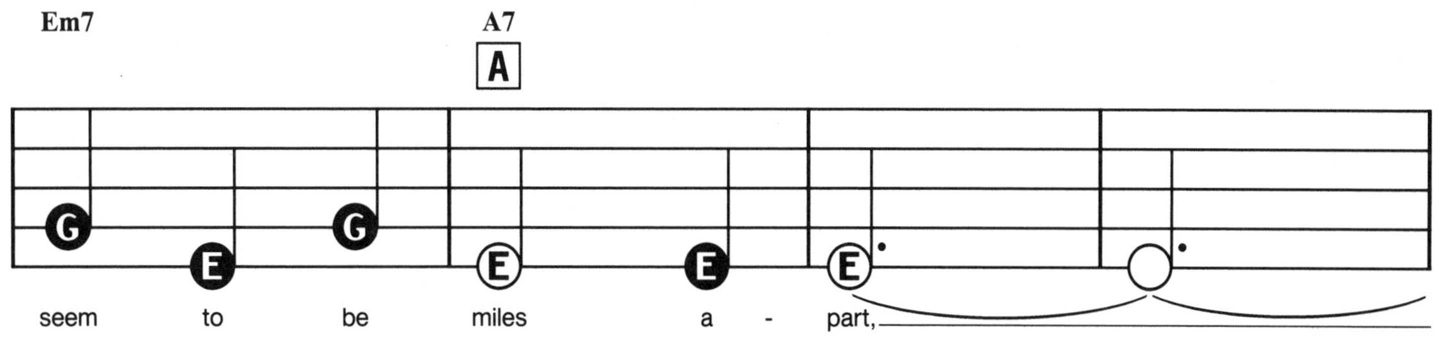
Em7
A7
A
G
E
G
E
E
E
seem to be miles a - part,

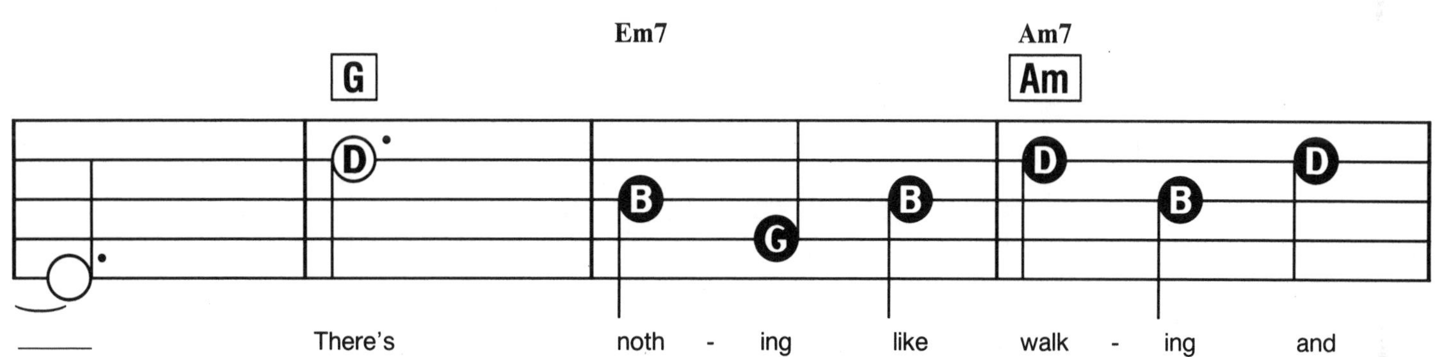
G
Em7
Am7
Am
D
B
G
B
D
B
D
There's noth - ing like walk - ing and

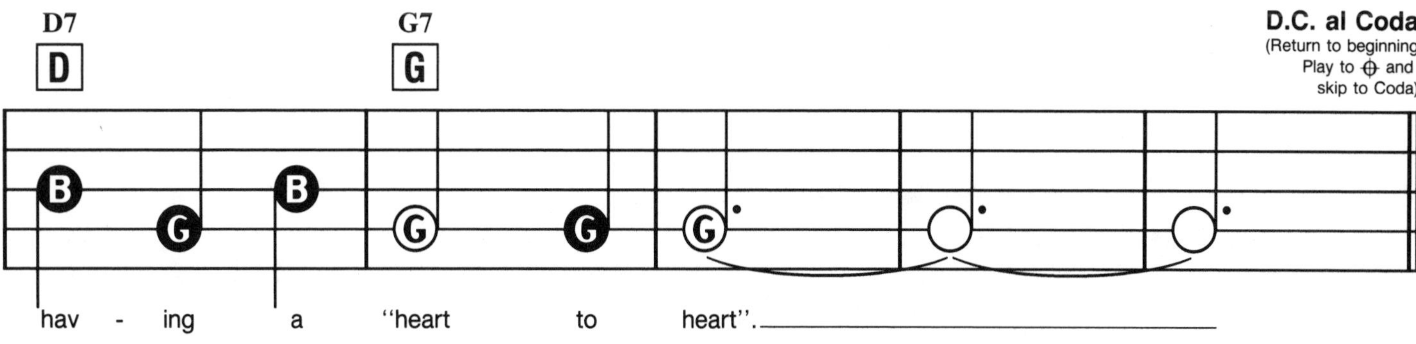
D7
D
G7
G
D.C. al Coda
(Return to beginning
Play to ⊕ and
skip to Coda)
B
G
B
G
G
G
hav - ing a "heart to heart".

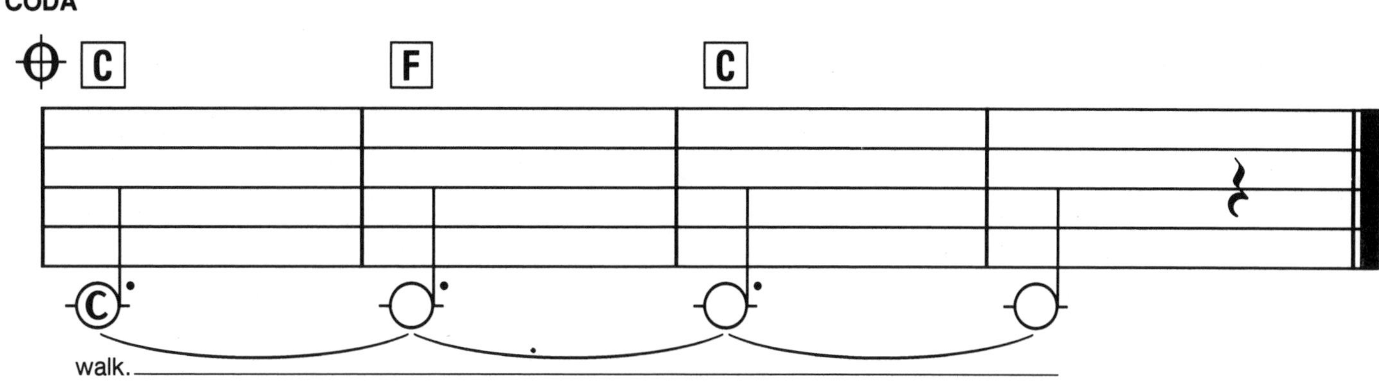
CODA
C
F
C
C
walk.

Mandy

Registration 5
Rhythm: Swing

Words and Music by
Irving Berlin

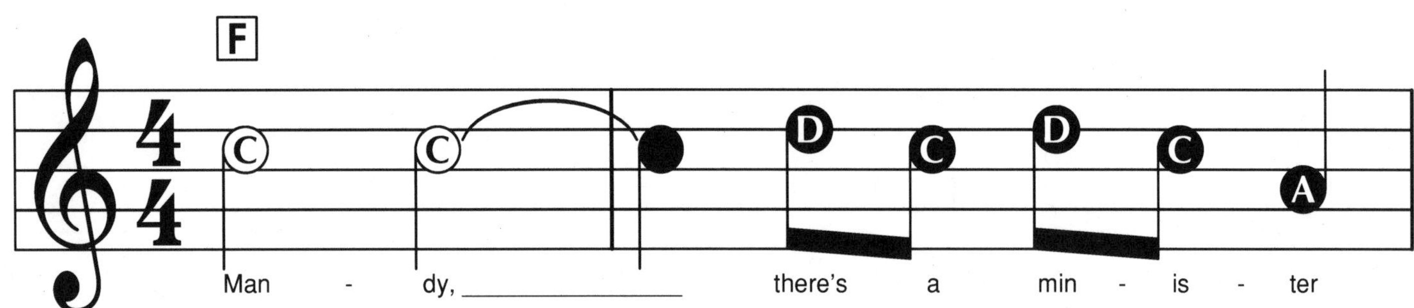

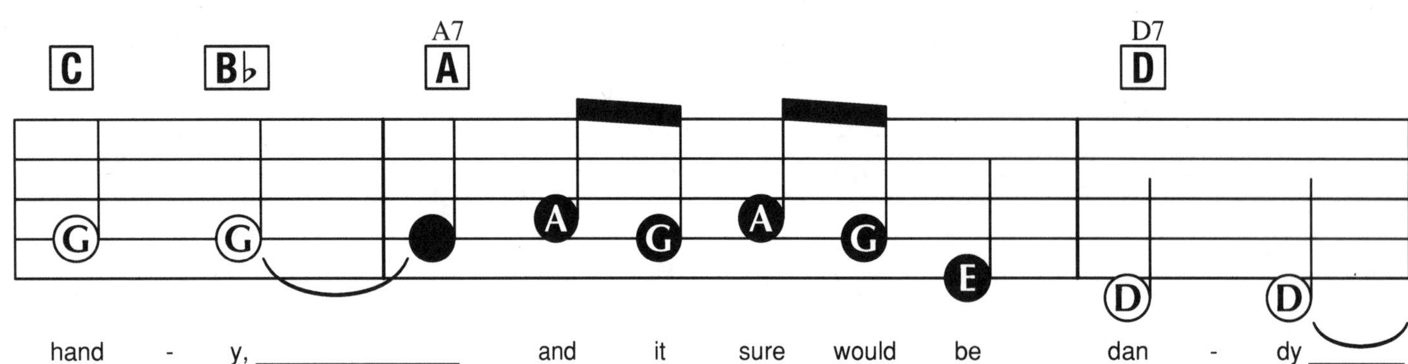

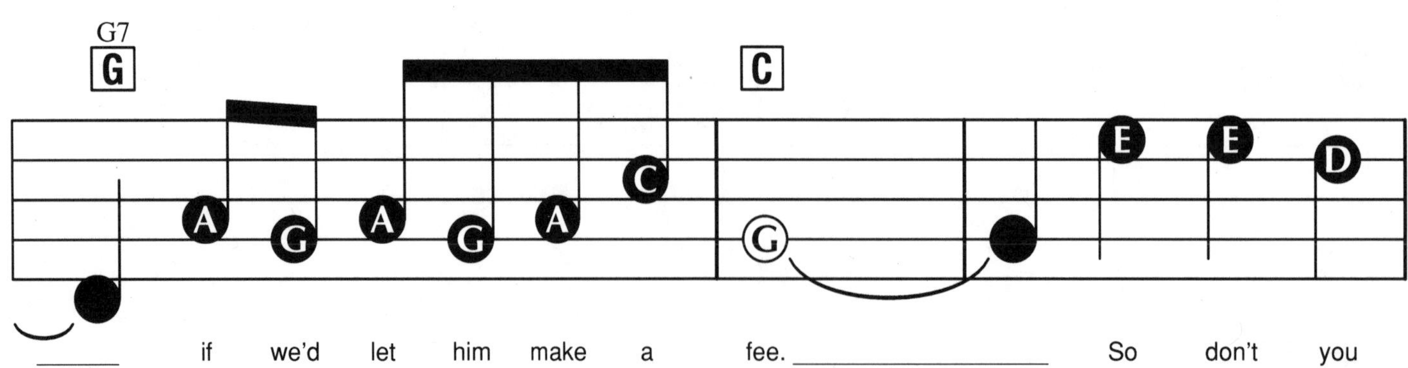

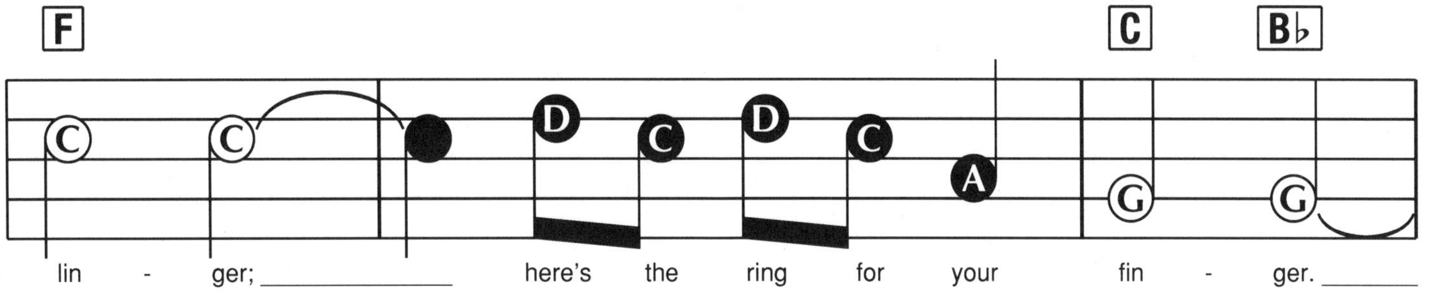
F
C
B♭
C
C
D
C
D
C
A
G
G
lin - ger; here's the ring for your fin - ger.

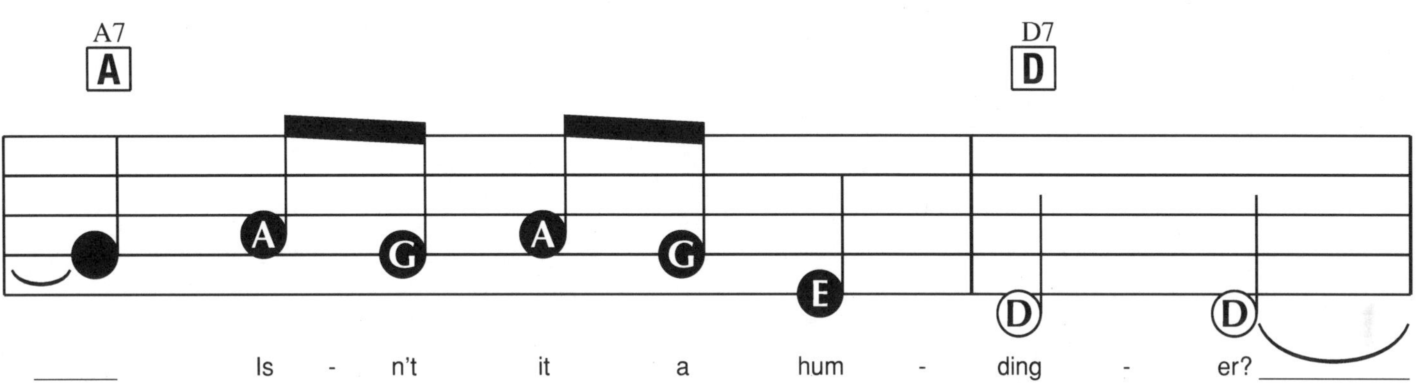
A7
A
D7
D
A
G
A
G
E
D
D
Is - n't it a hum - ding - er?

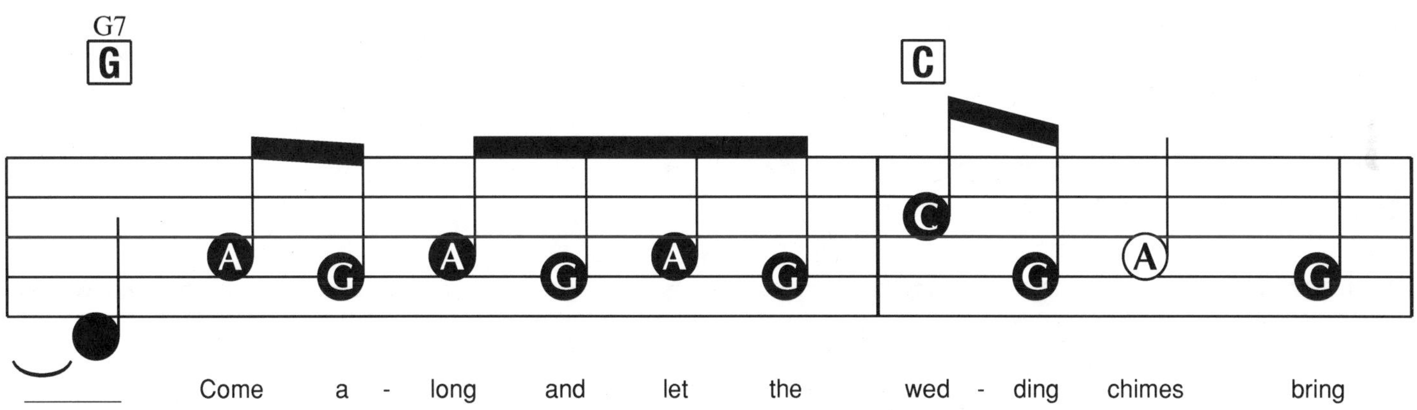
G7
G
C
A
G
A
G
A
G
C
G
A
G
Come a - long and let the wed - ding chimes bring

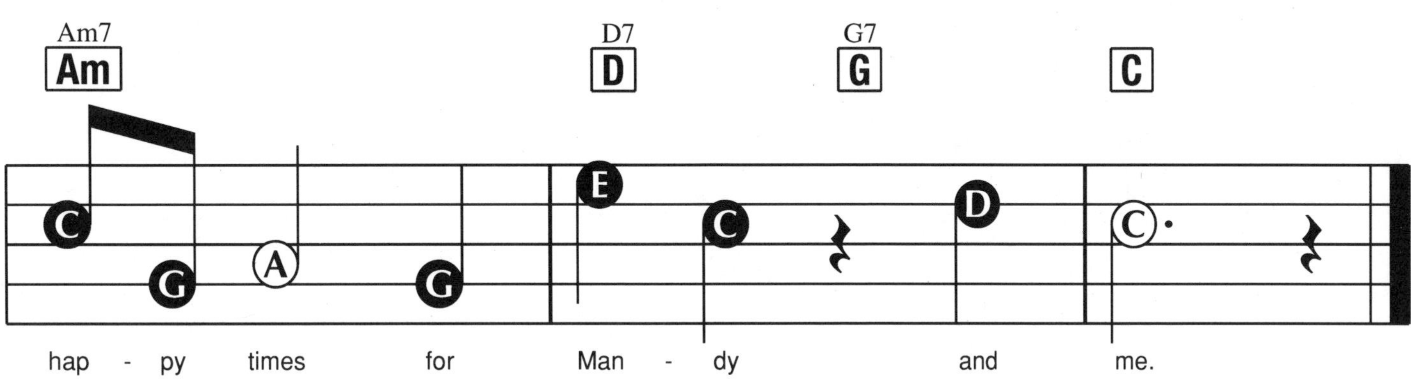
Am7
Am
D7
D
G7
G
C
C
G
A
G
E
C
D
C
hap - py times for Man - dy and me.

Marie

Registration 1
Rhythm: Fox Trot or Swing

Words and Music by
Irving Berlin

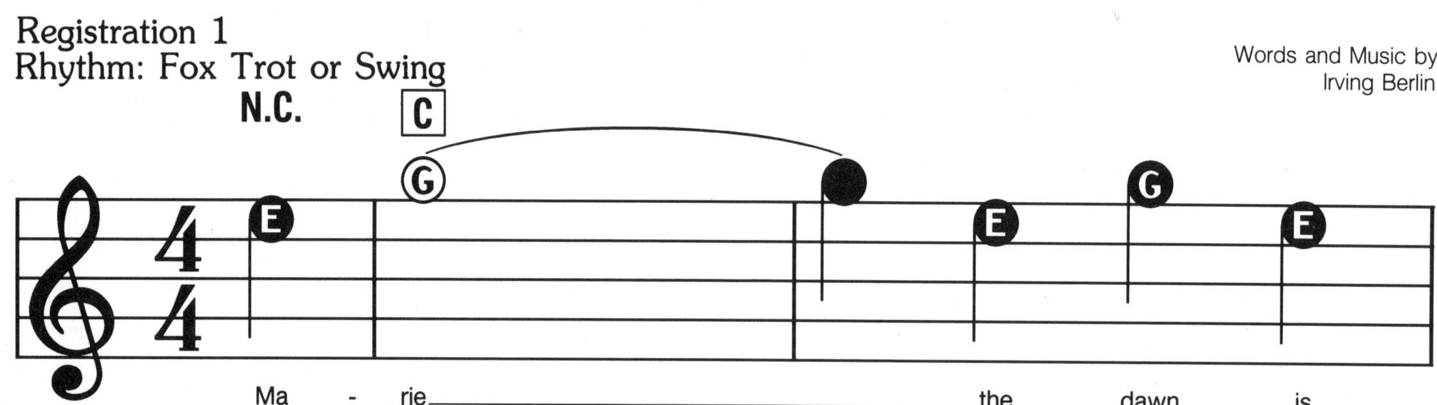

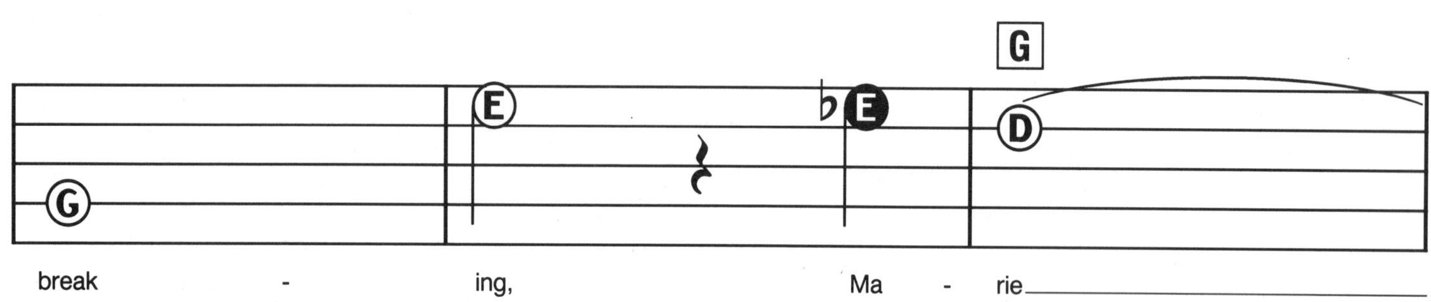

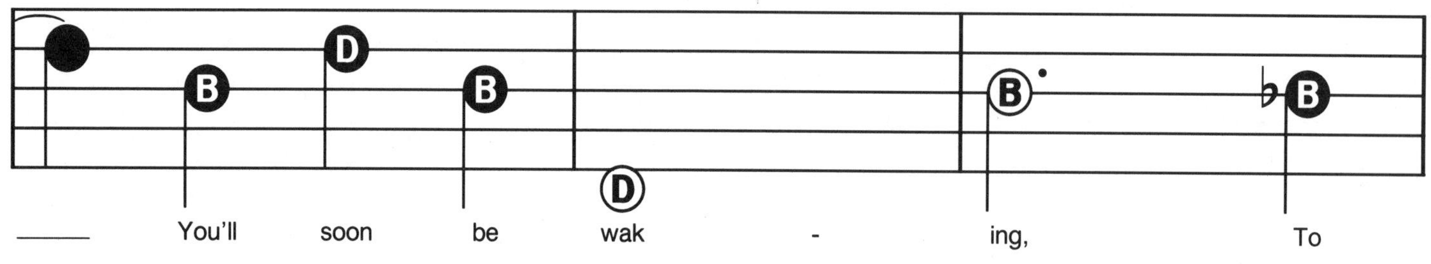

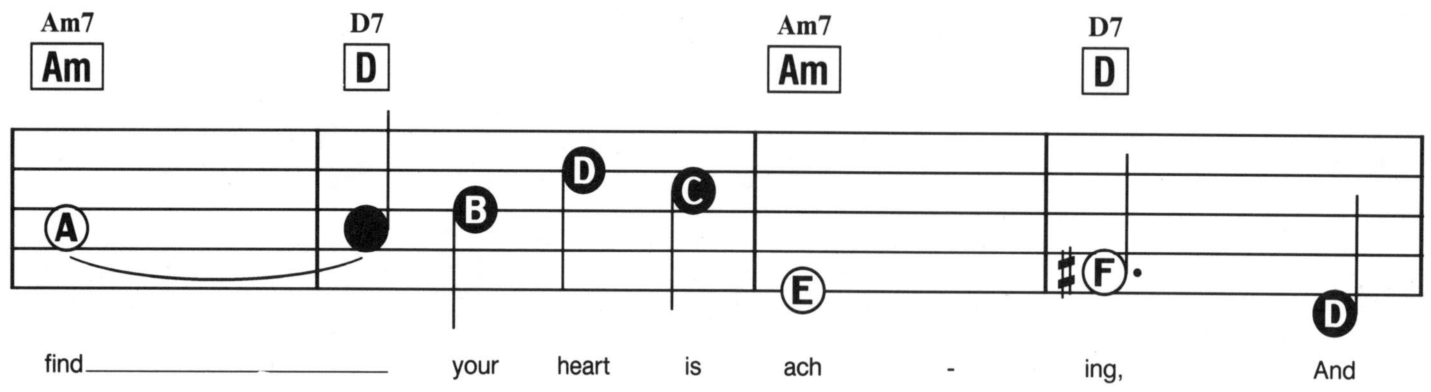

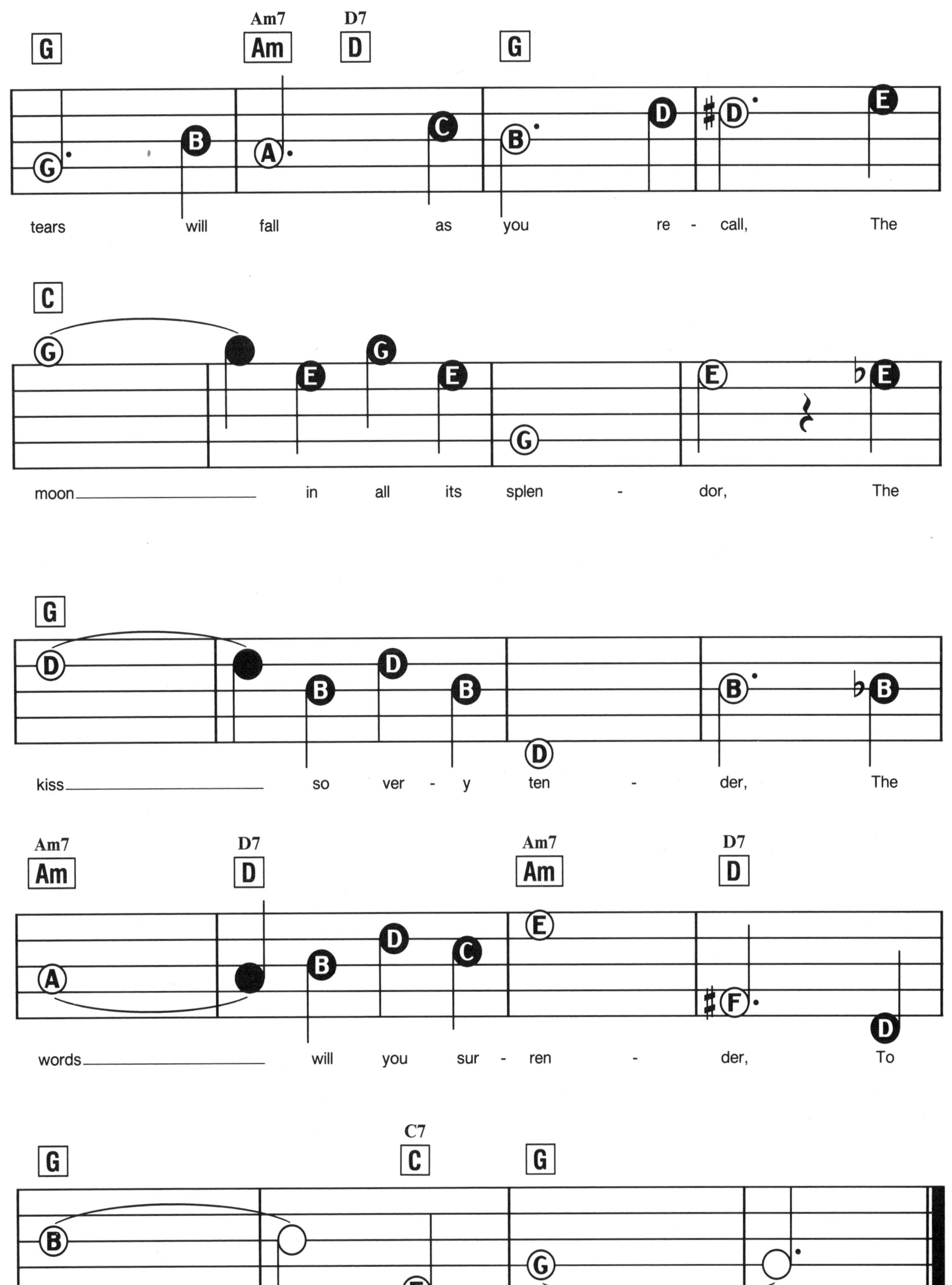
G
Am7
Am
D7
D
G
tears will fall as you re - call, The
C
moon in all its splen - dor, The
G
kiss so ver - y ten - der, The
Am7
Am
D7
D
Am7
Am
D7
D
words will you sur - ren - der, To
G
C7
C
G
me Ma - rie.

Oh! How I Hate To Get Up In The Morning

Registration 2
Rhythm: 6/8 March

Words and Music by
Irving Berlin

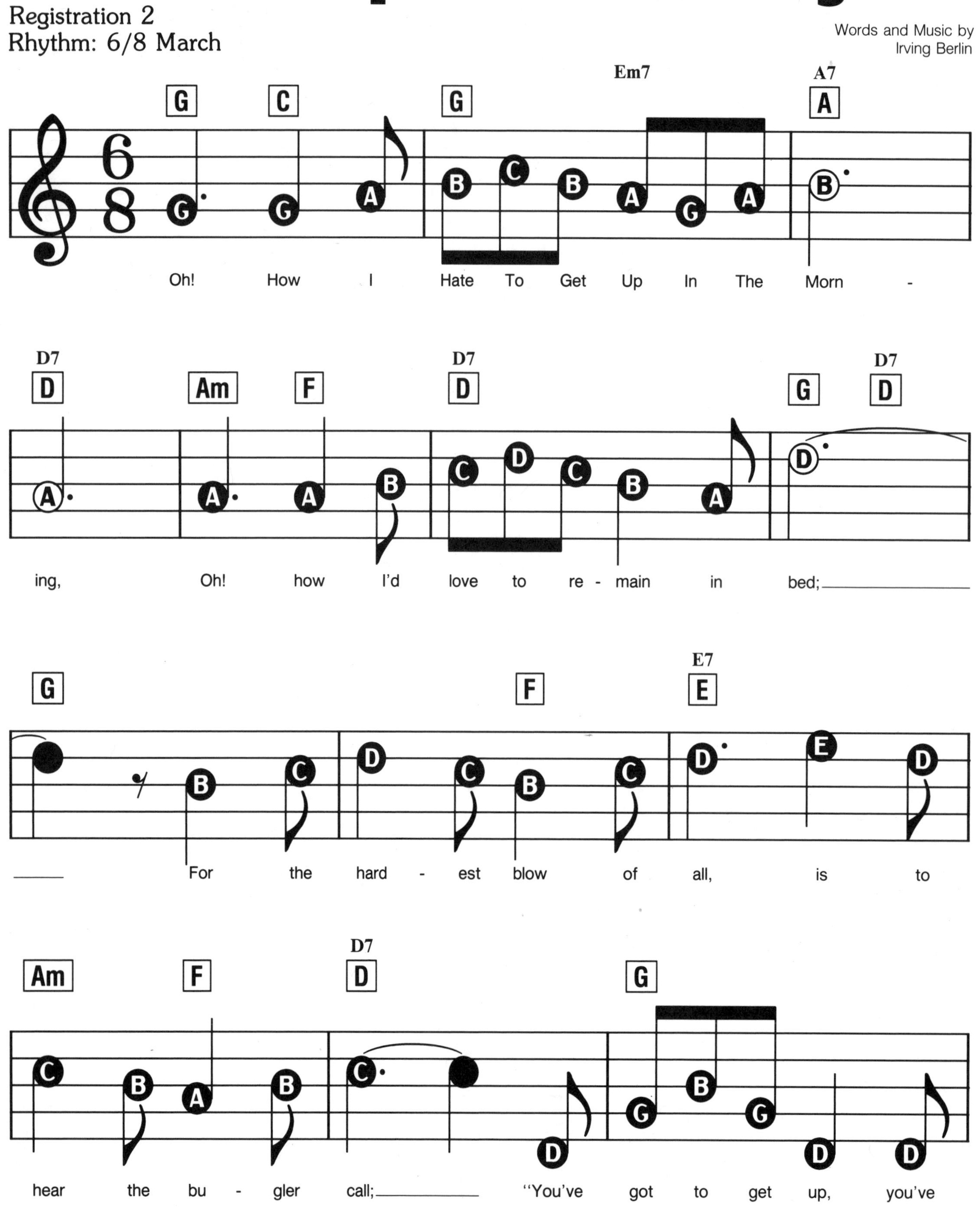

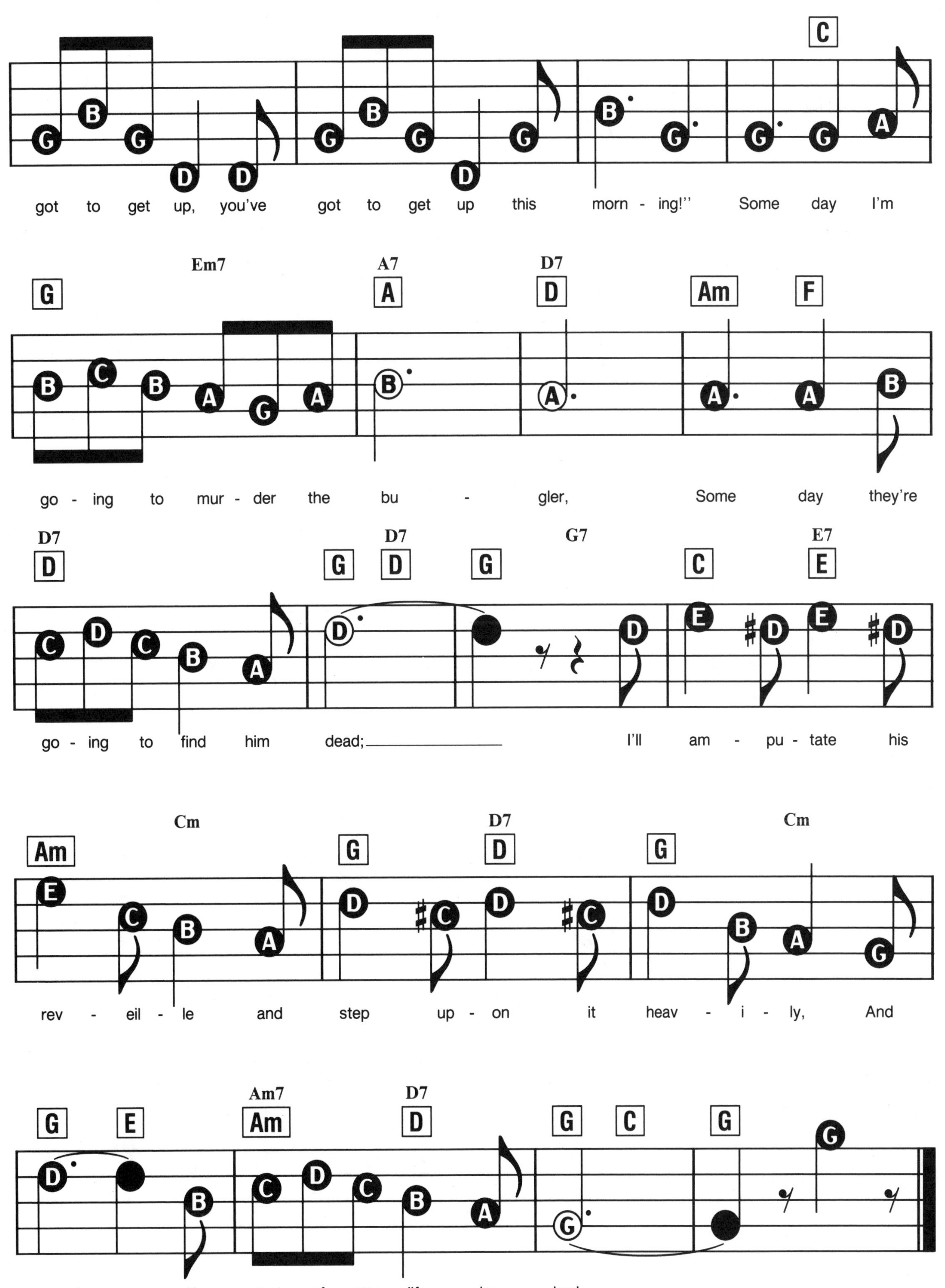
C
got to get up, you've got to get up this morn - ing!'' Some day I'm
G
Em7
A7
A
D7
D
Am
F
go - ing to mur - der the bu - gler, Some day they're
D7
D
G
D7
D
G
G7
C
E7
E
go - ing to find him dead; I'll am - pu - tate his
Am
Cm
G
D7
D
G
Cm
rev - eil - le and step up - on it heav - i - ly, And
G
E
Am7
Am
D7
D
G
C
G
spend the rest of my life in bed.

Outside Of That I Love You

Registration 2
Rhythm: Swing

Words and Music by
Irving Berlin

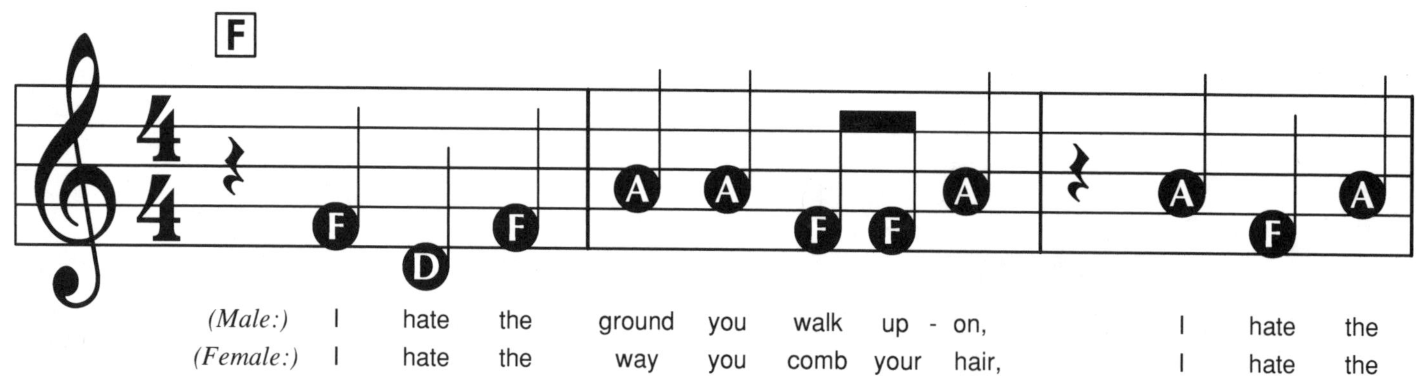

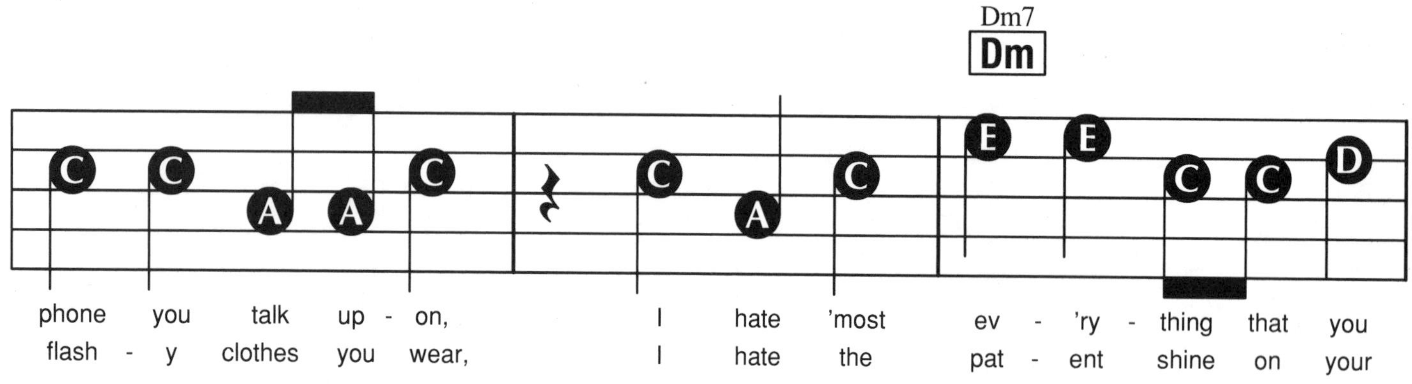

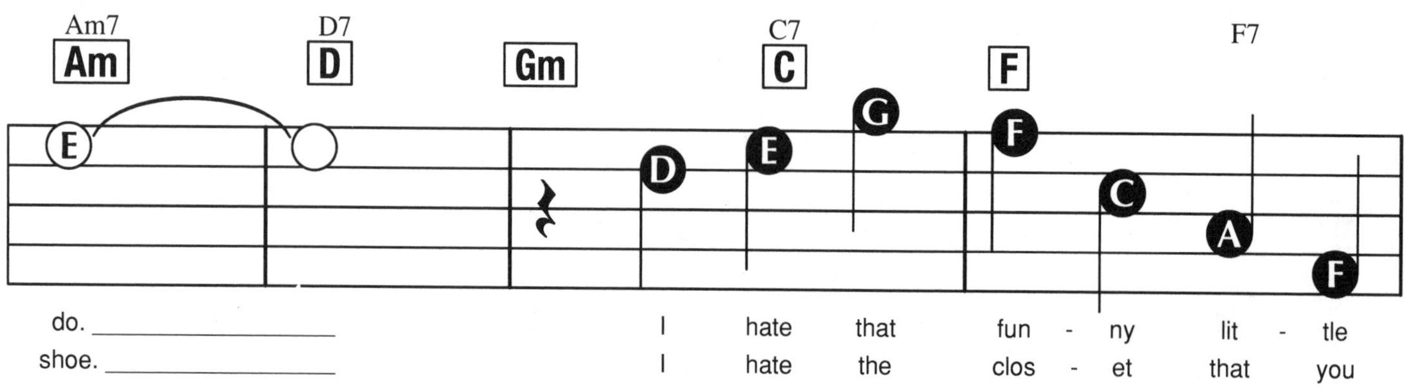

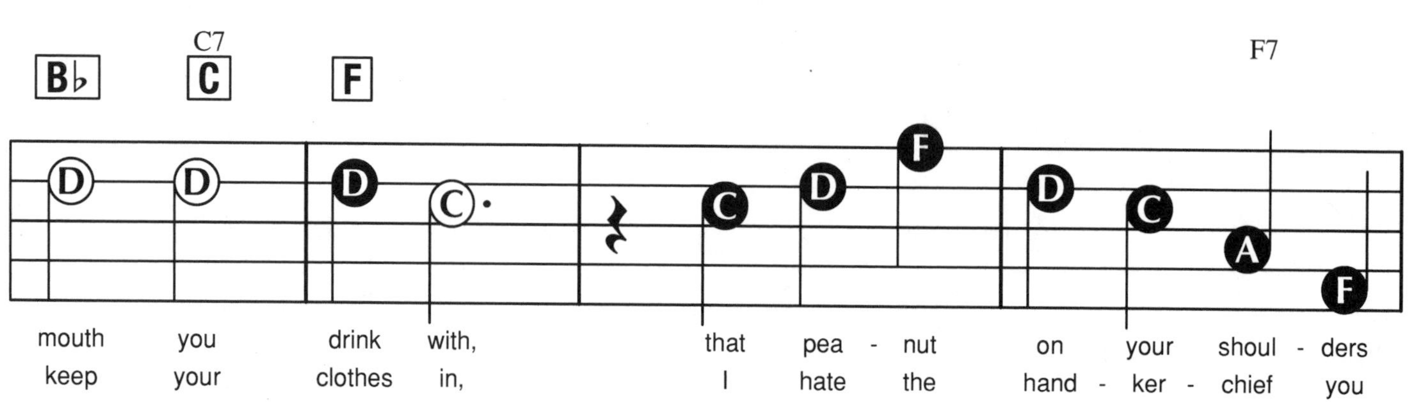

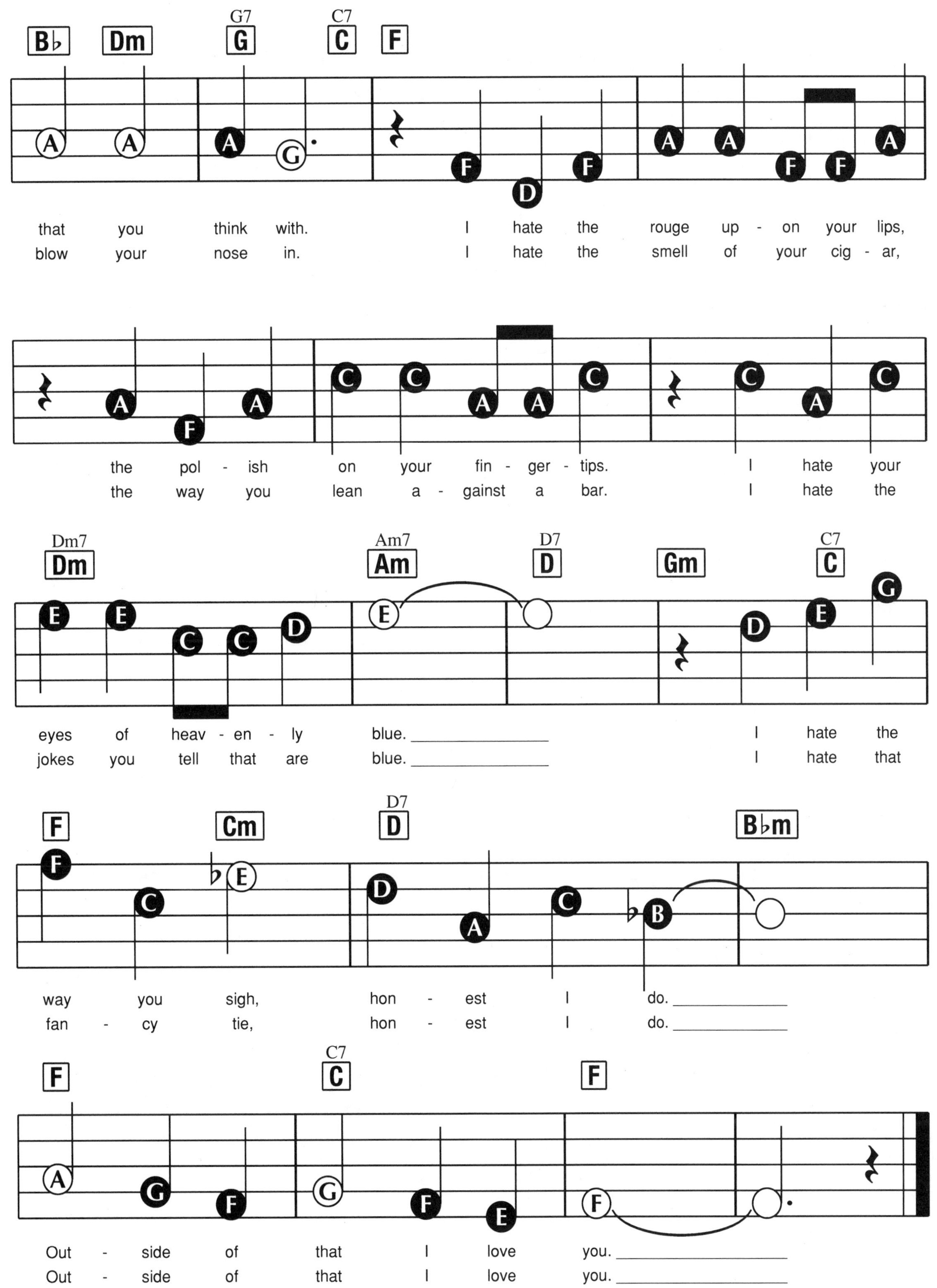
B♭ Dm G7 G C7 C F
that you think with. I hate the rouge up - on your lips,
blow your nose in. I hate the smell of your cig - ar,
the pol - ish on your fin - ger - tips. I hate your
the way you lean a - gainst a bar. I hate the
Dm7 Dm Am7 Am D7 D Gm C7 C
eyes of heav - en - ly blue. I hate the
jokes you tell that are blue. I hate that
F Cm D7 D B♭m
way you sigh, hon - est I do.
fan - cy tie, hon - est I do.
F C7 C F
Out - side of that I love you.
Out - side of that I love you.

No Strings (I'm Fancy Free)

Registration 7
Rhythm: Swing

Words and Music by
Irving Berlin

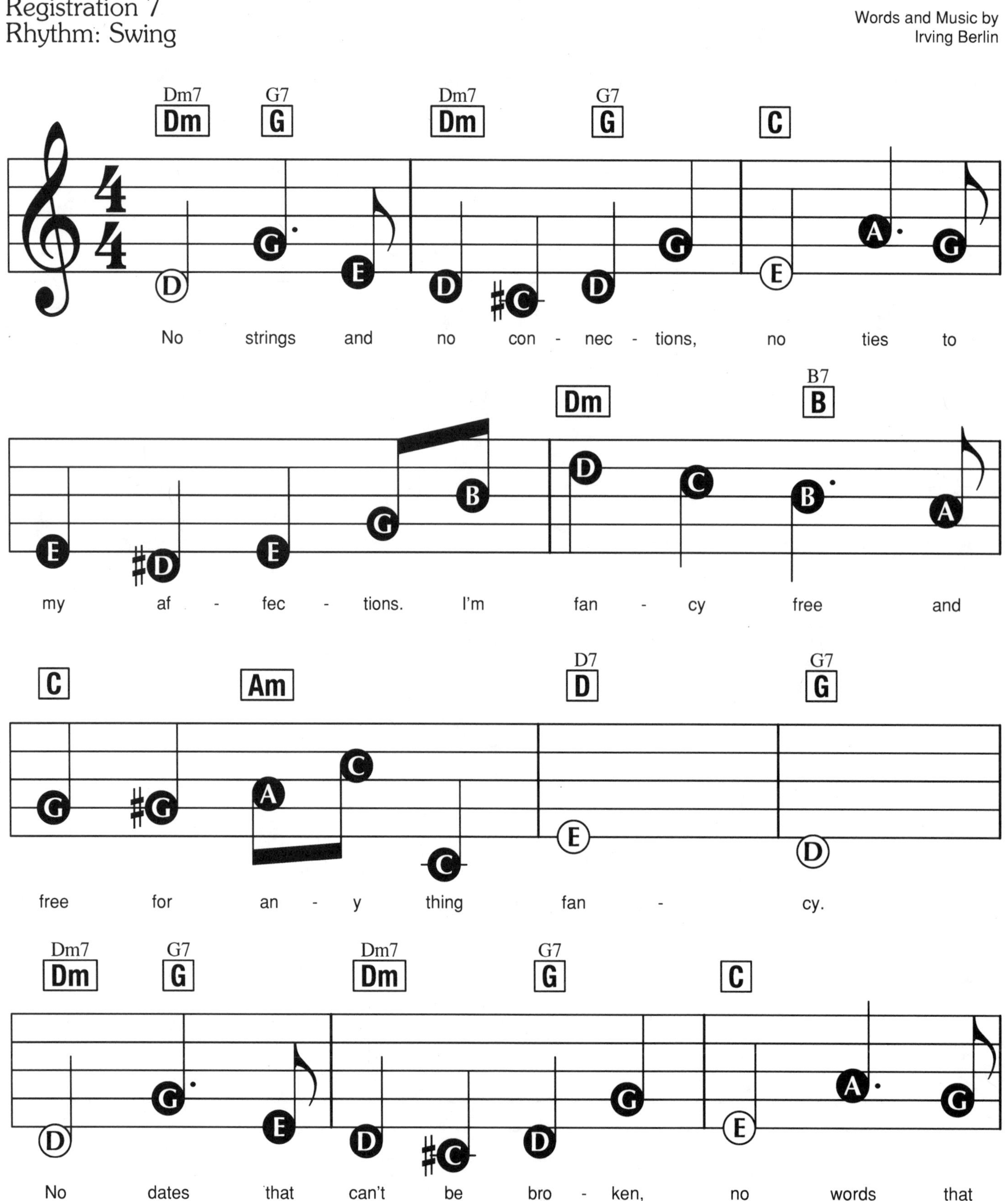

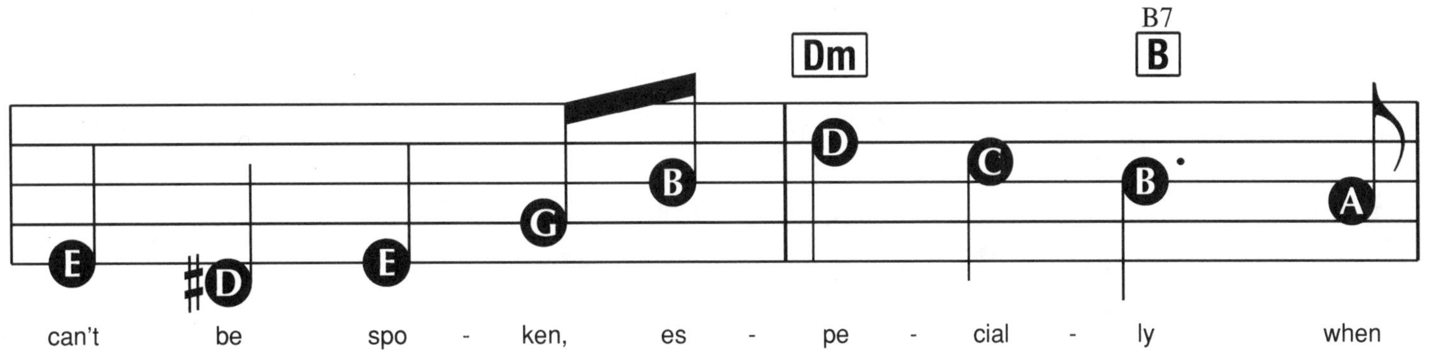
Dm
B7
B
E
D
E
G
B
D
C
B
A
can't be spo - ken, es - pe - cial - ly when

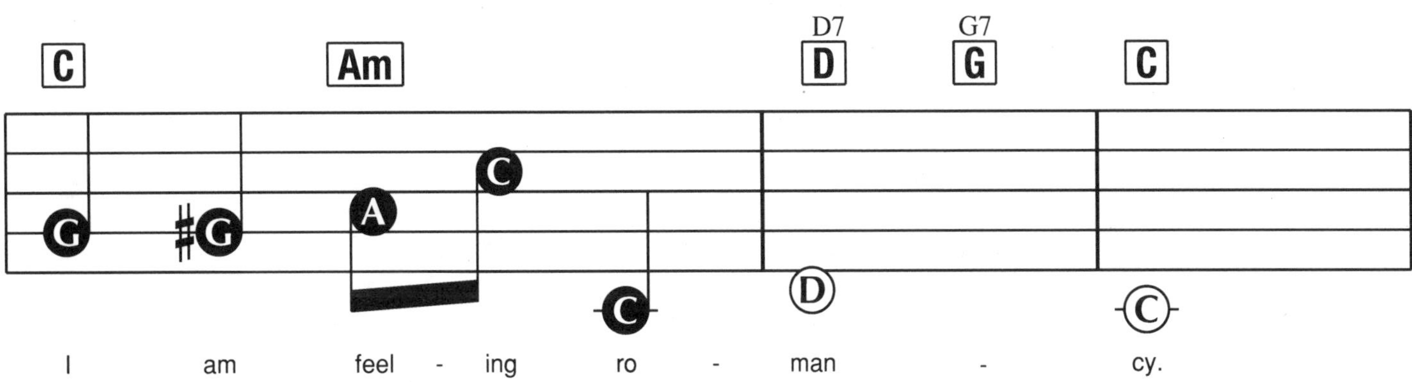
C
Am
D7
D
G7
G
C
G
G
A
C
C
D
C
I am feel - ing ro - man - cy.

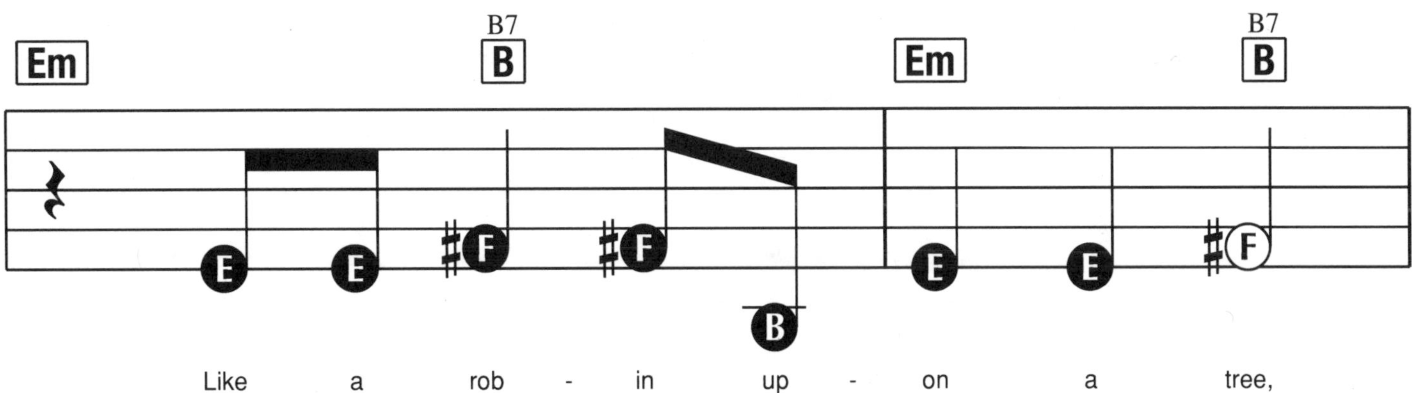
Em
B7
B
Em
B7
B
E
E
F
F
B
E
E
F
Like a rob - in up - on a tree,

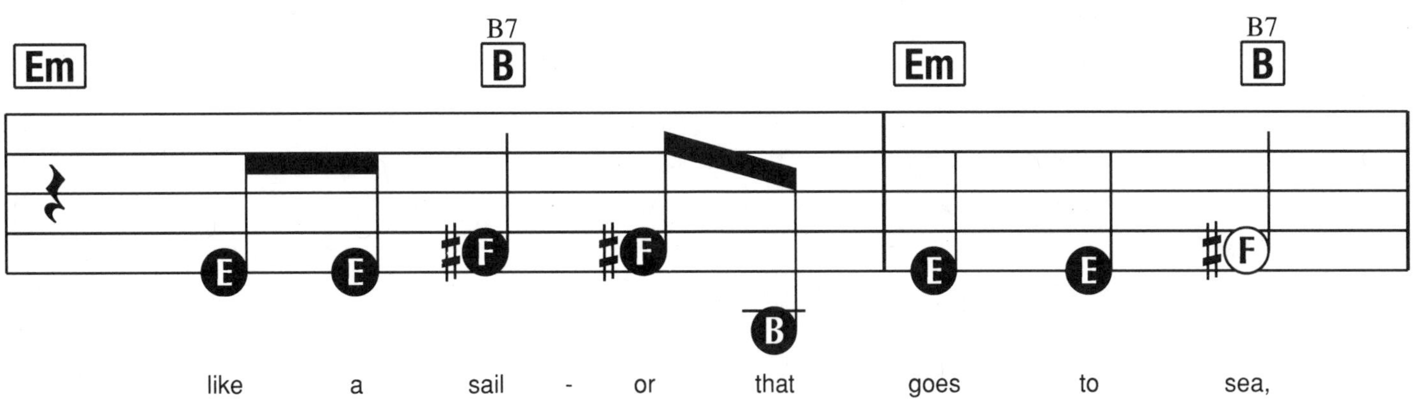
Em
B7
B
Em
B7
B
E
E
F
F
B
E
E
F
like a sail - or that goes to sea,

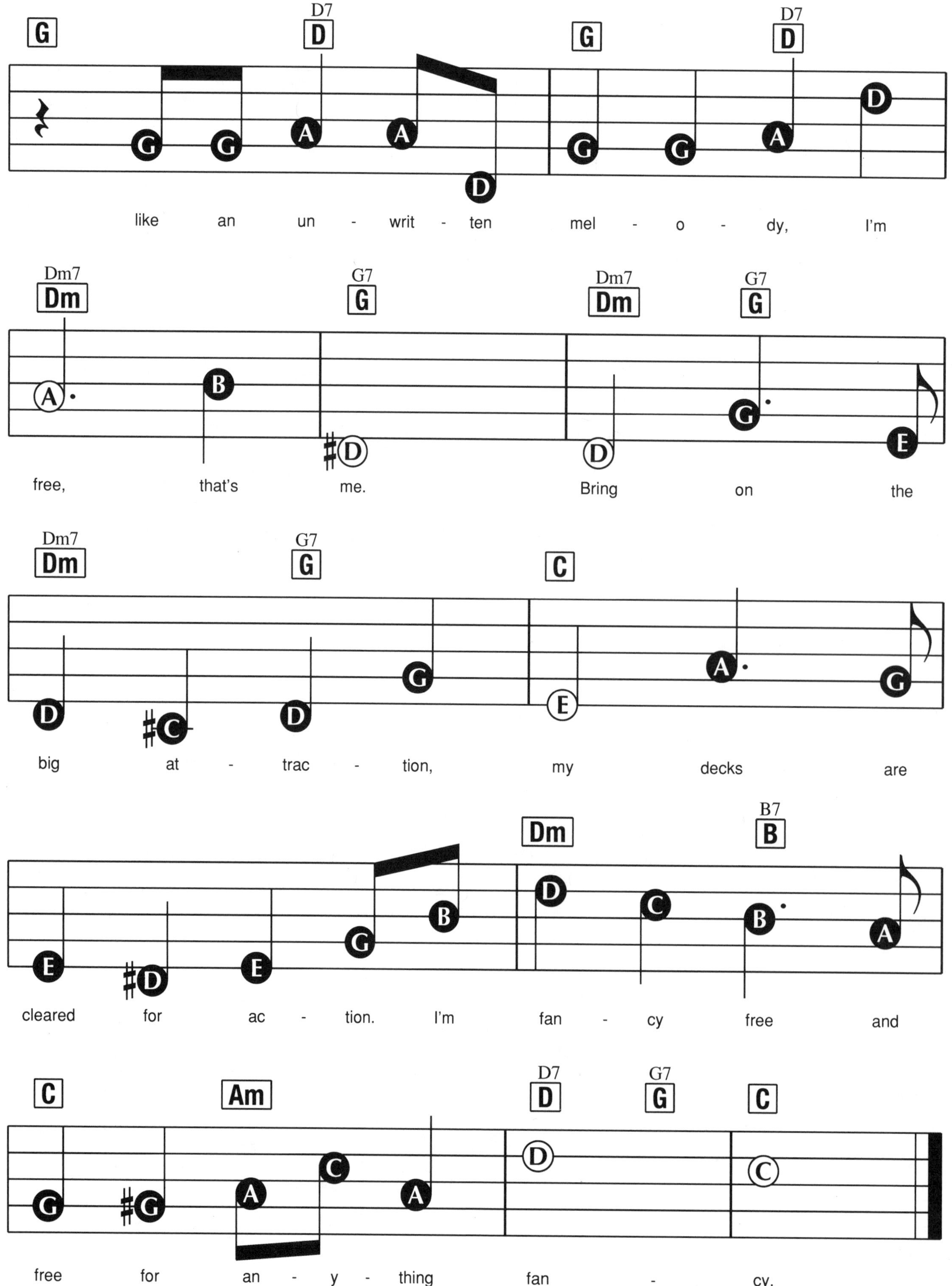
G
D7
D
G
D7
D
like an un - writ - ten mel - o - dy, I'm
Dm7
Dm
G7
G
Dm7
Dm
G7
G
free, that's me. Bring on the
Dm7
Dm
G7
G
C
big at - trac - tion, my decks are
Dm
B7
B
cleared for ac - tion. I'm fan - cy free and
C
Am
D7
D
G7
G
C
free for an - y - thing fan - cy.

Play A Simple Melody

Registration 1
Rhythm: Swing

Words and Music by
Irving Berlin

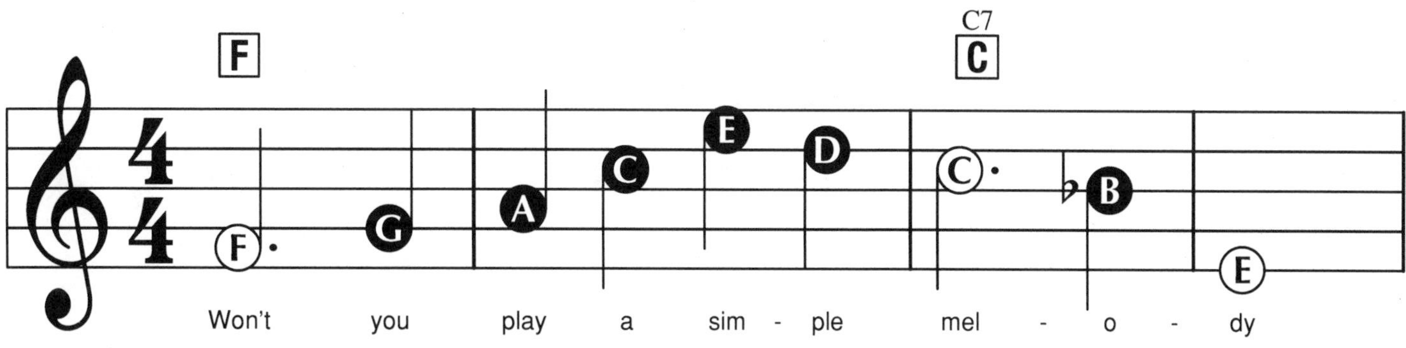

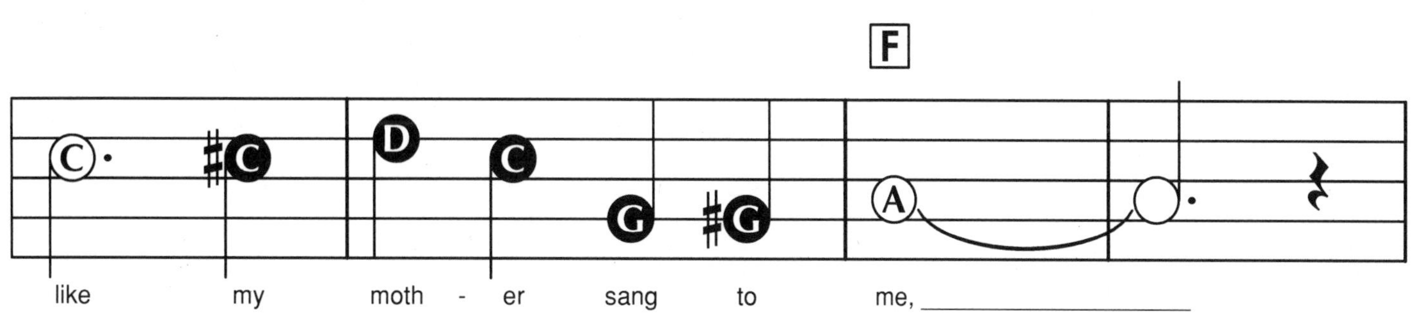

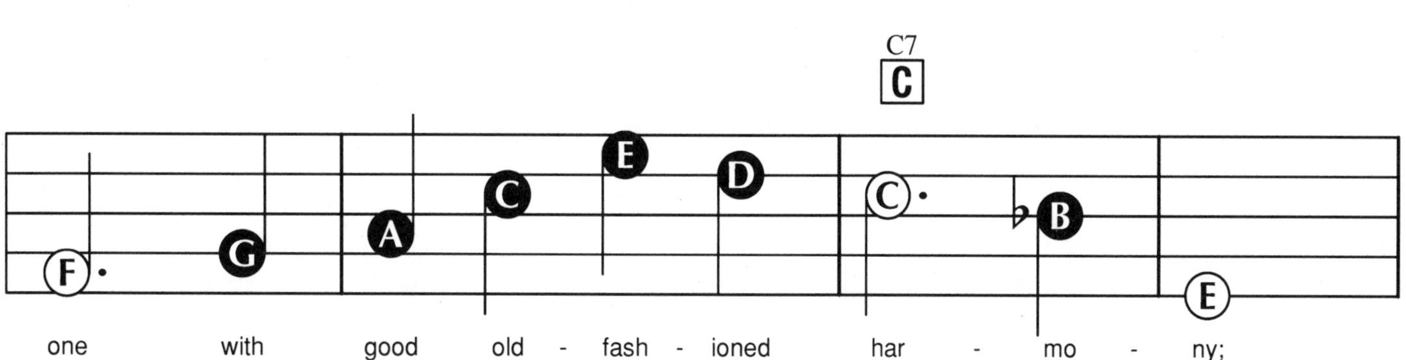

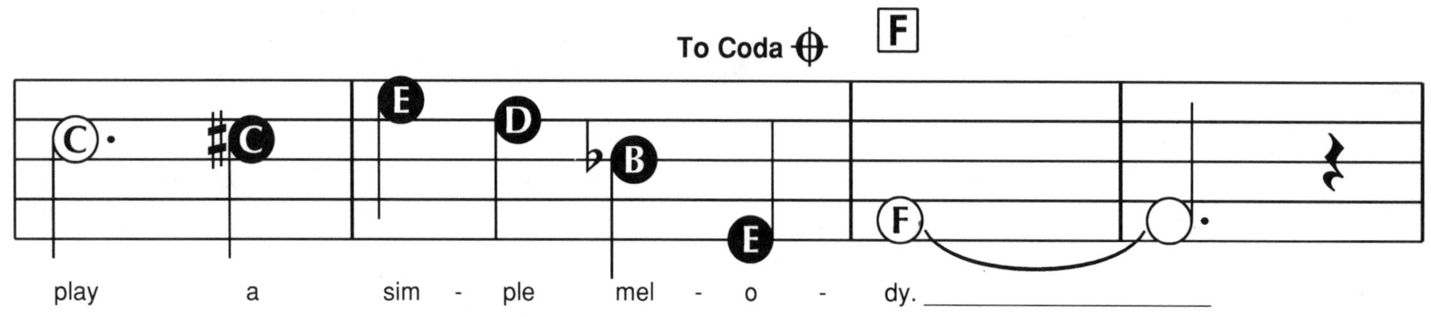
To Coda
F
C
C
E
D
B
E
F
play a sim - ple mel - o - dy.

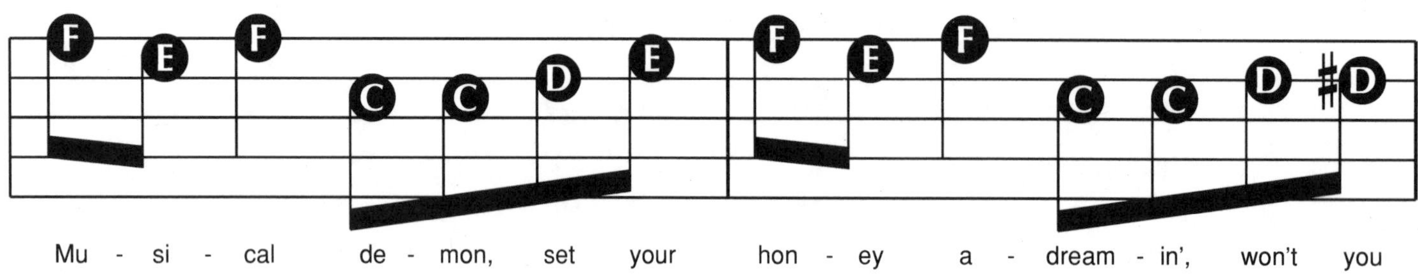
F
E
F
C
C
D
E
F
E
F
C
C
D
D
Mu - si - cal de - mon, set your hon - ey a - dream - in', won't you

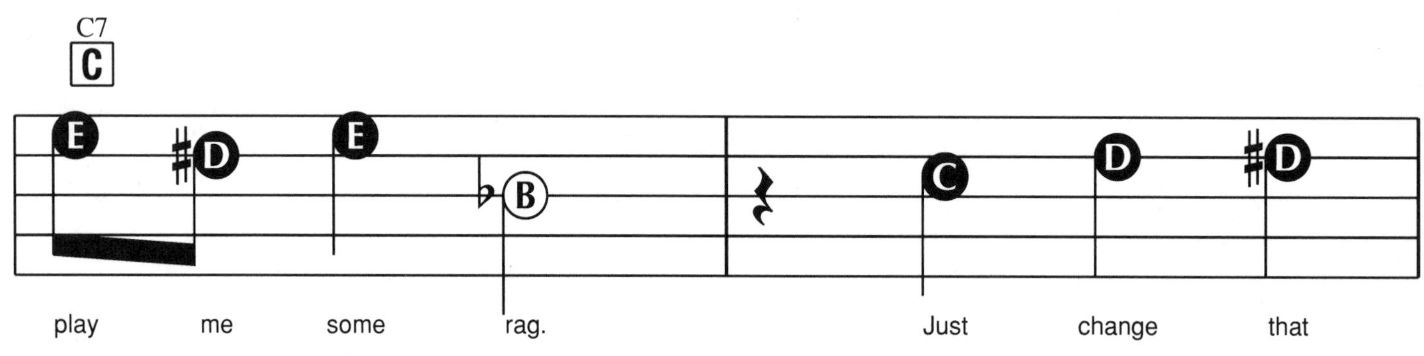
C7
C
E
D
E
B
C
D
D
play me some rag. Just change that

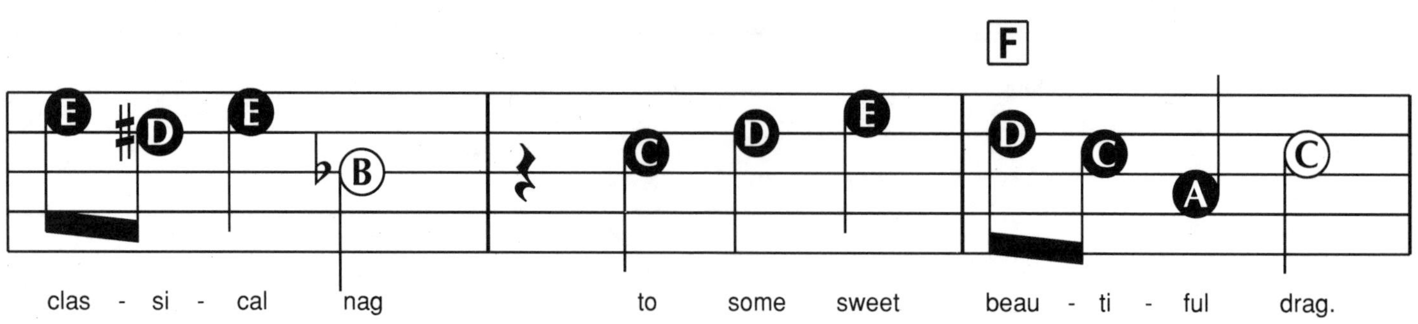
F
E
D
E
B
C
D
E
D
C
A
C
clas - si - cal nag to some sweet beau - ti - ful drag.

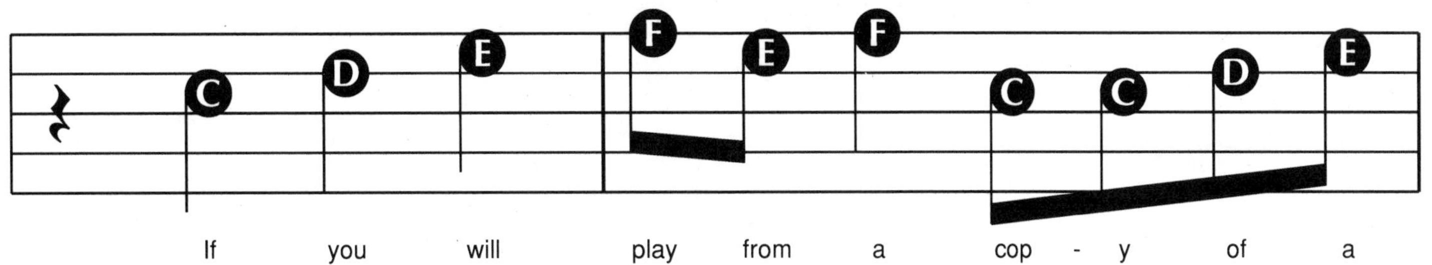
C D E F E F C C D E
If you will play from a cop - y of a

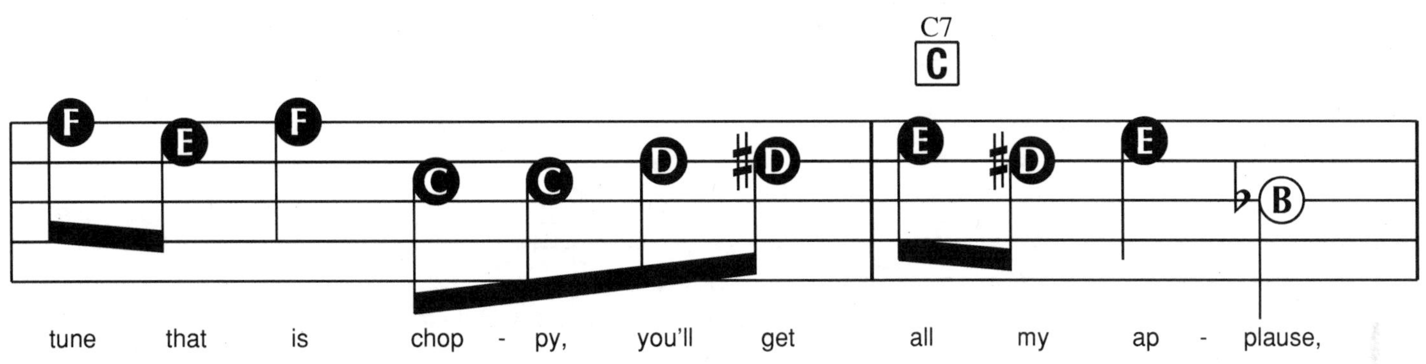
C7
C
F E F C C D ♯D E ♯D E ♭B
tune that is chop - py, you'll get all my ap - plause,

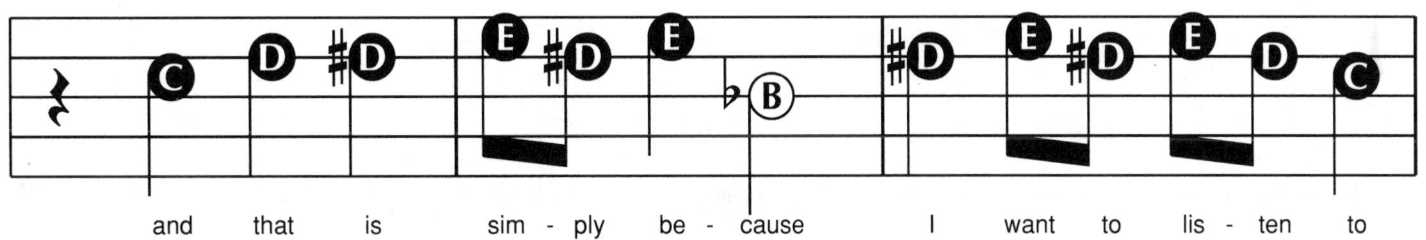
C D ♯D E ♯D E ♭B ♯D E ♯D E D C
and that is sim - ply be - cause I want to lis - ten to

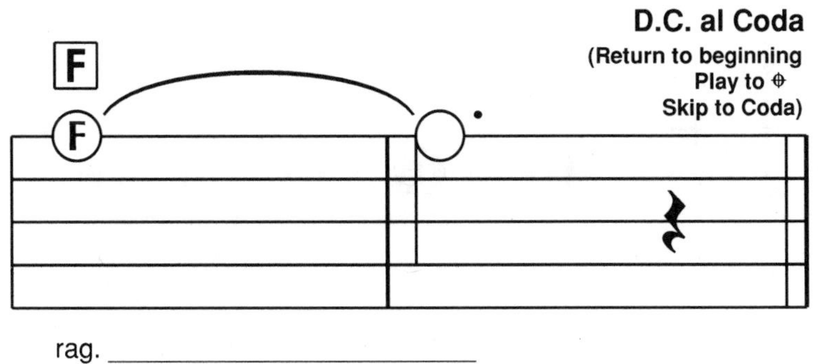
F
D.C. al Coda
(Return to beginning
Play to ⊕
Skip to Coda)
F
rag. ____________

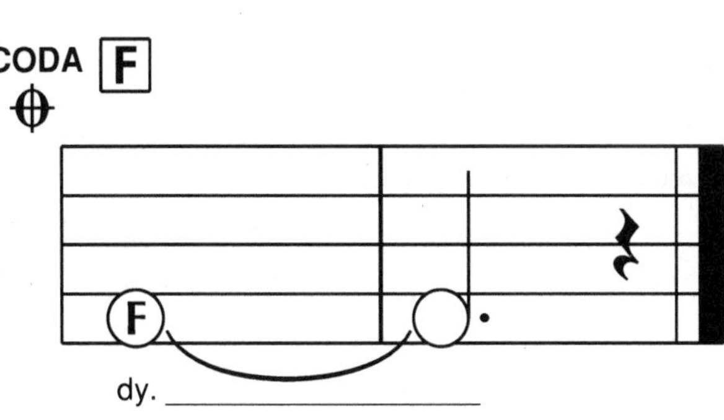
CODA F
⊕
F
dy. ____________

Plenty To Be Thankful For

Registration 4
Rhythm: Swing

Words and Music by
Irving Berlin

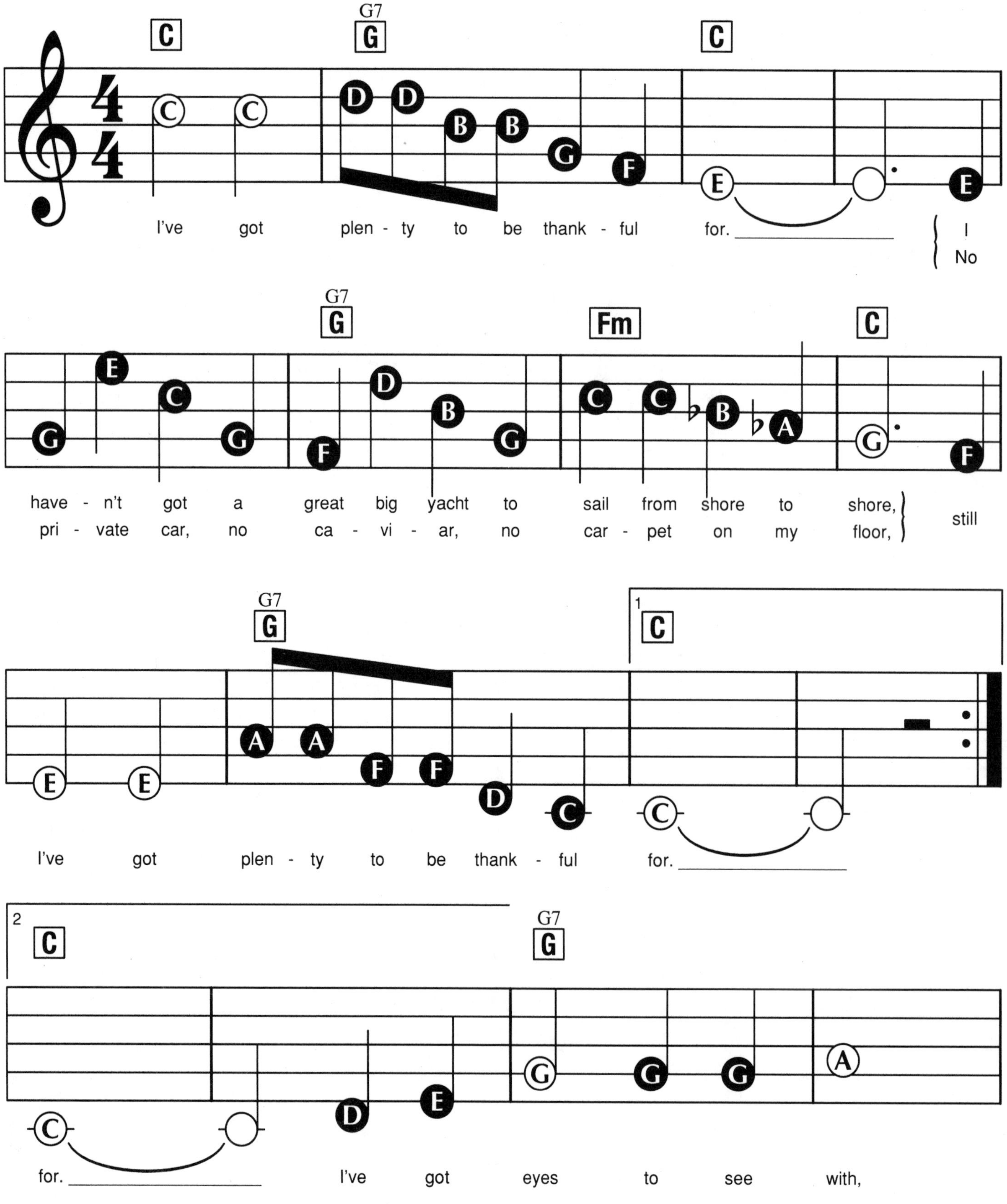
C
G7
G
C
I've got plen - ty to be thank - ful for.
I
No
G7
G
Fm
C
have - n't got a great big yacht to sail from shore to shore,
pri - vate car, no ca - vi - ar, no car - pet on my floor,
still
G7
G
1
C
I've got plen - ty to be thank - ful for.
2
C
G7
G
for. I've got eyes to see with,

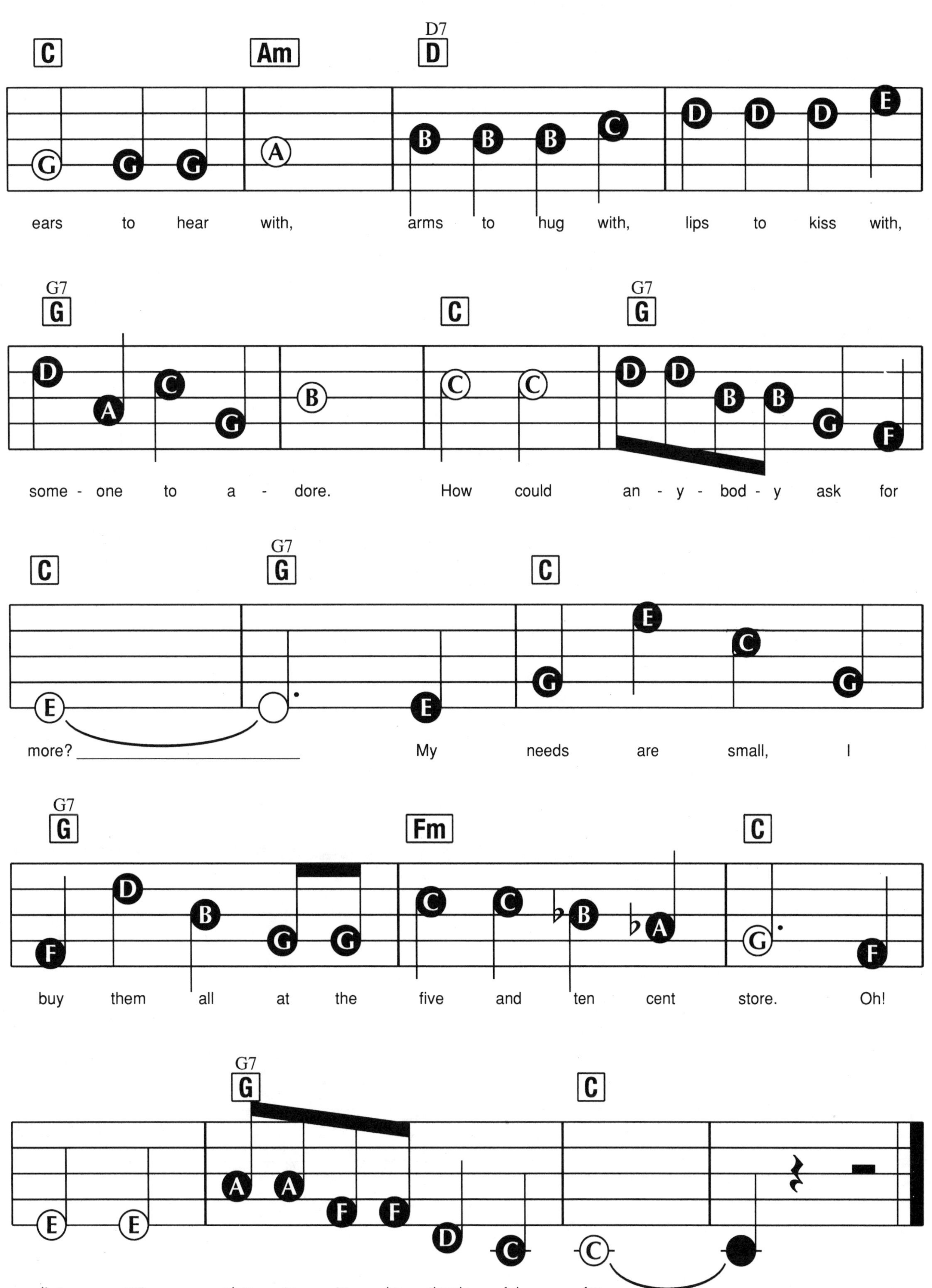
C
Am
D7
D
ears to hear with, arms to hug with, lips to kiss with,
G7
G
C
G7
G
some - one to a - dore. How could an - y - bod - y ask for
C
G7
G
C
more? My needs are small, I
G7
G
Fm
C
buy them all at the five and ten cent store. Oh!
G7
G
C
I've got plen - ty to be thank - ful for.

A Pretty Girl Is Like A Melody

Registration 8
Rhythm: Fox Trot or Ballad

Words and Music by
Irving Berlin

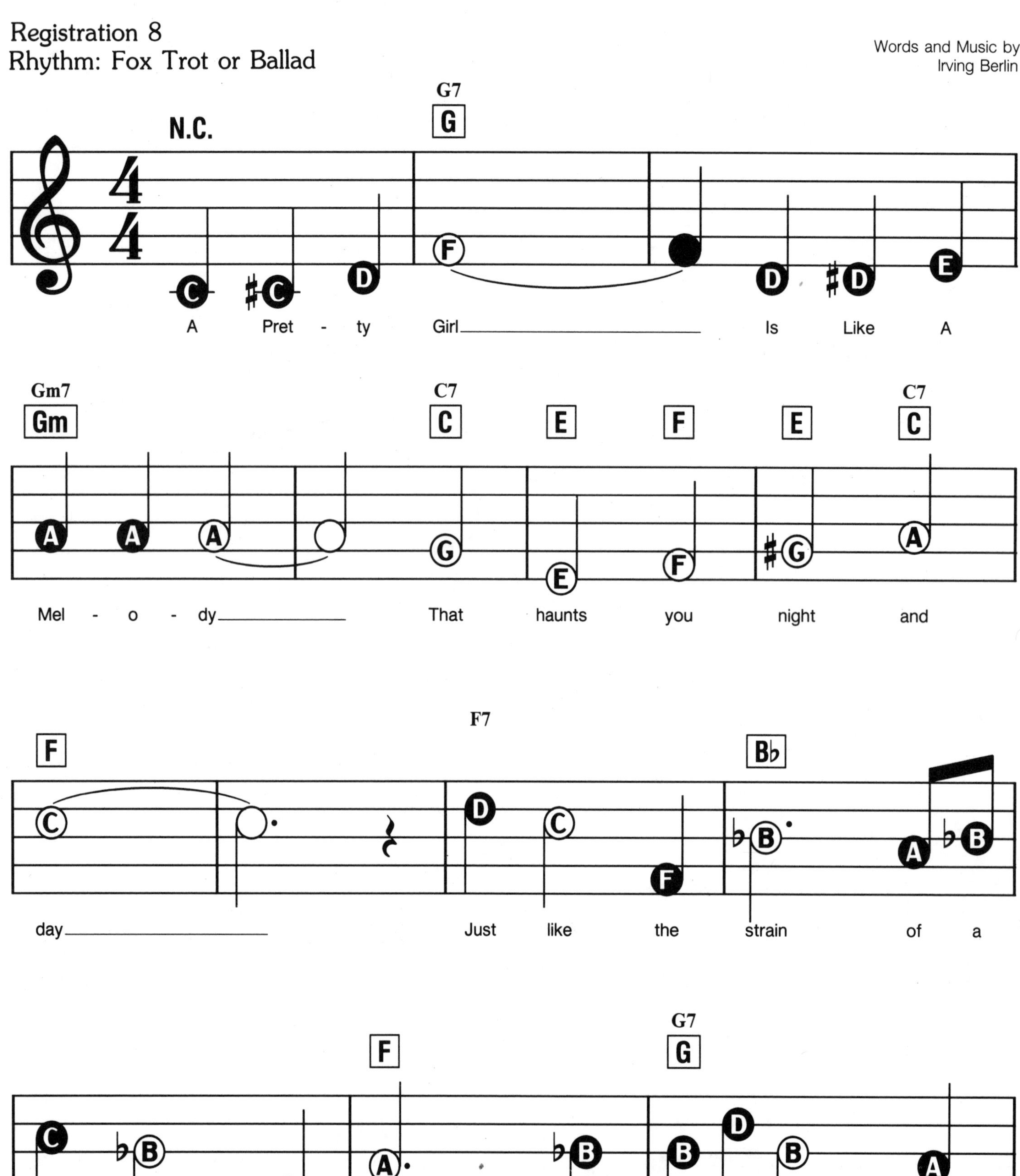

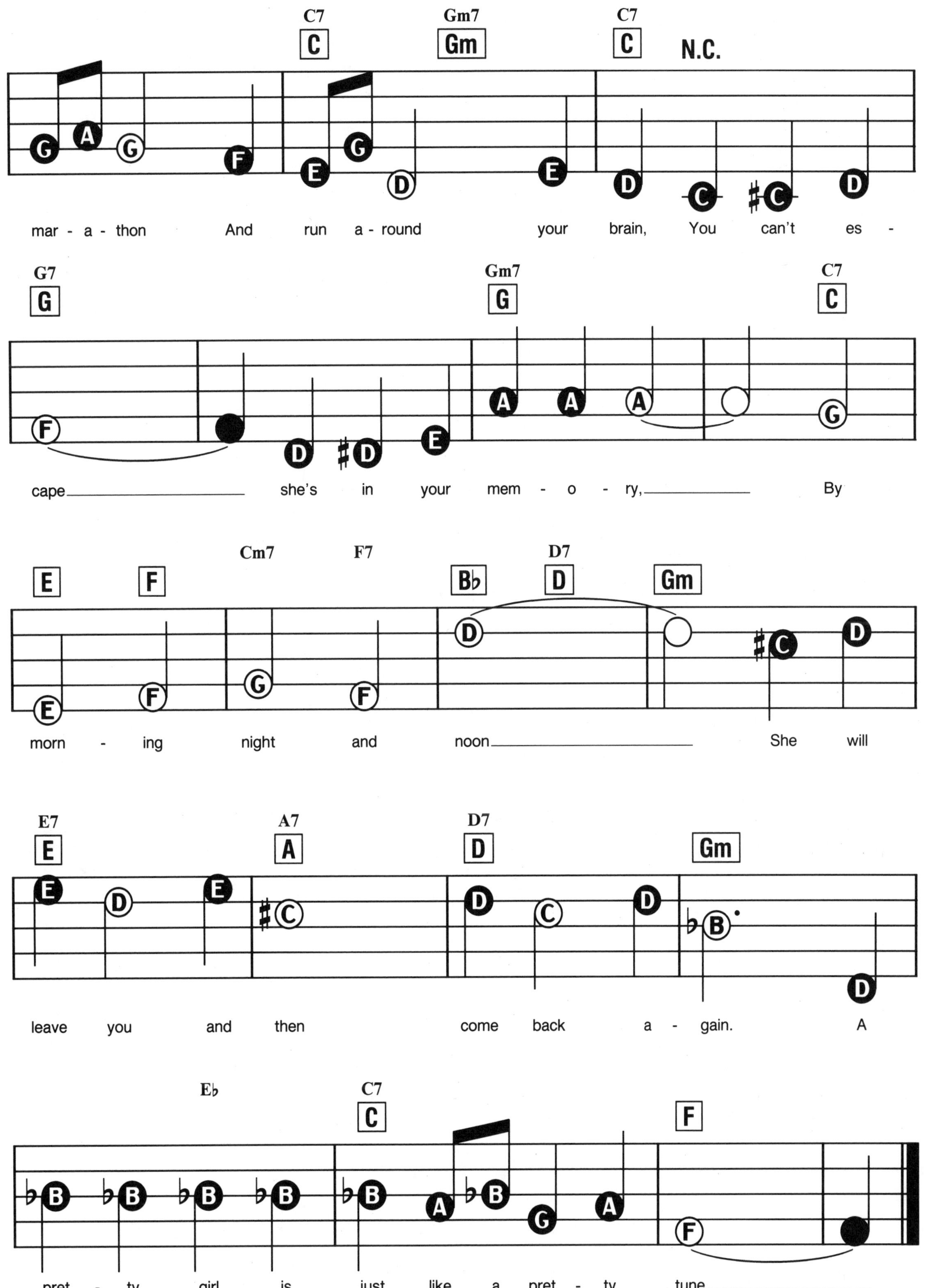
C7 C Gm7 Gm C7 C N.C.
G A G F E G D E D C ♯C D
mar - a - thon And run a - round your brain, You can't es -
G7 G Gm7 G C7 C
F D ♯D E A A A G
cape she's in your mem - o - ry, By
E F Cm7 F7 B♭ D7 D Gm
E F G F D ♯C D
morn - ing night and noon She will
E7 E A7 A D7 D Gm
E D E ♯C D C D ♭B D
leave you and then come back a - gain. A
E♭ C7 C F
♭B ♭B ♭B ♭B ♭B A ♭B G A F
pret - ty girl is just like a pret - ty tune.

Puttin' On The Ritz

Registration 7
Rhythm: Swing

Words and Music by
Irving Berlin

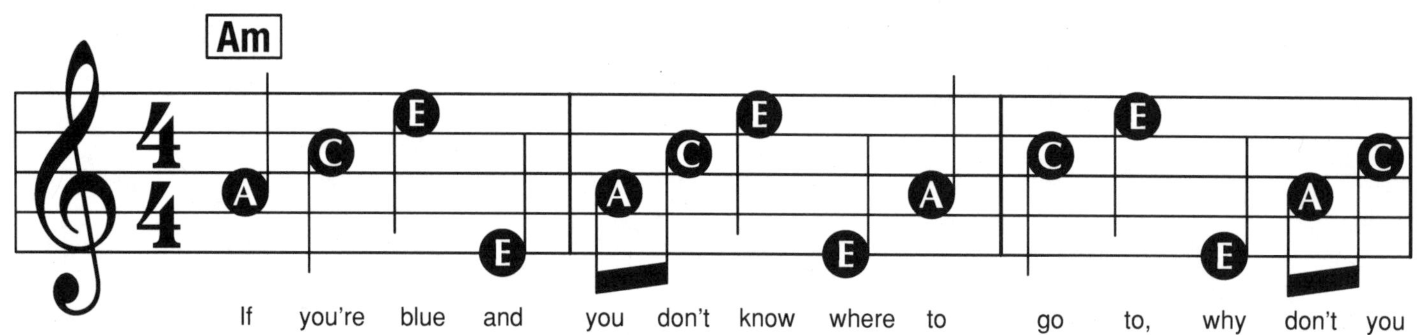

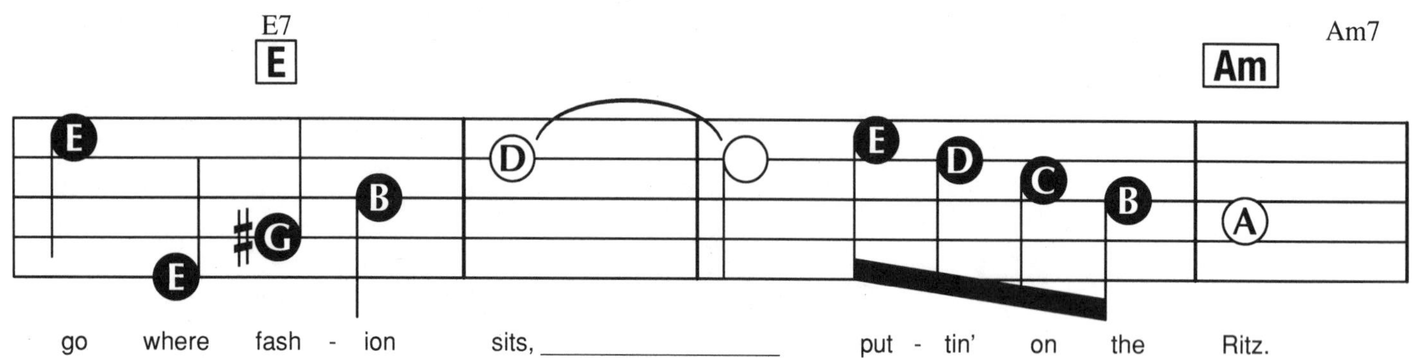

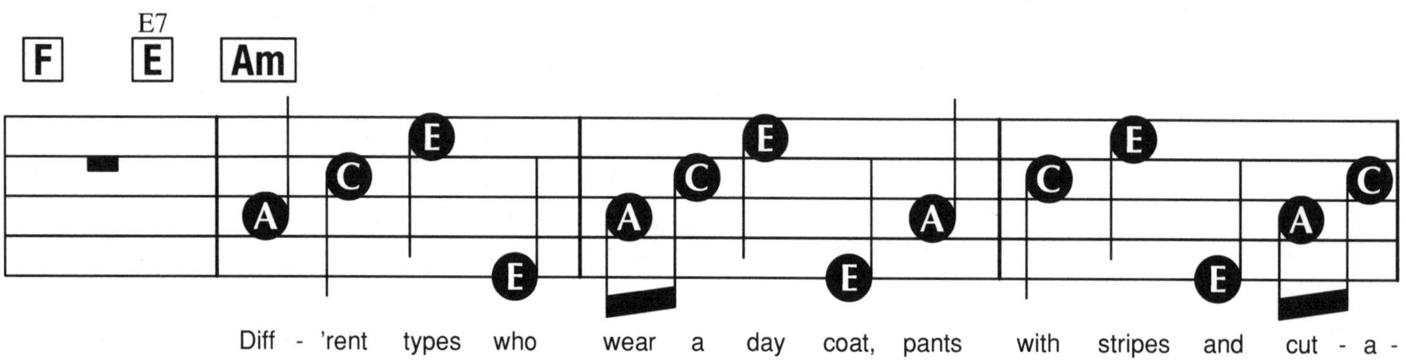

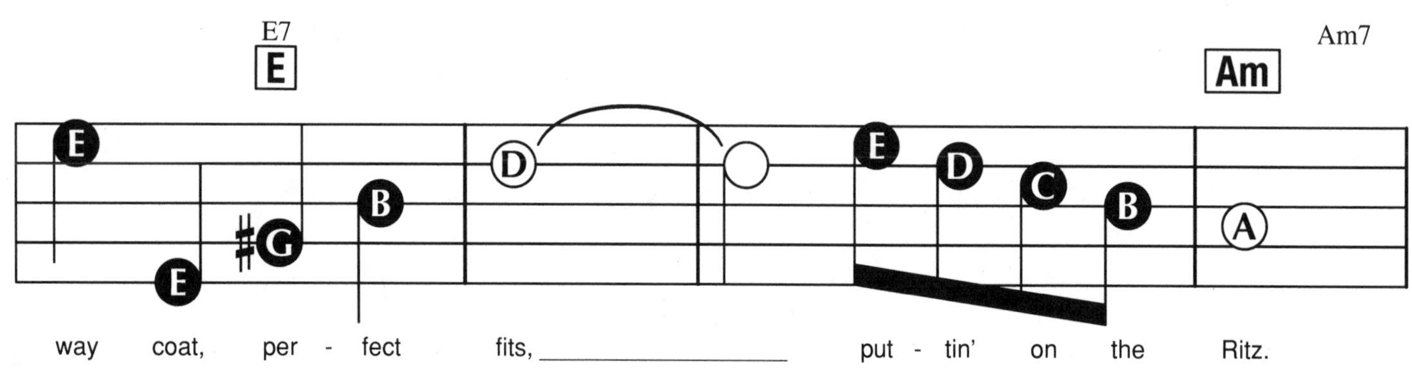

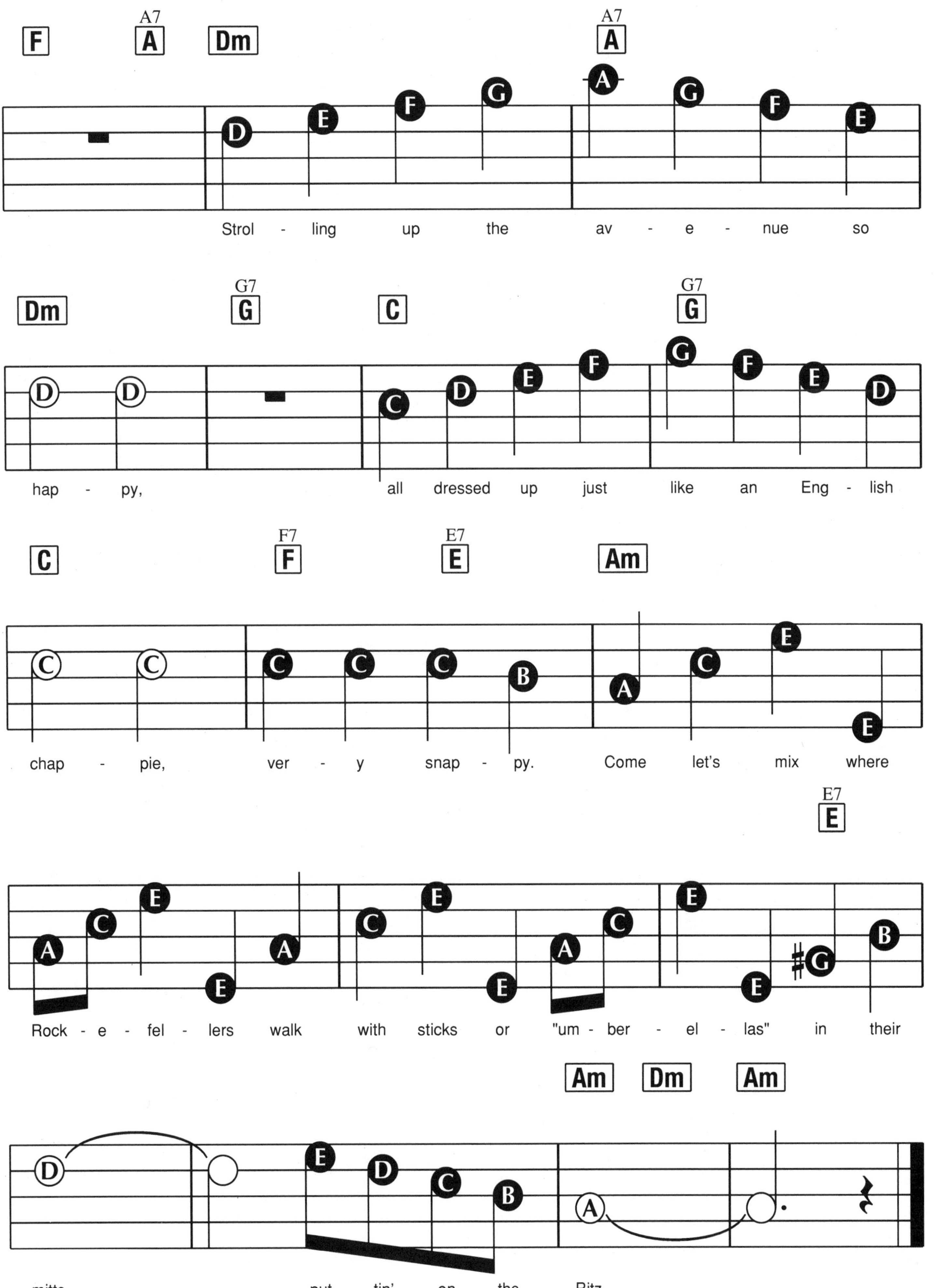
F
A7
A
Dm
A7
A
Strol - ling up the av - e - nue so
Dm
G7
G
C
G7
G
hap - py,
all dressed up just like an Eng - lish
C
F7
F
E7
E
Am
chap - pie,
ver - y snap - py.
Come let's mix where
E7
E
Rock - e - fel - lers walk
with sticks or "um - ber - el - las" in their
Am
Dm
Am
mitts,
put - tin' on the Ritz.

Remember

Registration 2
Rhythm: Waltz

Words and Music by
Irving Berlin

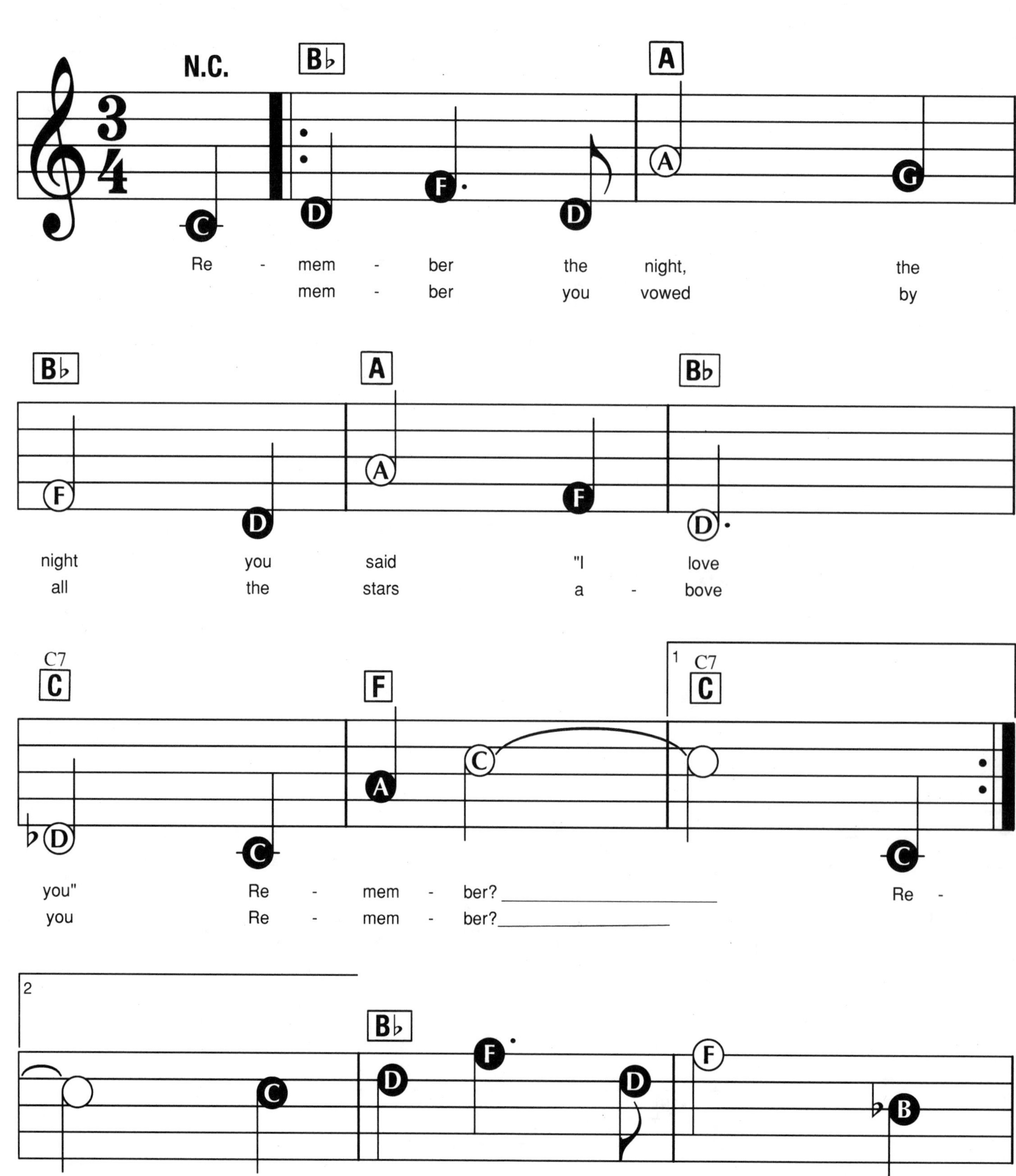

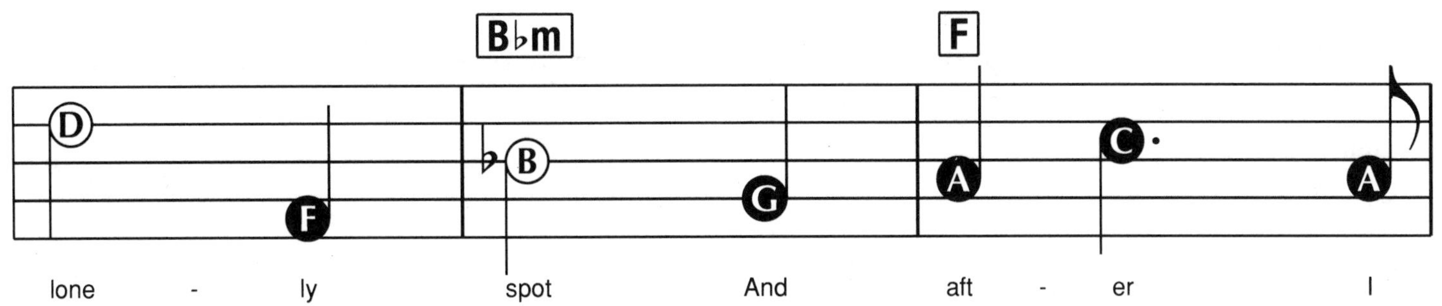
B♭m
F
D
F
B
G
A
C
A
lone - ly spot And aft - er I

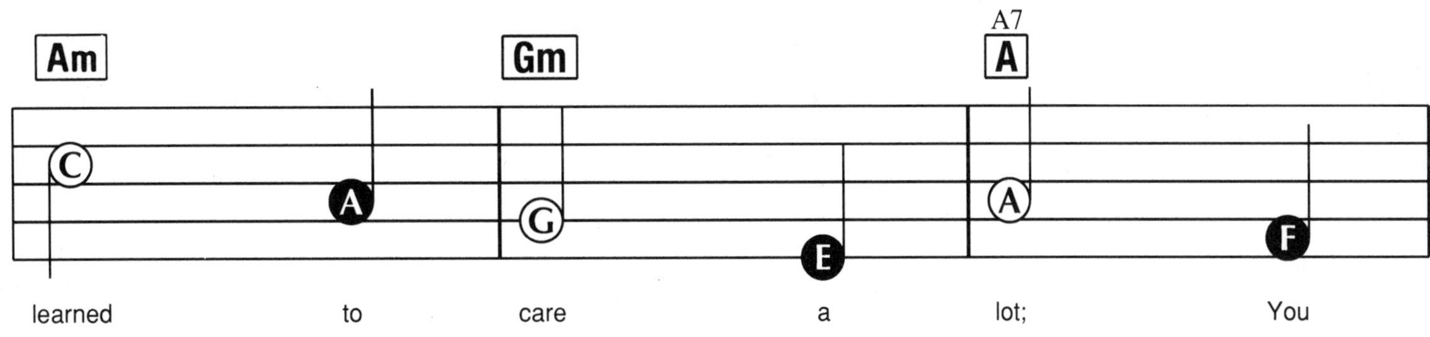
Am
Gm
A7
A
C
A
G
E
A
F
learned to care a lot; You

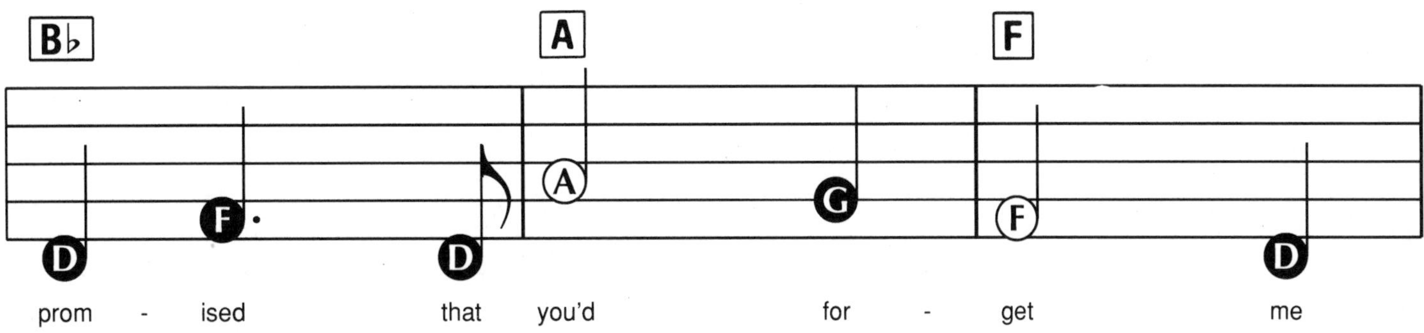
B♭
A
F
D
F
D
A
G
F
D
prom - ised that you'd for - get me

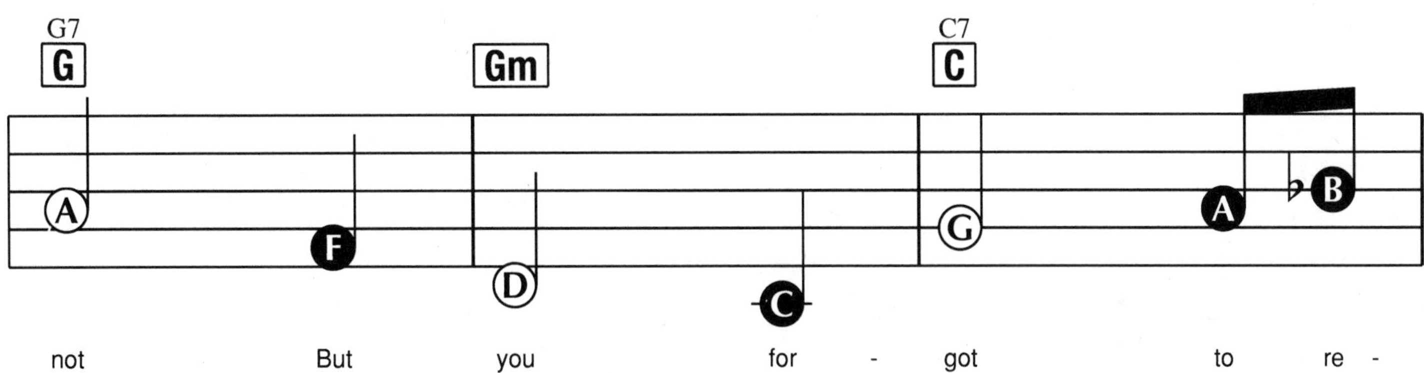
G7
G
Gm
C7
C
A
F
D
C
G
A
B
not But you for - got to re -

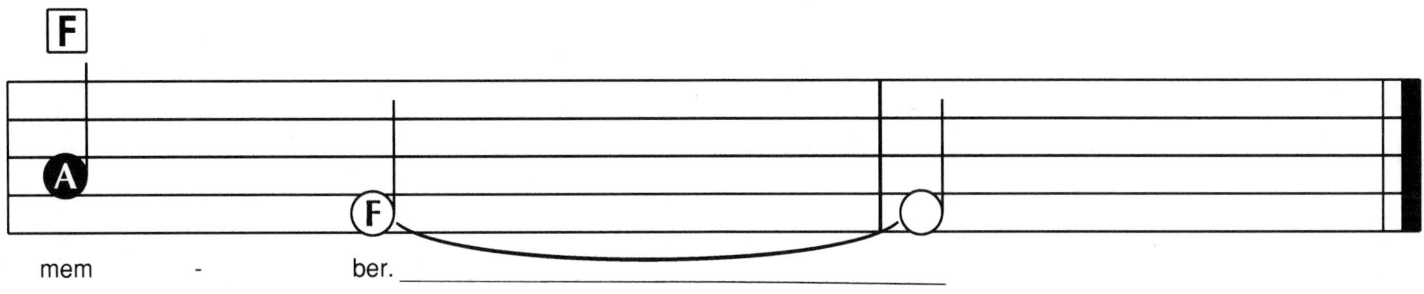
F
A
F
mem - ber.

Russian Lullaby

Registration 10
Rhythm: Waltz

Words and Music by
Irving Berlin

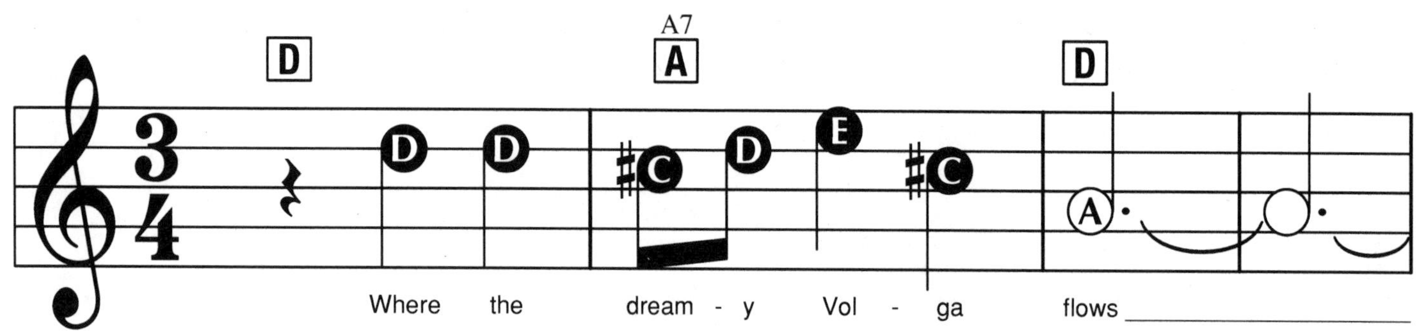

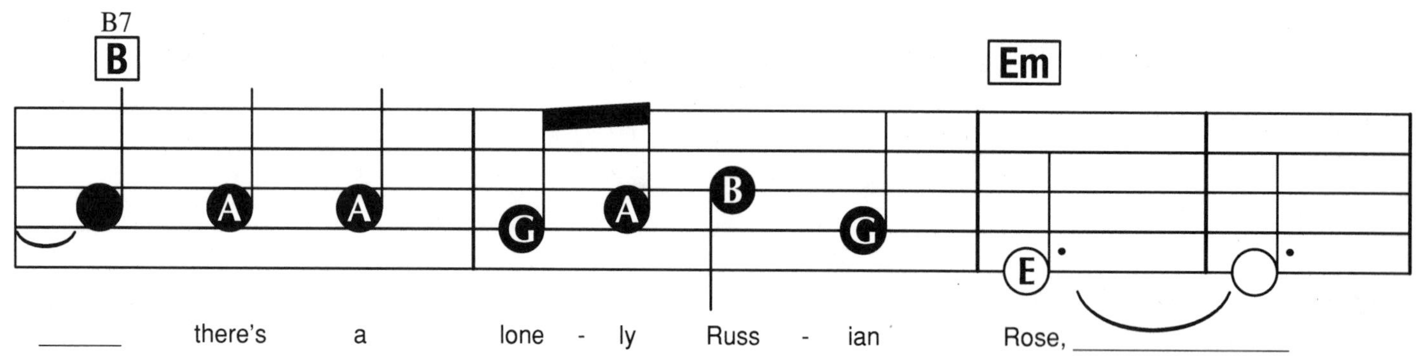

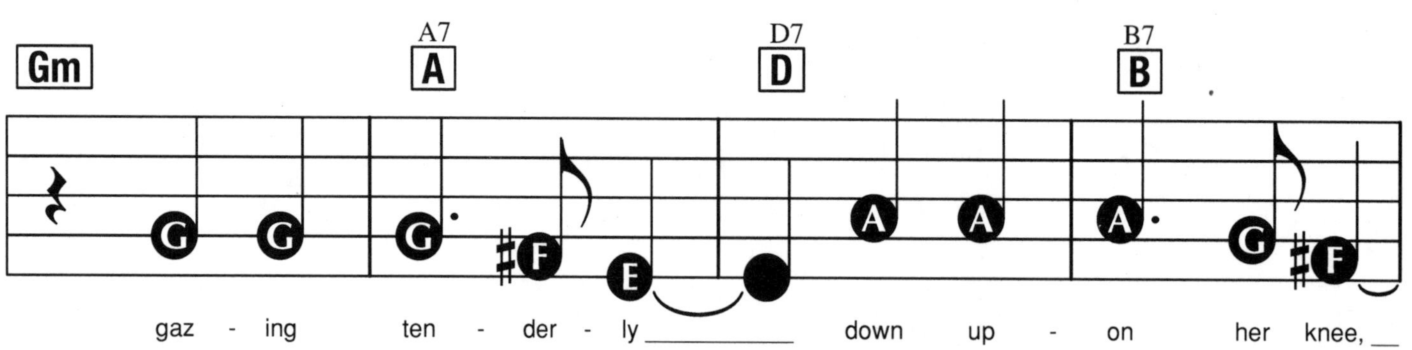

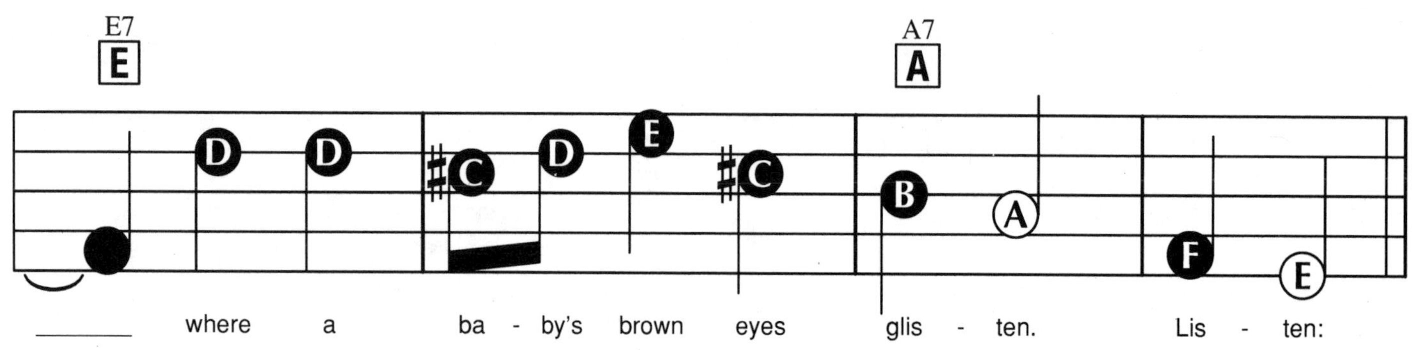

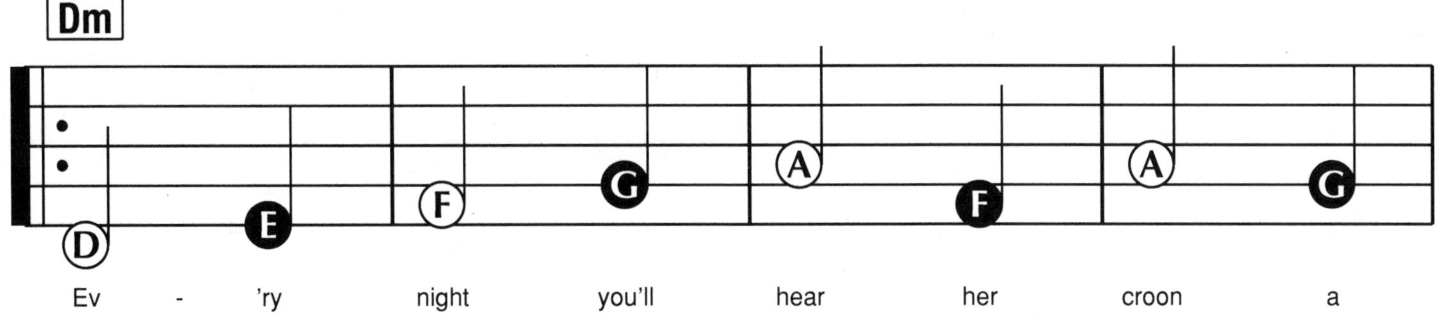
Dm
D E F G A F A G
Ev - 'ry night you'll hear her croon a

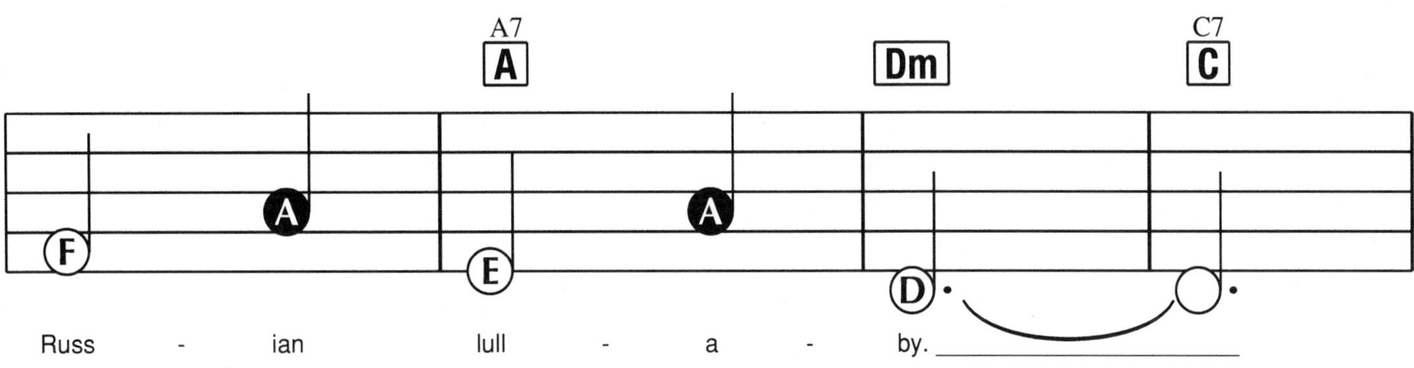
A7
A
Dm
C7
C
F A E A D
Russ - ian lull - a - by.

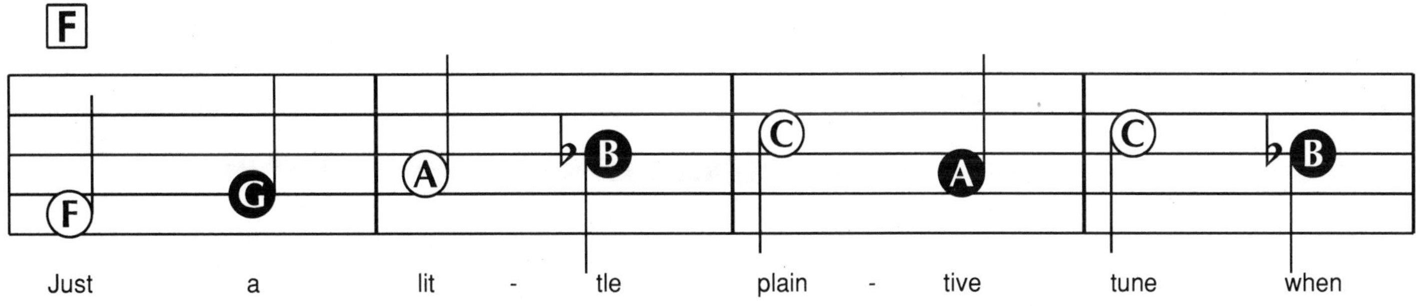
F
F G A B C A C B
Just a lit - tle plain - tive tune when

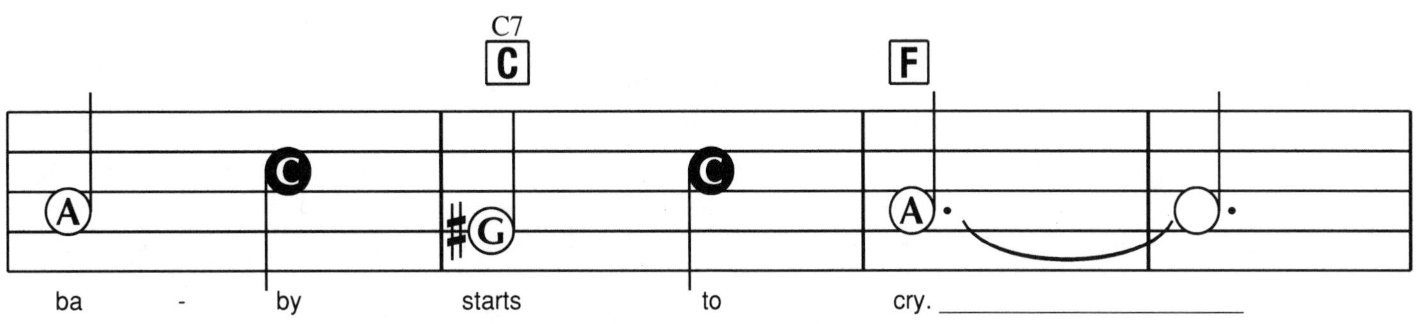
C7
C
F
A C G C A
ba - by starts to cry.

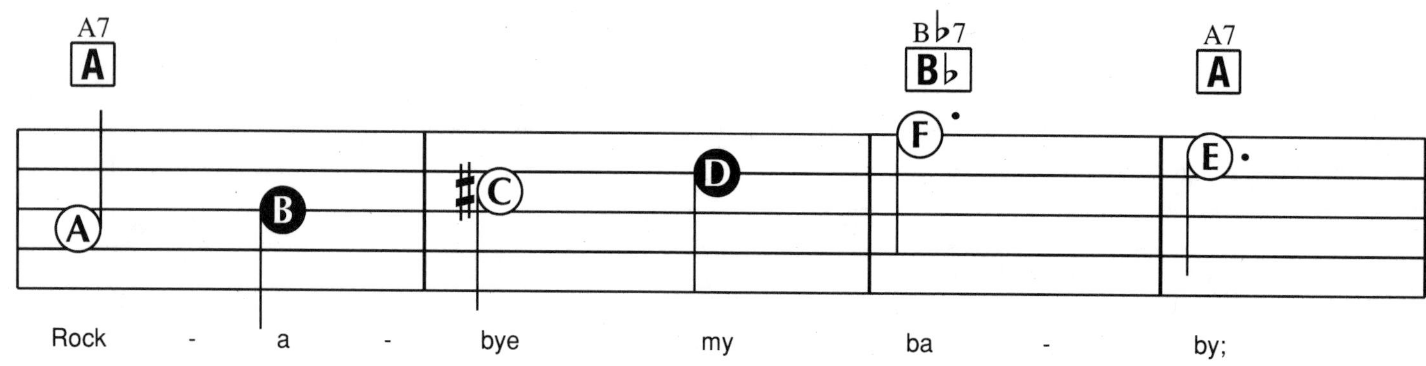
A7
A
B♭7
B♭
A7
A
A
B
♯C
D
F
E
Rock - a - bye my ba - by;

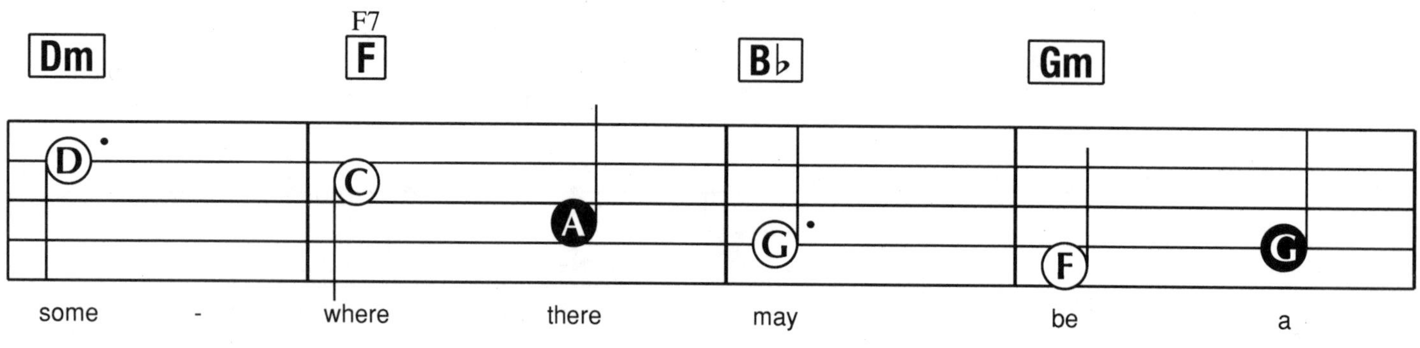
Dm
F7
F
B♭
Gm
D
C
A
G
F
G
some - where there may be a

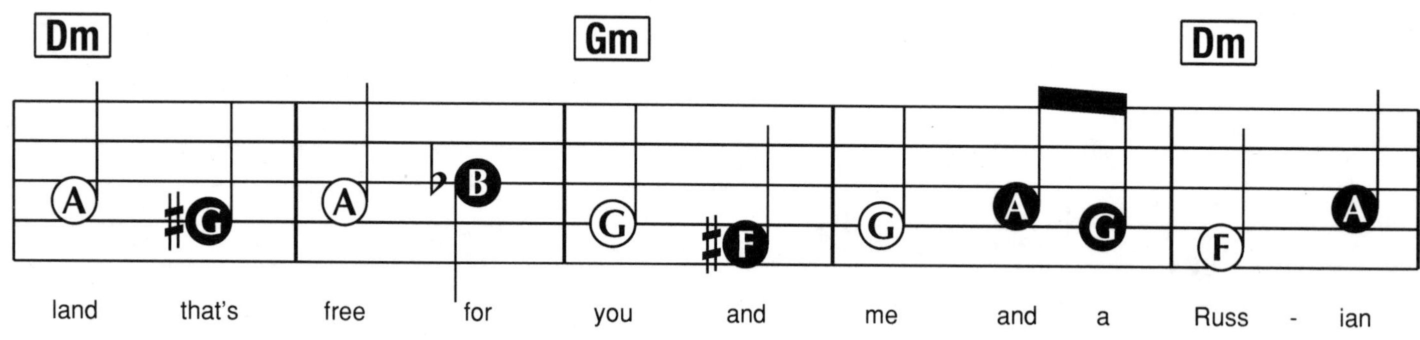
Dm
Gm
Dm
A
♯G
A
♭B
G
♯F
G
A
G
F
A
land that's free for you and me and a Russ - ian

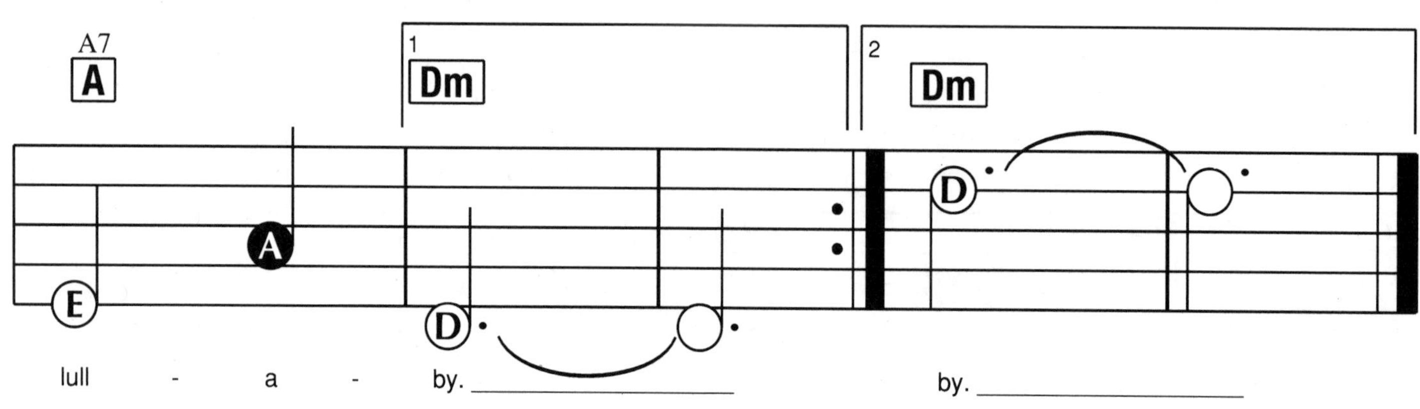
A7
A
1
Dm
2
Dm
E
A
D
D
lull - a - by.
by.

Steppin' Out With My Baby

Registration 9
Rhythm: Swing

Words and Music by
Irving Berlin

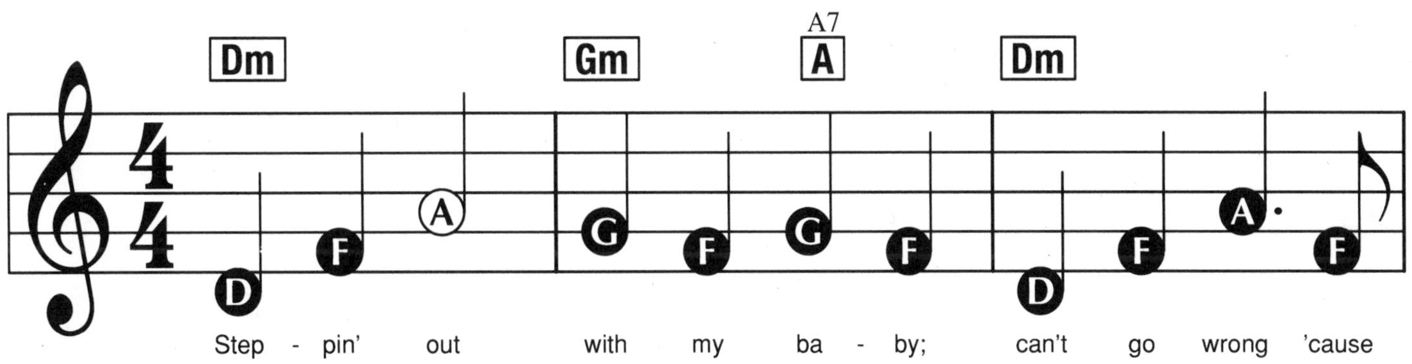

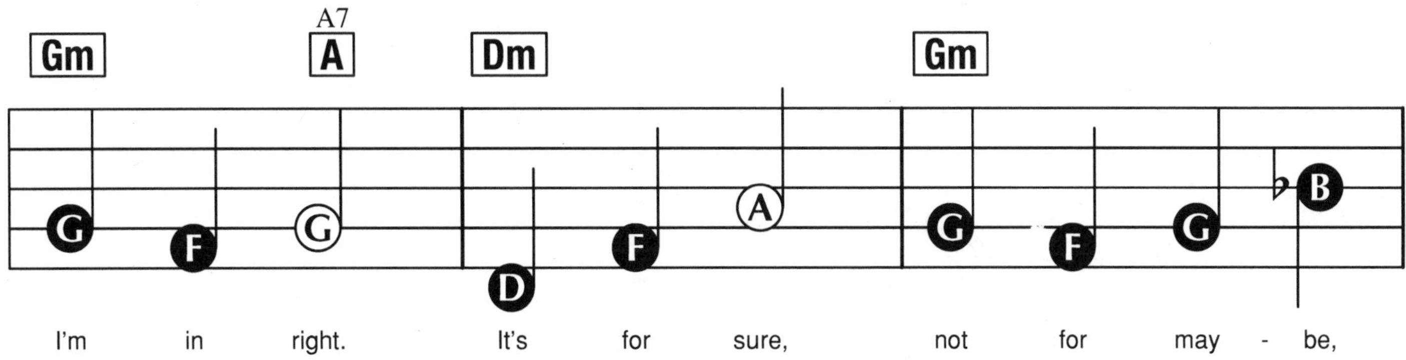

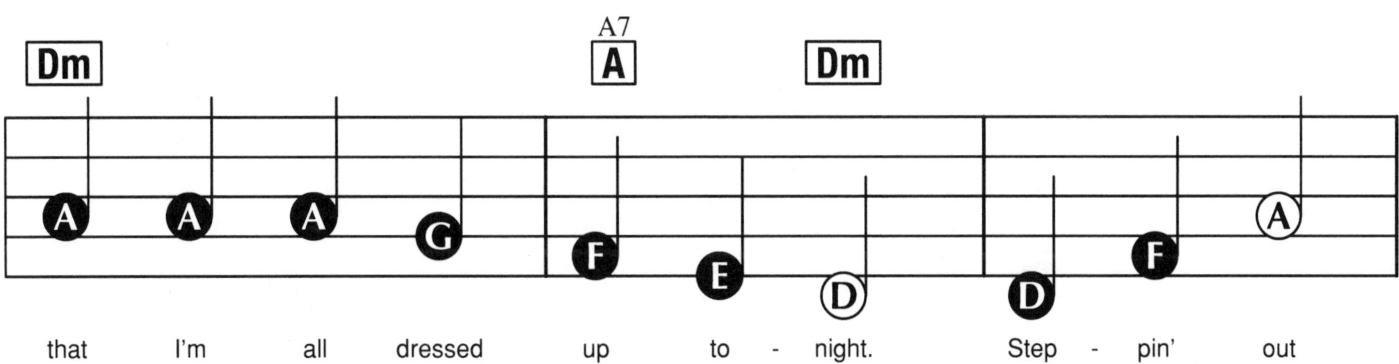

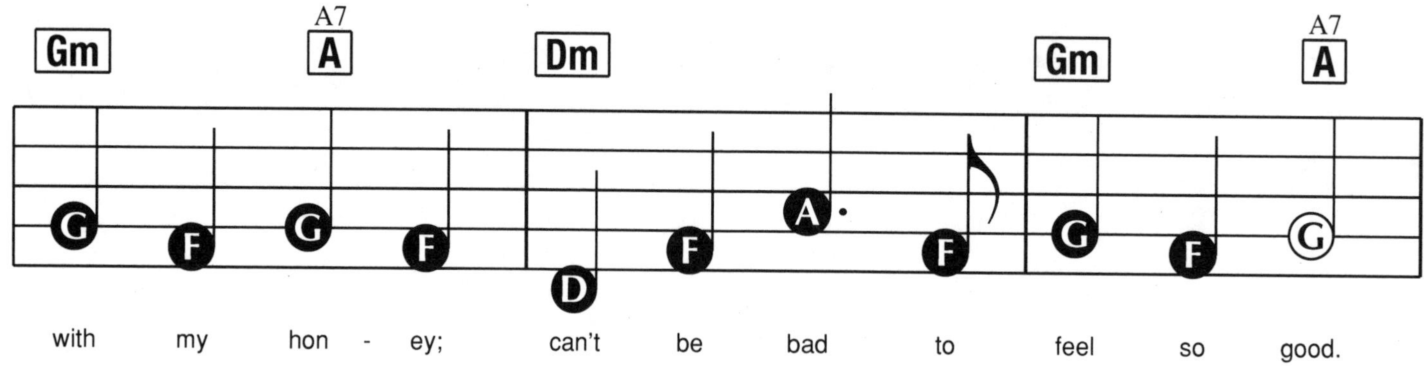

Gm
A7
A
Dm
Gm
A7
A
G F G F D F A F G F G
with my hon - ey; can't be bad to feel so good.

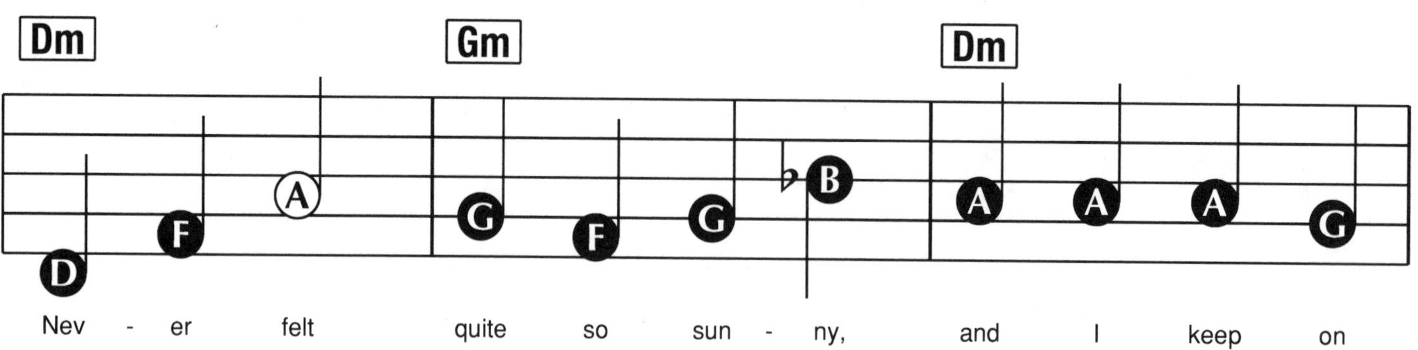

Dm
Gm
Dm
D F A G F G B A A A G
Nev - er felt quite so sun - ny, and I keep on

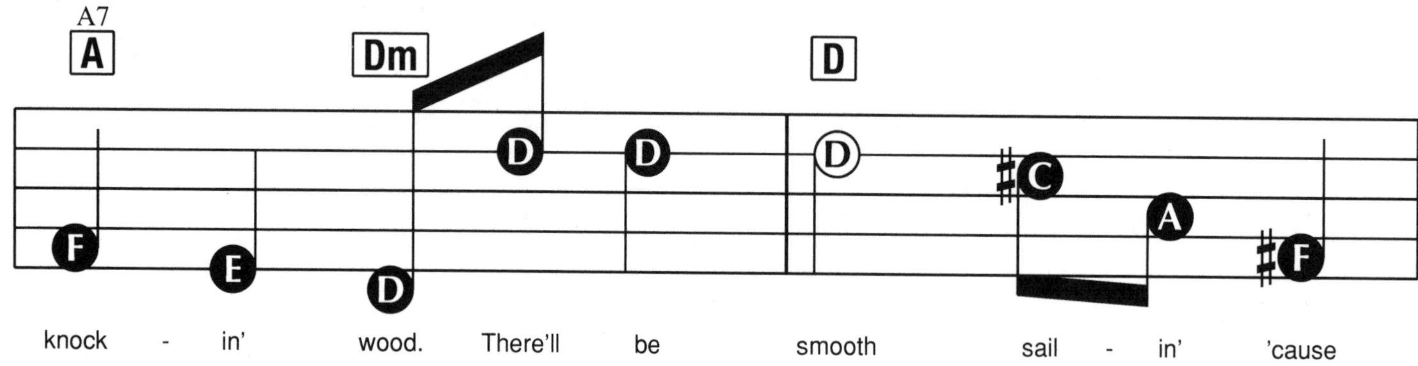

A7
A
Dm
D
F E D D D D C A F
knock - in' wood. There'll be smooth sail - in' 'cause

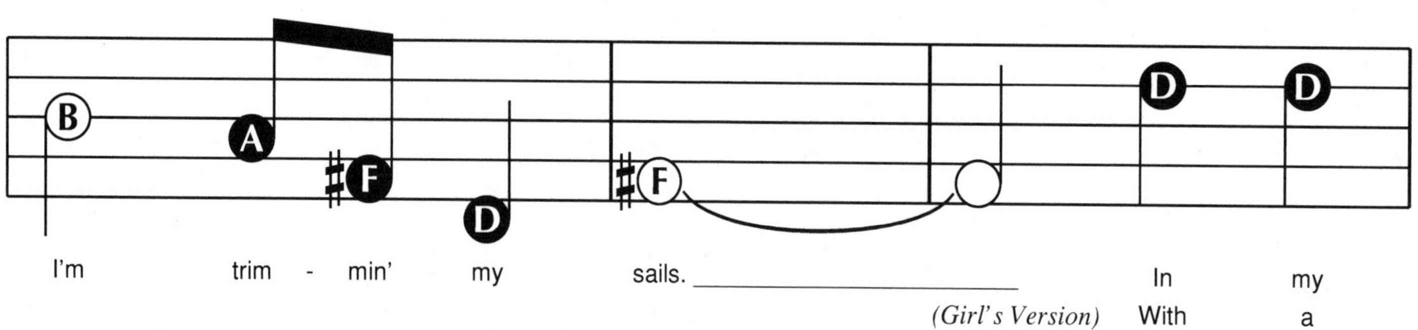

B A F D F D D
I'm trim - min' my sails. In my
(Girl's Version) With a

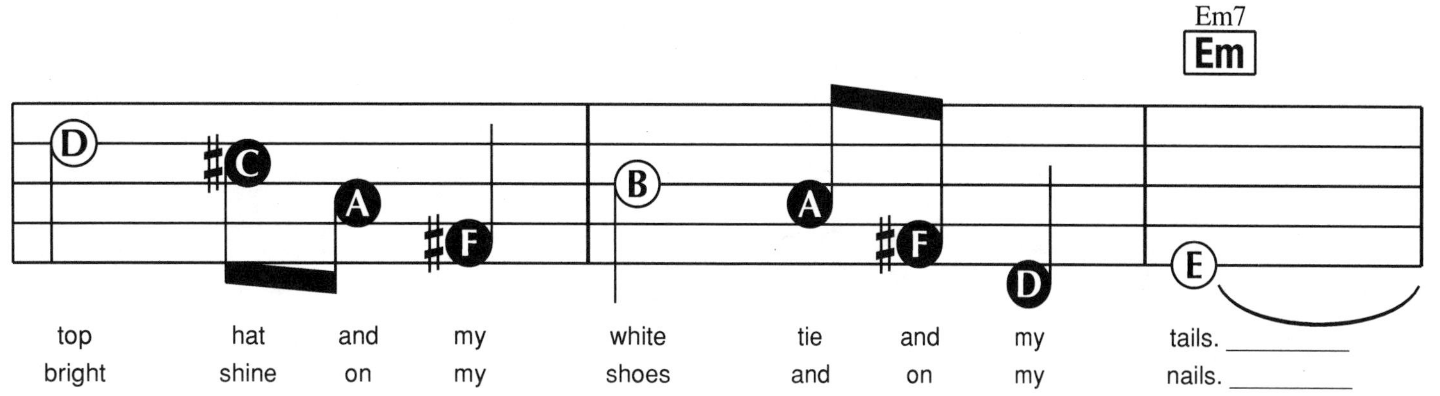
Em7
Em
D
C
A
F
B
A
F
D
E
top hat and my white tie and my tails.
bright shine on my shoes and on my nails.

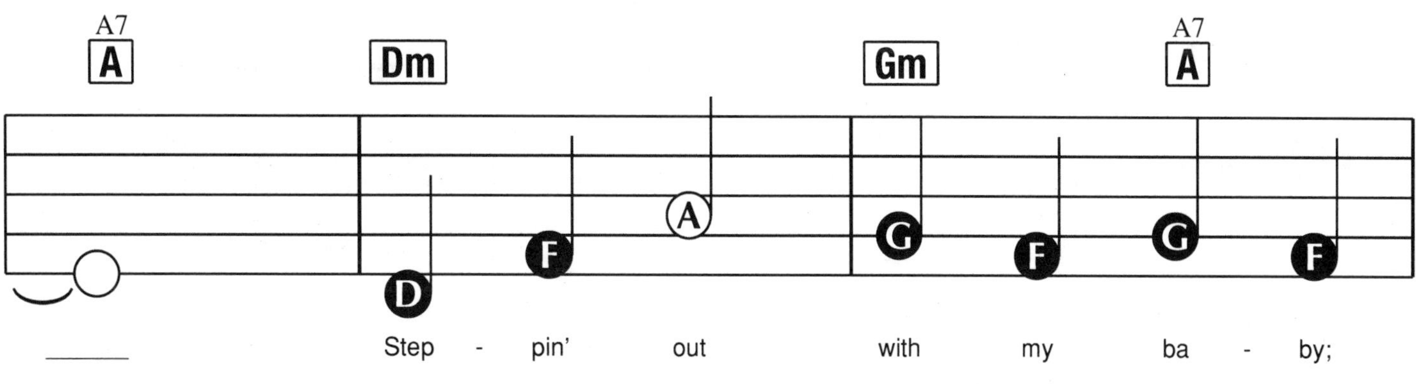
A7
A
Dm
Gm
A7
A
D
F
A
G
F
G
F
Step - pin' out with my ba - by;

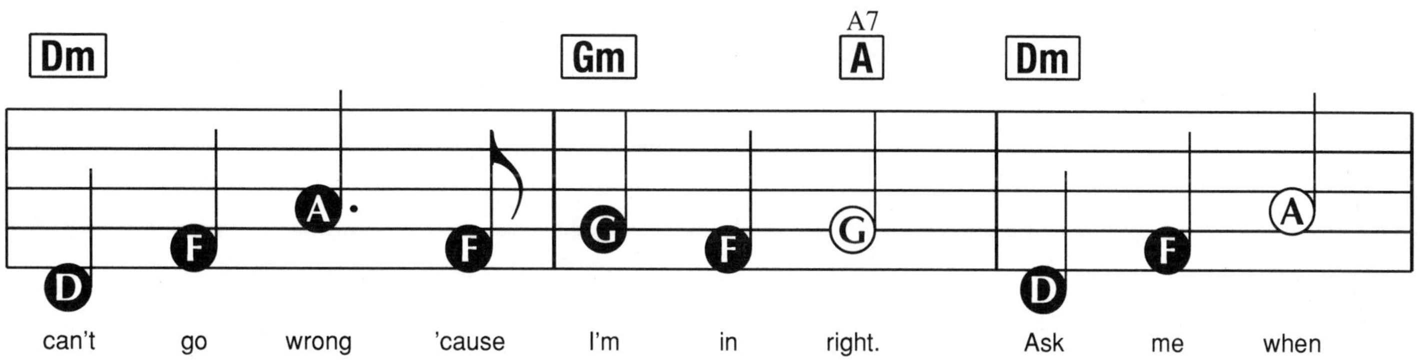
Dm
Gm
A7
A
Dm
D
F
A
F
G
F
G
D
F
A
can't go wrong 'cause I'm in right. Ask me when

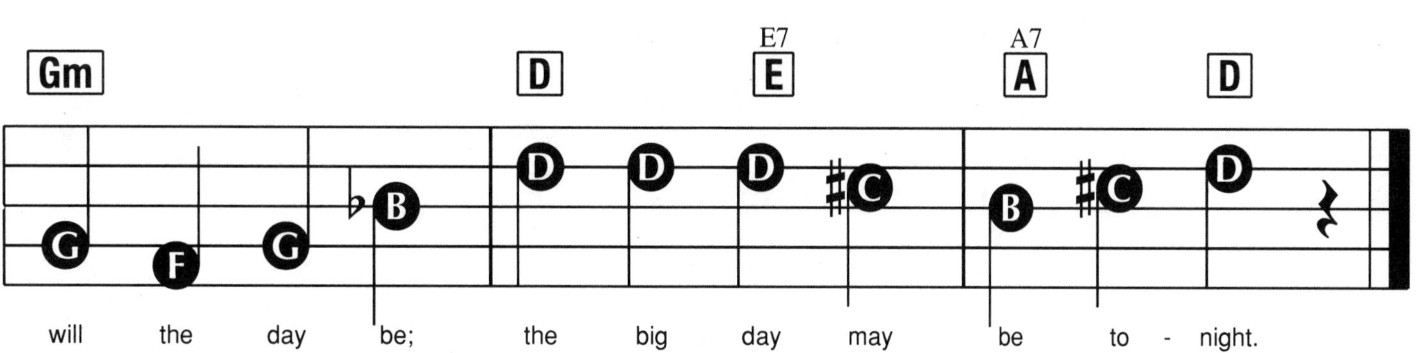
Gm
D
E7
E
A7
A
D
G
F
G
B
D
D
D
C
B
C
D
will the day be; the big day may be to - night.

Say It Isn't So

Registration 10
Rhythm: Fox Trot or Ballad

Words and Music by
Irving Berlin

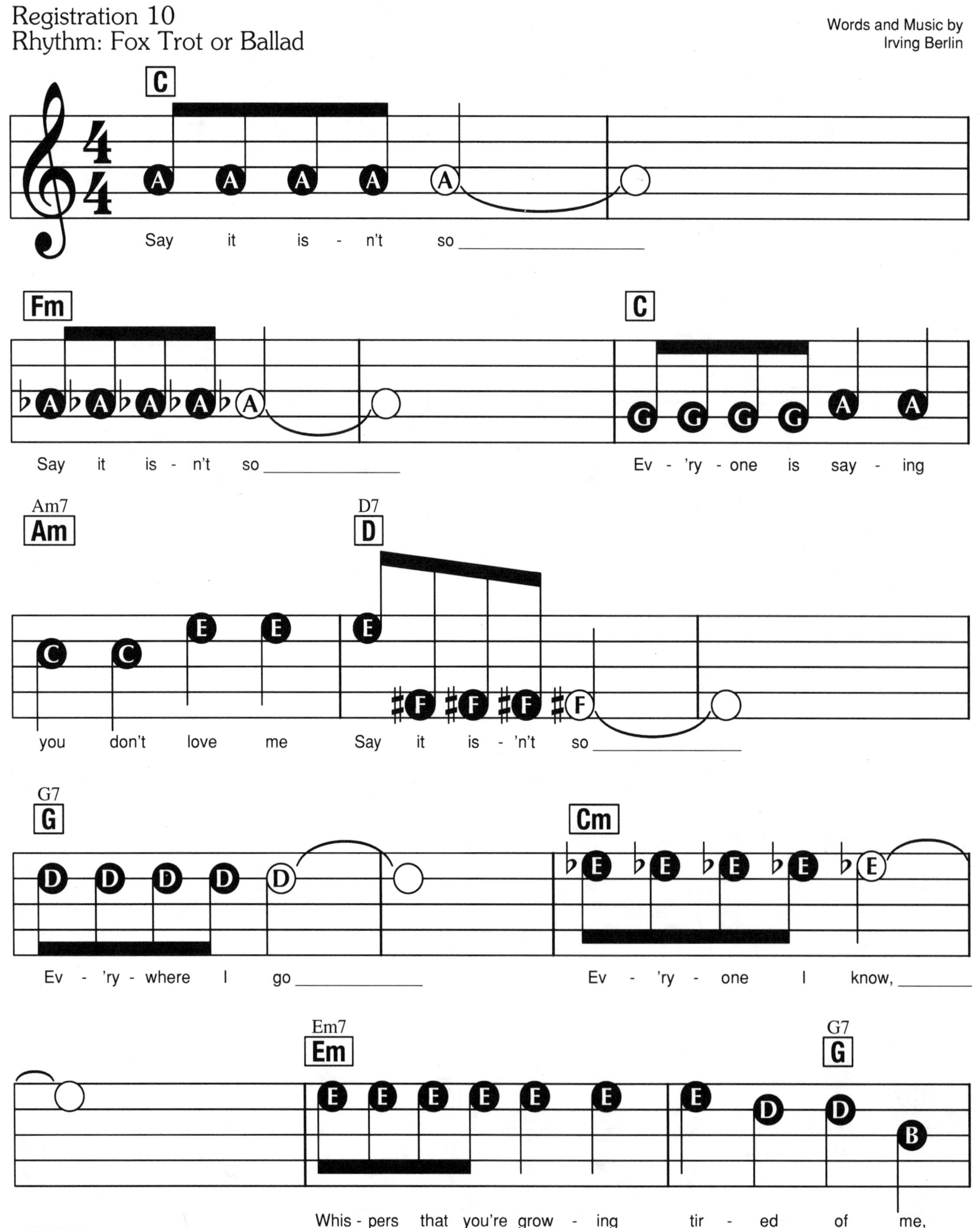

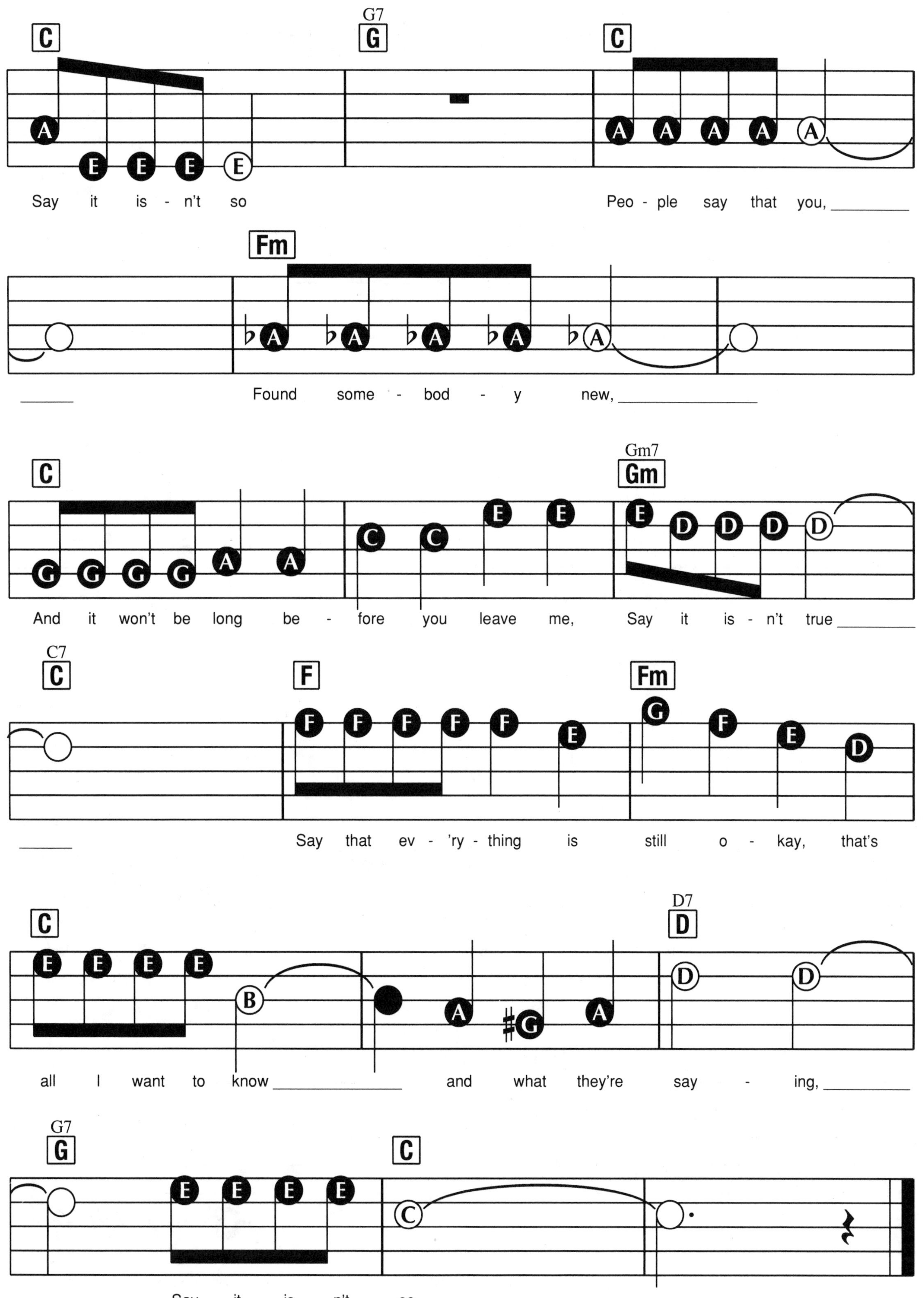
C
G7
G
C
A E E E E
A A A A A
Say it is - n't so
Peo - ple say that you,
Fm
Found some - bod - y new,
C
Gm7
Gm
G G G G A A C C E E E D D D D
And it won't be long be - fore you leave me,
Say it is - n't true
C7
C
F
Fm
F F F F F E G F E D
Say that ev - 'ry - thing is still o - kay, that's
C
D7
D
E E E E B A G A D D
all I want to know
and what they're say - ing,
G7
G
C
E E E E C
Say it is - n't so.

Say It With Music

Registration 2
Rhythm: Swing

Words and Music by Irving Berlin

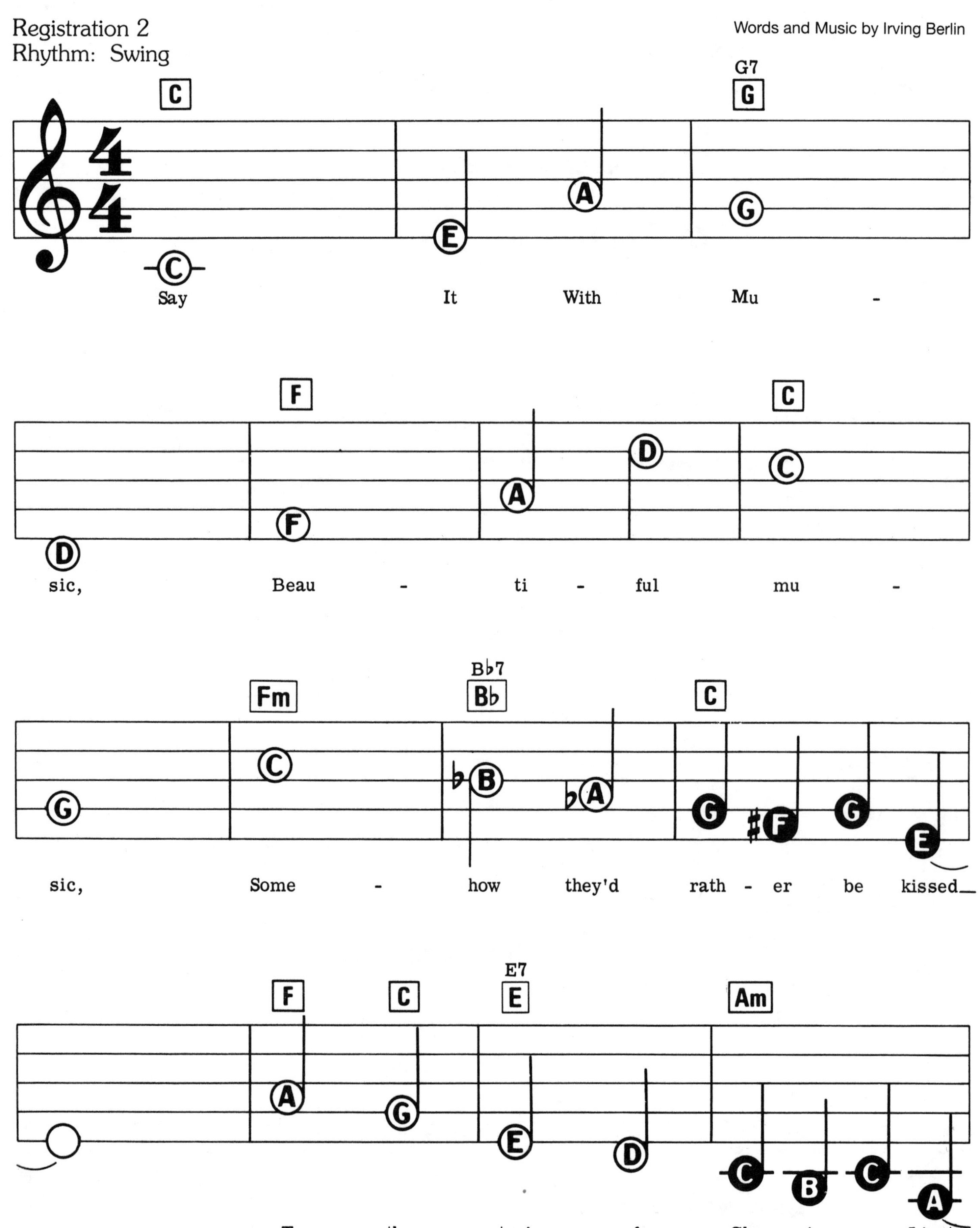

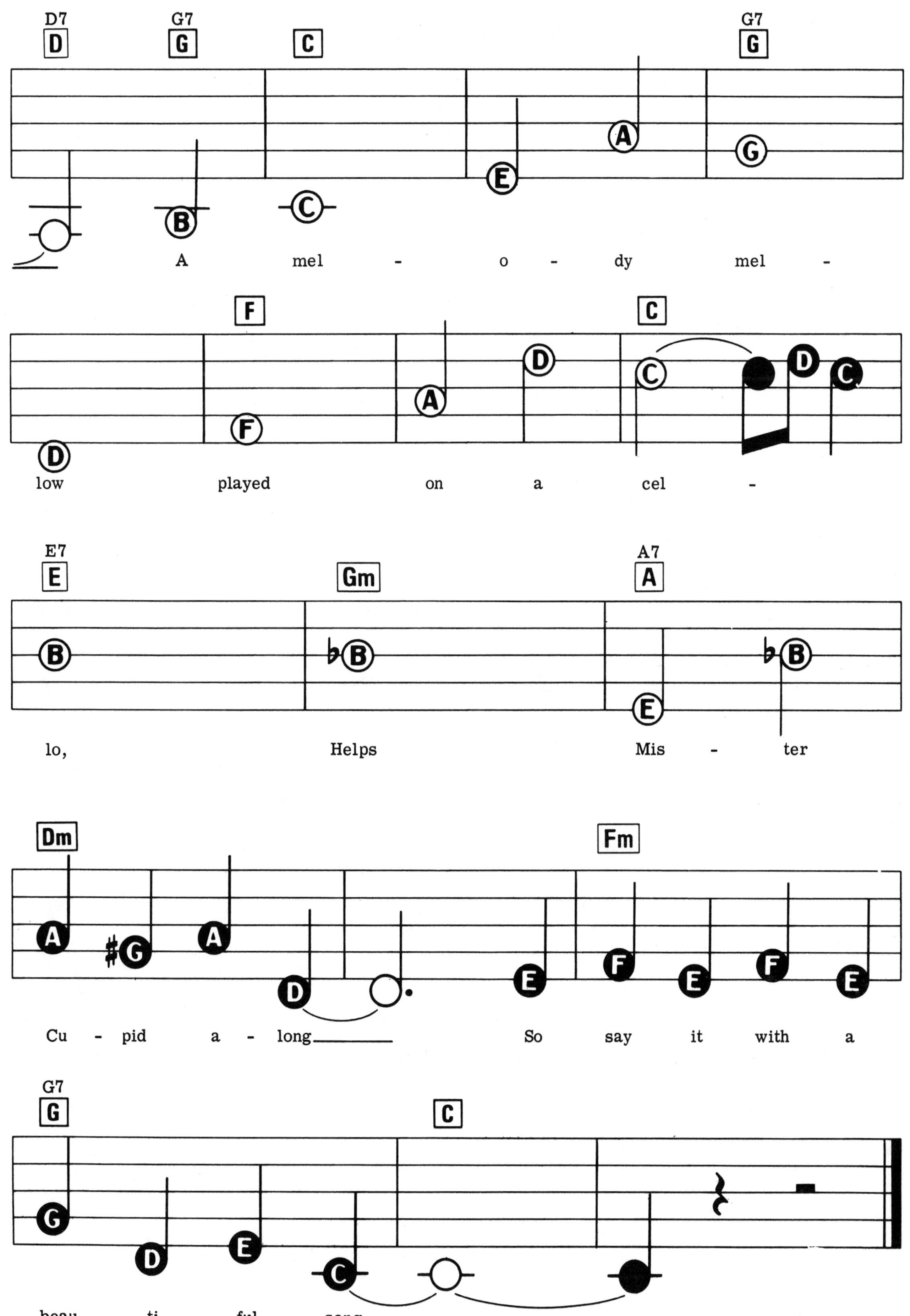
D7 D
G7 G
C
G7 G
A mel - o - dy mel -
F
C
low played on a cel -
E7 E
Gm
A7 A
lo, Helps Mis - ter
Dm
Fm
Cu - pid a - long
So say it with a
G7 G
C
beau - ti - ful song.

Sayonara

Registration 1
Rhythm: Rock

Words and Music by
Irving Berlin

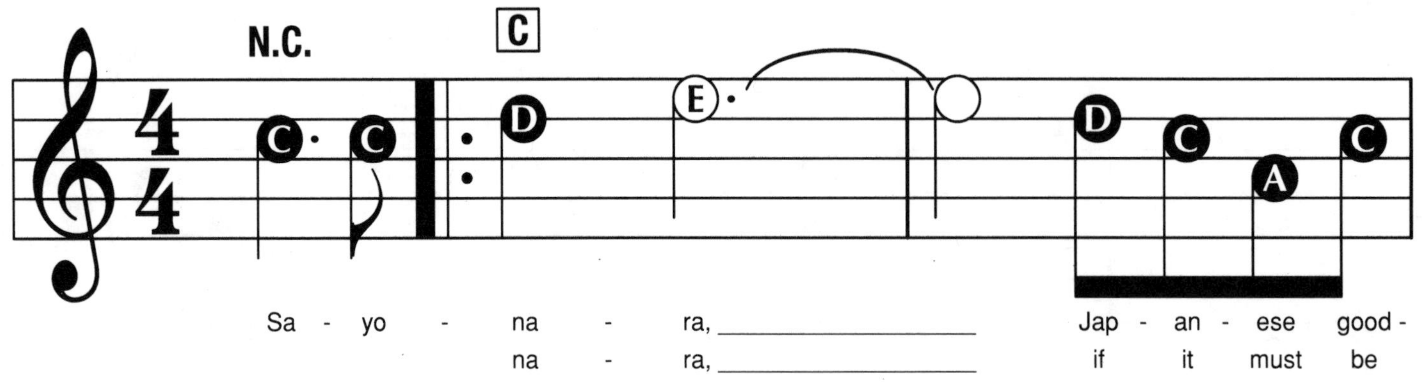

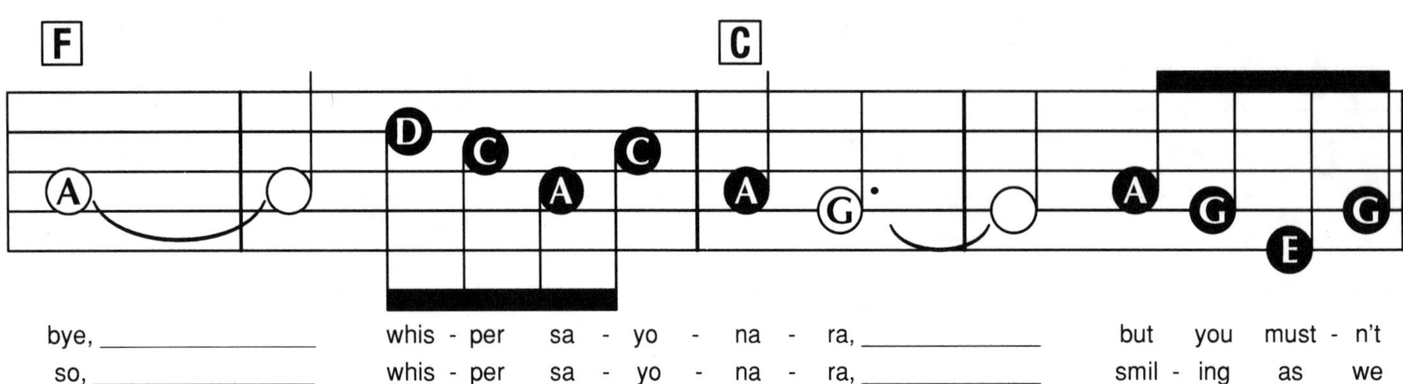

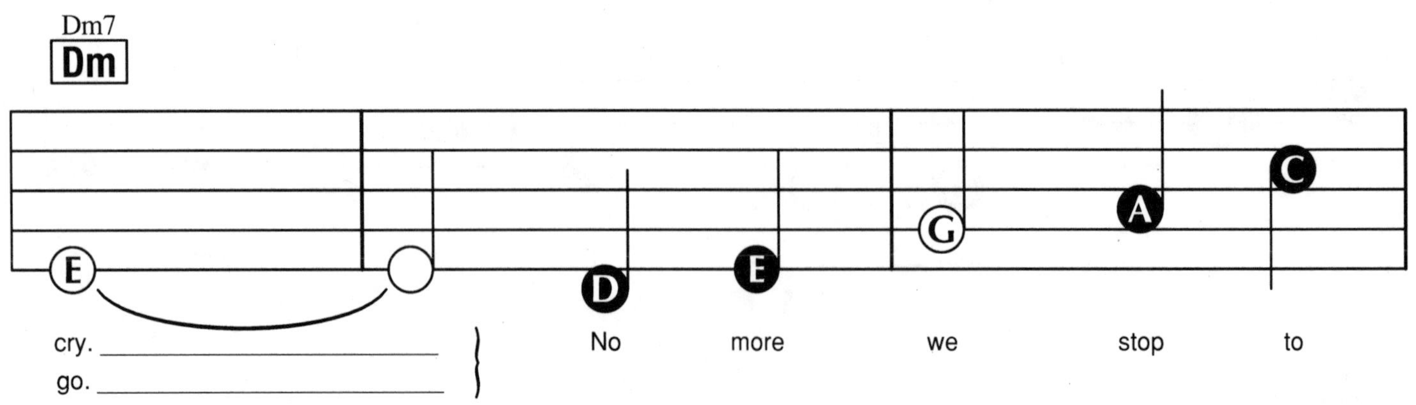

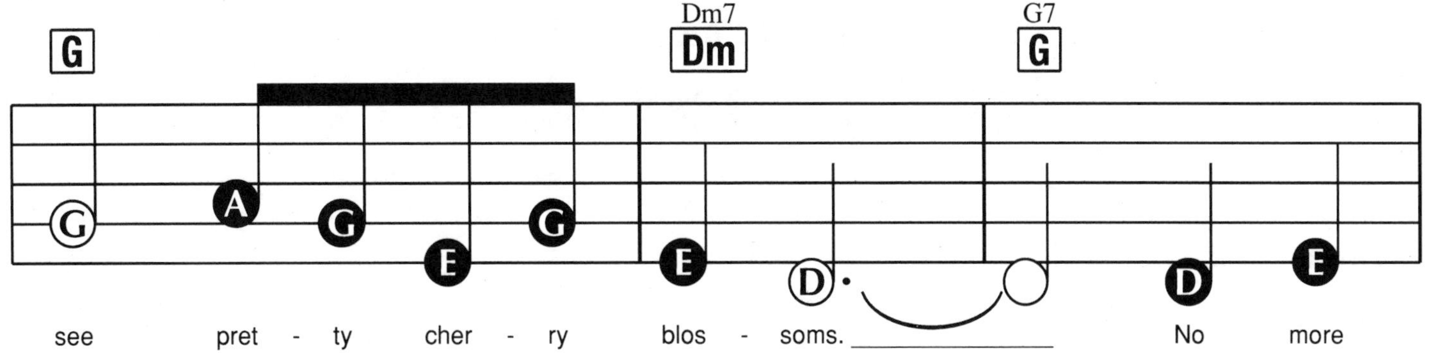
G
Dm7
Dm
G7
G
see pret - ty cher - ry blos - soms.
No more

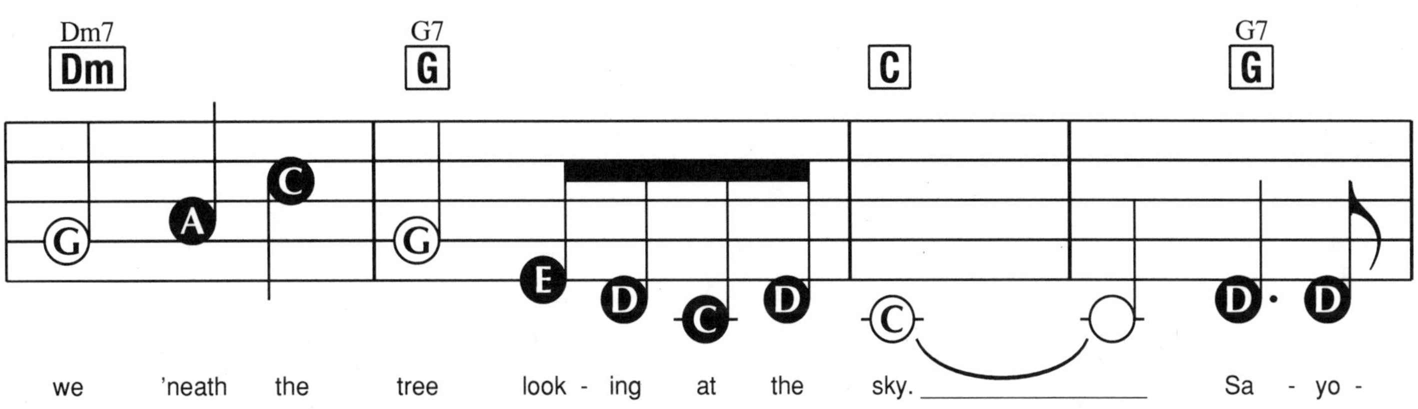
Dm7
Dm
G7
G
C
G7
G
we 'neath the tree look - ing at the sky.
Sa - yo -

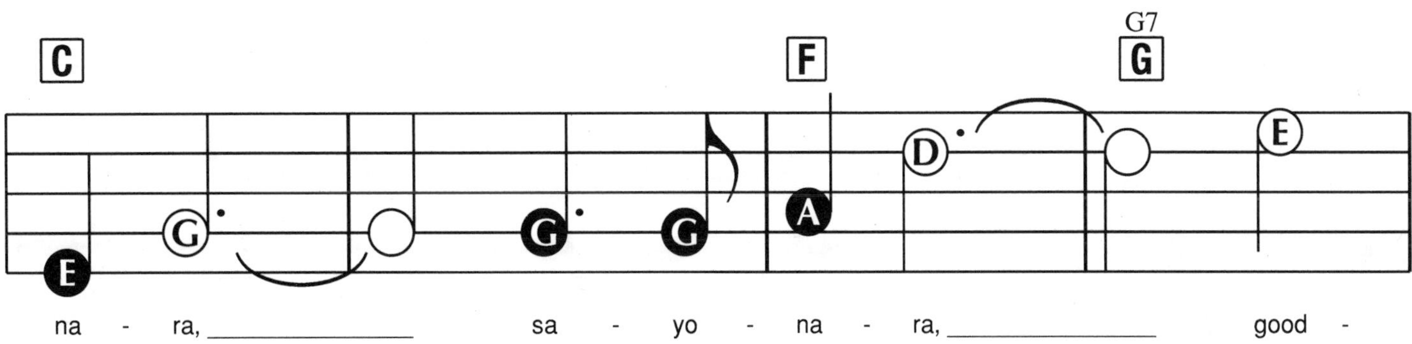
C
F
G7
G
na - ra,
sa - yo - na - ra,
good -

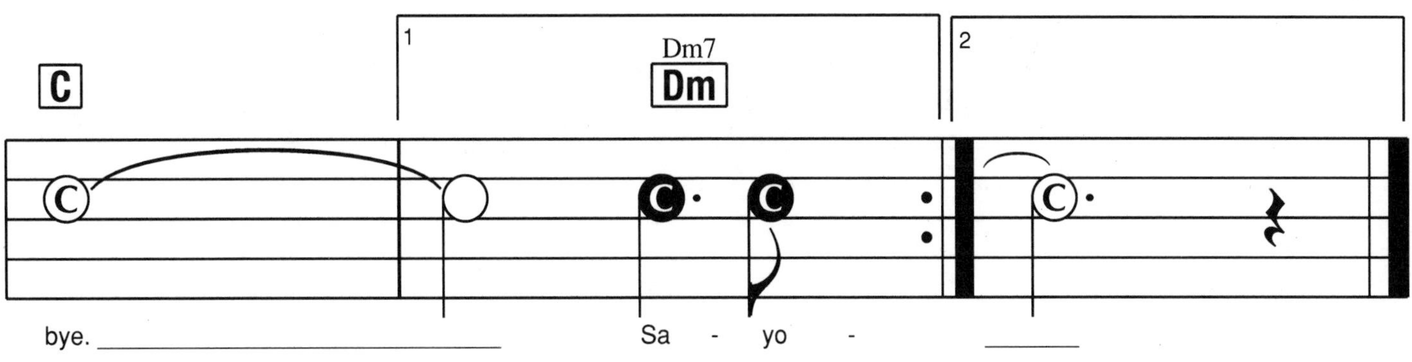
C
1
Dm7
Dm
2
bye.
Sa - yo -

Serenade To An Old Fashioned Girl

Registration 3
Rhythm: Swing

Words and Music by
Irving Berlin

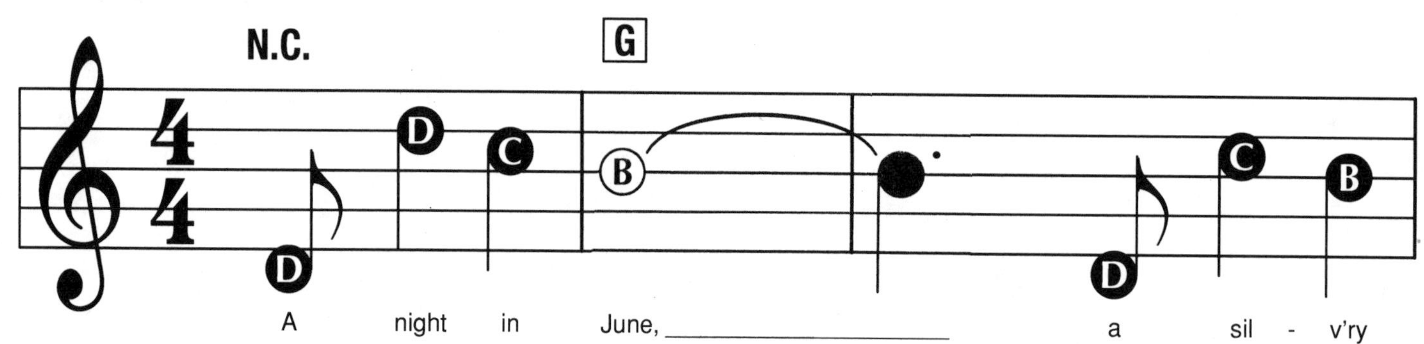

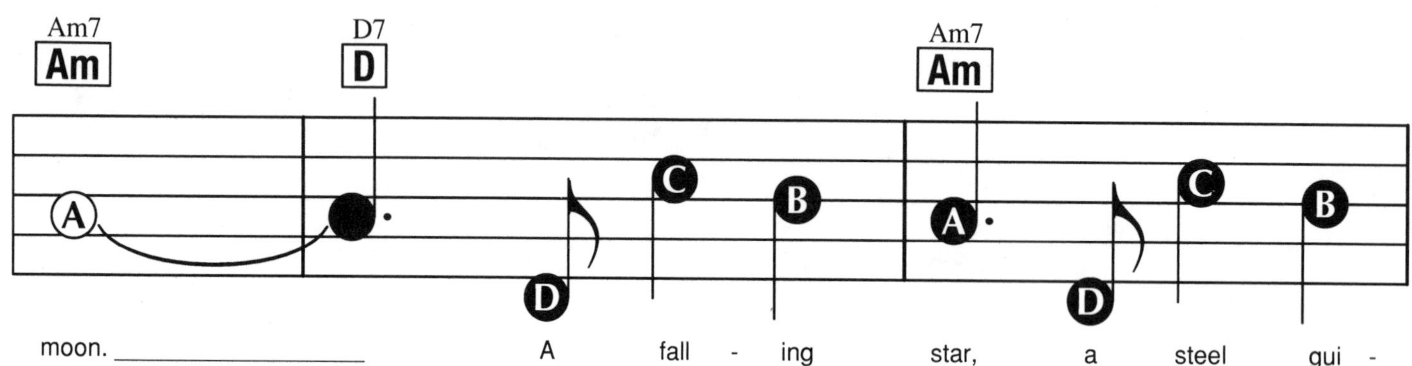

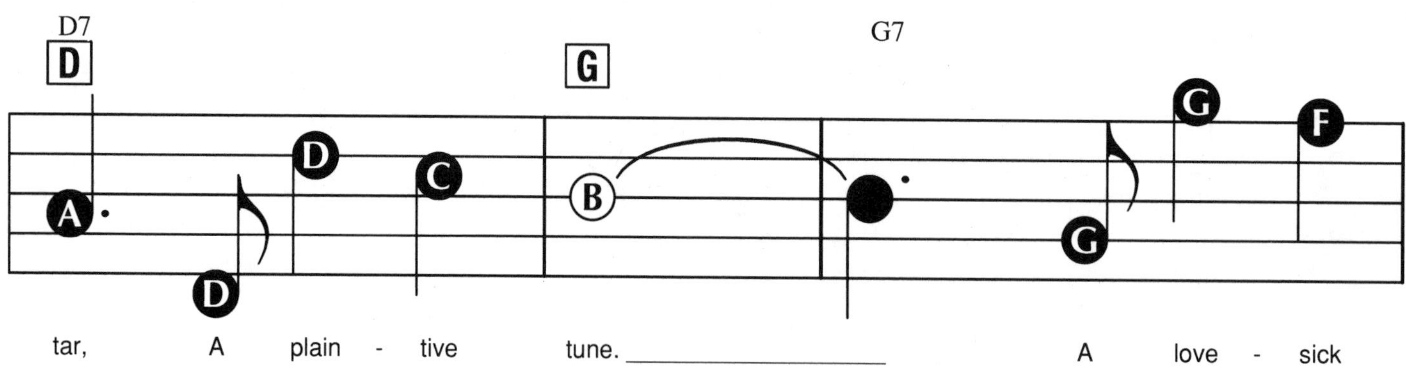

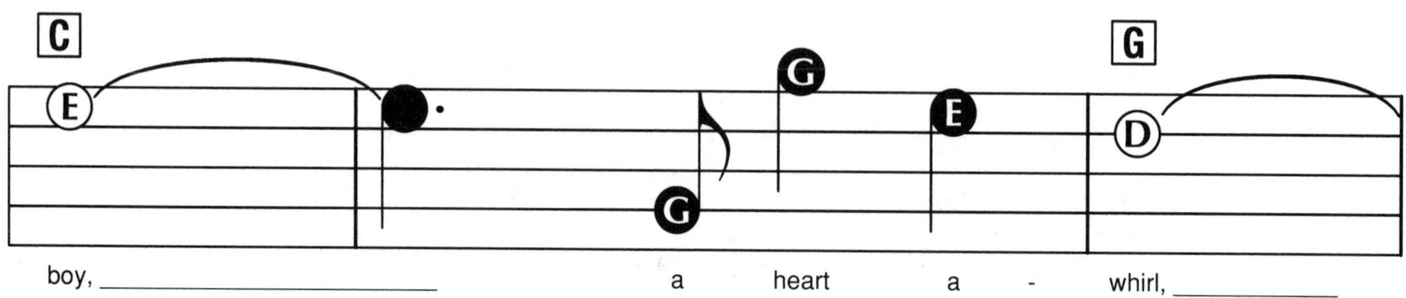

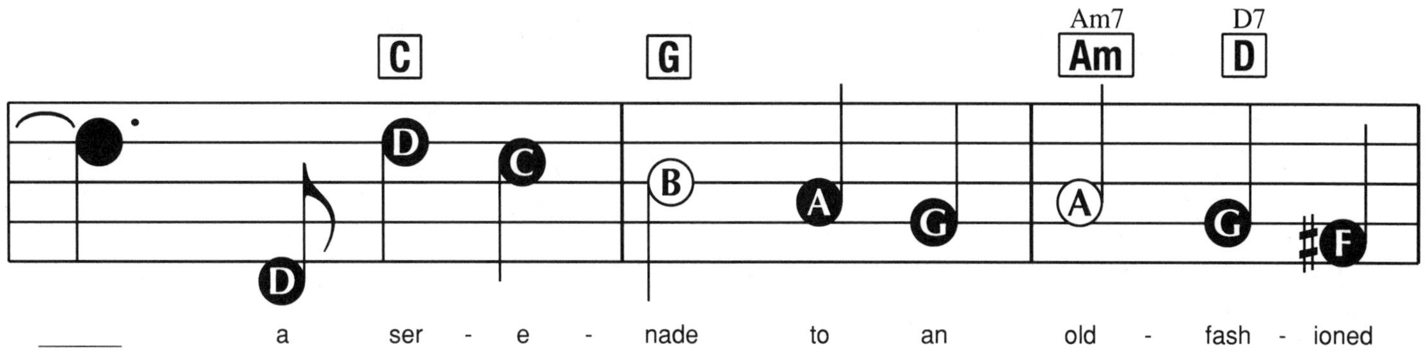
Am7
D7
C
G
Am
D
D
D
C
B
A
G
A
G
F
a ser - e - nade to an old - fash - ioned

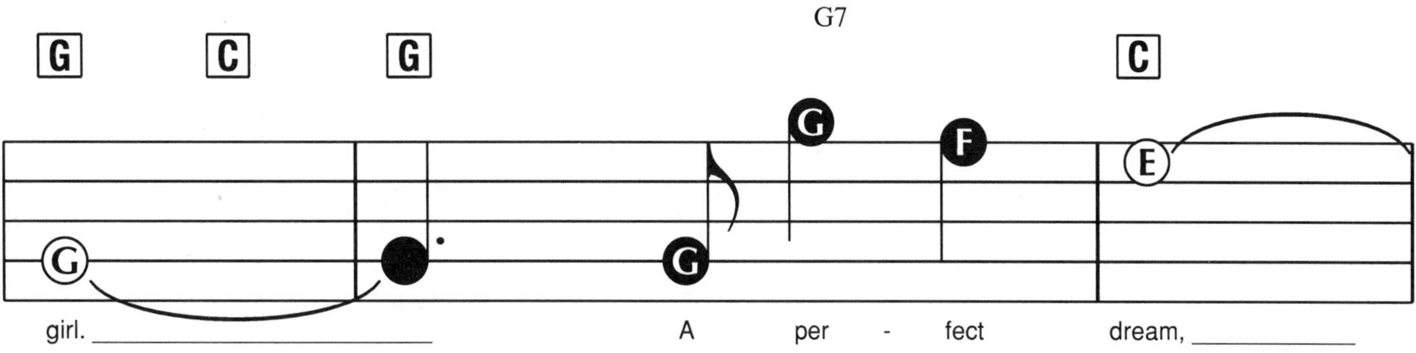
G7
G
C
G
C
G
G
G
F
E
girl. A per - fect dream,

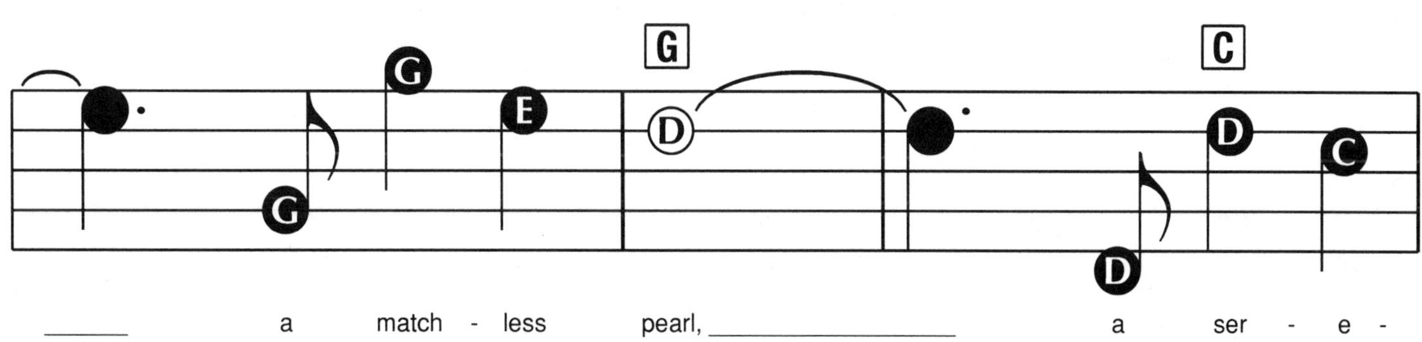
G
C
G
G
E
D
D
D
C
a match - less pearl, a ser - e -

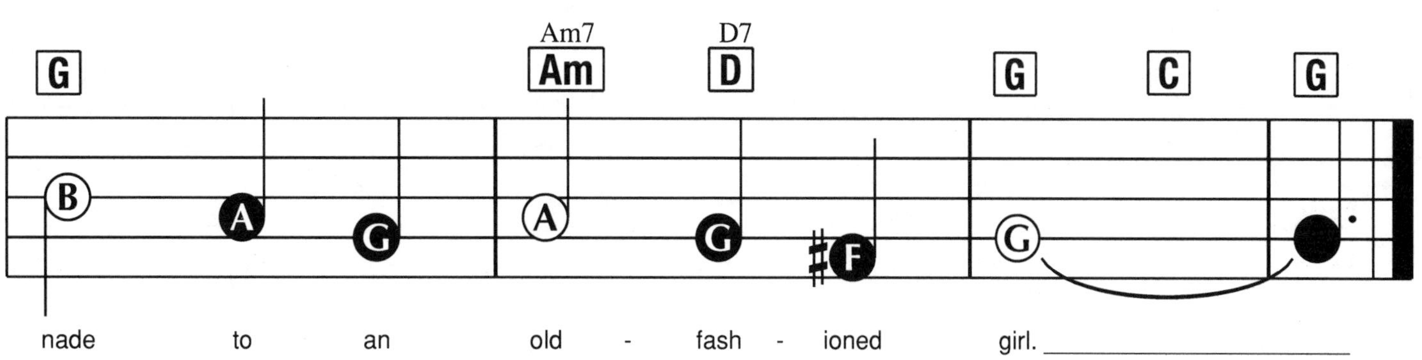
Am7
D7
G
Am
D
G
C
G
B
A
G
A
G
F
G
nade to an old - fash - ioned girl.

Shaking The Blues Away

Registration 7
Rhythm: Swing

Words and Music by
Irving Berlin

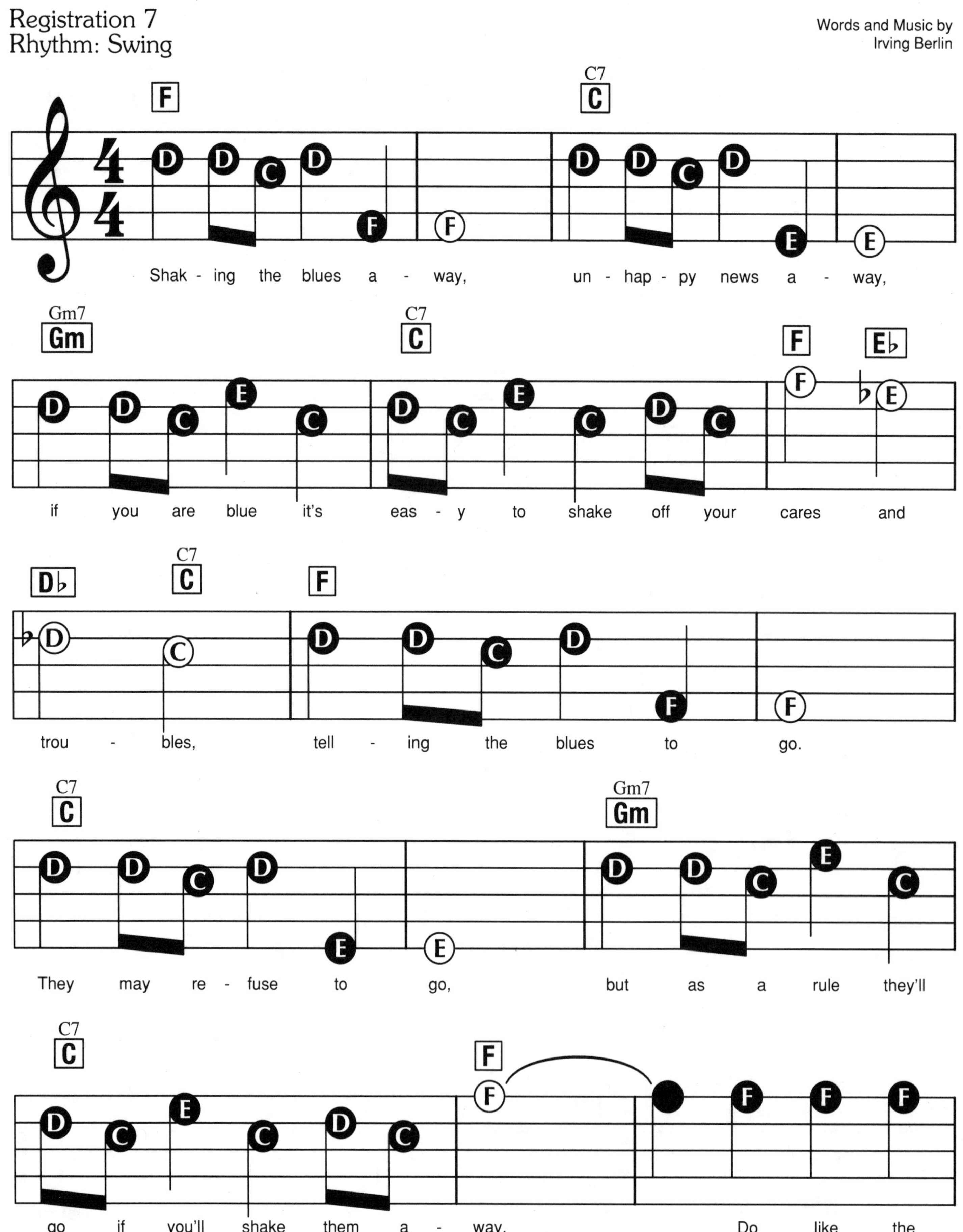

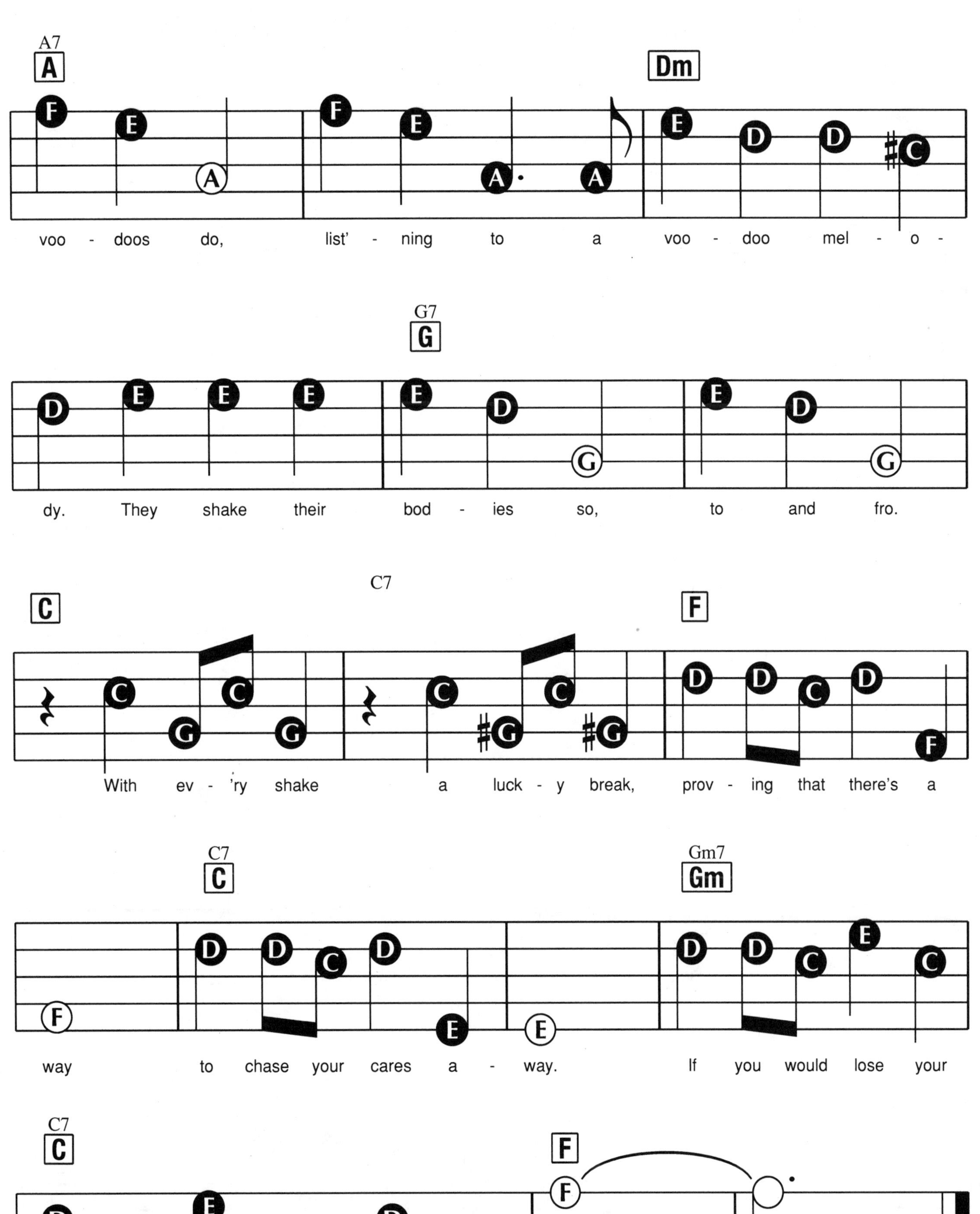
A7
A
Dm
voo - doos do, list' - ning to a voo - doo mel - o -
G7
G
dy. They shake their bod - ies so, to and fro.
C
C7
F
With ev - 'ry shake a luck - y break, prov - ing that there's a
C7
C
Gm7
Gm
way to chase your cares a - way. If you would lose your
C7
C
F
wear - y blues, shake 'em a - way.

Soft Lights And Sweet Music

Registration 1
Rhythm: Fox Trot or Ballad

Words and Music by
Irving Berlin

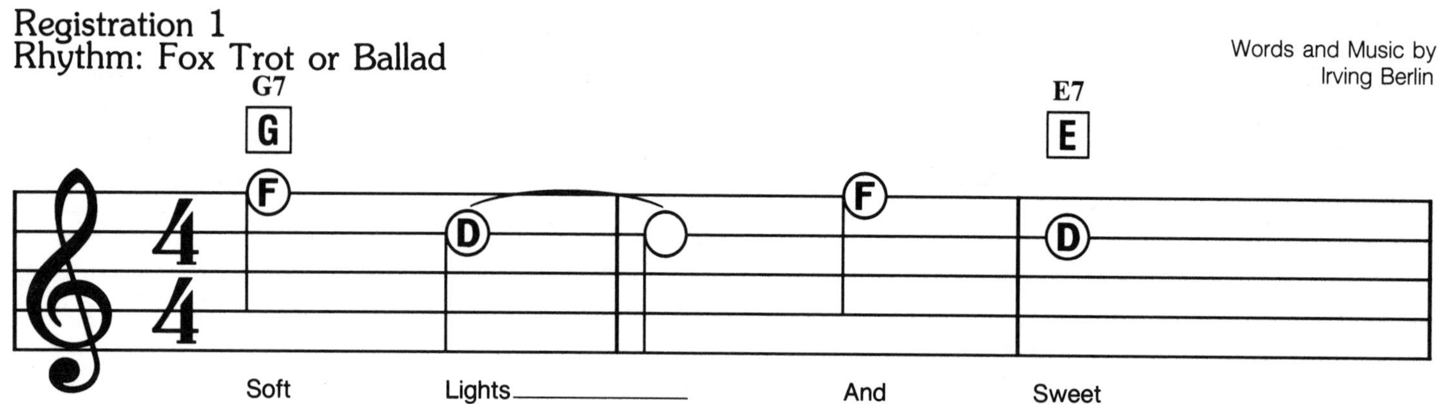

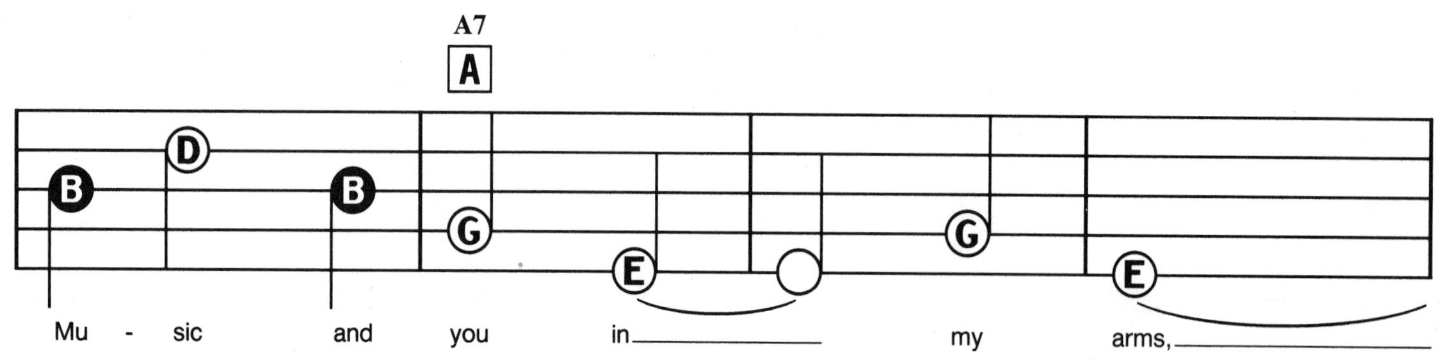

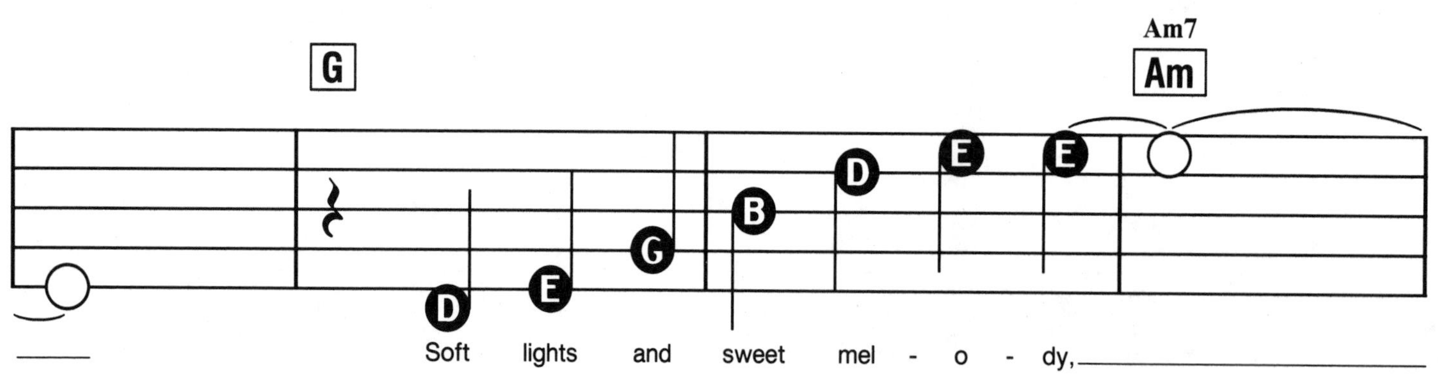

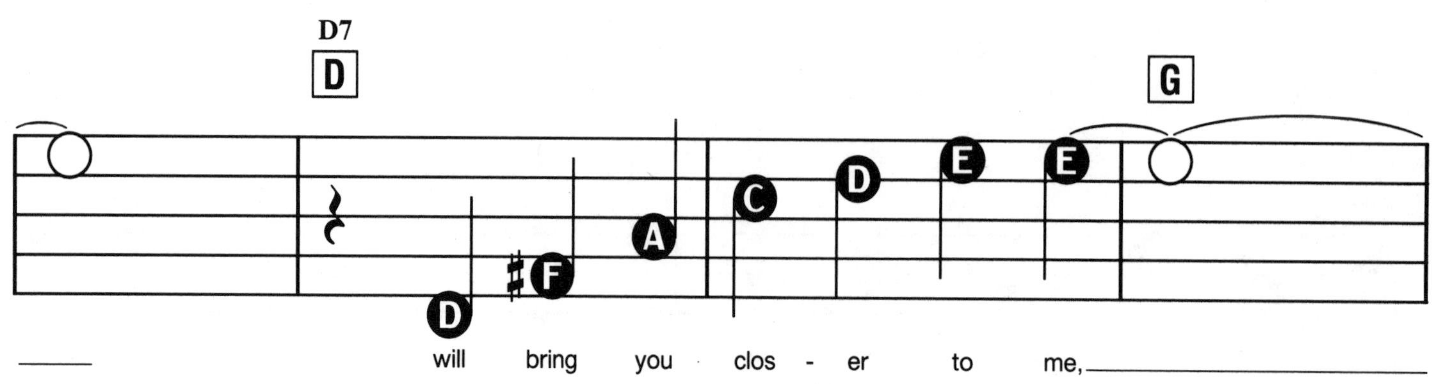

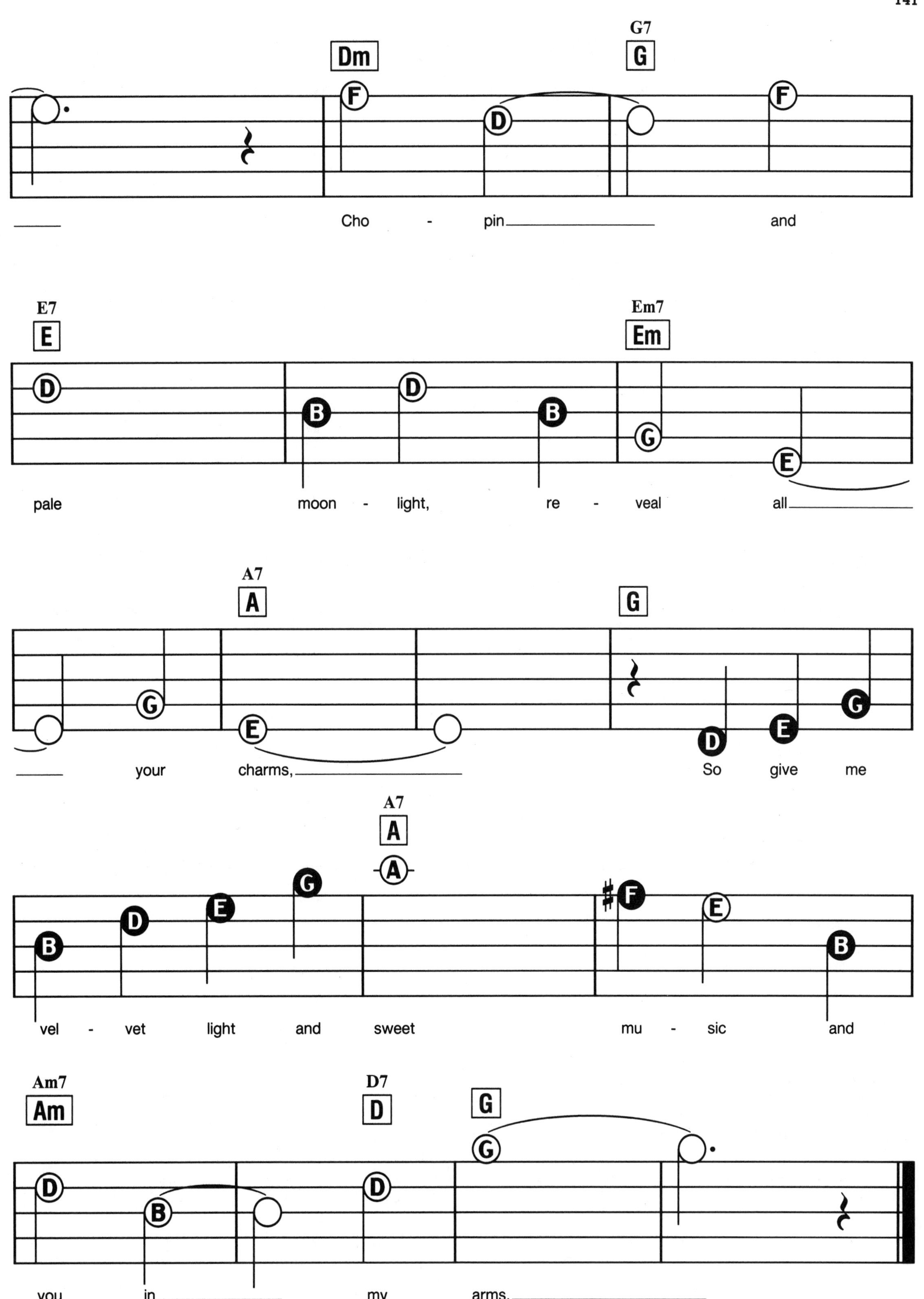
Dm
G7
G
F
D
F
Cho - pin and
E7
E
Em7
Em
D
B
D
B
G
E
pale moon - light, re - veal all
A7
A
G
G
E
E
D
E
G
your charms, So give me
A7
A
A
B
D
E
G
♯F
E
B
vel - vet light and sweet mu - sic and
Am7
Am
D7
D
G
D
B
D
G
you in my arms.

The Song Is Ended
(But The Melody Lingers On)

Registration 10
Rhythm: Waltz

Words and Music by Irving Berlin

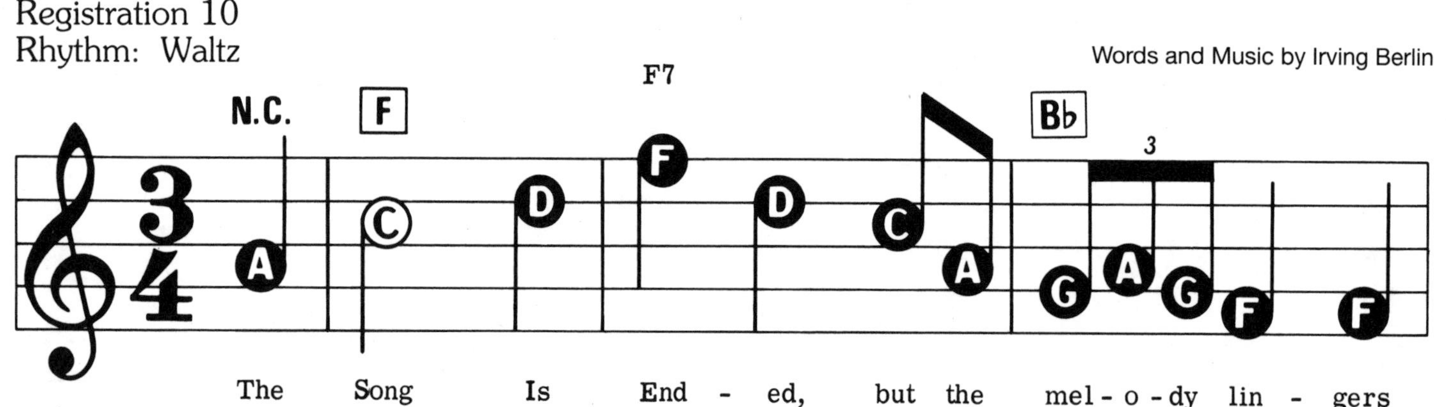

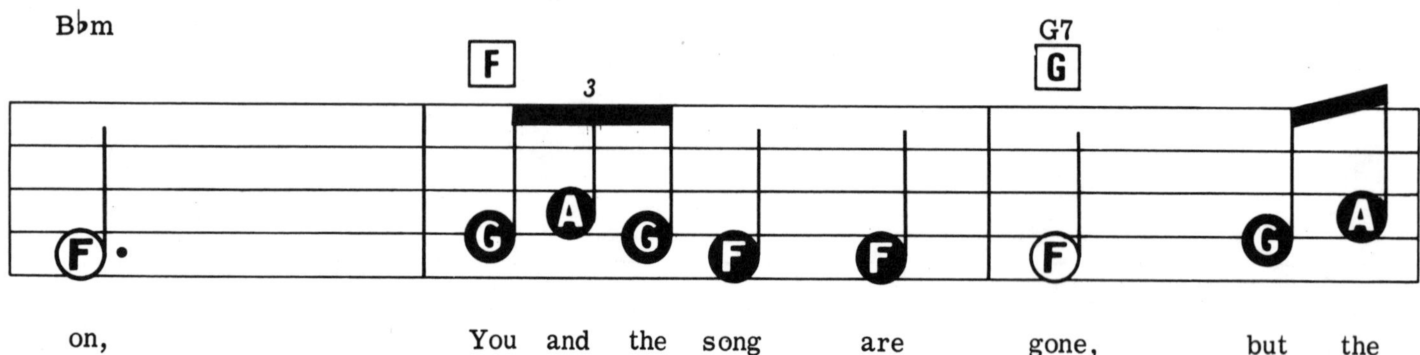

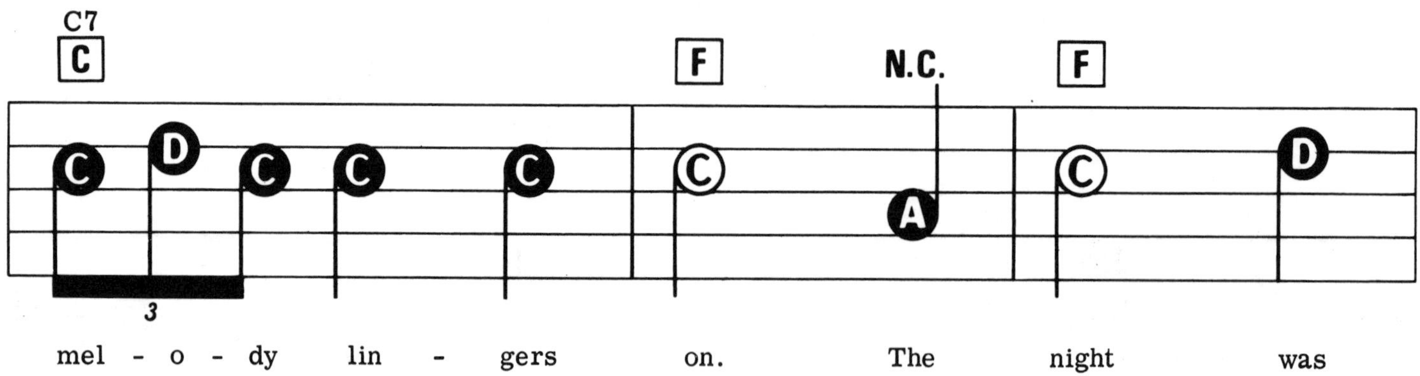

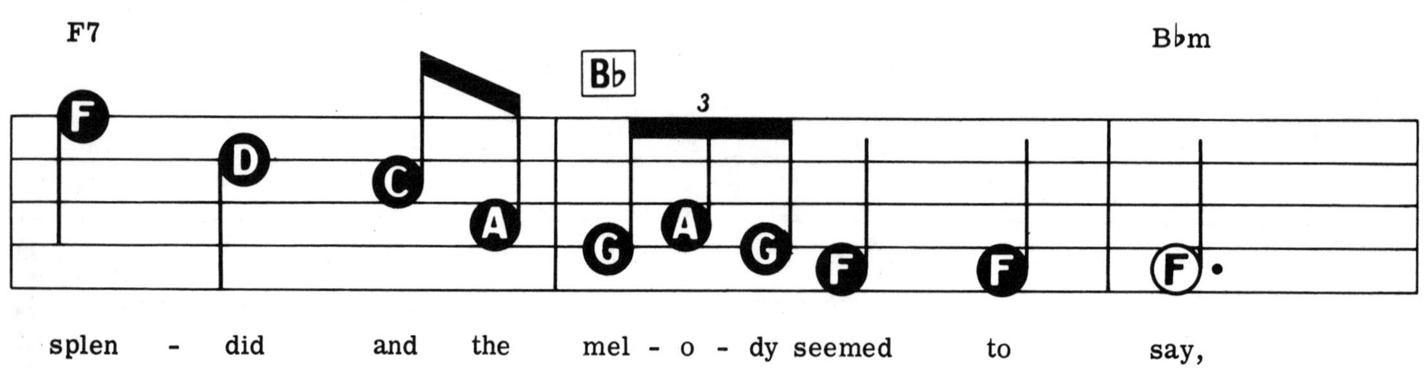

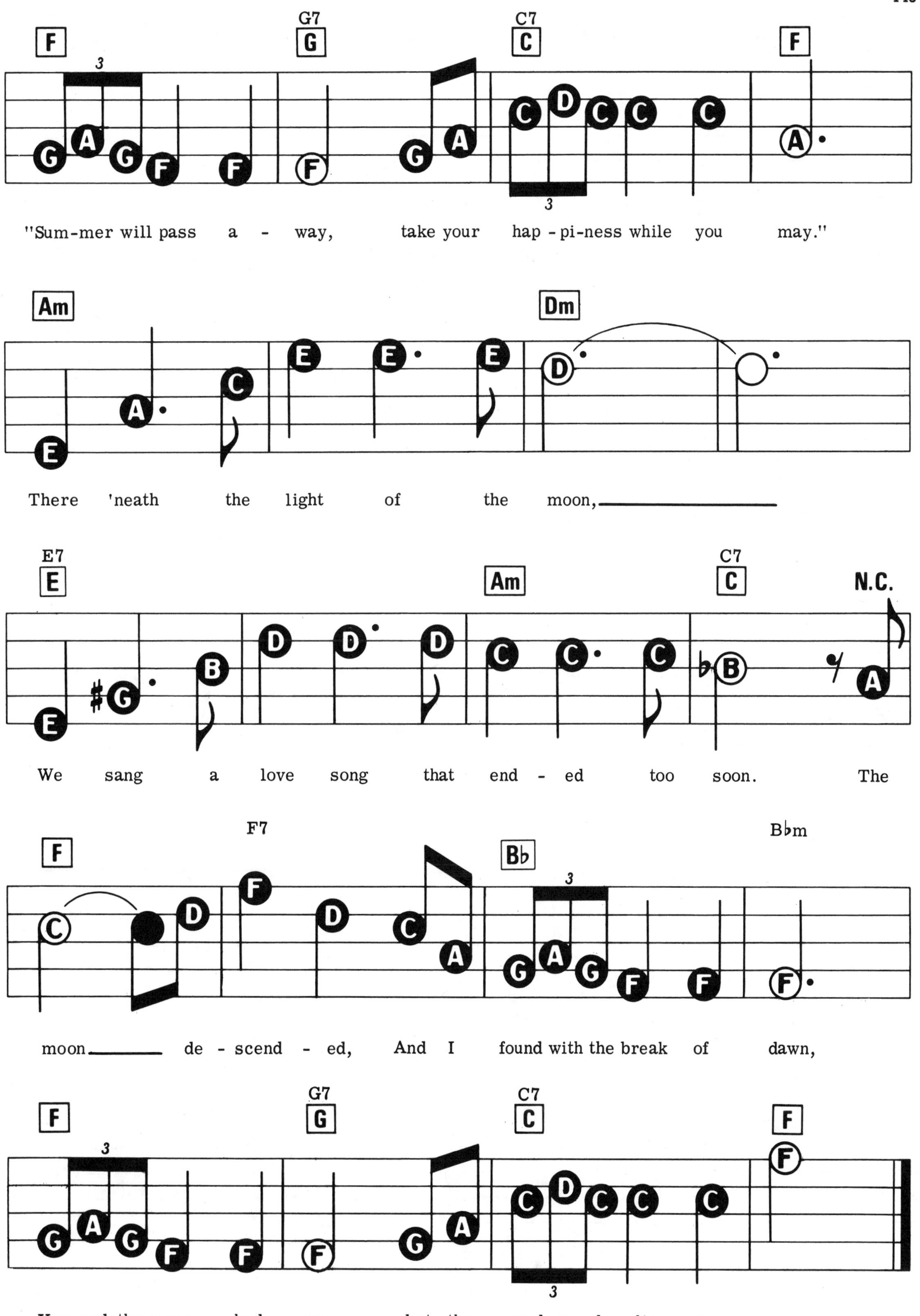
F
G7
G
C7
C
F
"Sum-mer will pass a - way, take your hap - pi-ness while you may."
Am
Dm
There 'neath the light of the moon,
E7
E
Am
C7
C
N.C.
We sang a love song that end - ed too soon. The
F
F7
B♭
B♭m
moon de - scend - ed, And I found with the break of dawn,
F
G7
G
C7
C
F
You and the song had gone, but the mel - o - dy lin - gers on.

There's No Business Like Show Business

Registration 2
Rhythm: Fox Trot

Words and Music by
Irving Berlin

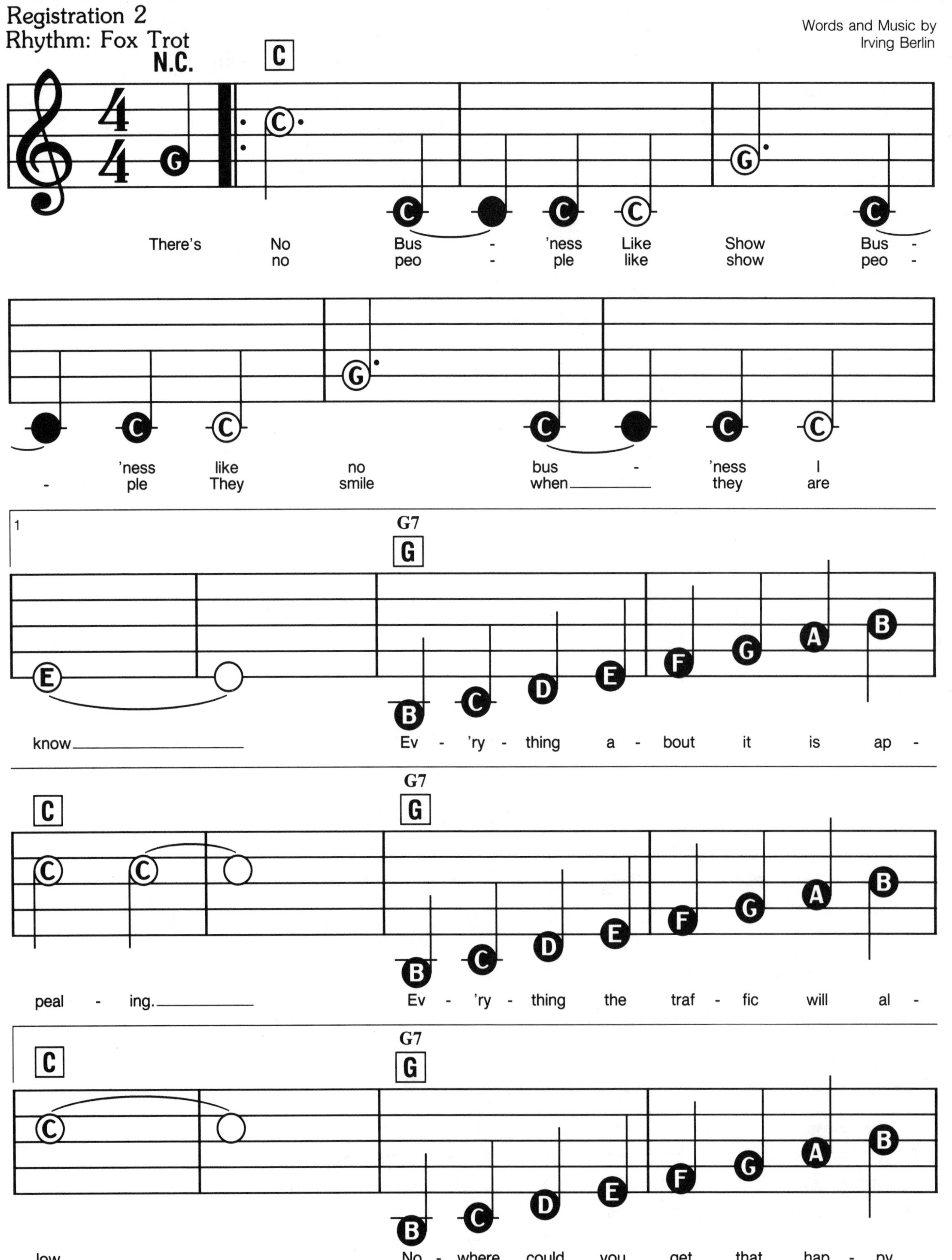

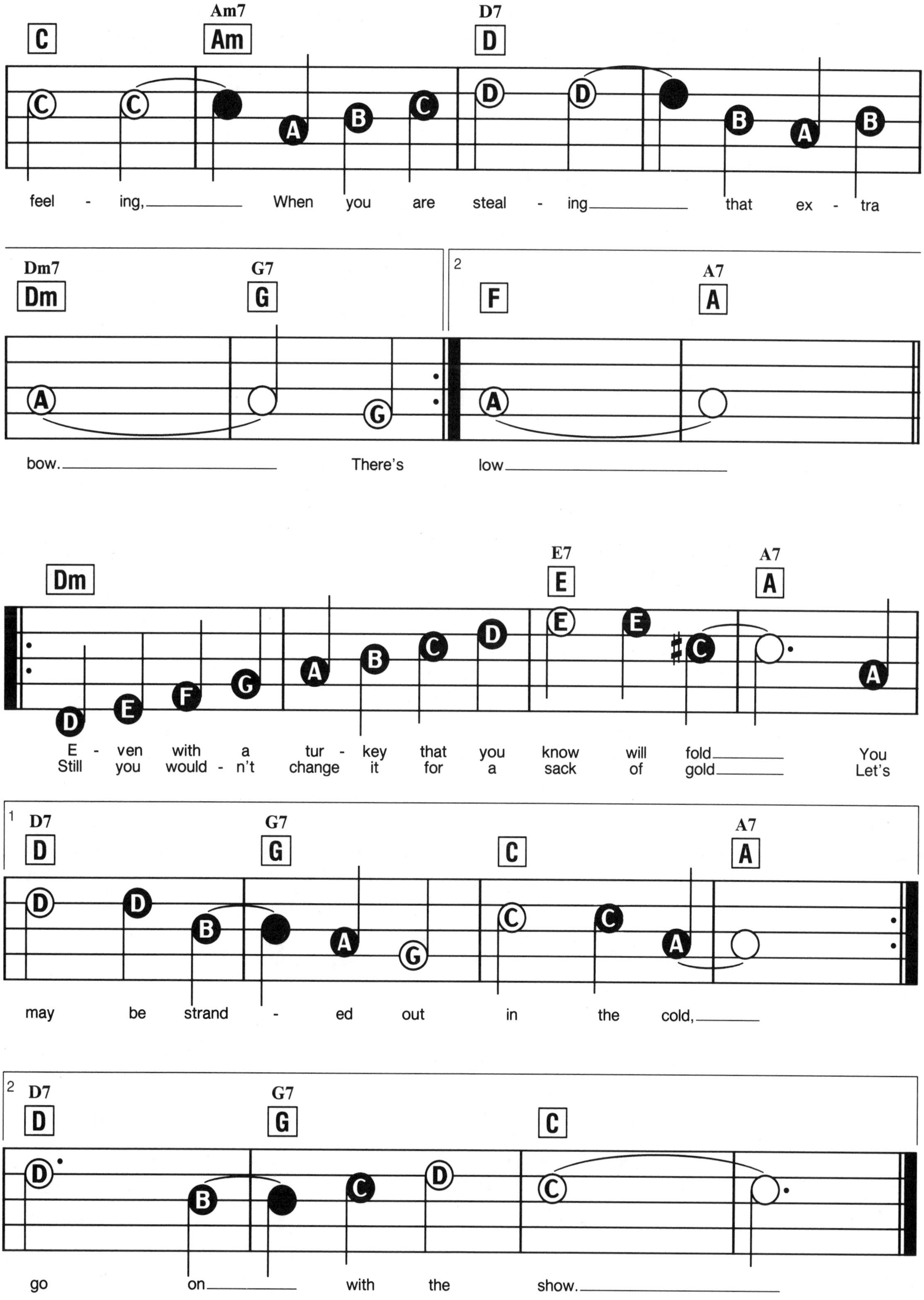

C | Am7 Am | D7 D

feel - ing, ___ When you are steal - ing ___ that ex - tra

Dm7 Dm | G7 G | 2 F | A7 A

bow. ___ There's low ___

Dm | E7 E | A7 A

E - ven with a tur - key that you know will fold ___ You
Still you would - n't change it for a sack of gold ___ Let's

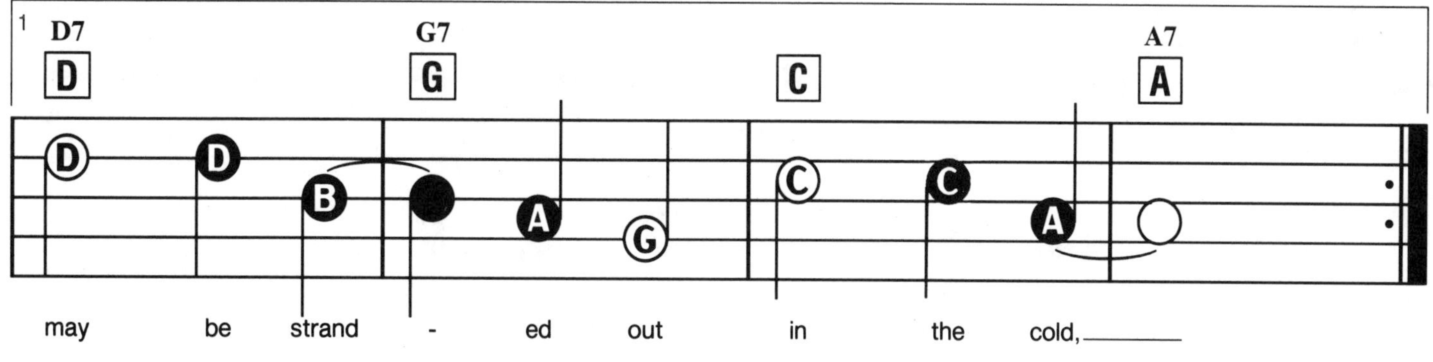

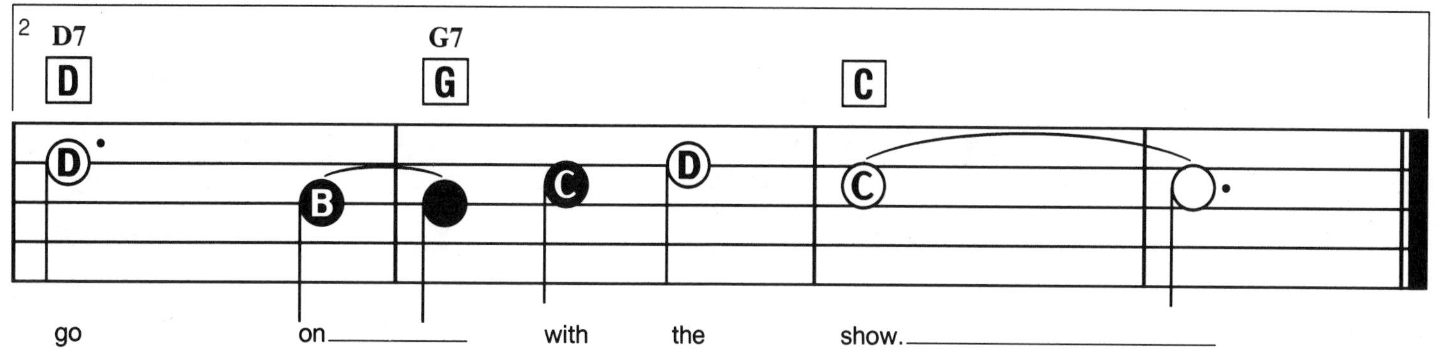

This Is The Army, Mr. Jones

Registration 5
Rhythm: March or Polka

Words and Music by Irving Berlin

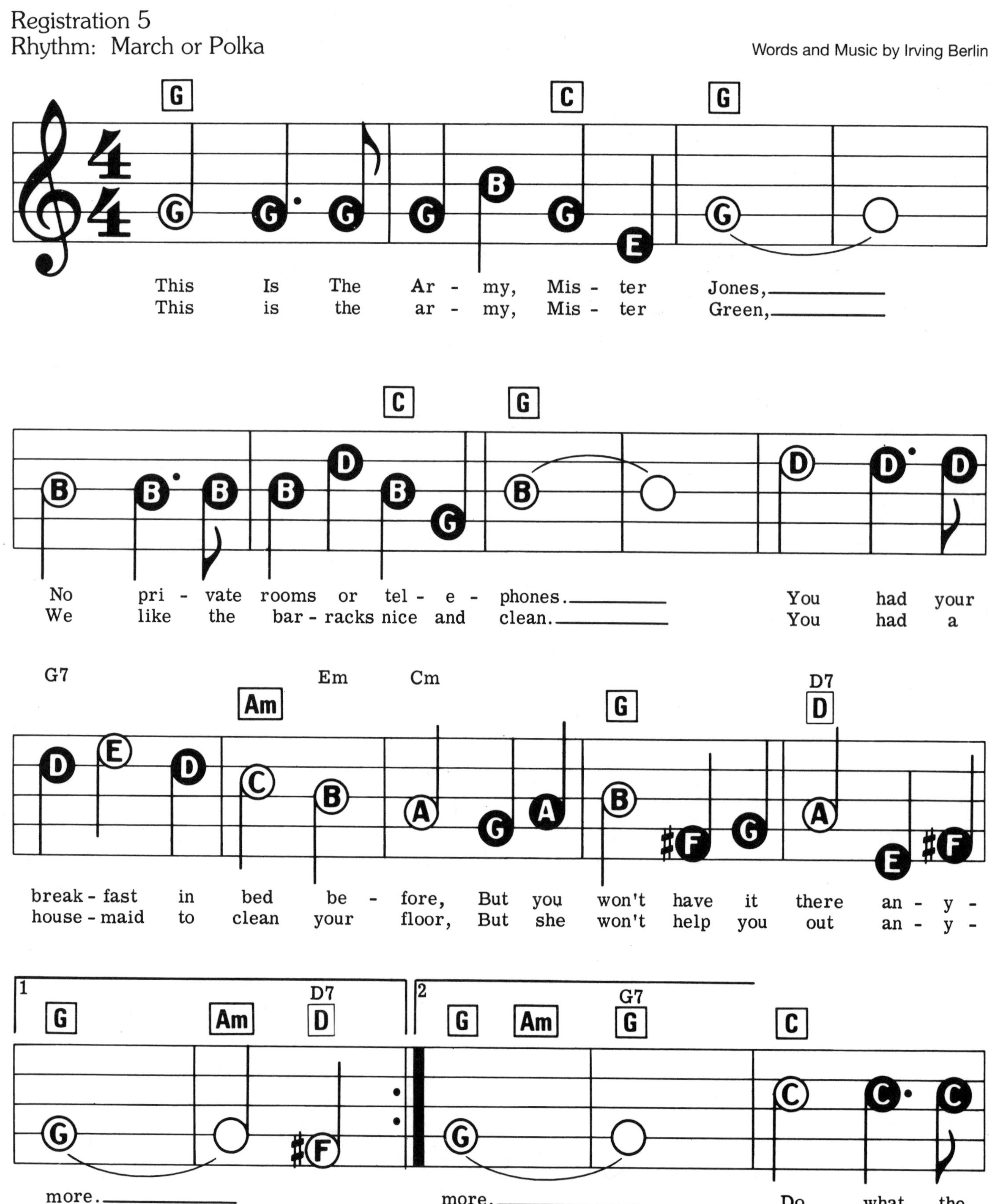

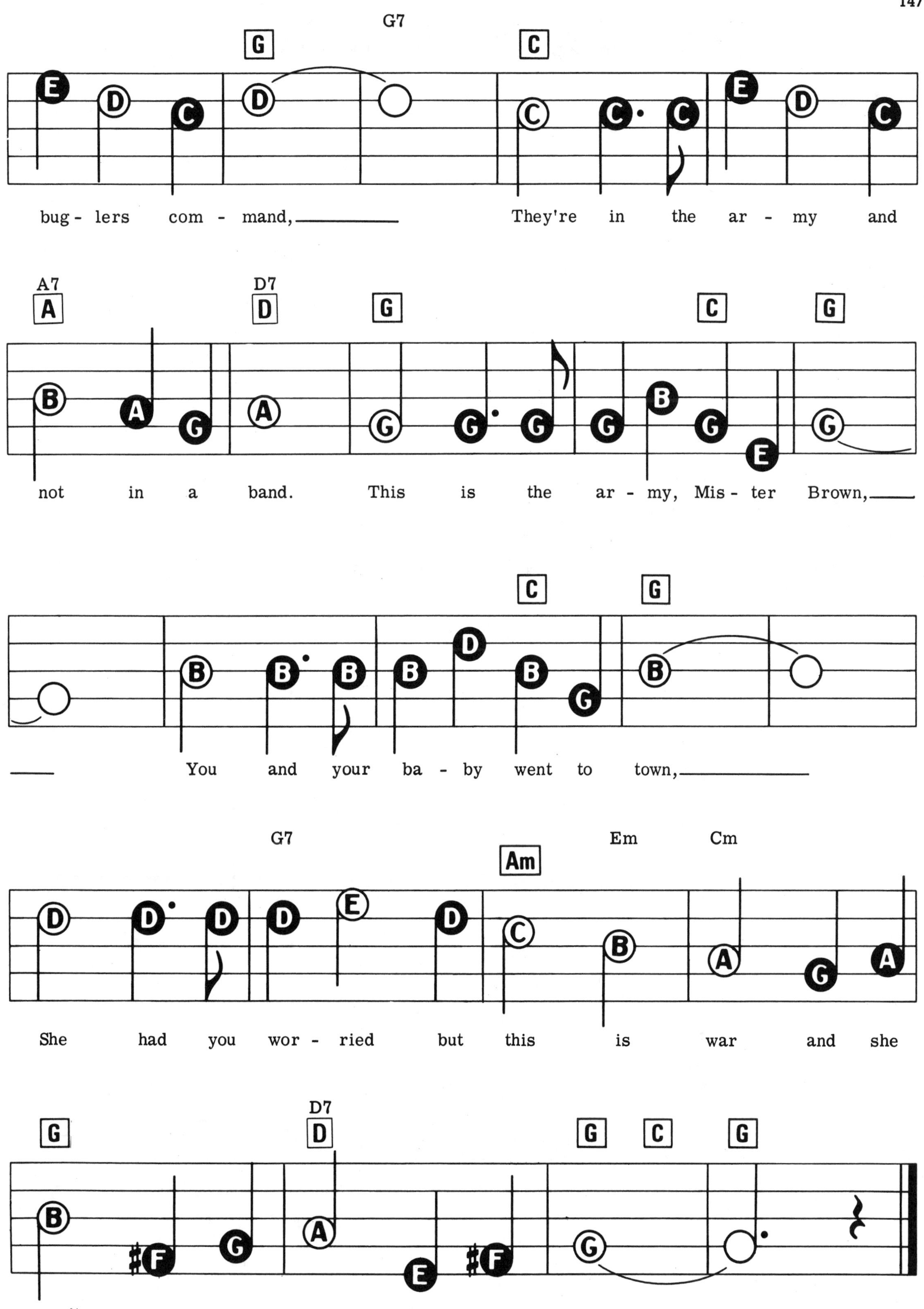
G7
G
C
bug - lers com - mand,
They're in the ar - my and
A7
A
D7
D
G
C
G
not in a band. This is the ar - my, Mis - ter Brown,
C
G
You and your ba - by went to town,
G7
Am
Em
Cm
She had you wor - ried but this is war and she
G
D7
D
G
C
G
won't wor - ry you an - y - more.

They Say It's Wonderful

Registration 10
Rhythm: Fox Trot or Ballad

Words and Music by
Irving Berlin

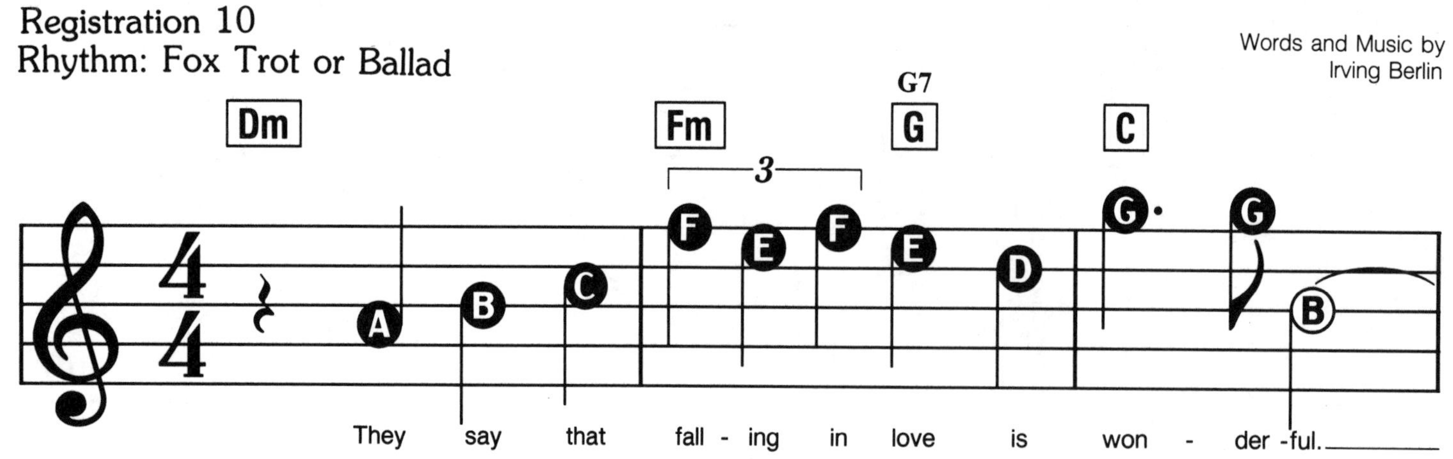

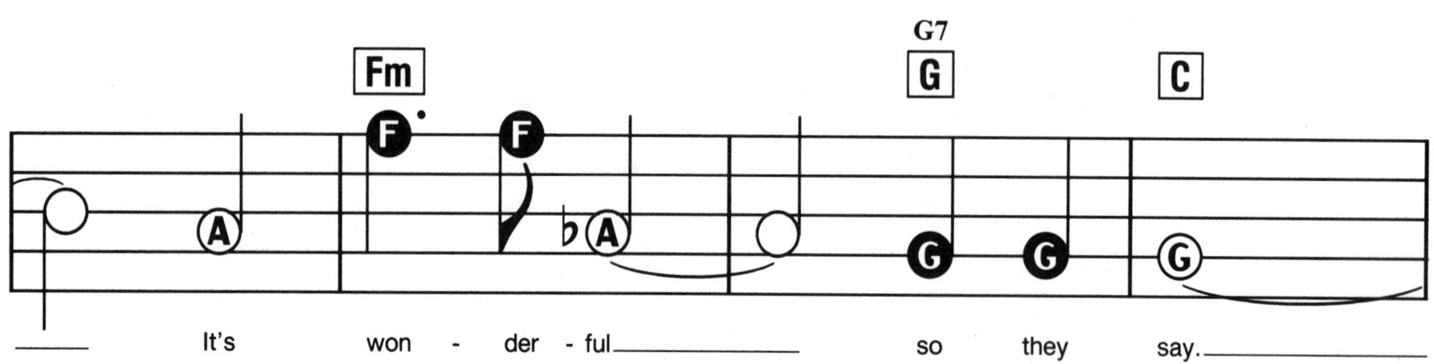

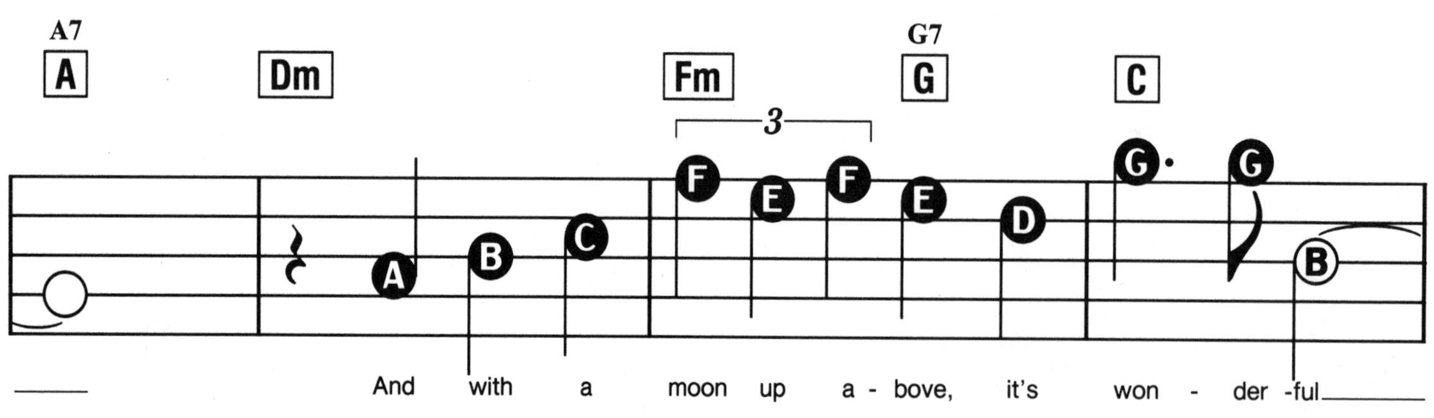

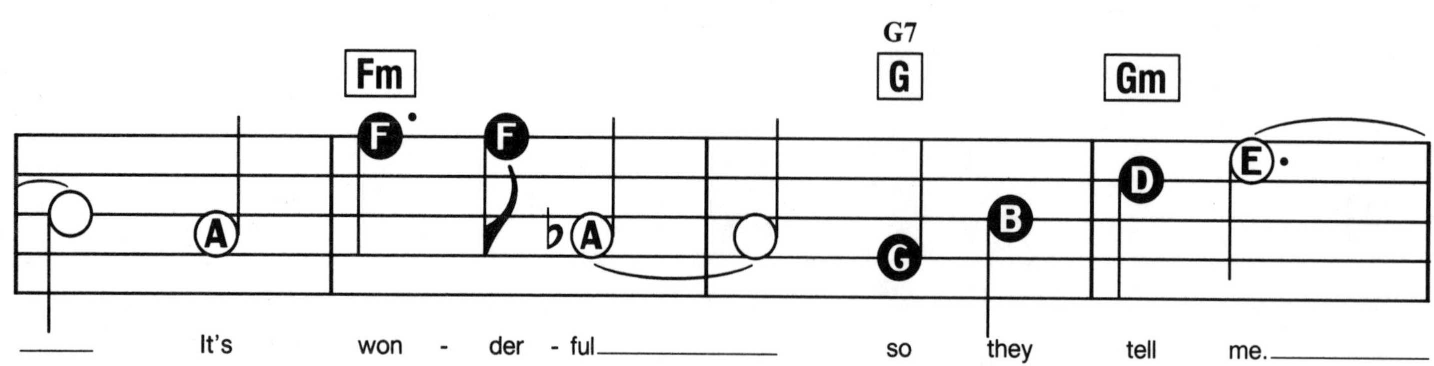

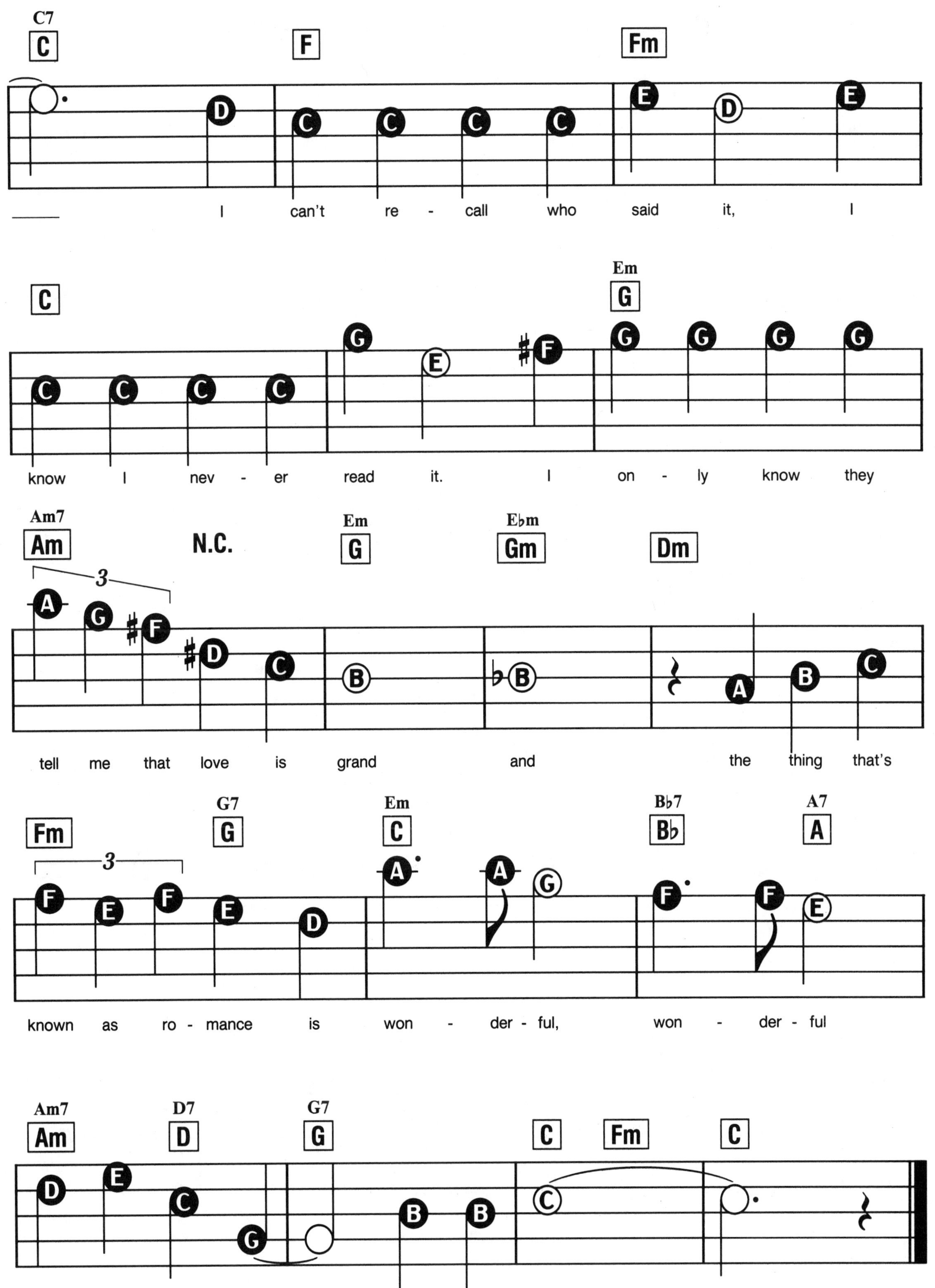
C7
C
F
Fm
I can't re - call who said it, I
C
Em
G
know I nev - er read it. I on - ly know they
Am7
Am
N.C.
Em
G
E♭m
Gm
Dm
3
tell me that love is grand and the thing that's
Fm
G7
G
Em
C
B♭7
B♭
A7
A
3
known as ro - mance is won - der - ful, won - der - ful
Am7
Am
D7
D
G7
G
C
Fm
C
in ev - 'ry way so they say.

This Is A Great Country

Registration 1
Rhythm: March or Polka

Words and Music by
Irving Berlin

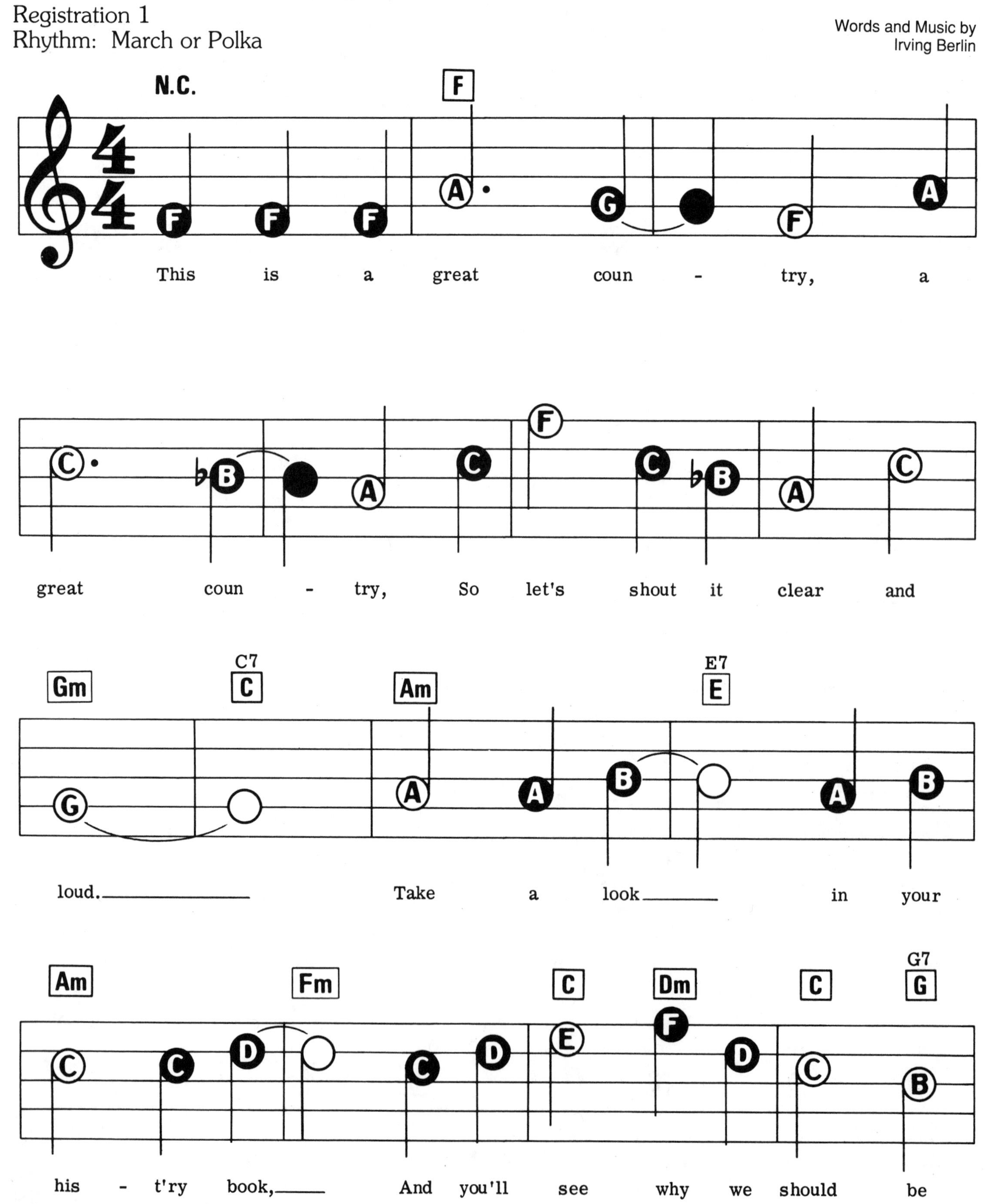

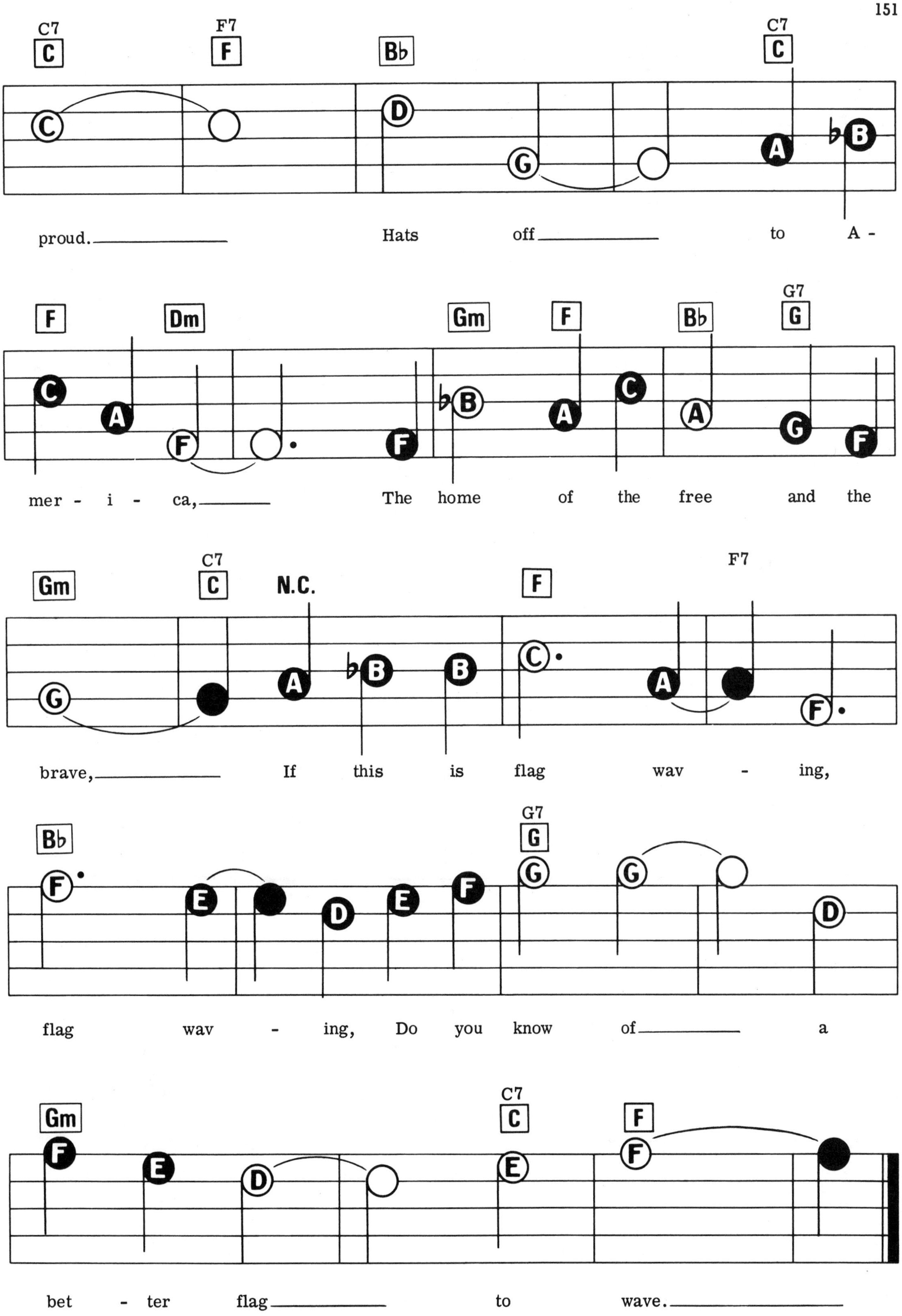

C7 C F7 F B♭ C7 C

proud._____ Hats off_____ to A -

F Dm Gm F B♭ G7 G

mer - i - ca,_____ The home of the free and the

Gm C7 C N.C. F F7

brave,_____ If this is flag wav - ing,

B♭ G7 G

flag wav - ing, Do you know of_____ a

Gm C7 C F

bet - ter flag_____ to wave._____

This Year's Kisses

Registration 2
Rhythm: Swing

Words and Music by
Irving Berlin

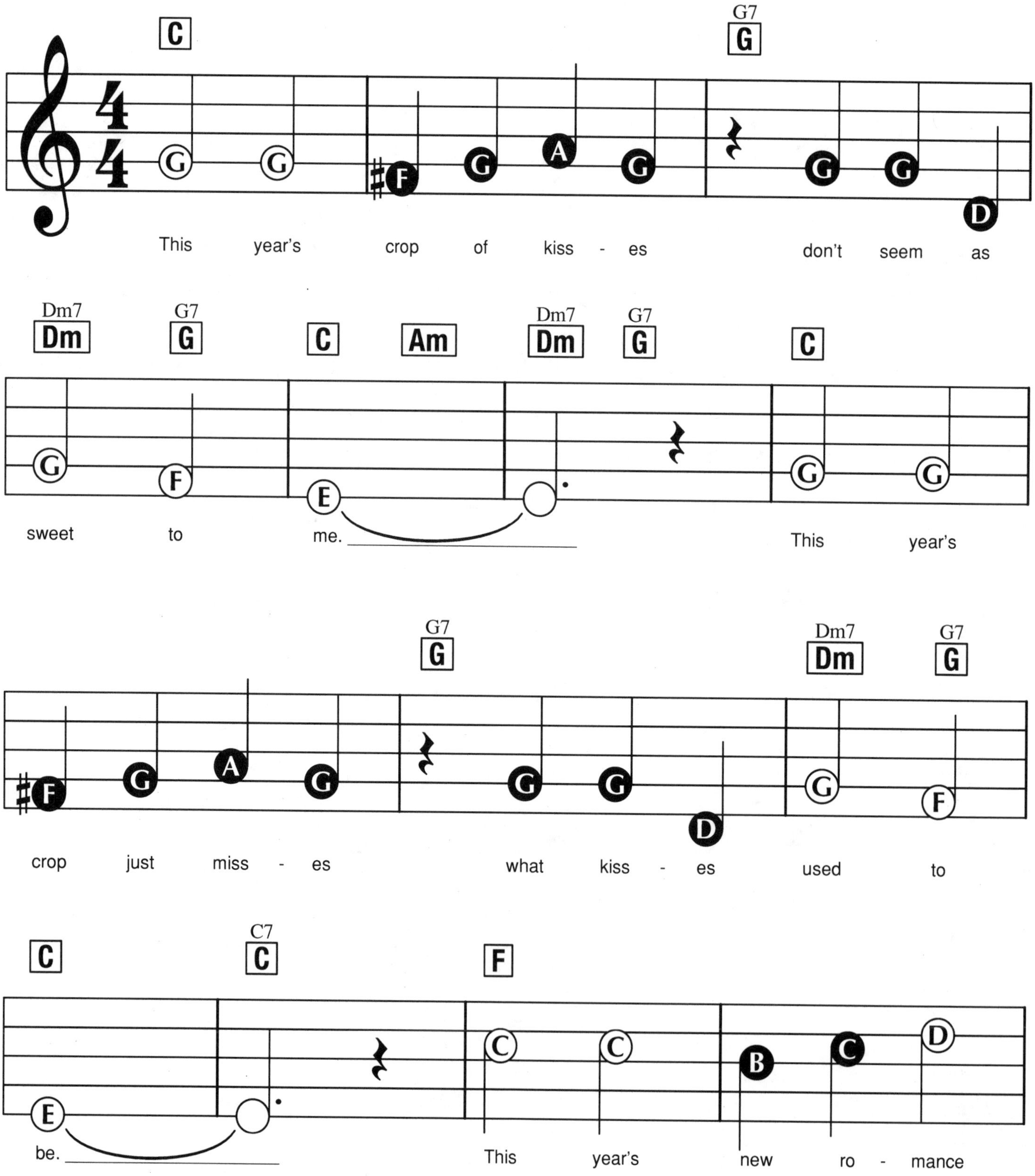

C G7 G

This year's crop of kiss - es don't seem as

Dm7 Dm G7 G C Am Dm7 Dm G7 G C

sweet to me. This year's

G7 G Dm7 Dm G7 G

crop just miss - es what kiss - es used to

C C7 C F

be. This year's new ro - mance

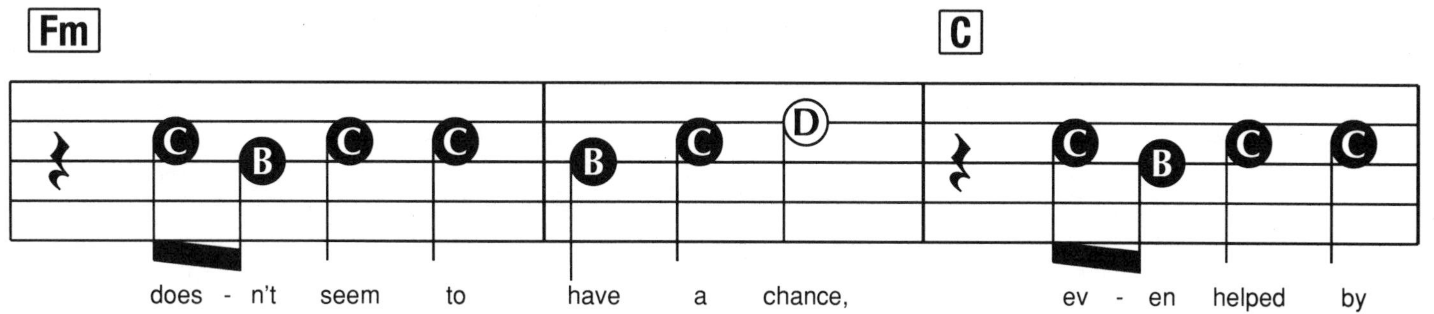
Fm
C
C
B
C
C
B
C
D
C
C
B
C
C
does - n't seem to have a chance, ev - en helped by

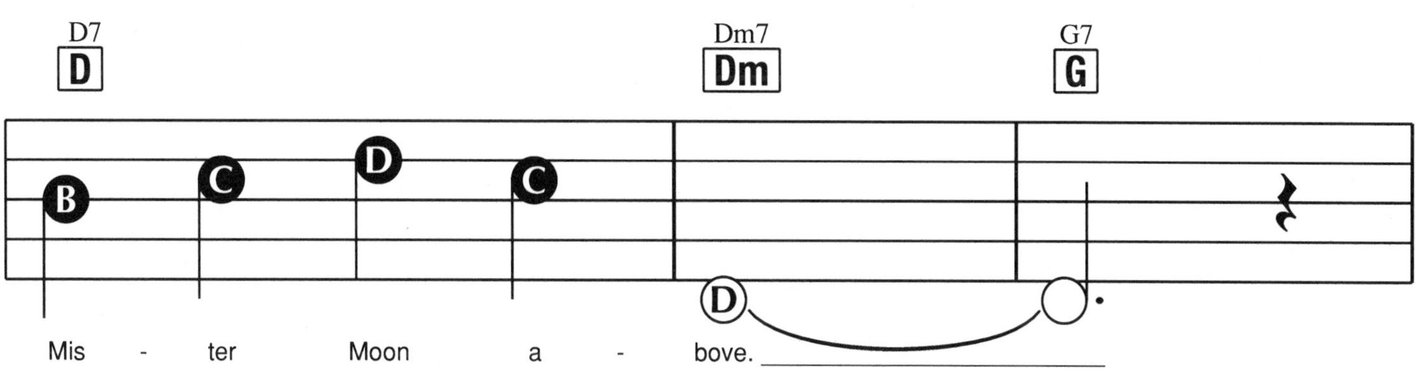
D7
D
Dm7
Dm
G7
G
B
C
D
C
D
Mis - ter Moon a - bove.

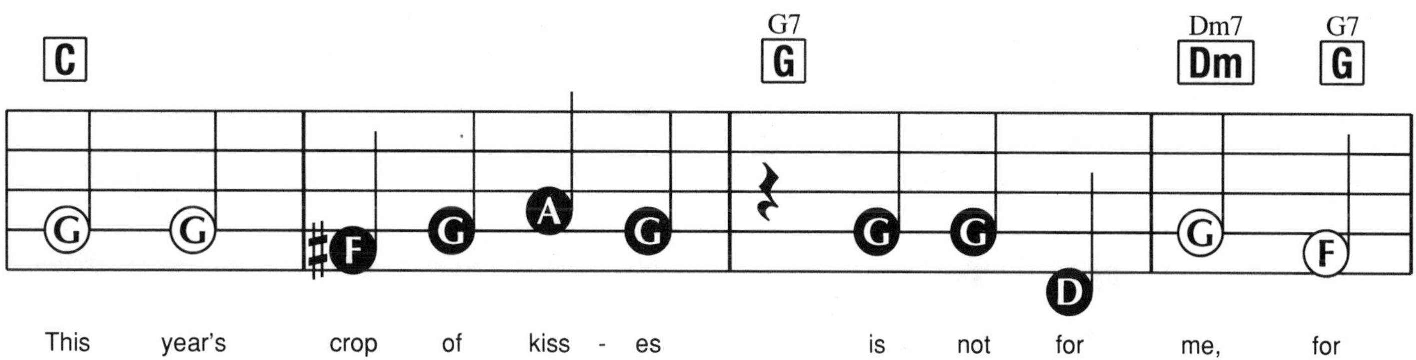
C
G7
G
Dm7
Dm
G7
G
G
G
F
G
A
G
G
G
D
G
F
This year's crop of kiss - es is not for me, for

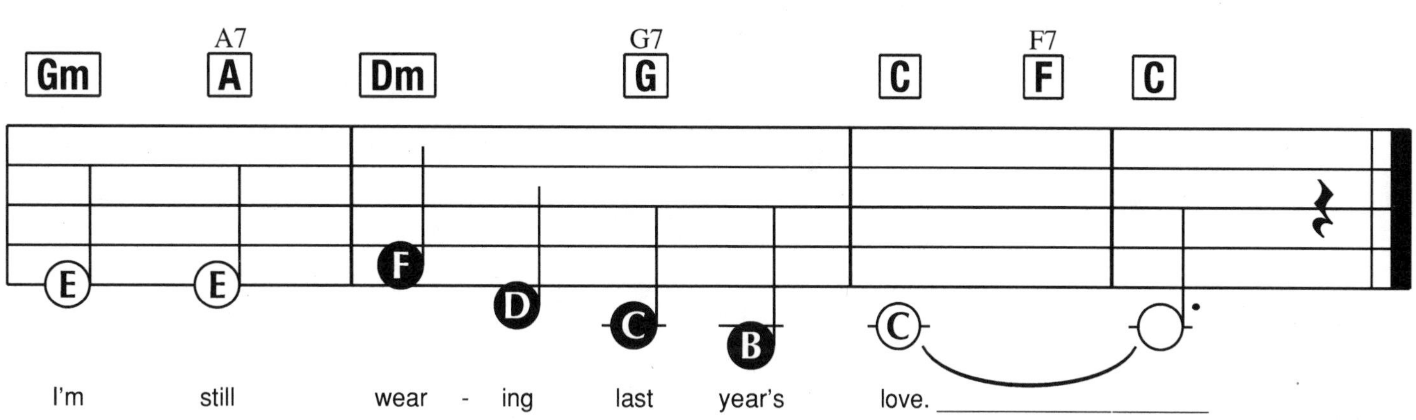
Gm
A7
A
Dm
G7
G
C
F7
F
C
E
E
F
D
C
B
C
I'm still wear - ing last year's love.

What'll I Do?

Registration 3
Rhythm: Waltz

Words and Music by
Irving Berlin

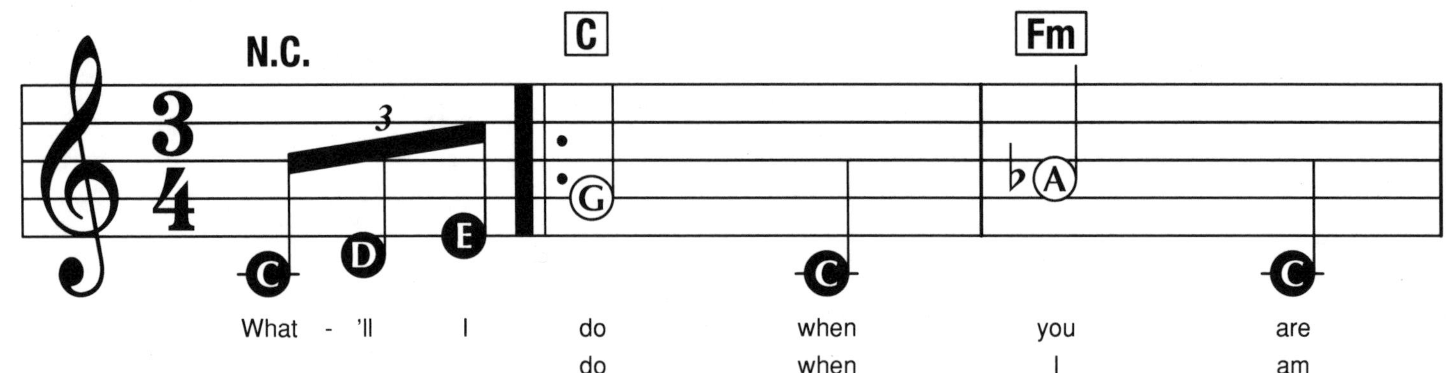

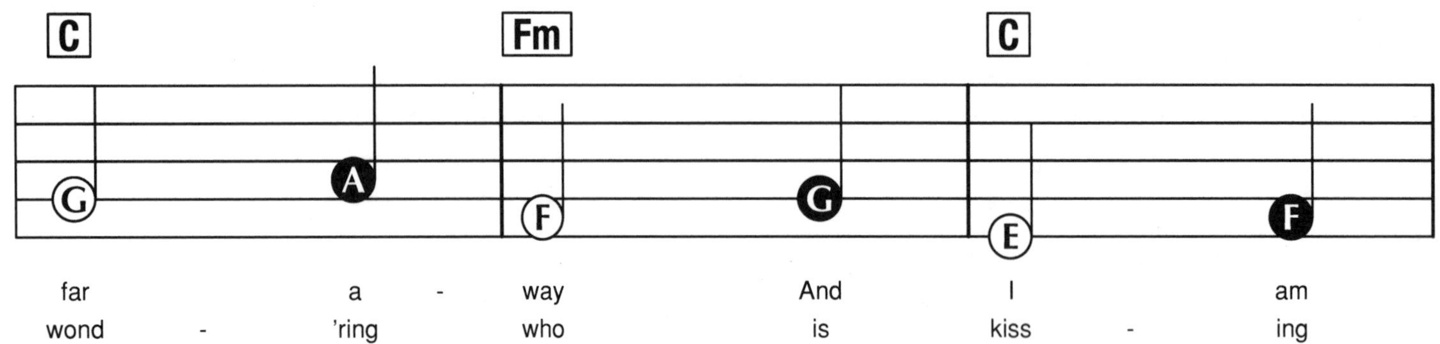

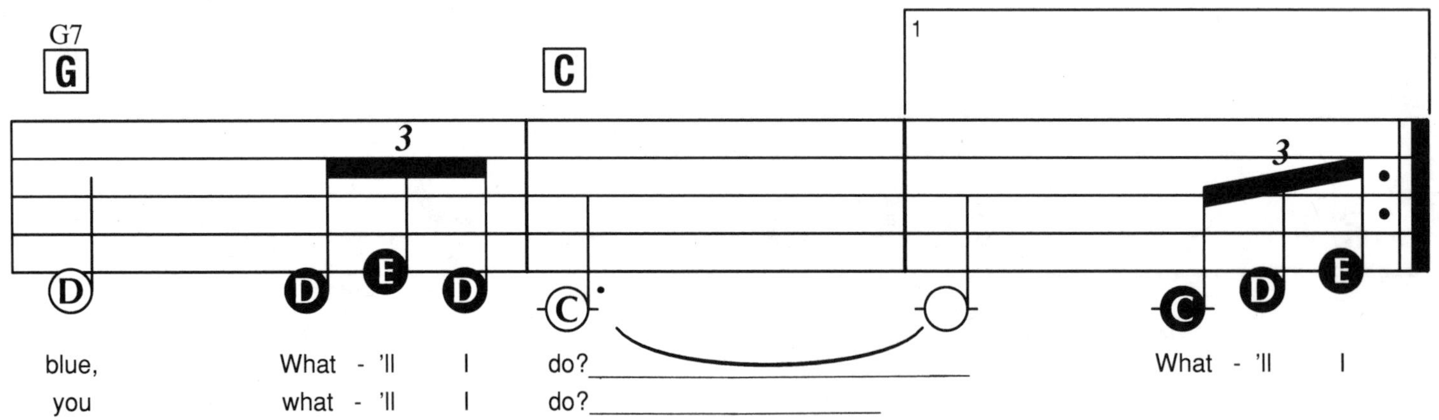

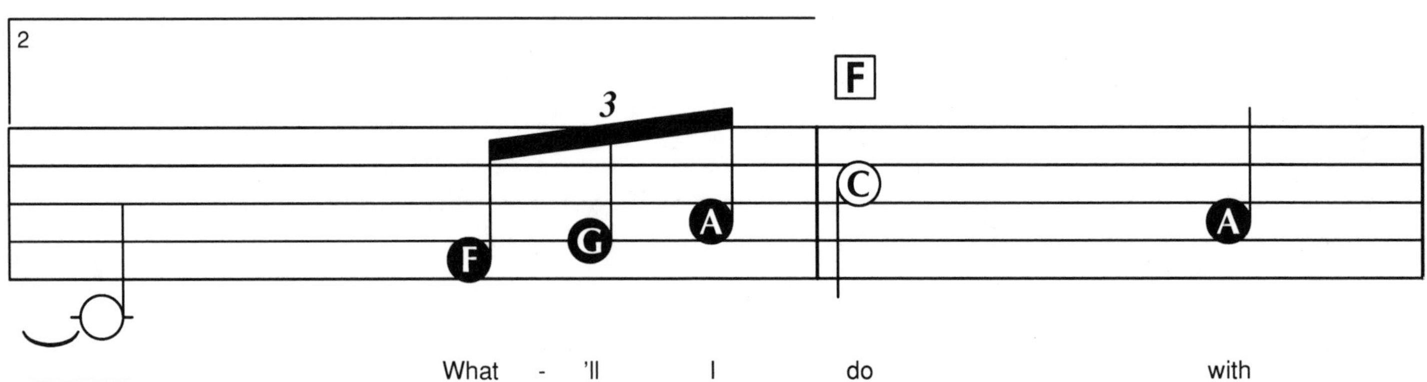

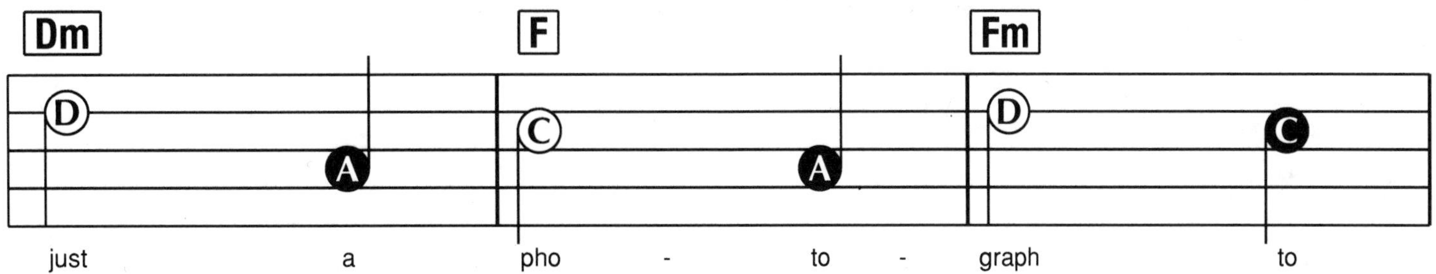
Dm
F
Fm
D
A
C
A
D
C
just
a
pho
-
to
-
graph
to

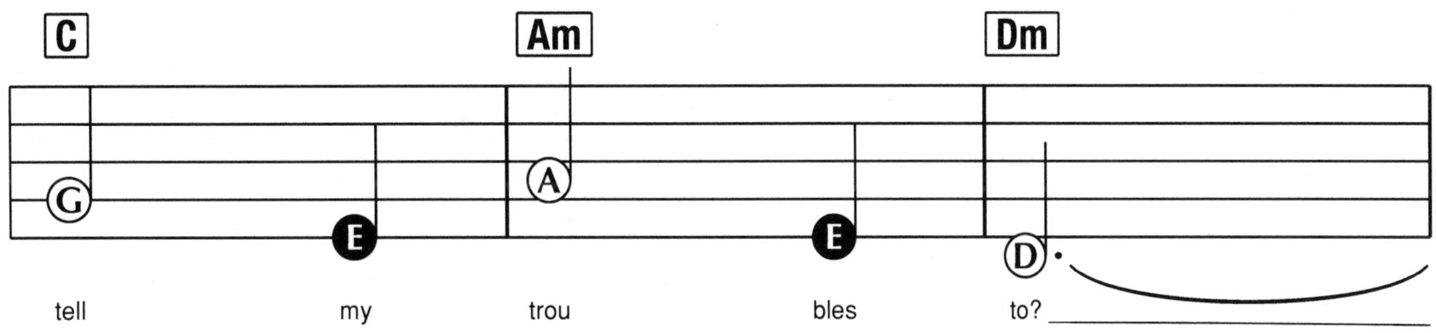
C
Am
Dm
G
E
A
E
D
tell
my
trou
bles
to?

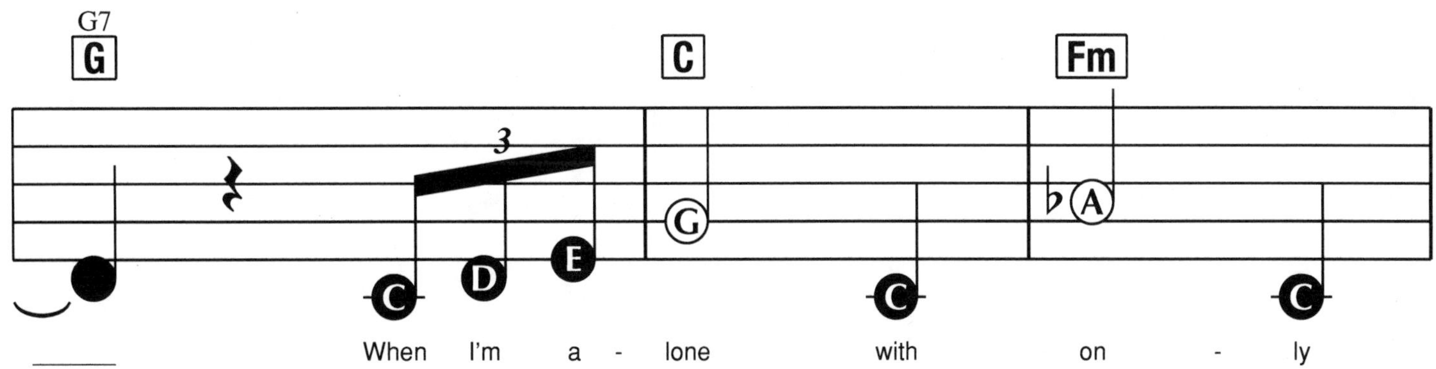
G7
G
C
Fm
3
C
D
E
G
C
A
C
When
I'm
a
-
lone
with
on
-
ly

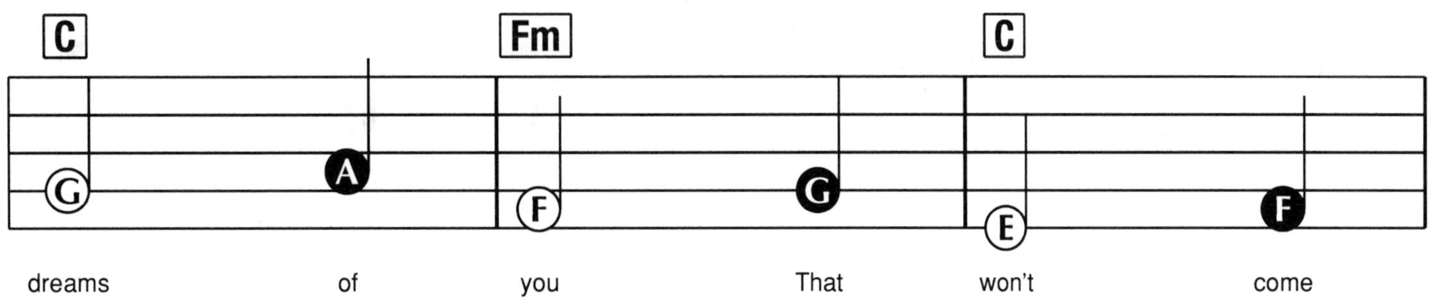
C
Fm
C
G
A
F
G
E
F
dreams
of
you
That
won't
come

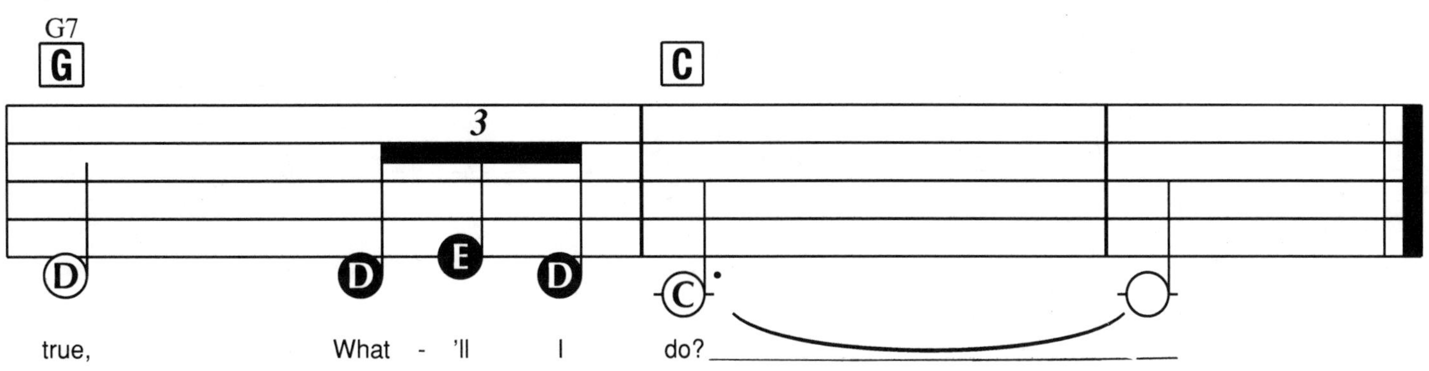
G7
G
C
3
D
D
E
D
C
true,
What
-
'll
I
do?

White Christmas

Registration 2
Rhythm: Fox Trot or Swing

Words and Music by Irving Berlin

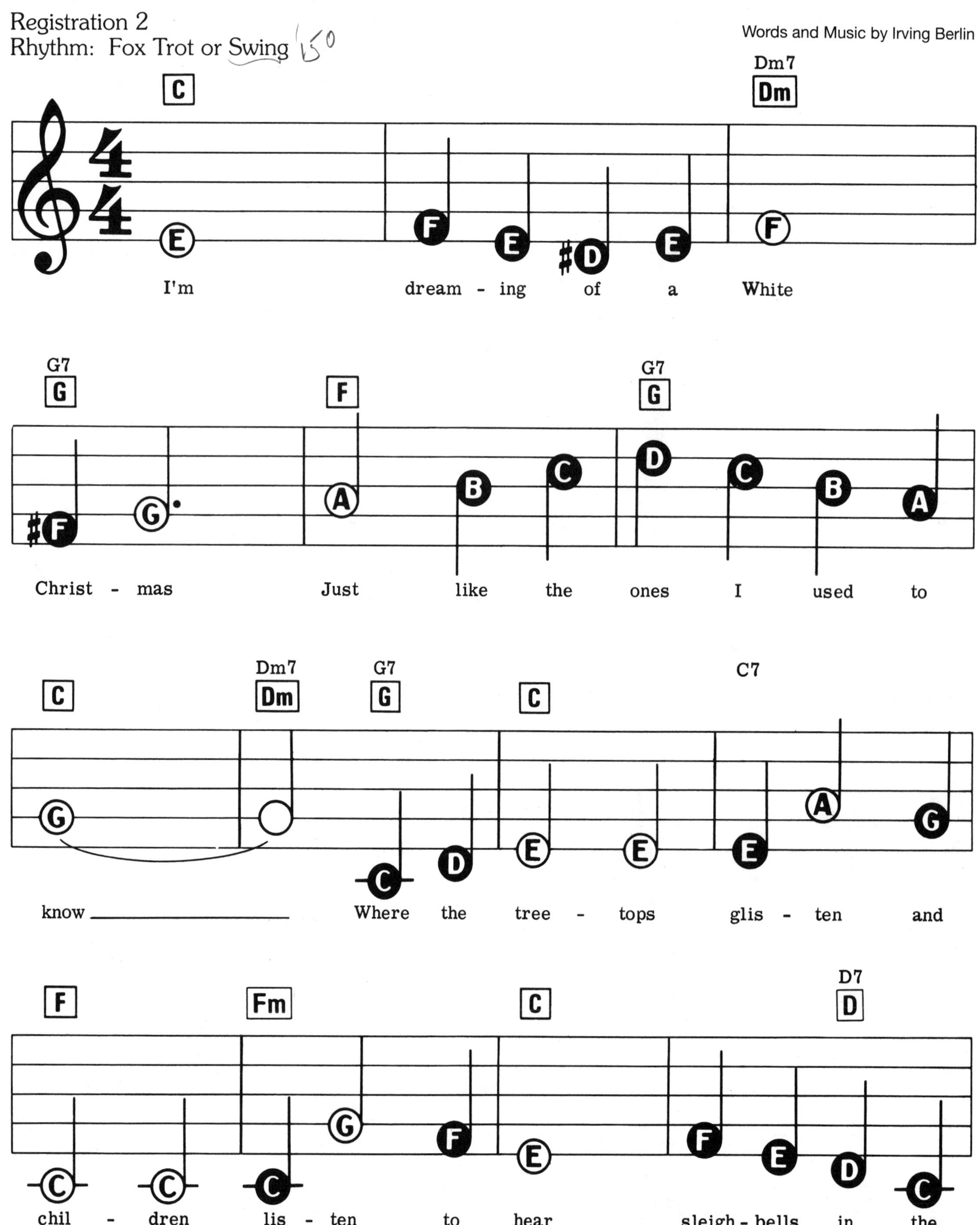

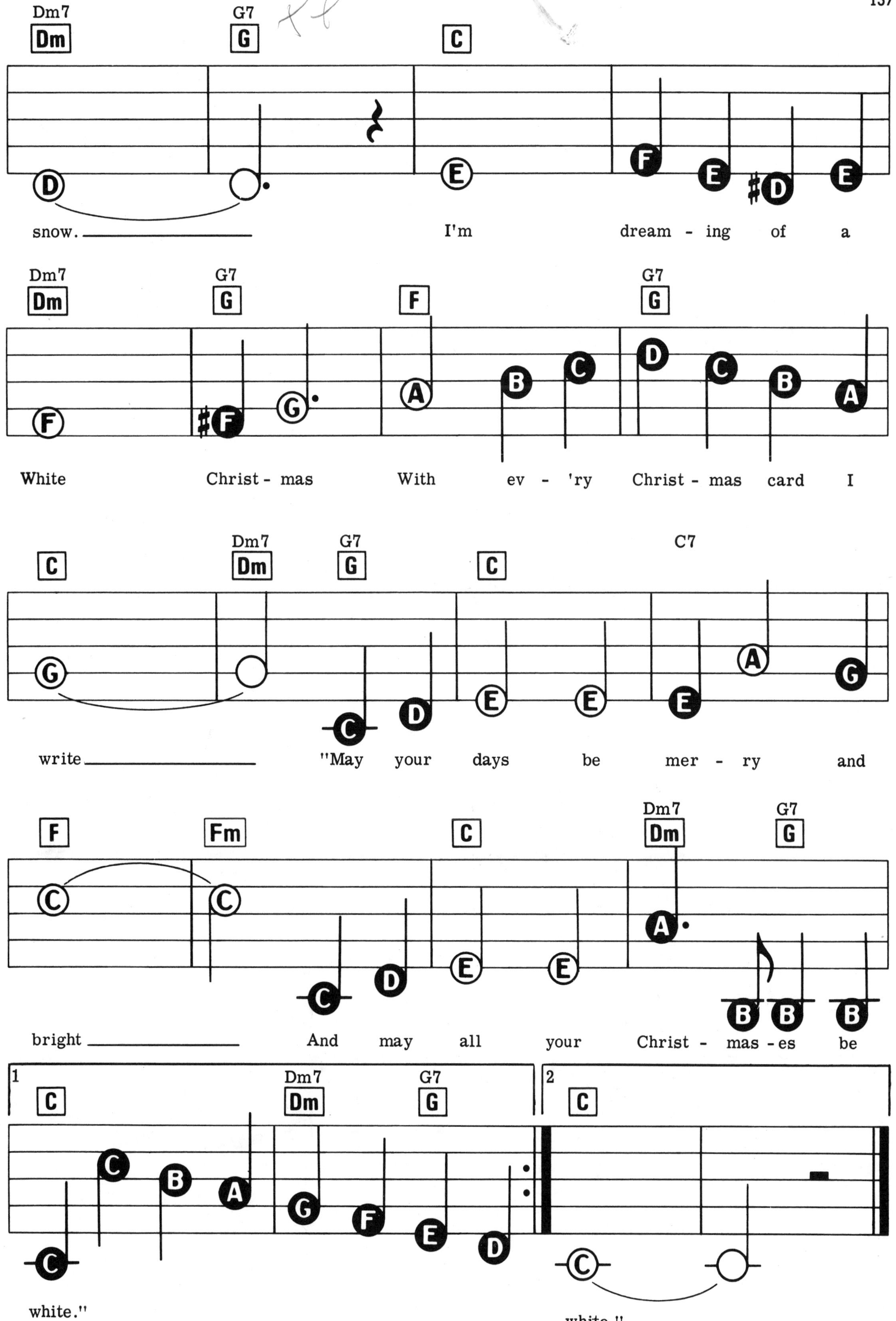
Dm7
Dm
G7
G
C
D
G
E
F
E
D
E
snow.
I'm
dream - ing of a
Dm7
Dm
G7
G
F
G7
G
F
F
G
A
B
C
D
C
B
A
White
Christ - mas
With
ev - 'ry
Christ - mas card I
C
Dm7
Dm
G7
G
C
C7
G
C
D
E
E
E
A
G
write
"May your days be mer - ry and
F
Fm
C
Dm7
Dm
G7
G
C
C
C
D
E
E
A
B
B
B
bright
And may all your Christ - mas - es be
1
C
Dm7
Dm
G7
G
2
C
C
C
B
A
G
F
E
D
C
white."
white."

Who

Registration 2
Rhythm: Swing

Words and Music by
Irving Berlin

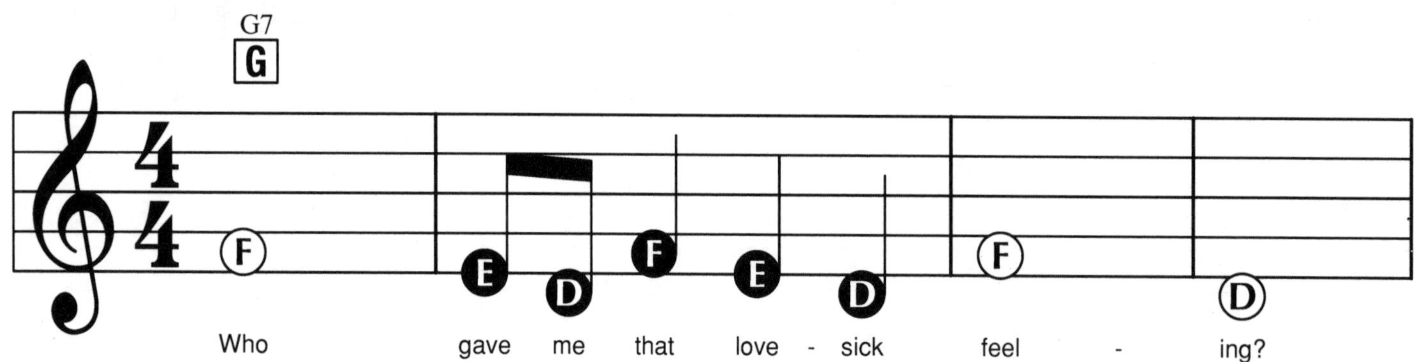

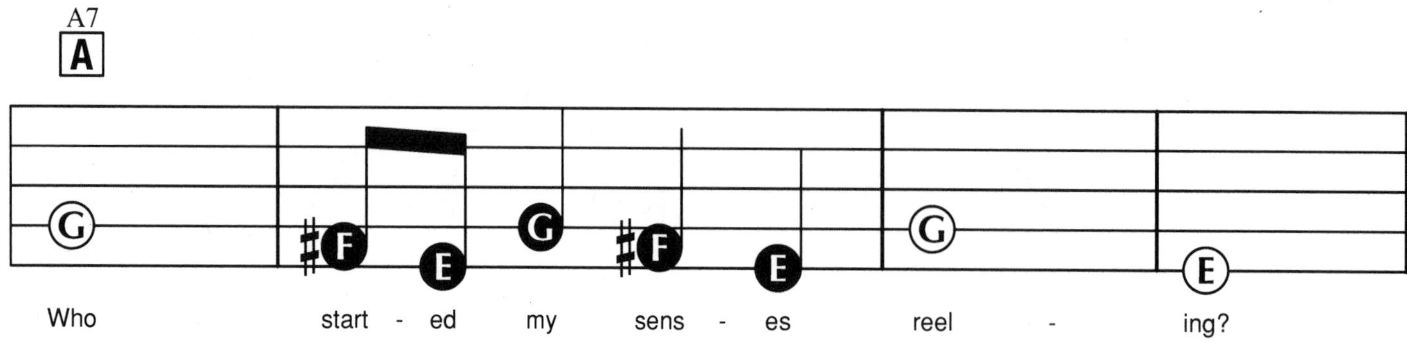

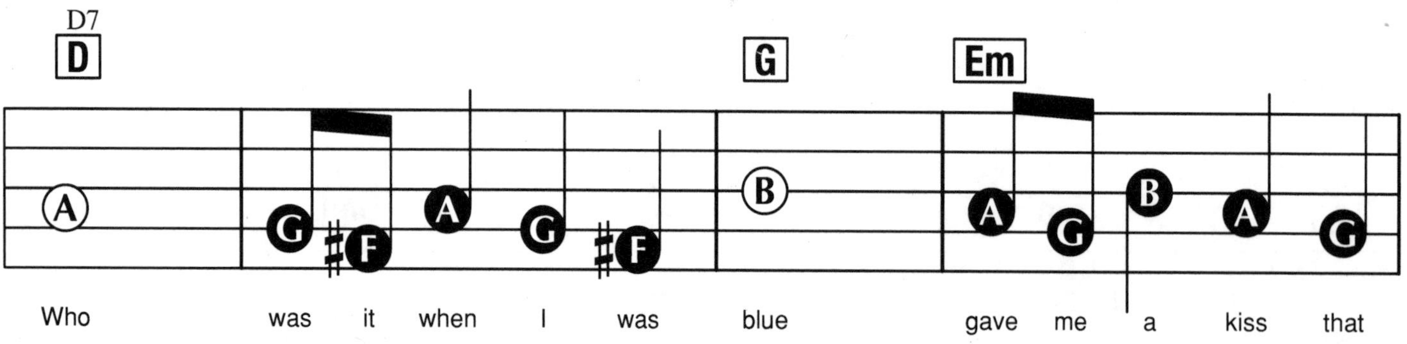

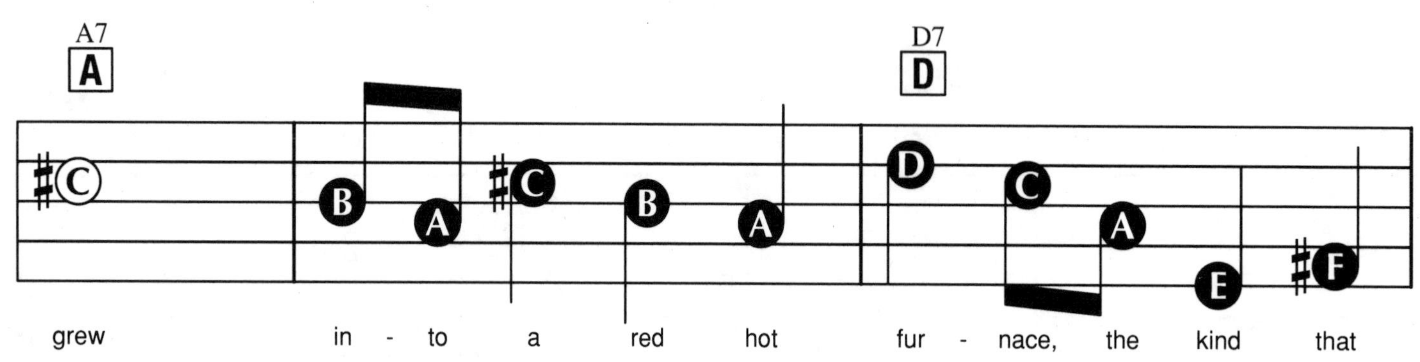

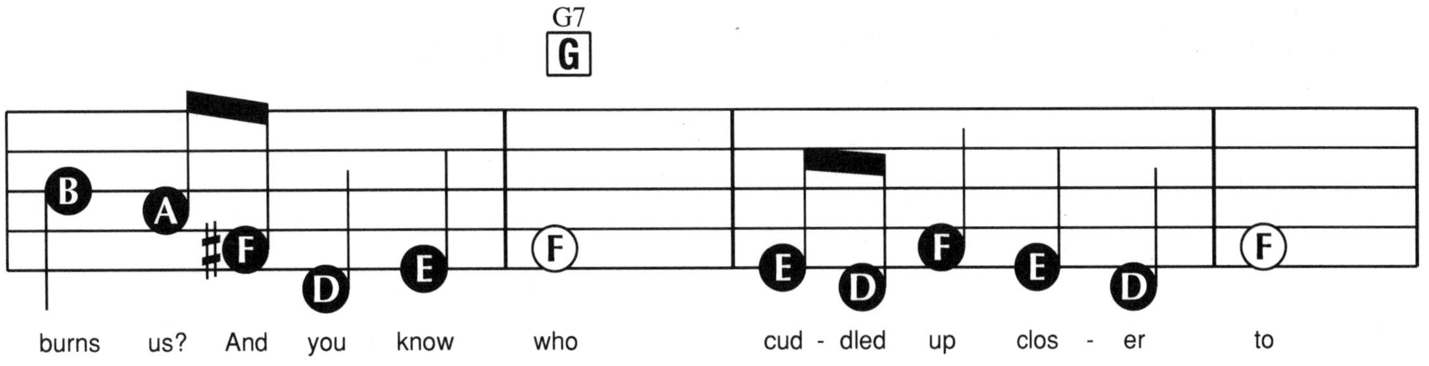
G7
G
B
A
♯F
D
E
F
E
D
F
E
D
F
burns us? And you know who cud - dled up clos - er to

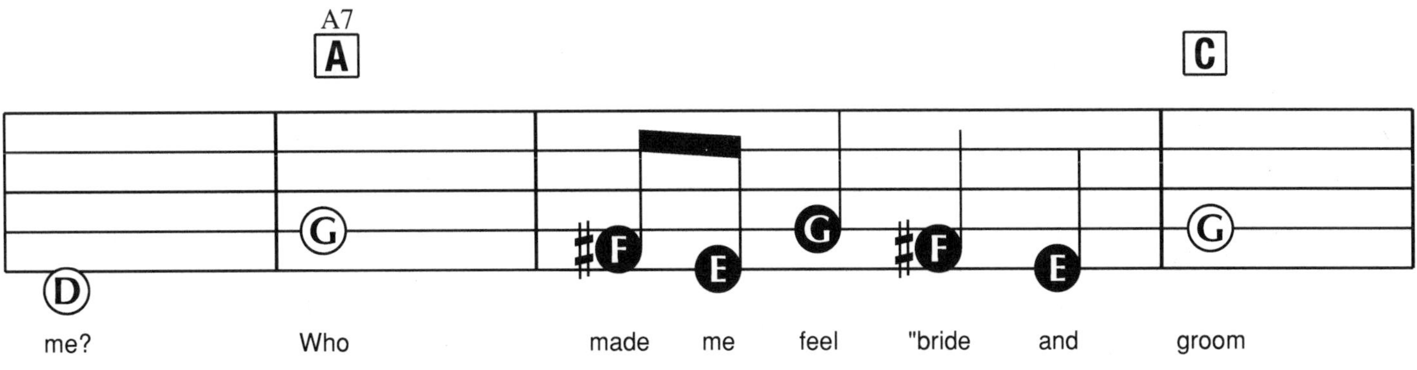
A7
A
C
D
G
♯F
E
G
♯F
E
G
me? Who made me feel "bride and groom

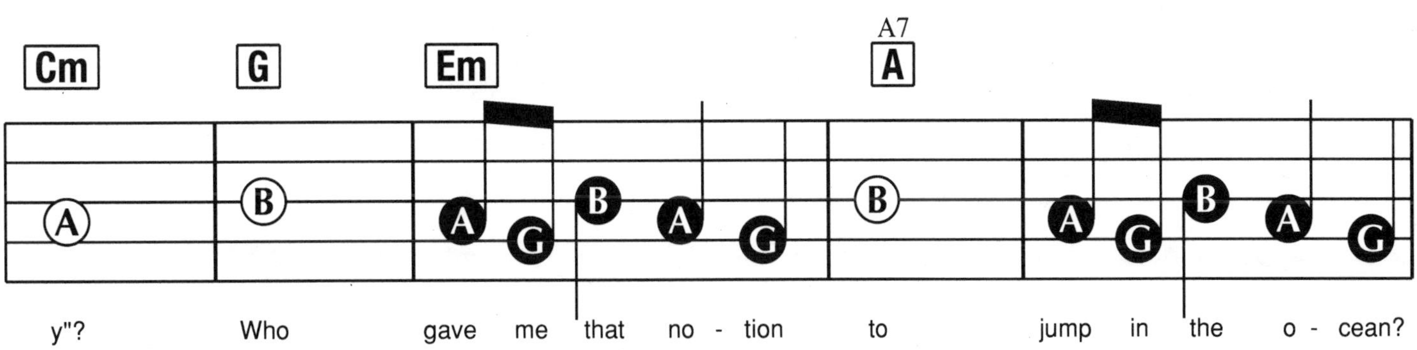
Cm
G
Em
A7
A
A
B
A
G
B
A
G
B
A
G
B
A
G
y"? Who gave me that no - tion to jump in the o - cean?

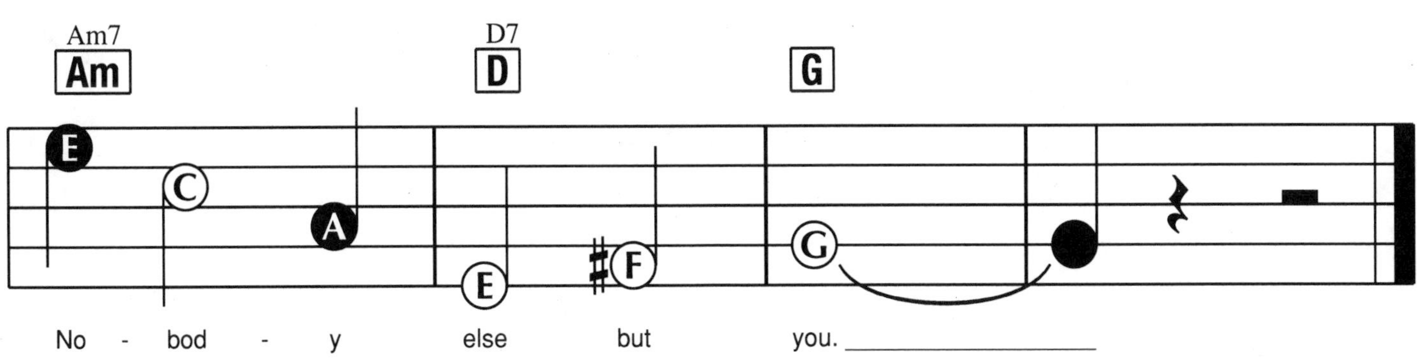
Am7
Am
D7
D
G
E
C
A
E
♯F
G
No - bod - y else but you.

Top Hat, White Tie And Tails

Registration 1
Rhythm: Swing

Words and Music by
Irving Berlin

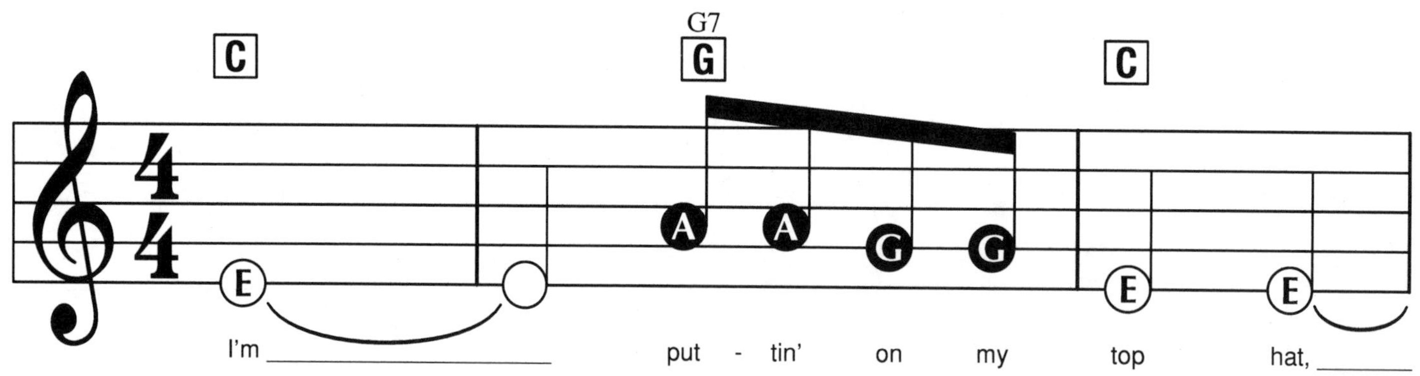

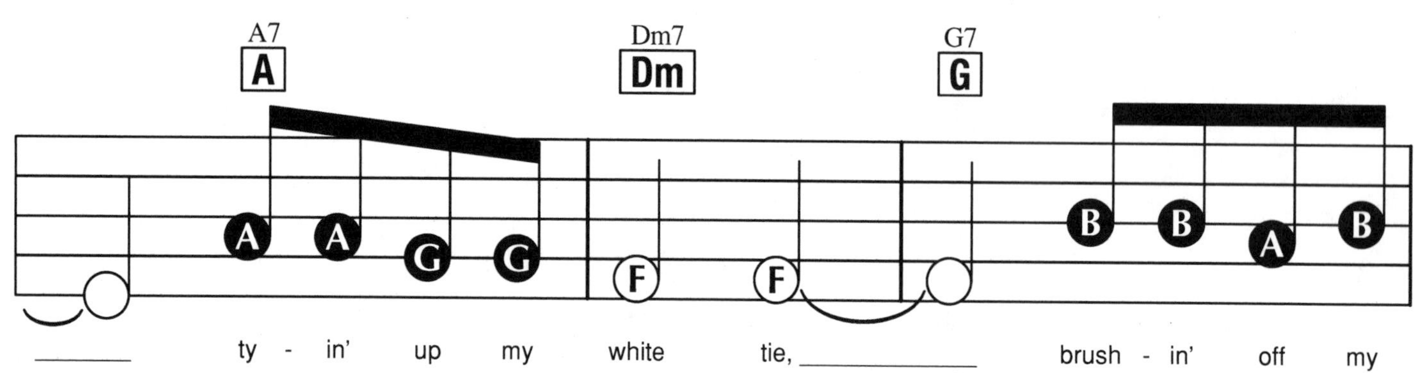

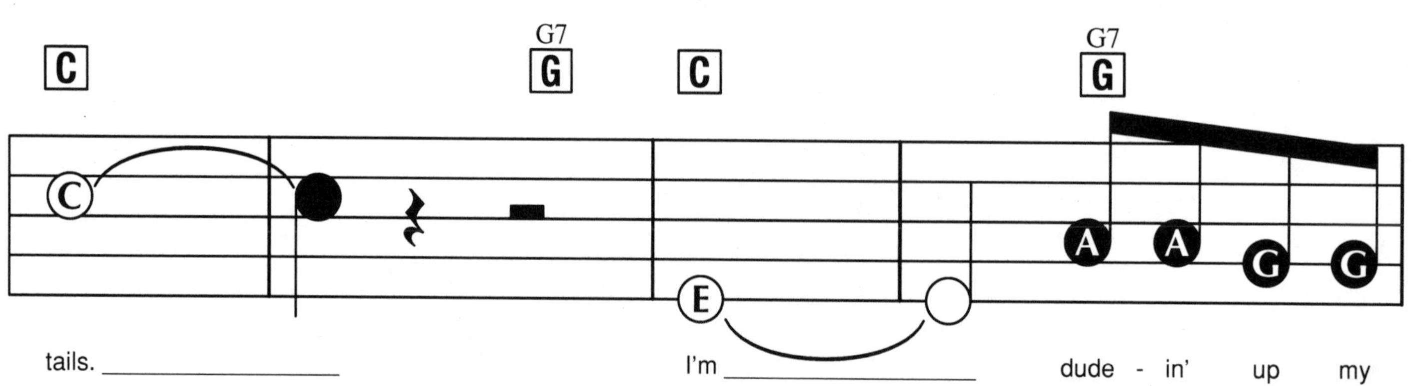

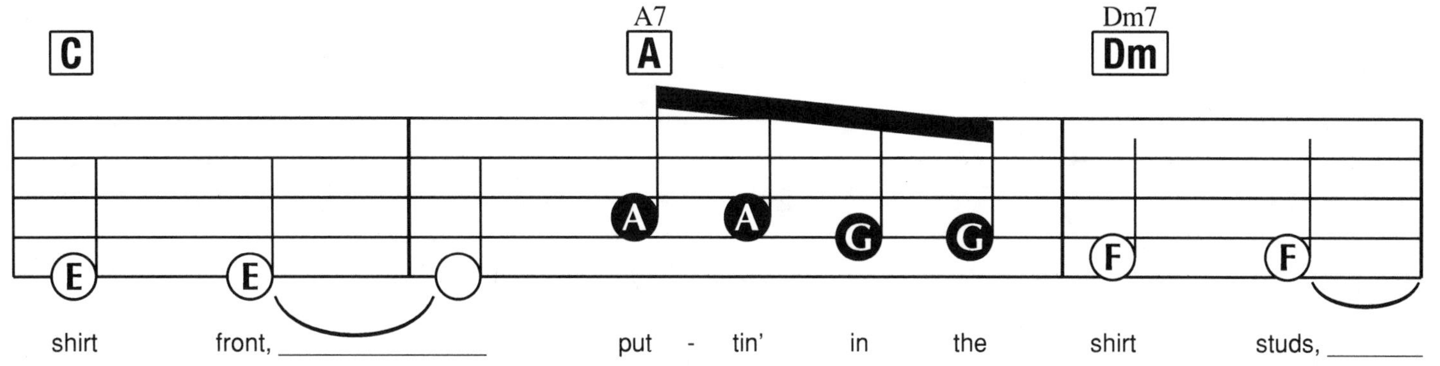
C
A7
A
Dm7
Dm
shirt front, put - tin' in the shirt studs,

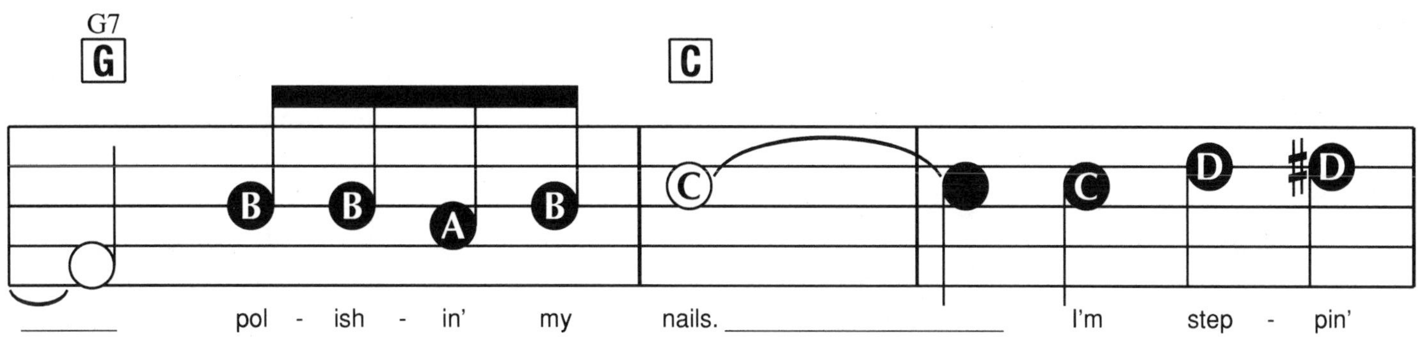
G7
G
C
pol - ish - in' my nails. I'm step - pin'

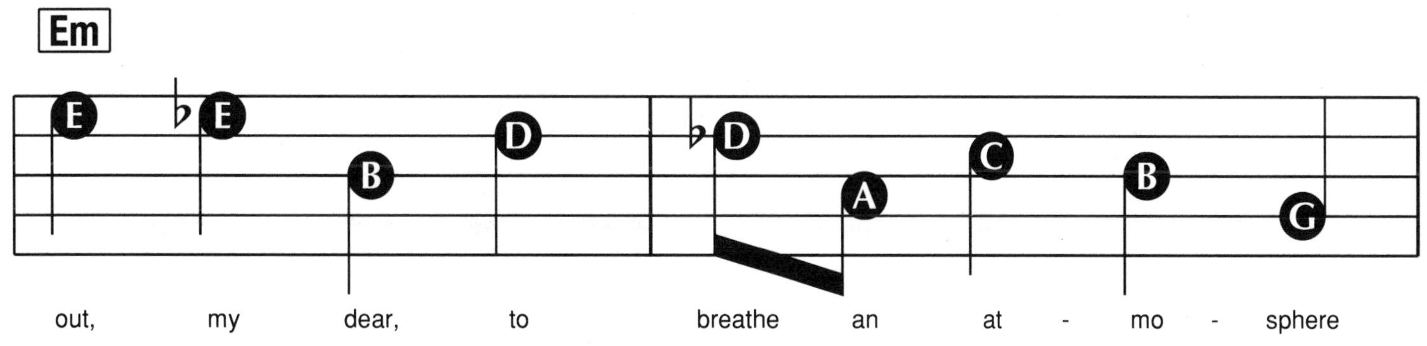
Em
out, my dear, to breathe an at - mo - sphere

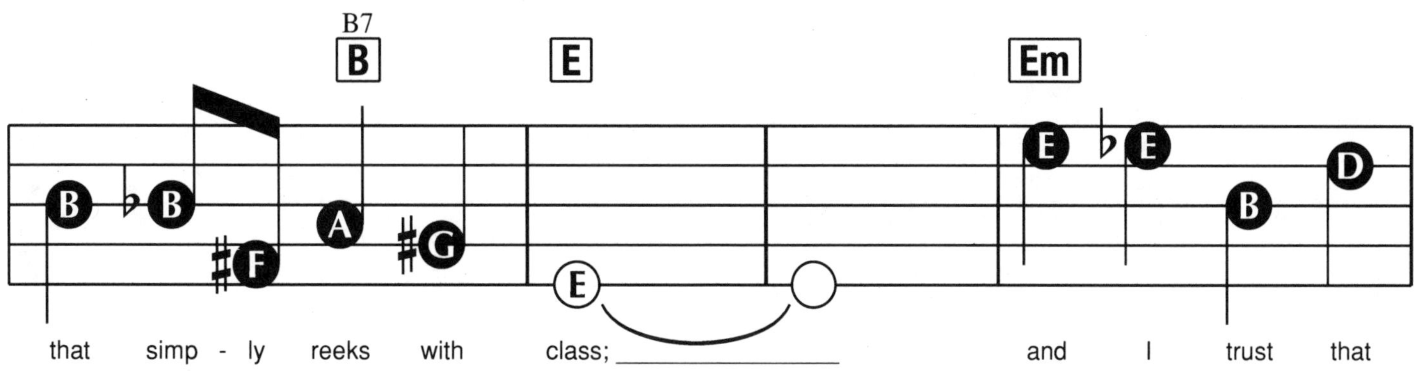
B7
B
E
Em
that simp - ly reeks with class; and I trust that

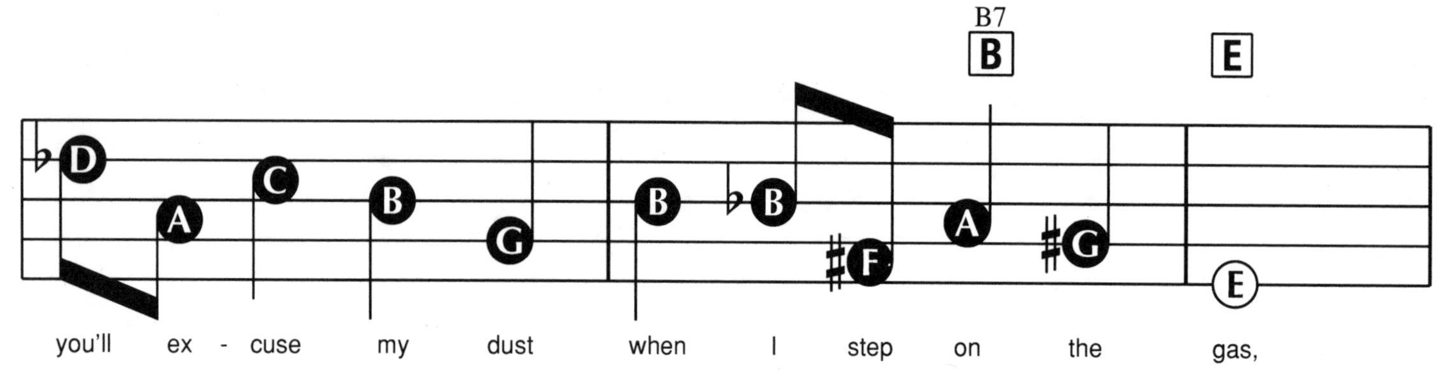
B7
B
E
D
A
C
B
G
B
B
F
A
G
E
you'll ex - cuse my dust when I step on the gas,

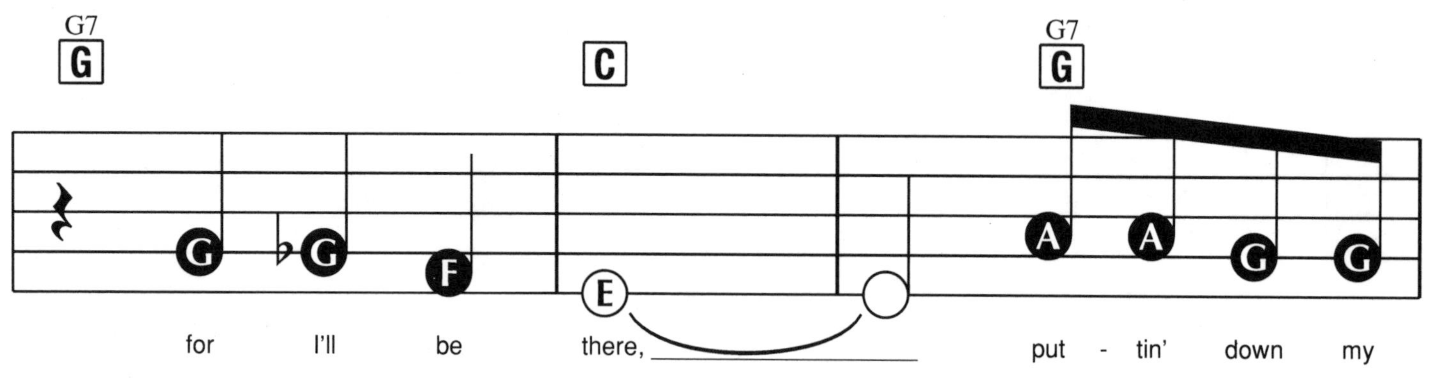
G7
G
C
G7
G
G
G
F
E
A
A
G
G
for I'll be there, put - tin' down my

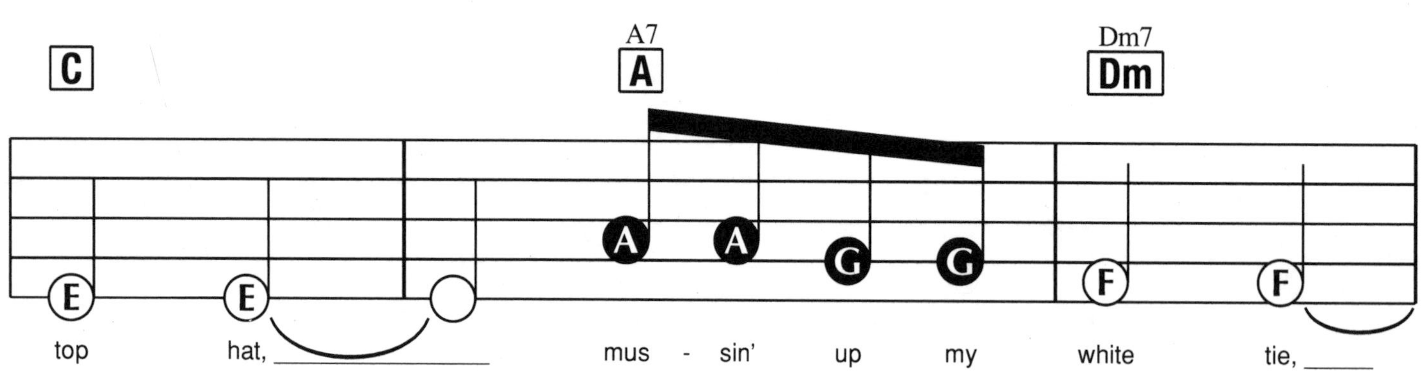
C
A7
A
Dm7
Dm
E
E
A
A
G
G
F
F
top hat, mus - sin' up my white tie,

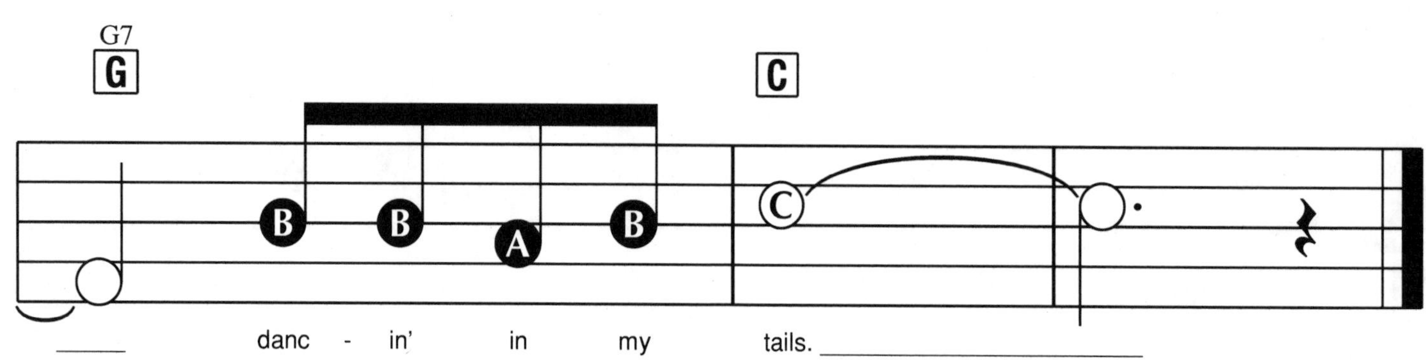
G7
G
C
B
B
A
B
C
danc - in' in my tails.

You'd Be Surprised

Registration 8
Rhythm: Swing

Words and Music by
Irving Berlin

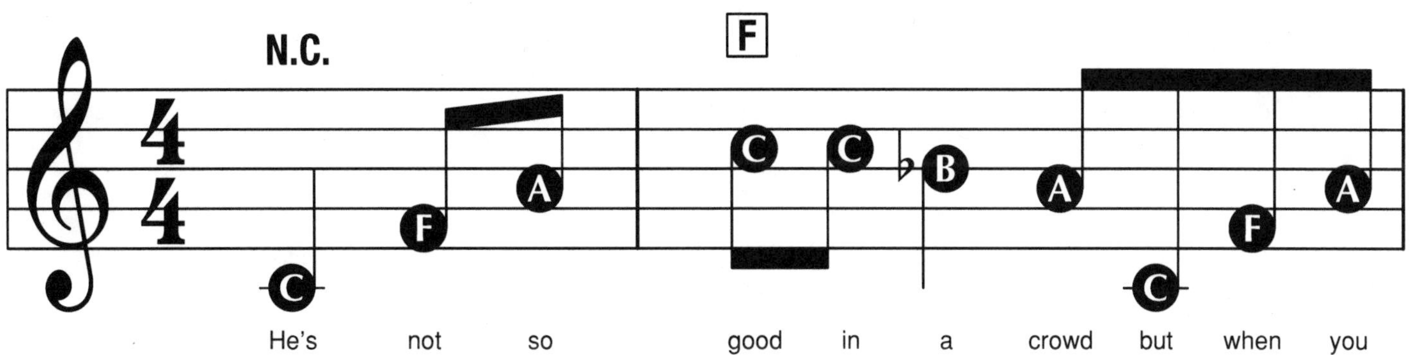

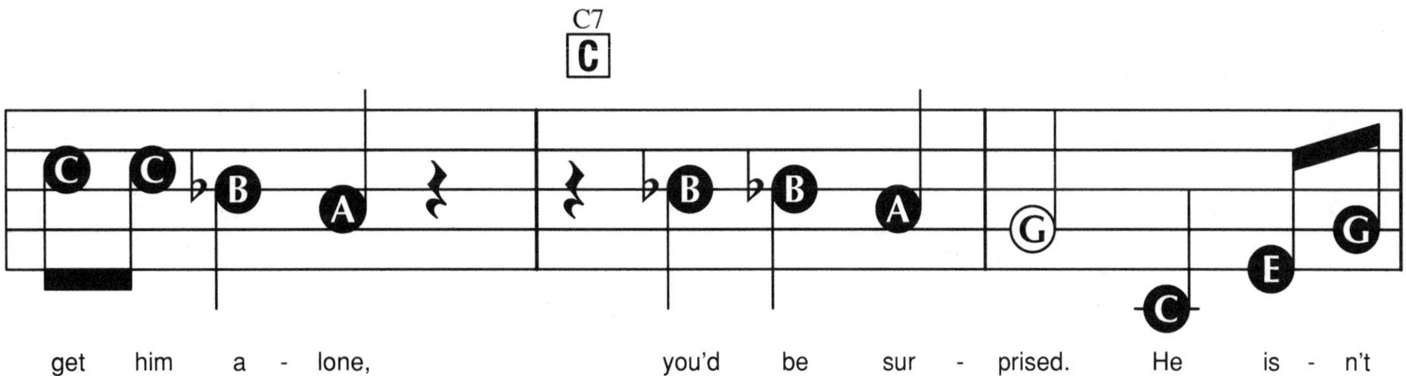

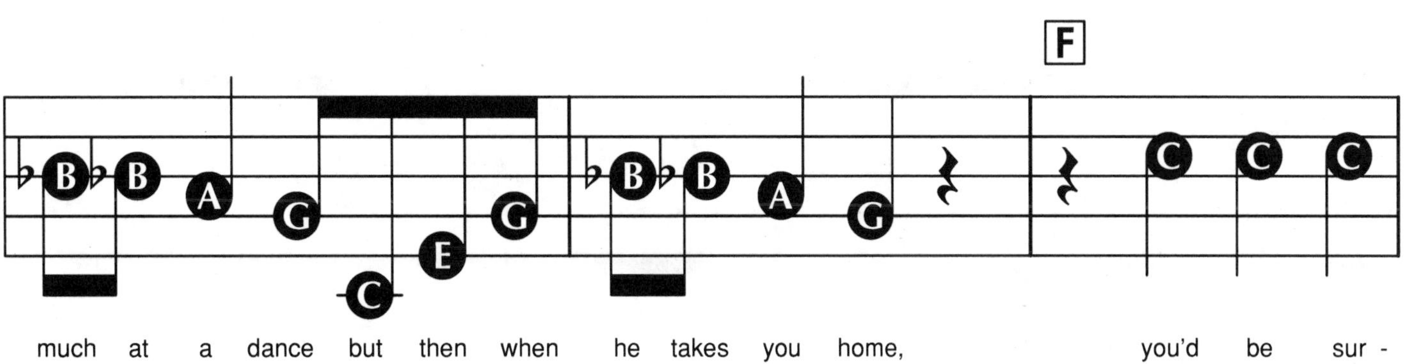

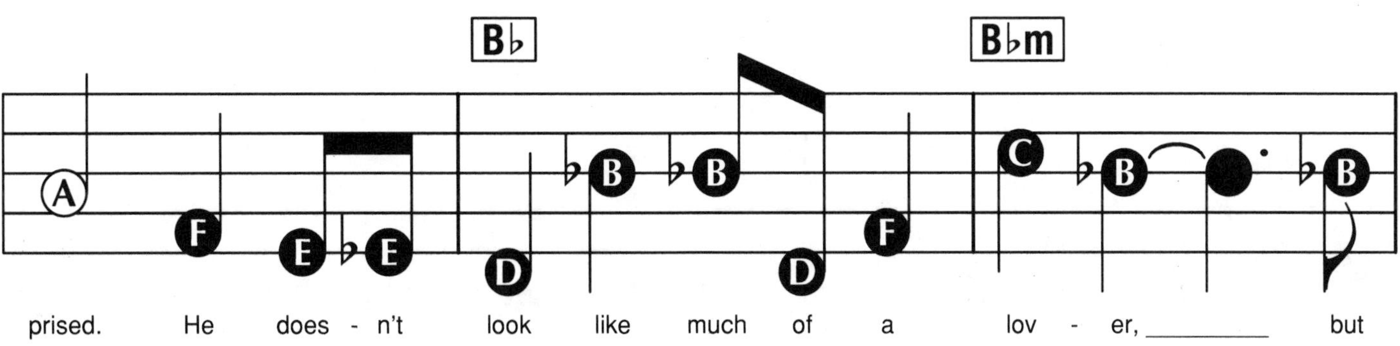

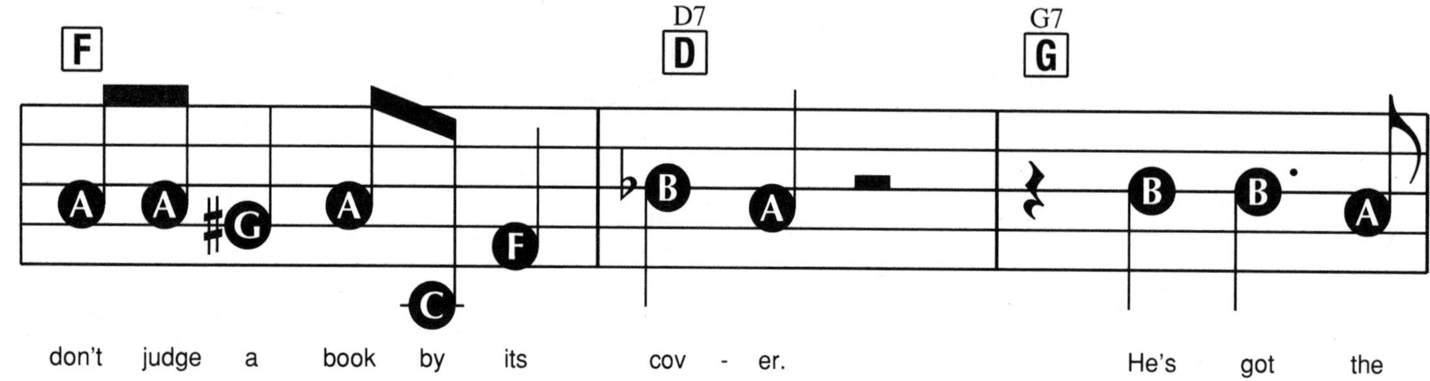
F
D7
D
G7
G
A A G A C F B A B B A
don't judge a book by its cov - er. He's got the

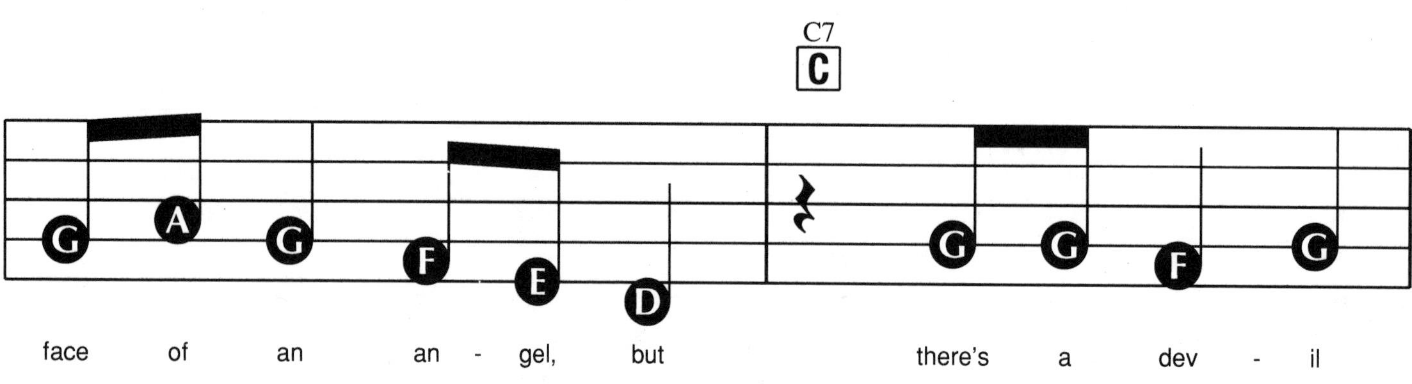
C7
C
G A G F E D G G F G
face of an an - gel, but there's a dev - il

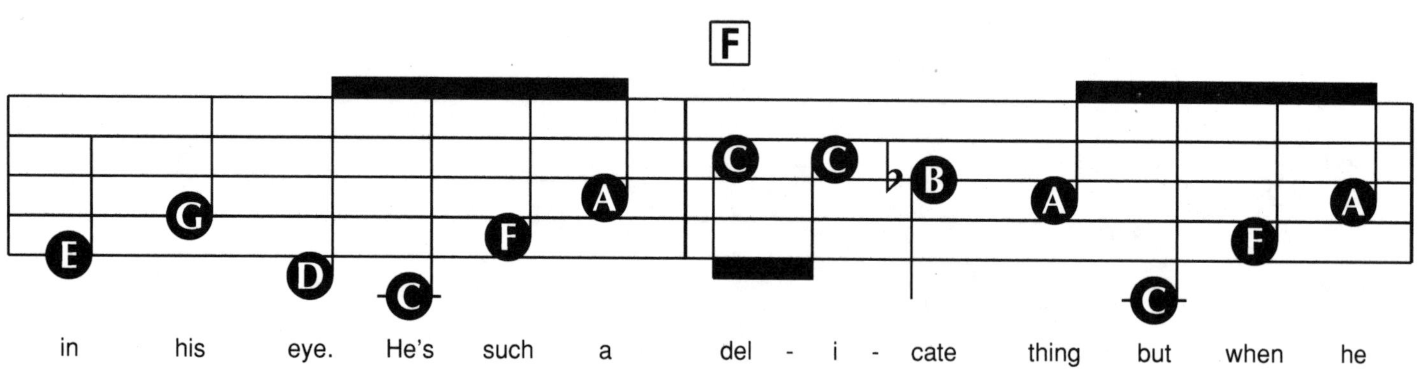
F
E G D C F A C C B A C F A
in his eye. He's such a del - i - cate thing but when he

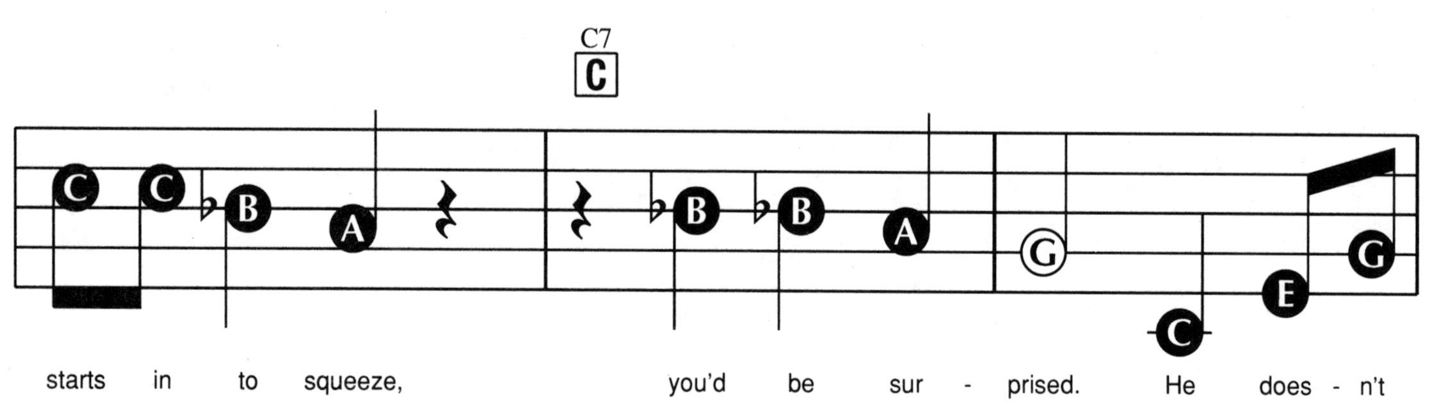
C7
C
C C B A B B A G C E G
starts in to squeeze, you'd be sur - prised. He does - n't

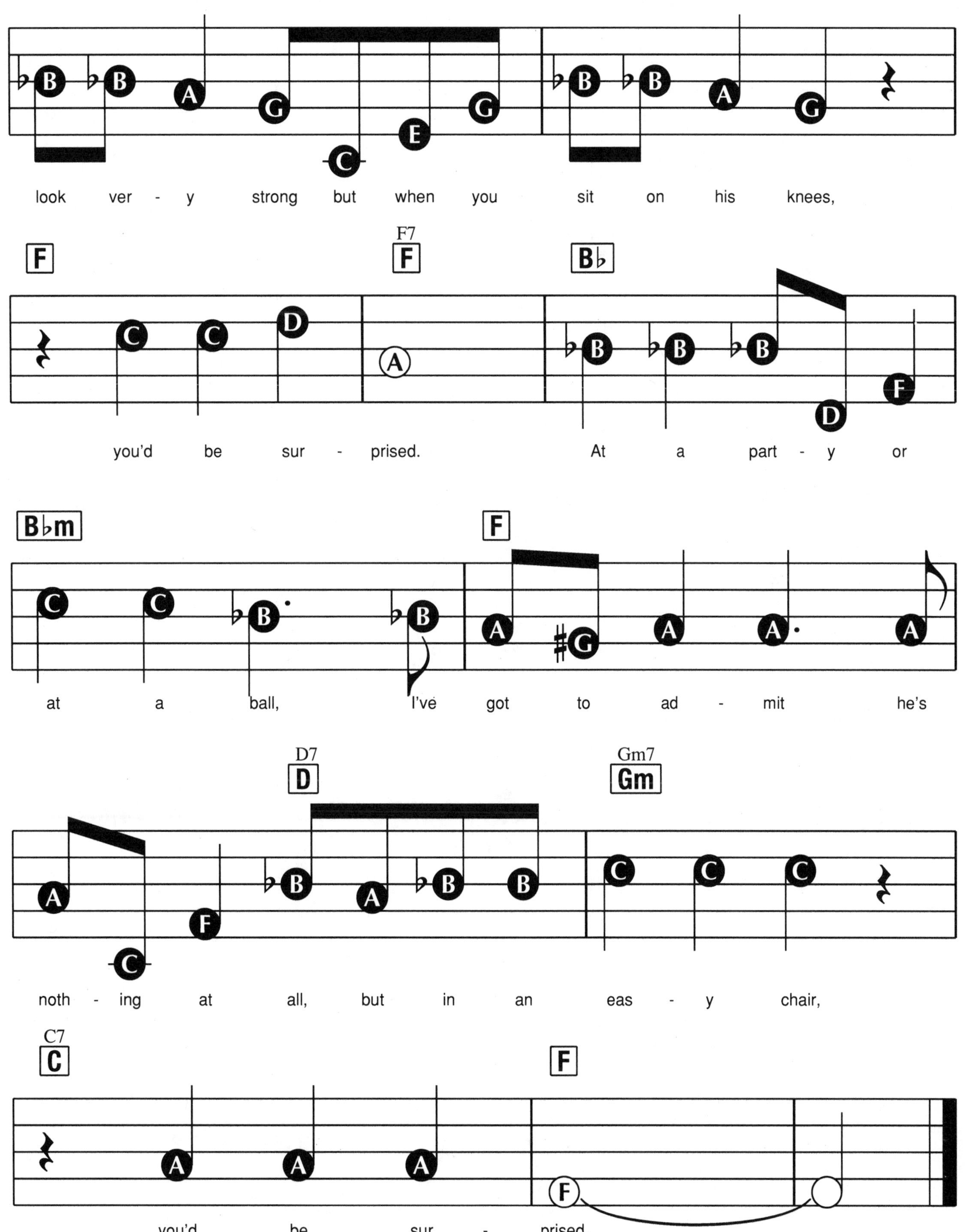

look ver - y strong but when you sit on his knees,
F
F7
F
B♭
you'd be sur - prised. At a part - y or
B♭m
F
at a ball, I've got to ad - mit he's
D7
D
Gm7
Gm
noth - ing at all, but in an eas - y chair,
C7
C
F
you'd be sur - prised.

You Can't Get A Man With A Gun

Registration 4
Rhythm: March

Words and Music by
Irving Berlin

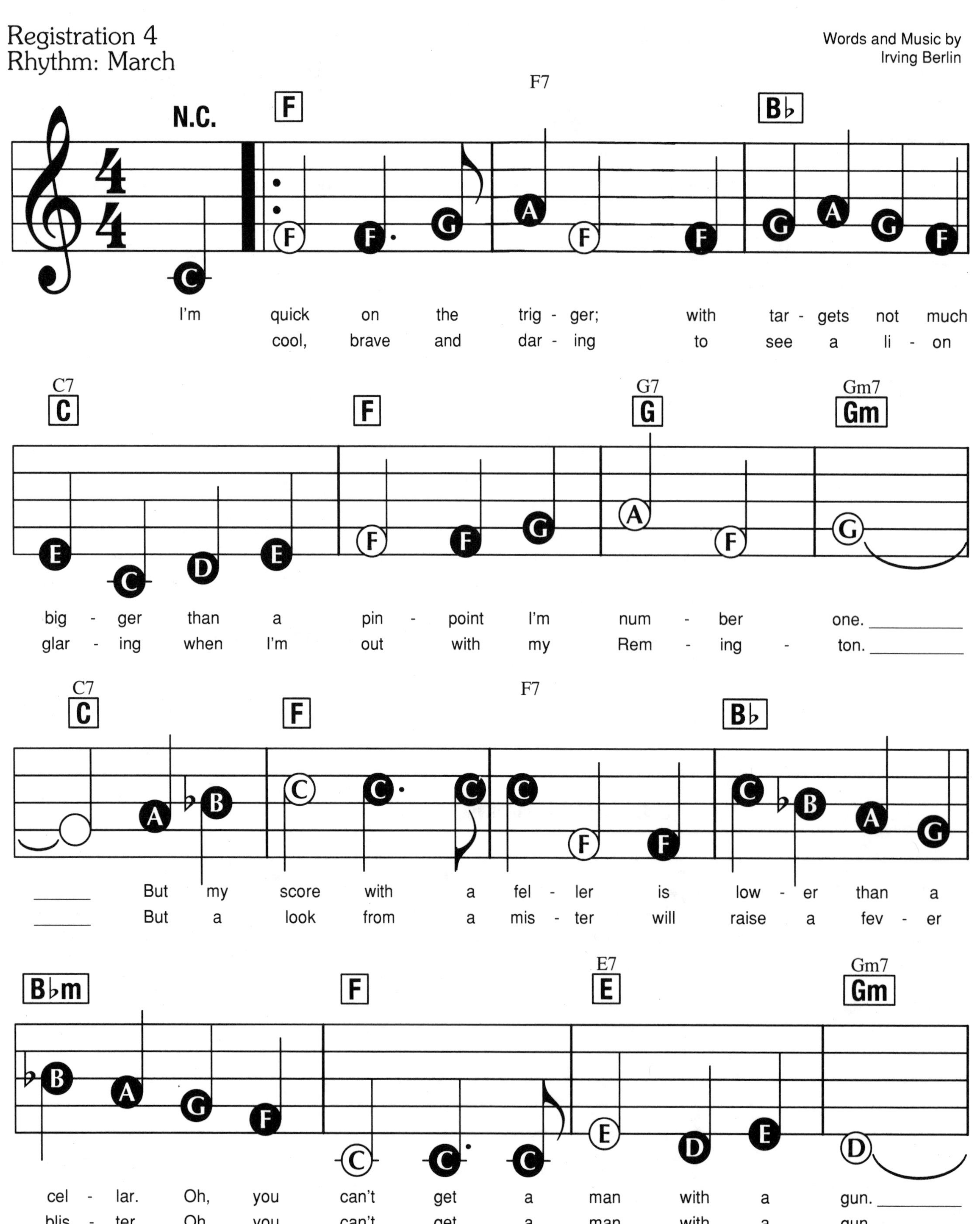

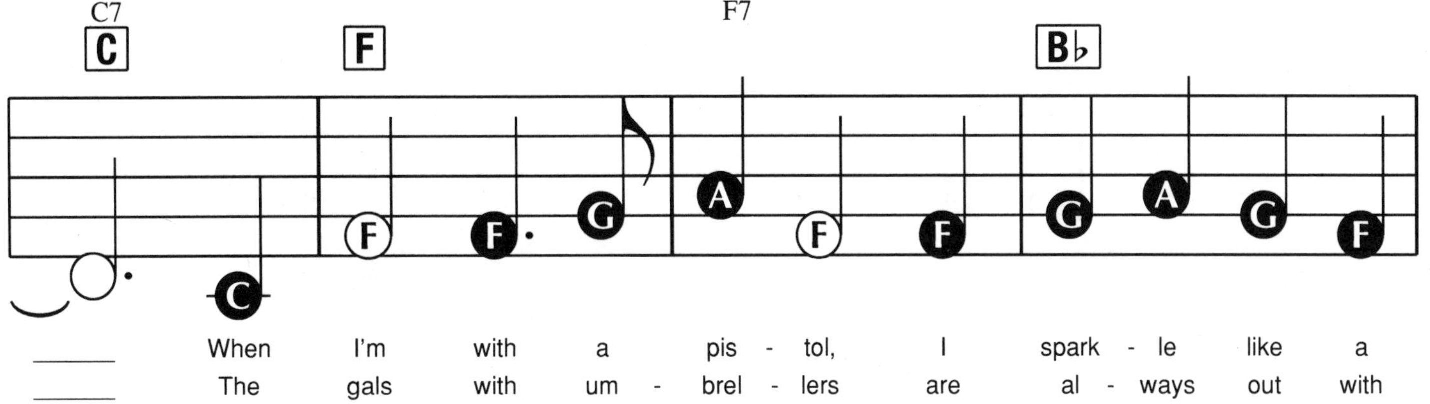
C7
C
F
F7
B♭
F
F
G
A
F
F
G
A
G
F
C
When I'm with a pis - tol, I spark - le like a
The gals with um - brel - lers are al - ways out with

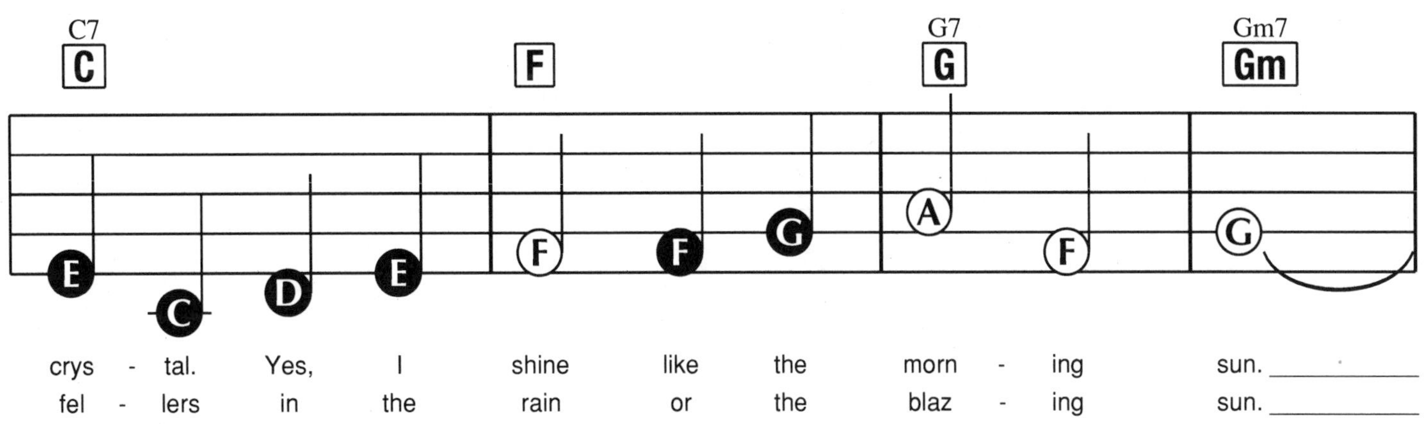
C7
C
F
G7
G
Gm7
Gm
E
C
D
E
F
F
G
A
F
G
crys - tal. Yes, I shine like the morn - ing sun.
fel - lers in the rain or the blaz - ing sun.

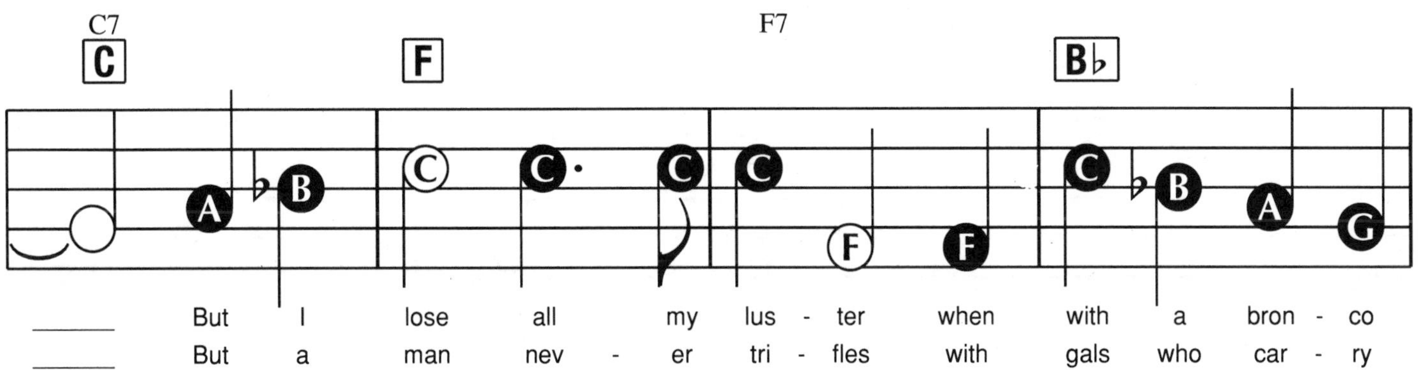
C7
C
F
F7
B♭
A
B
C
C
C
C
F
F
C
B
A
G
But I lose all my lus - ter when with a bron - co
But a man nev - er tri - fles with gals who car - ry

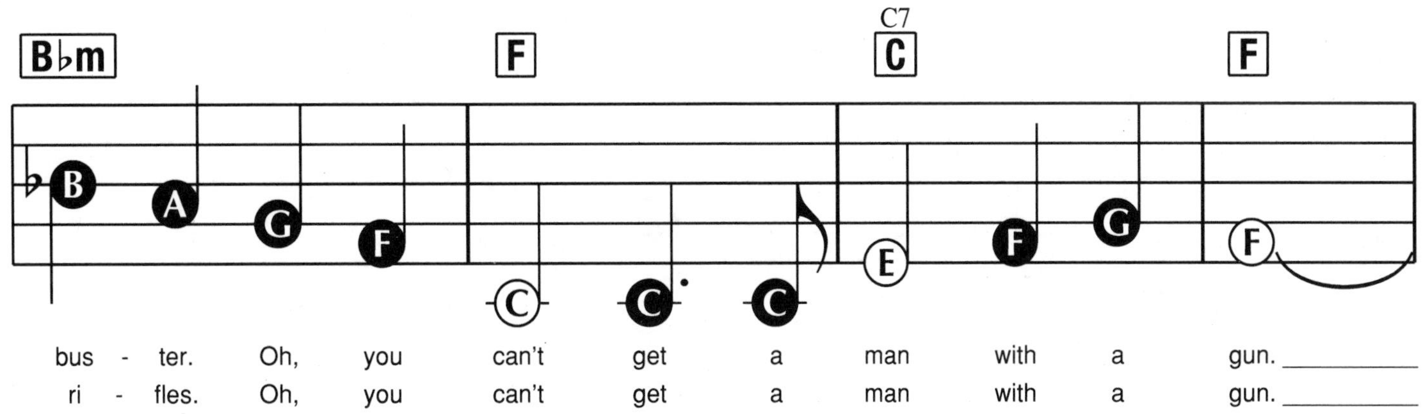
B♭m
F
C7
C
F
B
A
G
F
C
C
C
E
F
G
F
bus - ter. Oh, you can't get a man with a gun.
ri - fles. Oh, you can't get a man with a gun.

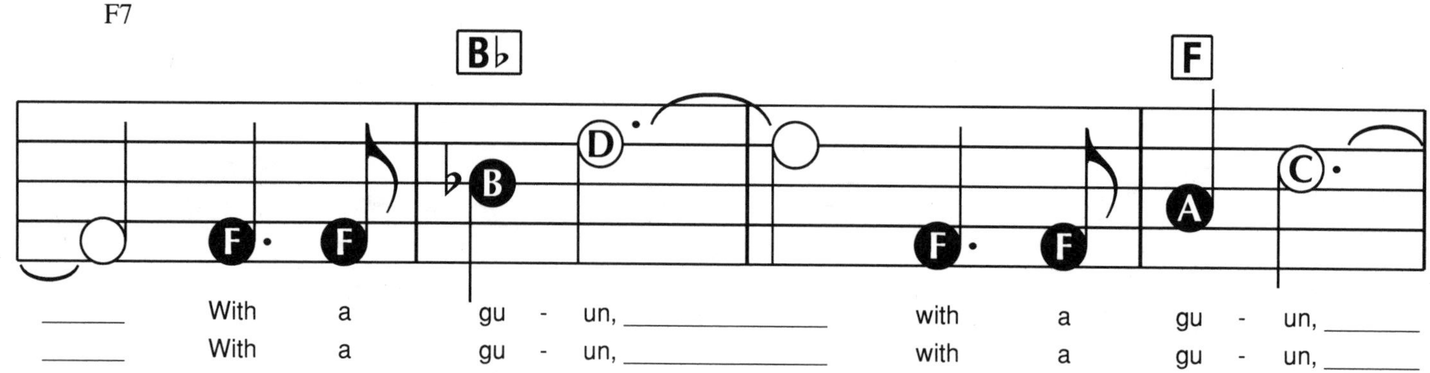
F7
B♭
F
With a gu - un, with a gu - un,
With a gu - un, with a gu - un,

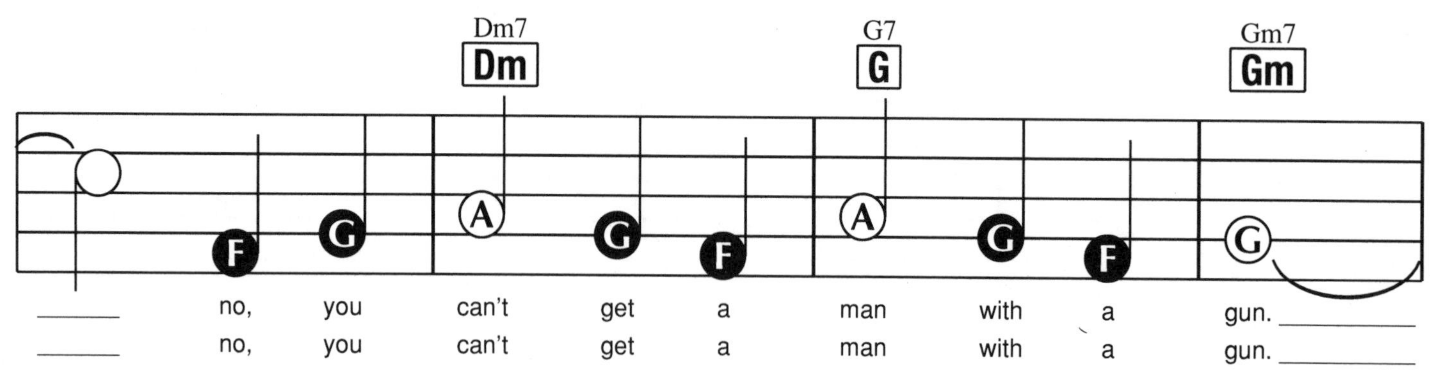
Dm7
Dm
G7
G
Gm7
Gm
no, you can't get a man with a gun.
no, you can't get a man with a gun.

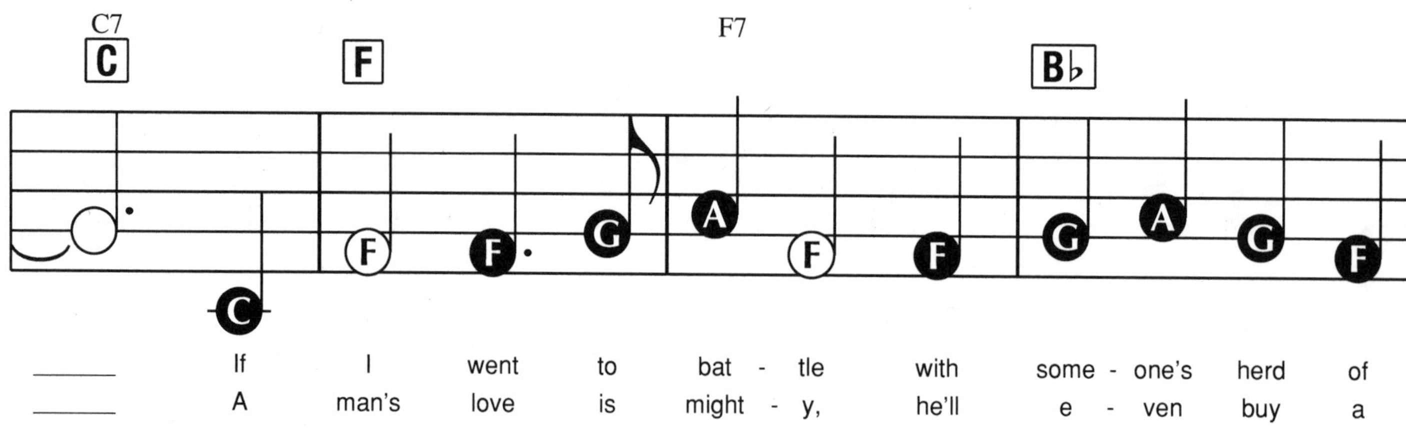
C7
C
F
F7
B♭
If I went to bat - tle with some - one's herd of
A man's love is might - y, he'll e - ven buy a

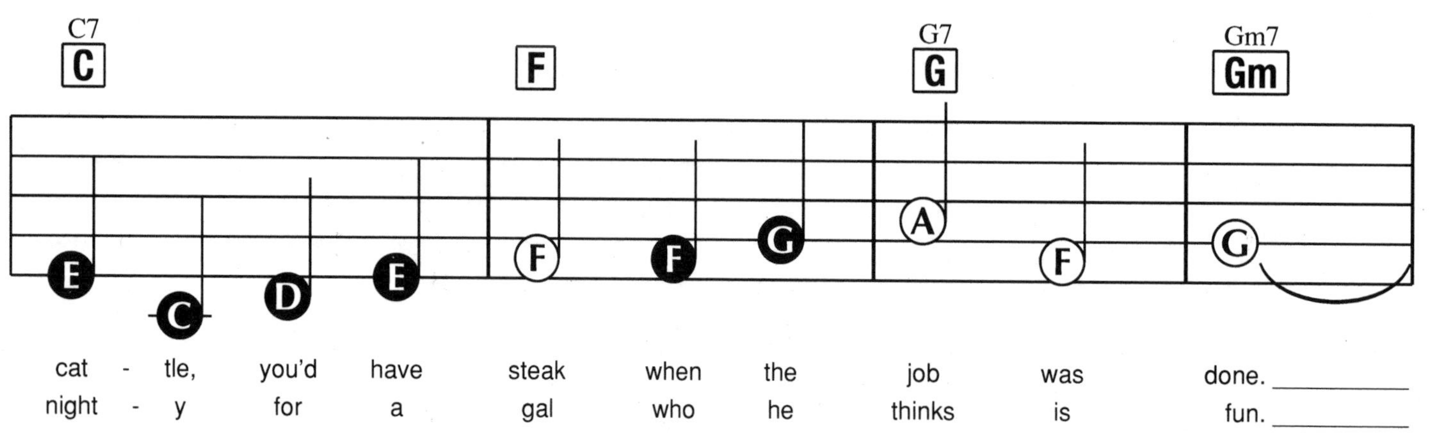
C7
C
F
G7
G
Gm7
Gm
cat - tle, you'd have steak when the job was done.
night - y for a gal who he thinks is fun.

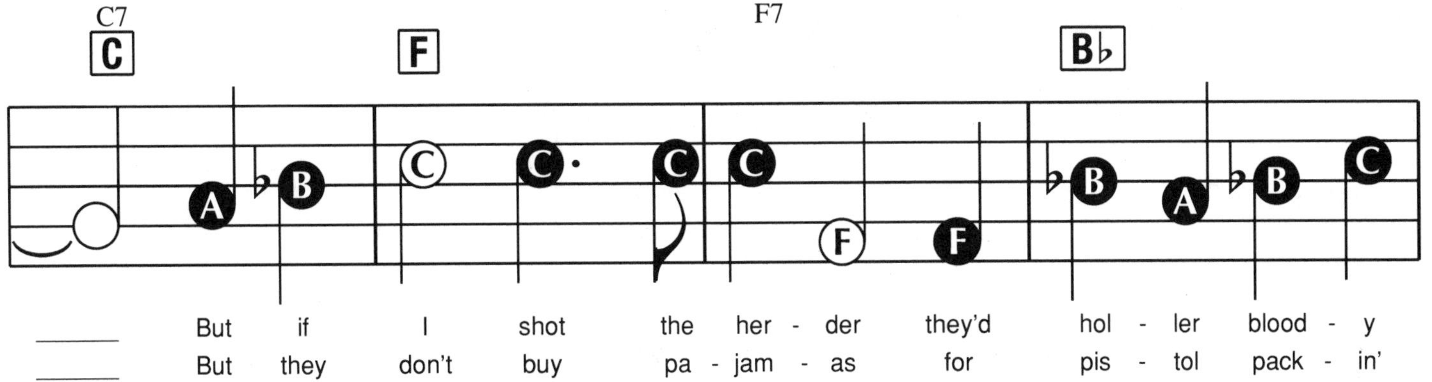
C7
C
F
F7
B♭
But if I shot the her - der they'd hol - ler blood - y
But they don't buy pa - jam - as for pis - tol pack - in'

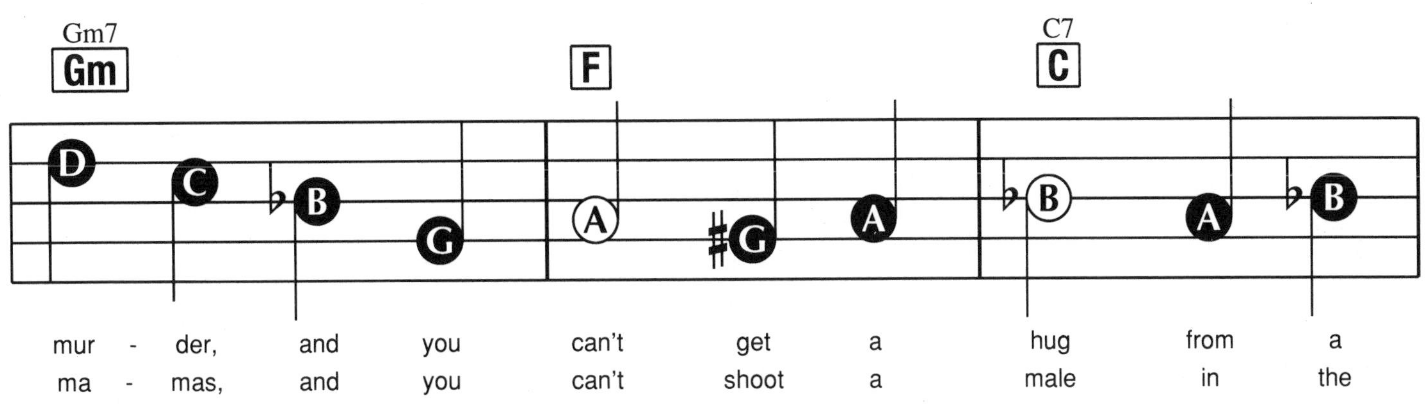
Gm7
Gm
F
C7
C
mur - der, and you can't get a hug from a
ma - mas, and you can't shoot a male in the

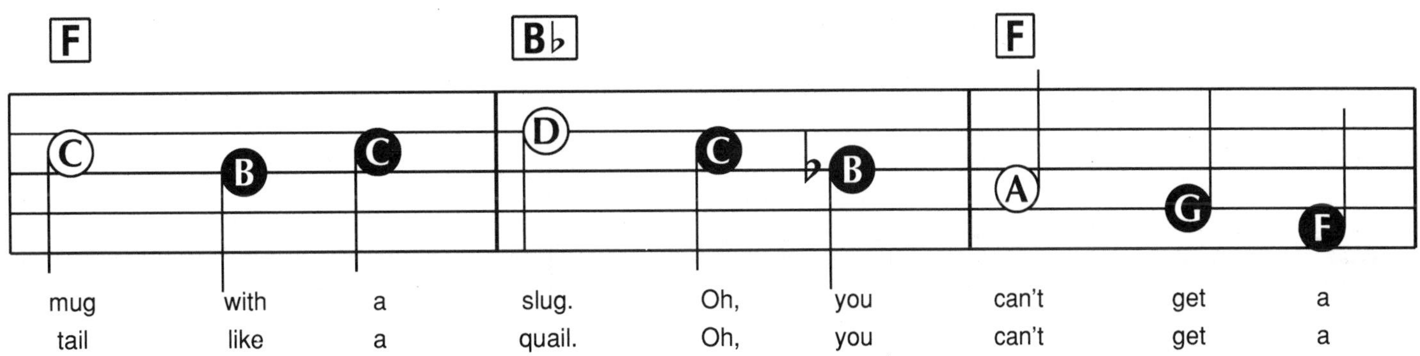
F
B♭
F
mug with a slug. Oh, you can't get a
tail like a quail. Oh, you can't get a

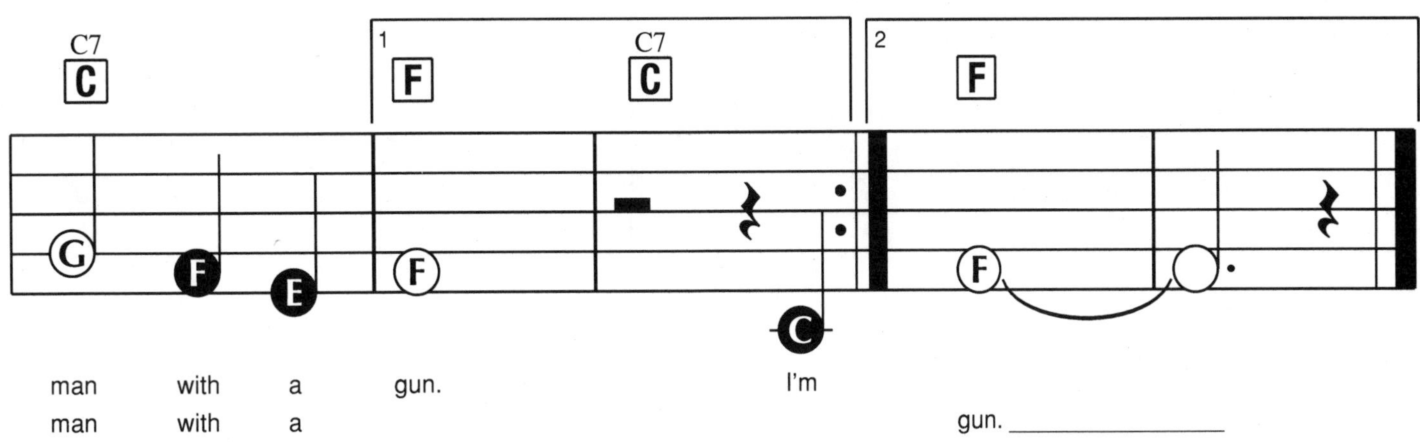
C7
C
1
F
C7
C
2
F
man with a gun. I'm
man with a gun.

You Keep Coming Back Like A Song

Registration 3
Rhythm: Swing

Words and Music by
Irving Berlin

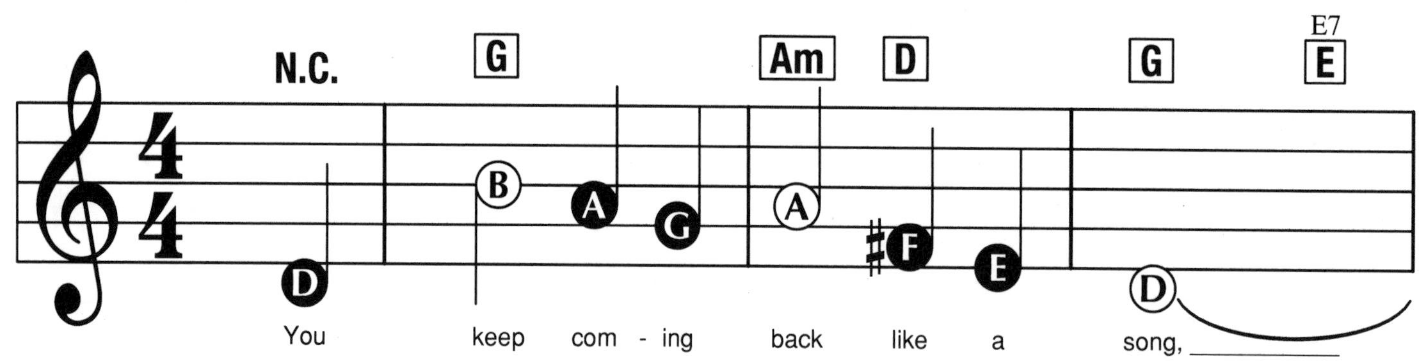

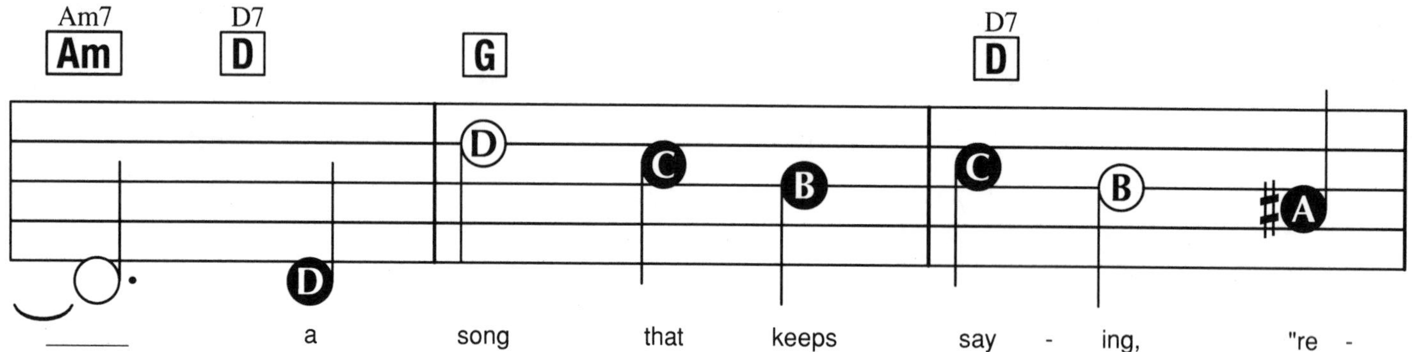

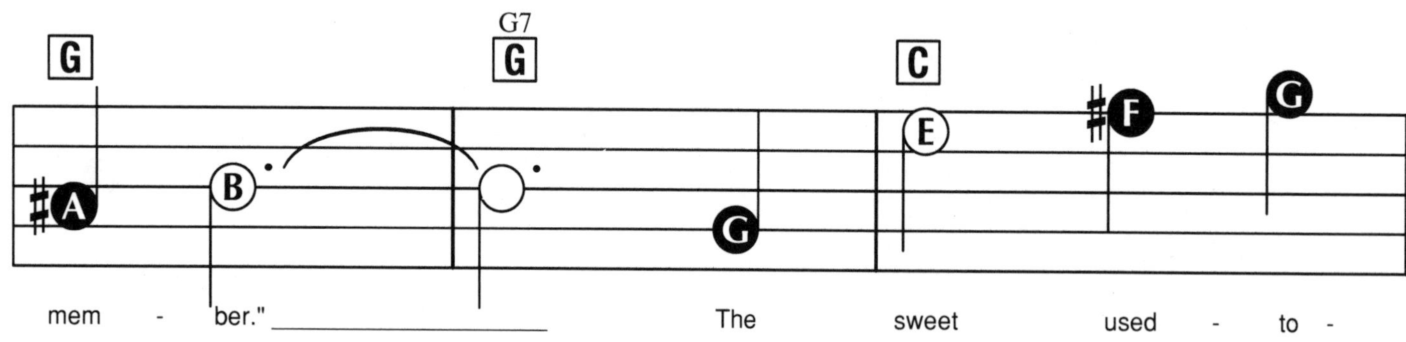

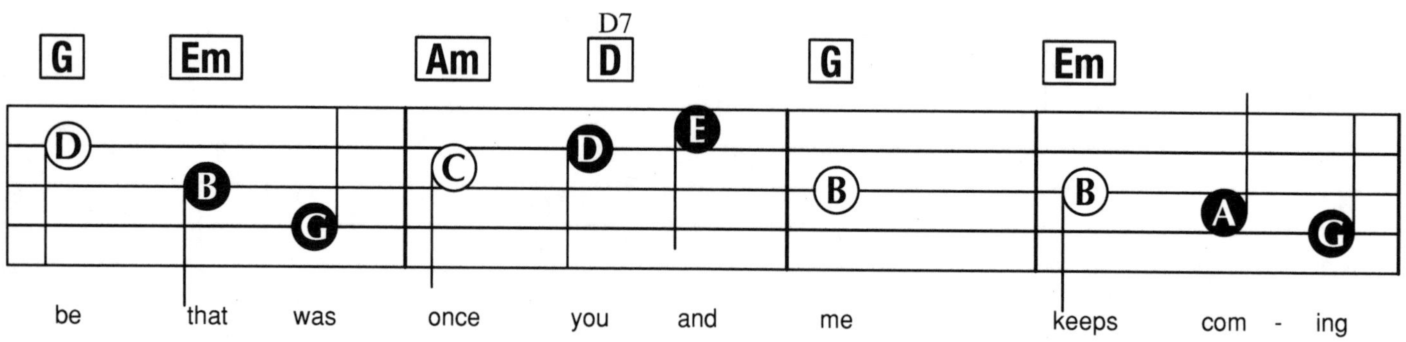

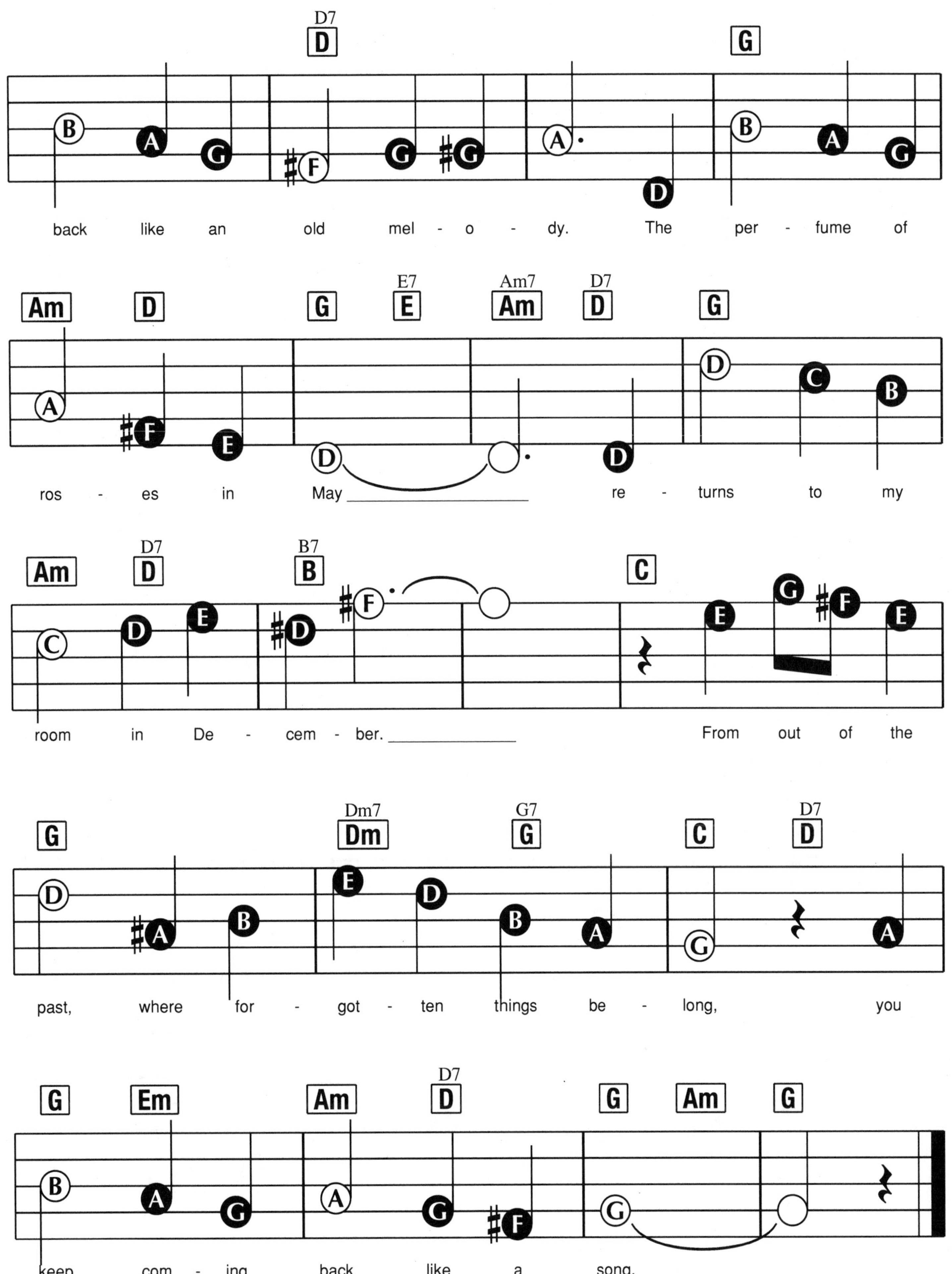
D7
D
G
back like an old mel - o - dy. The per - fume of
Am
D
G
E7
E
Am7
Am
D7
D
G
ros - es in May re - turns to my
Am
D7
D
B7
B
C
room in De - cem - ber. From out of the
G
Dm7
Dm
G7
G
C
D7
D
past, where for - got - ten things be - long, you
G
Em
Am
D7
D
G
Am
G
keep com - ing back like a song.

(I Wonder Why?)

You're Just In Love

Registration 2
Rhythm: Fox Trot or Ballad

Words and Music by
Irving Berlin

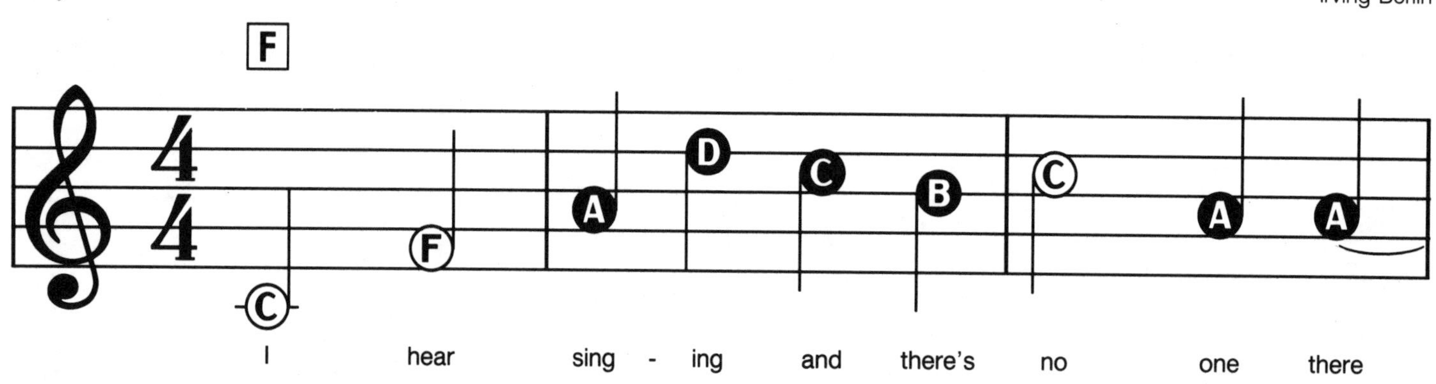

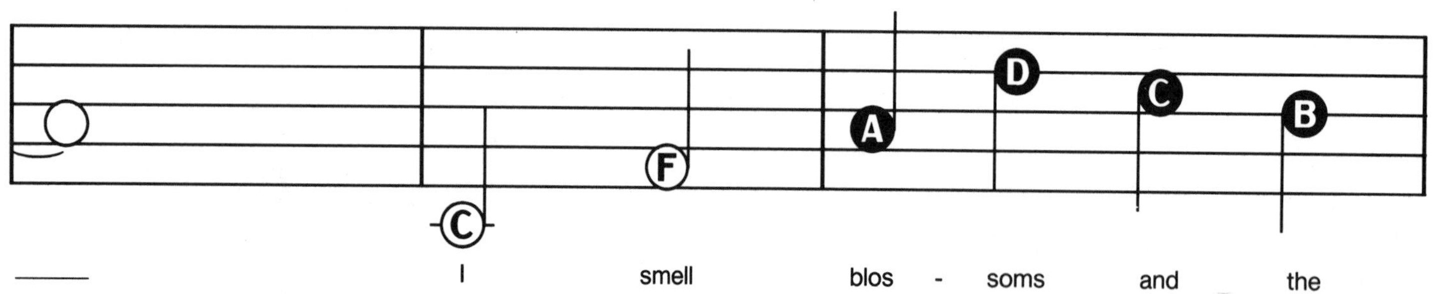

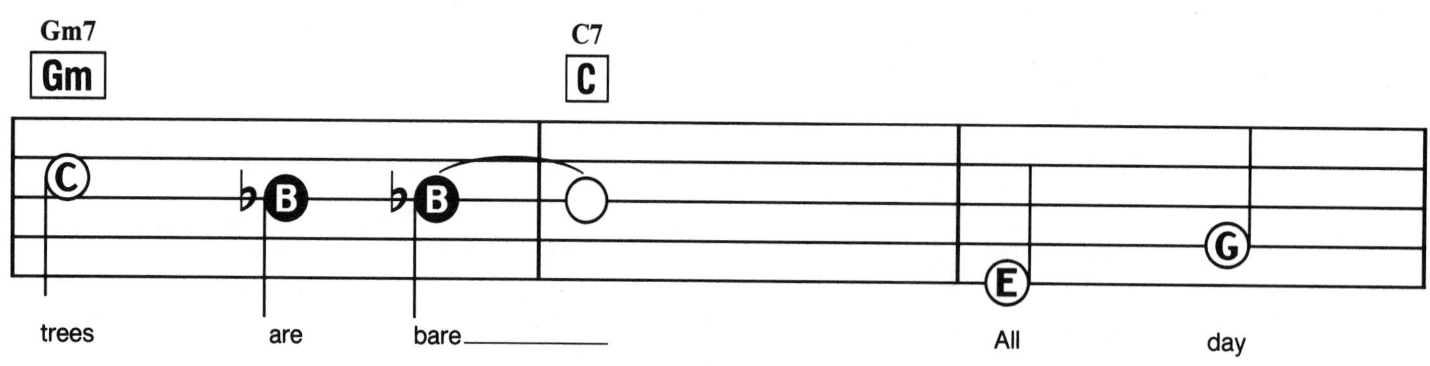

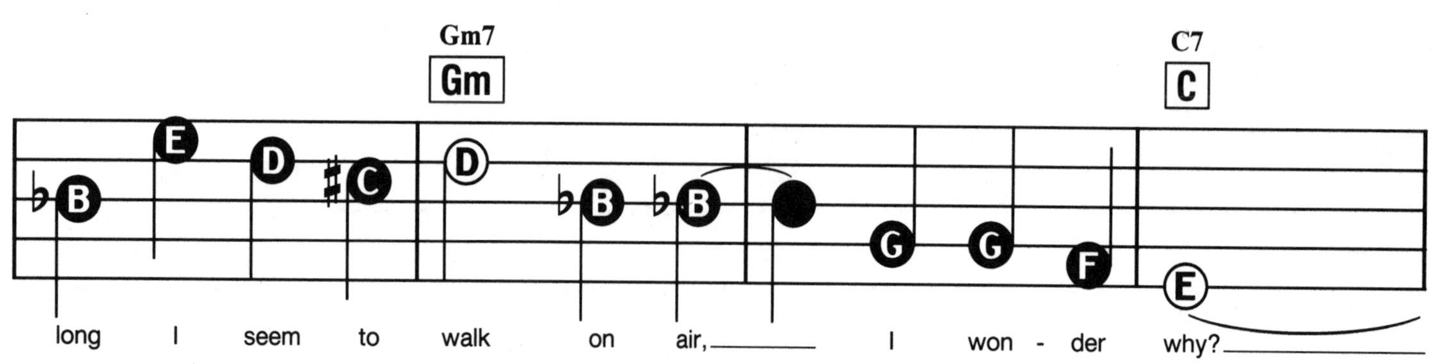

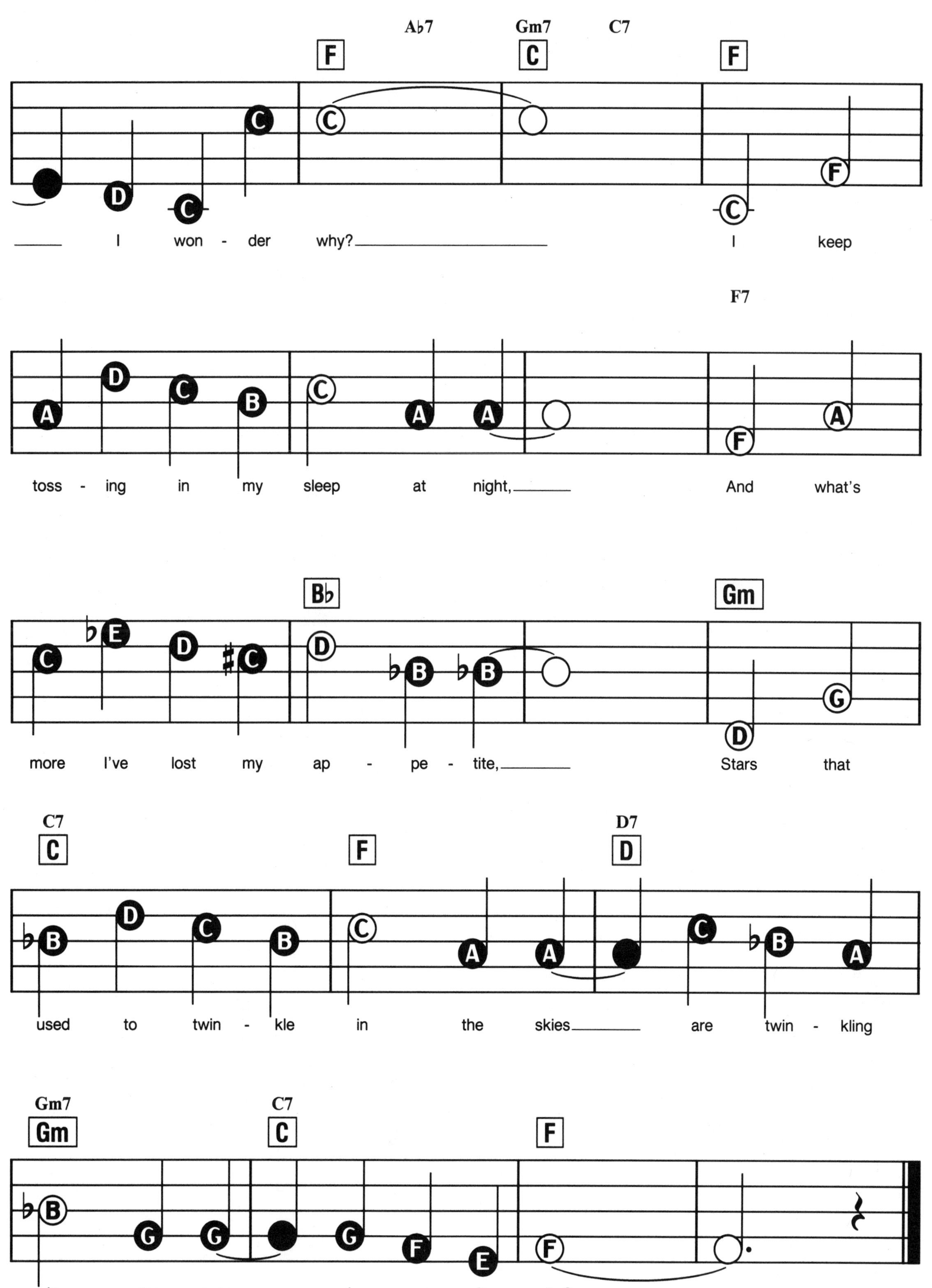
A♭7 Gm7 C7
F C F
I won - der why? I keep
F7
toss - ing in my sleep at night, And what's
B♭ Gm
more I've lost my ap - pe - tite, Stars that
C7 D7
C F D
used to twin - kle in the skies are twin - kling
Gm7 C7
Gm C F
in my eyes, I won - der why?

You're Lonely And I'm Lonely

Registration 9
Rhythm: Swing

Words and Music by
Irving Berlin

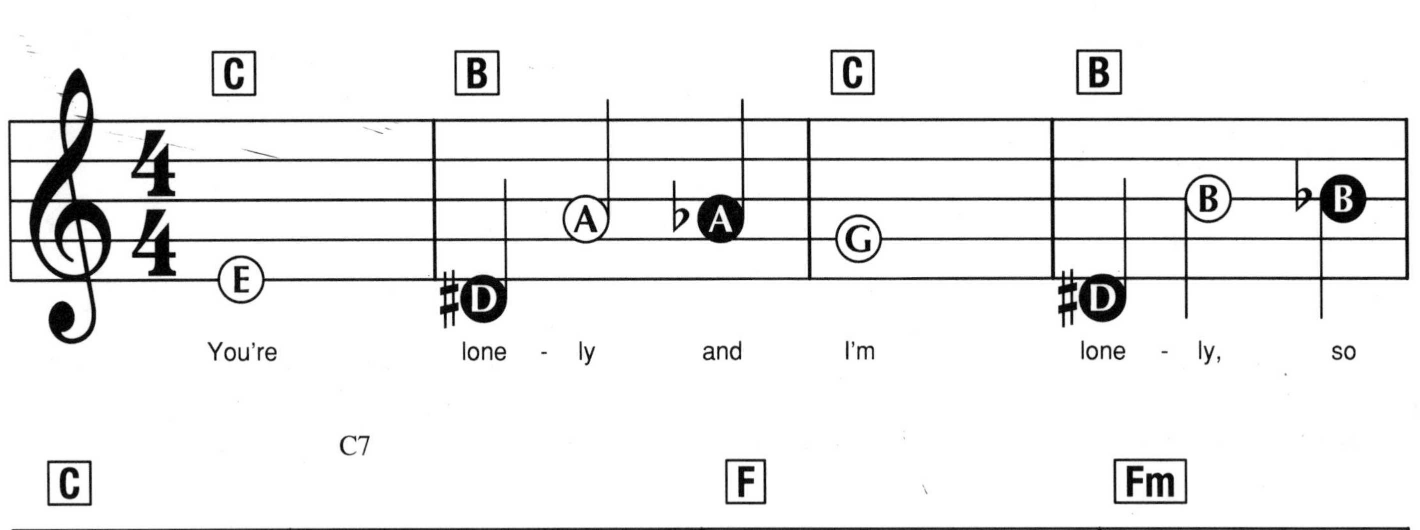

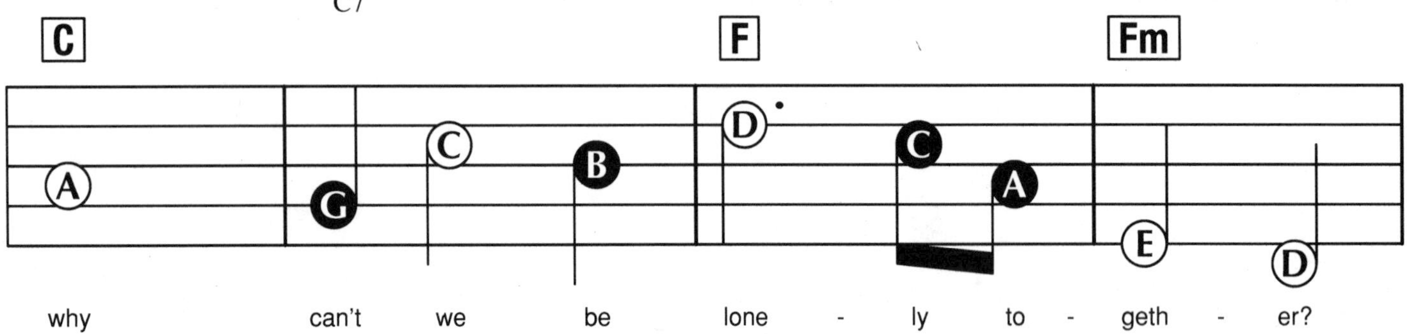

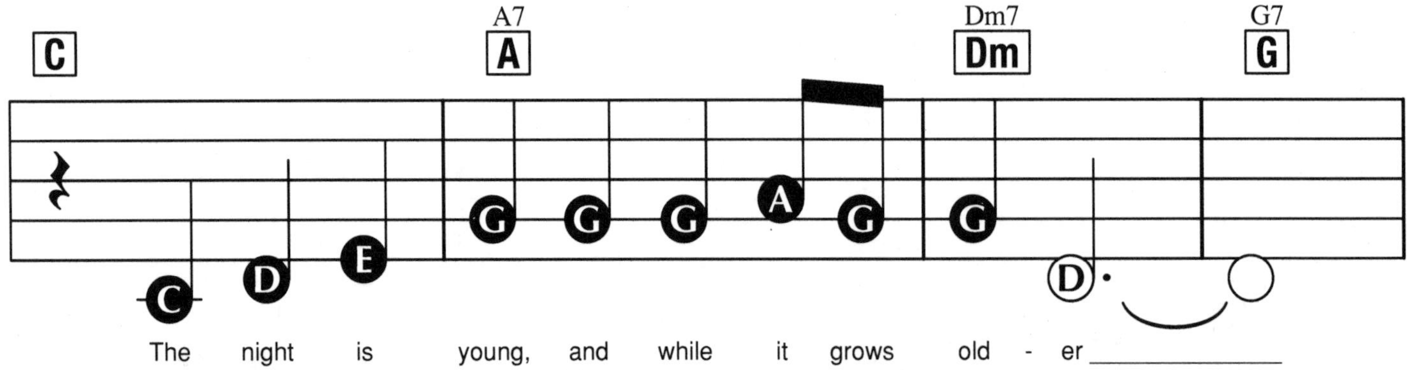

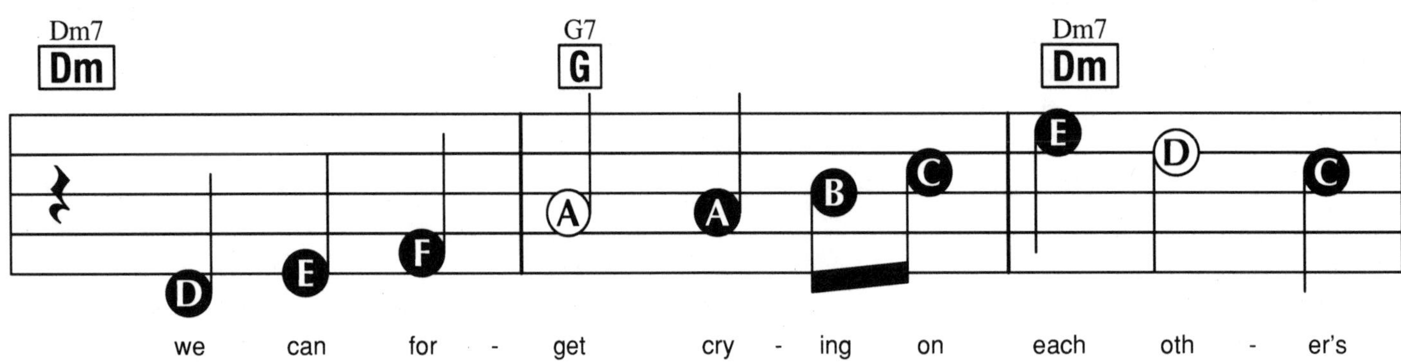

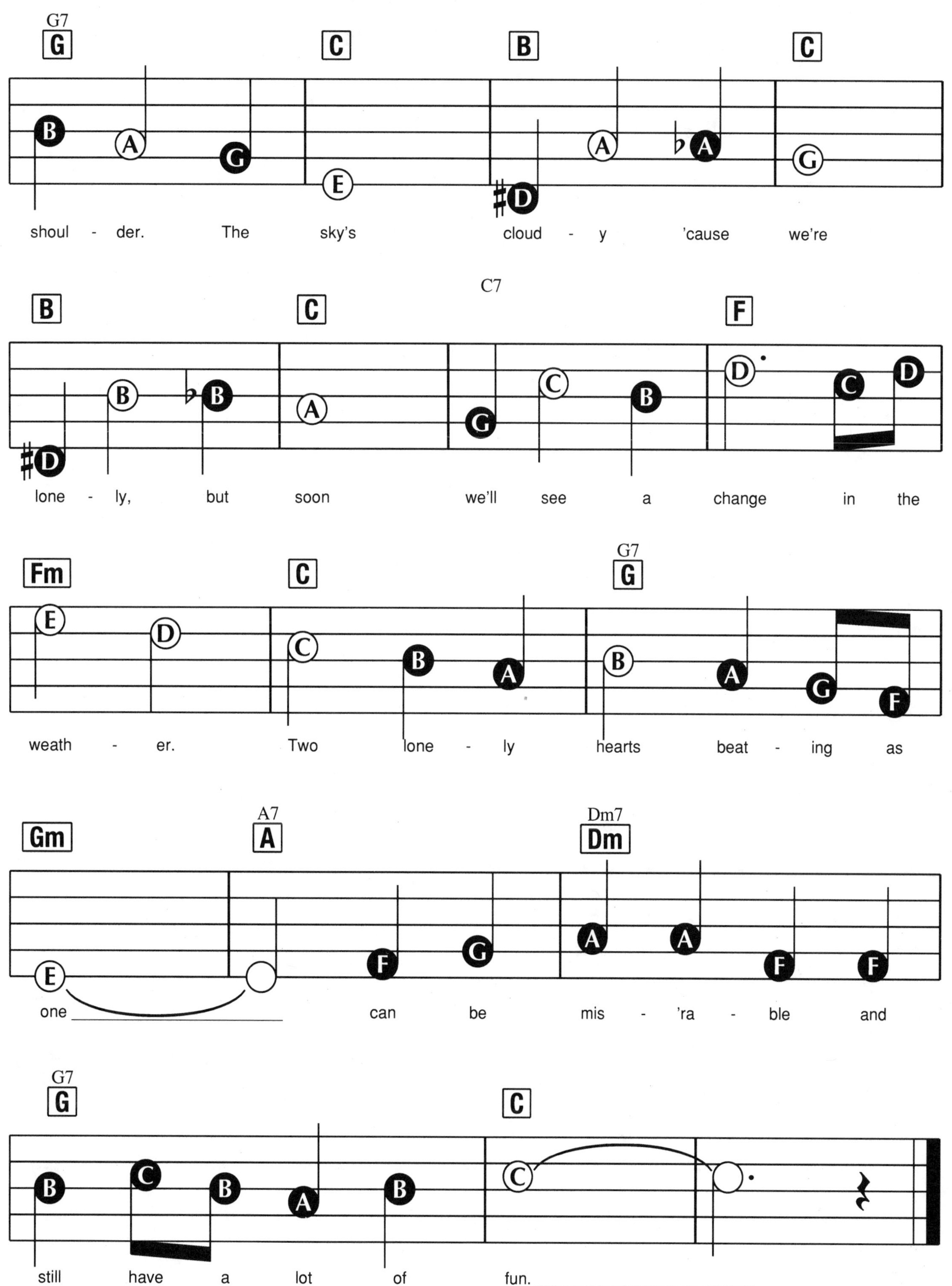

G7
G
C
B
C
shoul - der. The sky's cloud - y 'cause we're
B
C
C7
F
lone - ly, but soon we'll see a change in the
Fm
C
G7
G
weath - er. Two lone - ly hearts beat - ing as
Gm
A7
A
Dm7
Dm
one can be mis - 'ra - ble and
G7
G
C
still have a lot of fun.

Registration Guide

- Match the Registration number on the song to the corresponding numbered category below. Select and activate an instrumental sound available on your instrument.
- Choose an automatic rhythm appropriate to the mood and style of the song. (Consult your Owner's Guide for proper operation of automatic rhythm features.)
- Adjust the tempo and volume controls to comfortable settings.

Registration

1	Flute, Pan Flute, Jazz Flute
2	Clarinet, Organ
3	Violin, Strings
4	Brass, Trumpet
5	Synth Ensemble, Accordion, Brass
6	Pipe Organ, Harpsichord
7	Jazz Organ, Vibraphone, Vibes, Electric Piano, Jazz Guitar
8	Piano, Electric Piano
9	Trumpet, Trombone, Clarinet, Saxophone, Oboe
10	Violin, Cello, Strings